Skills for LITERARY analysis

Lessons in
Assessing
Writing
Structures

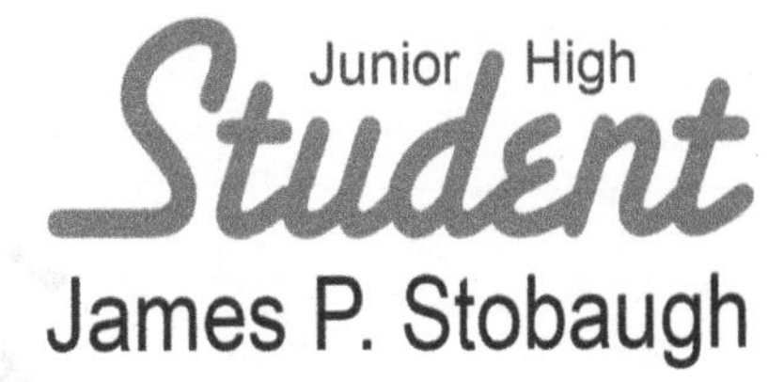

James P. Stobaugh

First printing: August 2013
Third printing: September 2015

Master Books®, P.O. Box 726, Green Forest, AR 72638
Master Books® is a division of the New Leaf Publishing Group, Inc.

ISBN: 978-0-89051-712-3
ISBN: 978-1-61458-320-2 (ebook)
Library of Congress Catalog Number: 2013938352

Cover design by Diana Bogardus.
Interior design by Terry White.

Please consider requesting that a copy of this volume be purchased by your local library system.

Printed in the United States of America

Please visit our website for other great titles:
www.masterbooks.com

For information regarding author interviews, please contact the publicity department at (870) 438-5288.

Acknowledgments

I thank my four children and my distance-learning students who so graciously allowed me to use their essays. Over the last 15 years it has been my great honor to teach some of the best writers in America. Finally, and most of all, I want to thank my best friend and lifelong editor, my wife, Karen. I also want to thank the students who have contributed to this book as well: J.B. Rutlemann, Joseph Stahl, Emily Miller, Benjamin Cobb, Rebecca Holscher, Sheridan Swathmore, Catelyn Mast, Ian Elliott Smith, Hannah Huynh, Daphnide McDermet, John Micah Braswell, Faith Baumann, Bethany Rishell, Anna Grace Knudsten, Stacia Hiramine, Megan Norman, Austin Allen, James Grinalds, Daniel Greenidge, Claire Atwood, Jaime Schimmer, Chris Loyd, Alouette Greenidge, and Josiah Keiter.

Everything is from God, who . . . gave us the ministry of reconciliation (2 Corinthians 5:18).

Contents

Using Your Student Textbook

How this course has been developed:

1. **Chapters:** This course has 34 chapters (representing 34 weeks of study).
2. **Lessons:** Each chapter has four instructive lessons, taking approximately 45 to 60 minutes each, with an exam or writing assignment due on Friday.
3. **Grading:** Depending on the grading option chosen, the parent/educator will grade the daily concept builders, and the weekly tests and essays.
4. **Course credit:** If a student has satisfactorily completed all assignments for this course, it is equivalent to one credit of writing and one credit of literature.

Throughout this course, you will find the following:

1. **Chapter learning objectives:** Always read the "First Thoughts" and "Chapter Learning Objectives" to comprehend the scope of the material to be covered in a particular week.
2. **Concept builders:** Students should complete a daily concept builder Monday through Thursday. These activities take 15 minutes or less and emphasize a particular concept that is vital to that particular chapter topic. These will relate to a subject covered in the chapter, though not necessarily in that day's lesson. Answers are available in the teacher guide.
3. **Weekly essay tests:** Students will write one essay per week. These are available in the teacher guide and online.
4. **Optional written assignments:** A parent/educator may select from varying options of literary criticism, biblical application and/or a challenge essay topic each week. These are found in the back of the teacher guide.
5. **Daily prayer journal:** Students are encouraged to write in a prayer journal every day. A parent/educator may include this in the overall grade. If so, it is encouraged that the grade be based on participation rather than on the content, since this is a deeply personal expression of a student's walk with God.
6. **Final project/portfolio:** Students will correct and rewrite their weekly essays for their final portfolio.
7. **Warm ups:** Daily warm up exercises will start each lesson, setting the tone of thought for the day.

What you will need each day:

1. A notepad or computer for your writing assignments.
2. A pen or pencil for taking notes and for essays.
3. A prayer journal so you can keep a record of your prayers and devotions.
4. Daily concept builders, weekly essays/speeches, and weekly essay tests and are available in the teacher guide.

Preface

Skills for Literary Analysis is a dialectic (examining opinion or ideas logically, often by the method of question and answer) or early rhetoric (using words effectively in writing or speaking) level, middle school or early high school, basic course. It is for the reluctant writer who nonetheless must be equipped with writing skills requisite for college and for the eager student who needs the same. Most college English professors do not assign essays with such titles as "What Did You Do for Summer Vacation?" Instead, they will ask you to write essay papers about literature. *Skills for Literary Analysis* teaches you how to write sophisticated literary analyses or criticisms.

Literary analysis or criticism is a way to talk about literature. It is a way to understand literature better so we can tell others about it.

Charles Osgood in his preface to Boswell's *Life of Johnson* states:

> Phillips Brooks once told the boys at Exeter that in reading a biography three men meet one another in close intimacy — the subject of the biography, the author, and the reader. Of the three, the most interesting is, of course, the man about whom the book is written. The most privileged is the reader, who is thus allowed to live familiarly with an eminent man. Least regarded of the three is the author. It is his part to introduce the others, and to develop between them an acquaintance, perhaps a friendship, while he, though ever busy and solicitous, withdraws into the background.[1]

Our task, likewise, is to bring the subject, the author, and the reader together. We presume to offer insights about different literature that will edify all three.

Every literary piece and every analysis of a literary piece concerns three elements: *ethos, logos,* and *pathos.*

Ethos means "character," and it implies "credibility." Great literature exhibits ethos, and great literary criticism exudes *ethos,* too! Ethos evidences beliefs or ideals that characterize a community, nation, or worldview. Literary criticism rises or falls on its ability to exhibit believable, credible analysis. For instance, the reader must ask, "Is Huw in *How Green Was my Valley* a credible, believable narrator?"

Logos concerns the argument. Every literary critical essay that you write will have an argument. What is the theme? What narrative approach does the author take? Does it work? These are only a few examples that a literary critic might argue. *Logos,* like all argumentation, must be mindful of logic and rhetoric. For instance, Jack London's *Call of the Wild* is not merely an adventure story about a sled dog — it is a book that presents an argument: a naturalistic argument. Readers and literary critics must be able to discern and to write about these arguments. No serious literary discussion of *Call of the Wild* can ignore the fact that London is advancing an evolutionary, naturalistic agenda.

Finally, every trustworthy literary piece has pathos, or "heart." Literary critics, and the literary pieces they are analyzing, should offer much more than sterile, persuasive rhetoric. Great literature, and effective literary analysis, exhibits empathy with the reader and insights about the human condition. For example, George Eliot's *Silas Marner* skillfully invites readers to enter the lonely world of old Silas Marner. Eliot causes the reader to feel, not simply to understand, the tragedy that drives Marner from his loving God and human community.

1 James Boswell, edited by Charles Osgood, *The Life of Samuel Johnson* (1917), preface.

Student Responsibilities

Read the assigned, whole literary piece before the first classroom literary analysis. You will have to read ahead. You cannot wait until two days before a literary analysis is due to read the material. You will be prompted throughout the text, but you will need to make sure you do the work in a timely way. Your parent/educator may try to help you with more difficult readings by providing unabridged audiobooks of the assigned text. Listening to an audiobook is not a replacement for actual reading unless there are specific limitations that make this arrangement necessary.

Discuss the literary term highlighted for the week with your parent/educator (e.g., "plot"). The highlighted term is defined in simple language and is illustrated by a readable example. If you need more information, access other literature texts.

Review the Grammar Review and Writing Style section. This would be a good time for you to review and to correct manifested grammar deficiencies. If you are still having difficulty with grammar specifics, your parent/educator may give you a worksheet to complete. Grammar review will be in addition to your regular Literary Analysis.

Weekly essays. You will be writing one, two, or three, two-page essays per week, depending on the level of accomplishment you and your parent educator decide upon. To experience the optimum from the course, you should attempt to write all three of the essays in most lessons.

Complete literary reviews. You will be assigned particular works to read during this course; however, as time allows, read additional books from the enclosed list (see appendix). You should read most of the books on the enclosed supplemental book list before you graduate from high school. After reading a literary work, for this course or for any other reason, complete a literary review (see appendix). Keep these reviews as a record of your high school reading. The supplemental book list is not meant to be exhaustive but is intended as a guide to good reading. A suggestion is to read 35 to 50 pages per night (or 200 pages per week), which includes reading the books for this course.

Collect challenging vocabulary words

Create 3x5 Vocabulary Cards

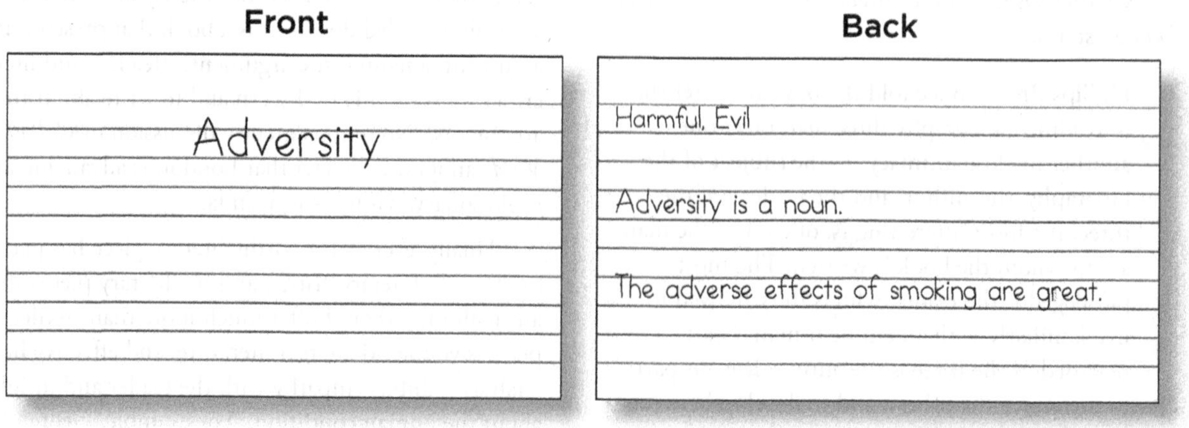

Front

Adversity

Back

Harmful, Evil

Adversity is a noun.

The adverse effects of smoking are great.

When you meet an unknown word for the first time,

- do your best to figure out the word in context;
- check your guess by looking in the dictionary; and
- write a sentence with the word in it.

Use the illustration above to formulate your vocabulary cards of new words.

Setting — *The Call of the Wild* (Jack London)

Chapter 1

First Thoughts

Jack London (1876–1916) lived and wrote in the last part of the 19th century and early part of the 20th century. He watched the final frontier of America — Alaska — disappear. He wrote in a style literary critics call *naturalism*. What is naturalism? *The Call of the Wild* is essentially the story of a dog named Buck. However, as the book unfolds, one notices that there is a lot more happening. Buck is invited back into his wild ancestry. In Jack London's opinion, this invitation is a metaphor for life itself.

Chapter Learning Objectives

In chapter 1 we will examine the literary concept setting and its use in Jack London's *The Call of the Wild*. We will also examine the impact of naturalism on world history.

As a result of this chapter study you will be able to . . .

1. Analyze the setting in Jack London's *The Call of the Wild*.
2. Evaluate the impact of a naturalism worldview.

Look Ahead for Friday

- Turn in a final copy of essay
- Take Weekly Test

Setting is Critical

Setting is the *time* and the *place* in which a literary piece occurs. The setting may be stated directly, or it may be implied. In any event, authors use the setting to reveal the character(s) and to advance the story. Read the following story.

The following is a portion of a short story by Jack London entitled "To Build a Fire," which first appeared in *The Century Magazine*, v. 76, August 1908. In this short story, the protagonist has foolishly tried to reach a distant location on the other side of a wilderness, in sub-zero weather. He failed and is very close to freezing to death.

The sight of the dog put a wild idea into his head. He remembered the tale of the man, caught in a blizzard, who killed a steer and crawled inside the carcass, and so was saved. He would kill the dog and bury his hands in the warm body until the numbness went out of them. Then he could build another fire. He spoke to the dog, calling it to him; but in his voice was a strange note of fear that frightened the animal, who had never known the man to speak in such way before. Something was the matter, and its suspicious nature sensed danger — it knew not what danger, but some-where, somehow, in its brain arose an apprehension of the man. It flattened its ears down at the sound of the man's voice, and its restless, hunching movements and the liftings and shiftings of its forefeet became more pronounced; but it would not come to the man. He got on his hands and knees and crawled toward the dog. This unusual posture again excited suspicion, and the animal sidled mincingly away.

The man sat up in the snow for a moment and struggled for calmness. Then he pulled on his mittens, by means of his teeth, and got upon his feet. He glanced down at first in order to assure himself that he was really standing up, for the absence of sensation in his feet left him unrelated to the earth. His erect position in itself started to drive the webs of suspicion from the dog's mind; and when he spoke peremptorily, with the sound of whiplashes in his voice, the dog rendered its customary allegiance and came to him. As it came within reaching distance, the man lost his control. His arms flashed out to the dog, and he experienced genuine surprise when he discovered that his hands could not clutch, that there was neither bend nor feeling in the fingers. He had forgotten for the moment that they were frozen and that they were freezing more and more. All this happened quickly, and before the animal could get away, he encircled its body with his arms. He sat down in the snow, and in this fashion held the dog, while it snarled and whined and struggled.

But it was all he could do, hold its body encircled in his arms and sit there. He realized that he could not kill the dog. There was no way to do it. With his helpless hands he could neither draw nor hold his sheath-knife nor throttle the animal. He released it, and it plunged wildly away, with tail between its legs, and still snarling. It halted forty feet away and surveyed him curiously, with ears sharply pricked forward. The man looked down at his hands in order to locate them, and found them hanging on the ends of his arms. It struck him as curious that one should have to use his eyes in order to find out where his hands were. He began threshing his arms back and forth, beating the mittened hands against his sides. He did this for five minutes, violently, and his heart pumped enough blood up to the surface to put a stop to his shivering. But no sensation was aroused in the hands. He had an impression that they hung like weights on the ends of his arms, but when he tried to run the impression down, he could not find it.

A certain fear of death, dull and oppressive, came to him. This fear quickly became poignant as he realized that it was no longer a mere matter of freezing his fingers and toes, or of losing his hands and feet, but that it was a matter of life and death with the chances against him. This threw him into a panic, and he turned and ran up the creek-bed along the old, dim trail. The dog joined in behind and kept up with him. He ran blindly, without intention, in fear such as he had never known in his life. Slowly, as he ploughed and floundered through the snow, he began to see things again — the banks of the creek, the old timber-jams, the leafless aspens, and the sky. The running made him feel better. He did not shiver. Maybe, if he ran on, his feet would thaw out; and, anyway, if he ran far enough, he would reach camp and the boys. Without doubt he would lose some fingers and toes and some of his face; but the boys would take care of him, and save the rest of him when he got there. And at the same time there was another thought in his mind that said he would never get to the camp and the boys; that it was too many miles away, that the freezing had too great a start on him, and that he would soon be stiff and dead. This thought he kept in the background and refused to consider. Sometimes it pushed itself forward and demanded to be heard, but he thrust it back and strove to think of other things.

Clearly the setting is critical! This sort of story could not occur in downtown Manhattan, New York City!

Daily Assignment

- Warm-up: The protagonist (main character) in this novel is Buck, a dog. Describe your pet. If you don't have one, describe a pet you wish you had.
- Students will complete Concept Builder 1-A.
- Prayer journal: Students are encouraged to write in their prayer journal every day.
- Students need to review their material for the next assignment
- Students should systematically review their vocabulary words daily.

Audience

Different audiences require different writing styles. It matters to whom you are writing a piece!

Choose the audience of each passage, and circle words that tell why you chose a particular audience. Hint: clues regarding audience lie in word choice and content.

B We conducted a single-center, randomized, controlled trial of arthroscopic surgery in patients with moderate-to-severe osteoarthritis of the knee.	A. Teachers
E Colston tried to continue playing with the injury during the Saints' 24-20 victory over the Bucs, but finished with only three catches for 26 yards.	B. Doctors
A What is editing? Ruth Culham of the Northwest Regional Education Laboratory separates revision (last month's column topic) from editing (spelling, grammar, capitalization, and punctuation).	C. Magazine for Women
D My guy loves music, and he had just bought himself a new iPod. He's obsessed with the painting *The Great Wave*, and I found an iPod skin with the exact painting on it. He loved it, and now he thinks of me every time he listens to his music!	D. Teenagers
C You want to look bright-eyed. Hide dark circles around the eye area with an apricot-tinted color, or if you have darker skin, one that's one shade lighter than your skin tone.	E. Football Fans
F Making the user interface for one device easy, slick, fun, and fast is a challenge. If you have multiple devices and they need to cooperate, the challenge increases dramatically. As wired and wireless communications hardware gets cheaper, the design opportunities for communicating devices become more common.	F. Computer Nerd

Lesson 2

Setting is Marginally Important

In some literary works, the setting is relatively unimportant. Neither the plot nor the character development is dependent upon a location or time. Such is the case with George Eliot's *Silas Marner*. The following is chapter 1. Readers are introduced to the main character, Silas Marner, who lives in a small English village, Raveloe. While this location is interesting and does in fact contribute to Marner's character development, readers are reminded that Marner's desperate condition is the focus of this novel and not dependent upon any particular setting. Marner would feel betrayed and bitter if this novel occurred in London, for instance. In fact, Eliot invests most of her time revealing and developing internal conflicts within the soul of Silas Marner himself and invests precious little time developing the setting in which this occurs. Authors who are more concerned about character and plot development, and less about the setting, will liberally employ coincidence. Eliot does exactly that.

In the days when the spinning-wheels hummed busily in the farmhouses — and even great ladies, clothed in silk and thread-lace, had their toy spinning-wheels of polished oak — there might be seen in districts far away among the lanes, or deep in the bosom of the hills, certain pallid undersized men, who, by the side of the brawny country-folk, looked like the remnants of a disinherited race. The shepherd's dog barked fiercely when one of these alien-looking men appeared on the upland, dark against the early winter sunset; for what dog likes a figure bent under a heavy bag? — and these pale men rarely stirred abroad without that mysterious burden. The shepherd himself, though he had good reason to believe that the bag held nothing but flaxen thread, or else the long rolls of strong linen spun from that thread, was not quite sure that this trade of weaving, indispensable though it was, could be carried on entirely without the help of the Evil One. In that far-off time superstition clung easily round every person or thing that was at all unwonted, or even intermittent and occasional merely, like the visits of the pedlar or the knife-grinder. No one knew where wandering men had their homes or their origin; and how was a man to be explained unless you at least knew somebody who knew his father and mother? To the peasants of old times, the world outside their own direct experience was a region of vagueness and mystery: to their untravelled thought a state of wandering was a conception as dim as the winter life of the swallows that came back with the spring; and even a settler, if he came from distant parts, hardly ever ceased to be viewed with a remnant of distrust, which would have prevented any surprise if a long course of inoffensive conduct on his part had ended in the commission of a crime; especially if he had any reputation for knowledge, or showed any skill in handicraft. All cleverness, whether in the rapid use of that difficult instrument the tongue, or in some other art unfamiliar to villagers, was in itself suspicious: honest folk, born and bred in a visible manner, were mostly not overwise or clever — at least, not beyond such a matter as knowing the signs of the weather; and the process by which rapidity and dexterity of any kind were acquired was so wholly hidden, that they partook of the nature of conjuring. In this way it came to pass that those scattered linen-weavers — emigrants from the town into the country — were to the last regarded as aliens by their rustic neighbours, and usually contracted the eccentric habits which belong to a state of loneliness.

In the early years of this century, such a linen-weaver, named Silas Marner, worked at his vocation in a stone cottage that stood among the nutty hedgerows near the village of Raveloe, and not far from the edge of a deserted stone-pit. The questionable sound of Silas's loom, so unlike the natural cheerful trotting of the winnowing-machine, or the simpler rhythm of the flail, had a half-fearful fascination for the Raveloe boys, who would often leave off their nutting or birds'-nesting to peep in at the window of the stone cottage, counterbalancing a certain awe at the mysterious action of the loom, by a pleasant sense of scornful superiority, drawn from the mockery of its alternating noises, along with the bent, tread-mill attitude of the weaver. But sometimes it happened that Marner, pausing to adjust an irregularity in his thread, became aware of the small scoundrels, and, though chary of his time, he liked their intrusion so ill that he would descend from his loom, and, opening the door, would fix on them a gaze that was always enough to make them take to their legs in terror. For how was it possible to believe that those large brown protuberant eyes in Silas Marner's pale face really saw nothing very distinctly that was not close to them, and not rather that their dreadful stare could dart cramp, or rickets, or a wry mouth at any boy who happened to be in the rear? They had, perhaps, heard their fathers and mothers hint that Silas Marner could cure folks' rheumatism if he had a mind, and add, still more darkly, that if you could only speak the devil fair enough, he might save you the cost of the doctor. Such strange lingering echoes of the old demon-worship might perhaps even now be caught by the diligent listener among the grey-haired peasantry; for the rude mind with difficulty associates the ideas of power and benignity. A shadowy conception of power that by much persuasion can be induced to refrain from inflicting harm, is the shape most easily taken by the sense of the Invisible in the minds of men who have always been pressed close by primitive wants, and to whom a life of hard toil has never been illuminated by any enthusiastic religious faith. To them pain and mishap present a far wider range of possibilities than gladness and enjoyment: their imagination is almost barren of the images that feed desire and hope, but is all overgrown by recollections that are a perpetual pasture to fear. "Is there anything you can fancy that you would like to eat?" I once said to an old labouring man, who was in his last illness, and who had refused all the food his wife had offered him. "No," he answered, "I've never been used to nothing but common victual, and I can't eat that." Experience had bred no fancies in him that could raise the phantasm of appetite.

And Raveloe was a village where many of the old echoes lingered, undrowned by new voices. Not that it was one of those barren parishes lying on the outskirts of civilization — inhabited by meagre sheep and thinly-scattered shepherds: on the contrary, it lay in the rich central plain of what we are pleased to call Merry England, and held farms which, speaking from a spiritual point of view, paid highly-desirable tithes. But it was nestled in a snug well-wooded hollow, quite an hour's journey on horseback from any turnpike, where it was never reached by the vibrations of the coach-horn, or of public opinion. It was an important-looking village, with a fine old church and large churchyard in the heart of it, and two or three large brick-and-stone homesteads, with well-walled orchards and ornamental weathercocks, standing close upon the road, and lifting more imposing fronts than the rectory, which peeped from among the trees on the other side of the churchyard — a village which showed at once the summits of its social life, and told the practised eye that there was no great park and manor-house in the vicinity, but that there were several chiefs in Raveloe who could farm badly quite at their ease, drawing enough money from their bad farming, in those war times, to live in a rollicking fashion, and keep a jolly Christmas, Whitsun, and Easter tide.

It was fifteen years since Silas Marner had first come to Raveloe; he was then simply a pallid young man, with prominent short-sighted brown eyes, whose appearance would have had nothing strange for people of average culture and experience, but for the villagers near whom he had come to settle it had mysterious peculiarities which corresponded with the exceptional nature of his occupation, and his advent from an unknown region called "North'ard." So had his way of life — he invited no comer to step across his door-sill, and he never strolled into the village to drink a pint at the Rainbow, or to gossip at the wheelwright's: he sought no man or woman, save for the purposes of his calling, or in order to supply himself with necessaries; and it was soon clear to the Raveloe lasses that he would never urge one of them to accept him against her will—quite as if he had heard them declare that they would never marry a dead man come to life again. This view of Marner's personality was not without another ground than his pale face and unexampled eyes; for Jem Rodney, the mole-catcher, averred that one evening as he was returning homeward, he saw Silas Marner leaning against a stile with a heavy bag on his back, instead of resting the bag on the stile as a man in his senses would have done; and that, on coming up to him, he saw that Marner's eyes were set like a dead man's, and he spoke to him, and shook him, and his limbs were stiff, and his hands clutched the bag as if they'd been made of iron; but just as he had made up his mind that the weaver was dead, he came all right again, like, as you might say, in the winking of an eye, and said "Goodnight," and walked off. All this Jem swore he had seen, more by token that it was the very day he had been mole-catching on Squire Cass's land, down by the old saw-pit. Some said Marner must have been in a "fit," a word which seemed to explain things otherwise incredible; but the argumentative Mr. Macey, clerk of the parish, shook his head, and asked if anybody was ever known to go off in a fit and not fall down. A fit was a stroke, wasn't it? and it was in the nature of a stroke to partly take away the use of a man's limbs and throw him on the parish, if he'd got no children to look to. No, no; it was no stroke that would let a man stand on his legs, like a horse between the shafts, and then walk off as soon as you can say "Gee!" But there might be such a thing as a man's soul being loose from his body, and going out and in, like a bird out of its nest and back; and that was how folks got over-wise, for they went to school in this shell-less state to those who could teach them more than their neighbours could learn with their five senses and the parson. And where did Master Marner get his knowledge of herbs from — and charms too, if he liked to give them away? Jem Rodney's story was no more than what might have been expected by anybody who had seen how Marner had cured Sally Oates, and made her sleep like a baby, when her heart had been beating enough to burst her body, for two months and more, while she had been under the doctor's care. He might cure more folks if he would; but he was worth speaking fair, if it was only to keep him from doing you a mischief.

It was partly to this vague fear that Marner was indebted for protecting him from the persecution that his singularities might have drawn upon him, but still more to the fact that, the old linen-weaver in the neighbouring parish of Tarley being dead, his handicraft made him a highly welcome settler to the richer housewives of the district, and even to the more provident cottagers, who had their little stock of yarn at the year's end. Their sense of his usefulness would have counteracted any repugnance or suspicion which was not confirmed by a deficiency in the quality or the tale of the cloth he wove for them. And the years had rolled on without producing any change in the impressions of the neighbours concerning Marner, except the change from novelty to habit. At the end of fifteen years the Raveloe men said just the same things about Silas Marner as at the beginning: they did not say them quite so often, but they believed them much more strongly when they did say them. There was only one important addition which the years had brought: it was, that Master Marner had laid by a fine sight of money somewhere, and that he could buy up "bigger men" than himself.

But while opinion concerning him had remained nearly stationary, and his daily habits had presented scarcely any visible change, Marner's inward life had been a history and a metamorphosis, as that of every fervid nature must be when it has fled, or been condemned, to solitude. His life, before he came to Raveloe, had been filled with the movement, the mental activity, and the close fellowship, which, in that day as in this, marked the life of an artisan early incorporated in a narrow religious sect, where the poorest layman has the chance of distinguishing himself by gifts of speech, and has, at the very least, the weight of a silent voter in the government of his community. Marner was highly thought of in that little hidden world, known to itself as the church assembling in Lantern Yard; he was believed to be a young man of exemplary life and ardent faith; and a peculiar interest had been centred in him ever since he had fallen, at a prayer-meeting, into a mysterious rigidity and suspension of consciousness, which, lasting for an hour or more, had been mistaken for death. To have sought a medical explanation for this phenomenon would have been held by Silas himself, as well as by his minister and fellow-members, a wilful self-exclusion from the spiritual significance that might lie therein. Silas was evidently a brother selected for a peculiar discipline; and though the effort to interpret this discipline was discouraged by the absence, on his part, of any spiritual vision during his outward trance, yet it was believed by himself and others that its effect was seen in an accession of light and fervour. A less truthful man than he might have been tempted into the subsequent creation of a vision in the form of resurgent memory; a less sane man might have believed in such a creation; but Silas was both sane and honest, though, as with many honest and fervent men, culture had not defined any channels for his sense of mystery, and so it spread itself over the proper pathway of inquiry and knowledge. He had inherited from his mother some acquaintance with medicinal herbs and their preparation—a little store of wisdom which she had imparted to him as a solemn bequest — but of late years he had had doubts about the lawfulness of applying this knowledge, believing that herbs could have no efficacy without prayer, and that prayer might suffice without herbs; so that the inherited delight he had in wandering in the fields in search of foxglove and dandelion and coltsfoot, began to wear to him the character of a temptation.

Among the members of his church there was one young man, a little older than himself, with whom he had long lived in such close friendship that it was the custom of their Lantern Yard brethren to call them David and Jonathan. The real name of the friend was William Dane, and he, too, was regarded as a shining instance of youthful piety, though somewhat given to over-severity towards weaker brethren, and to be so dazzled by his own light as to hold himself wiser than his teachers. But whatever blemishes others might discern in William, to his friend's mind he was faultless; for Marner had one of those impressible self-doubting natures which, at an inexperienced age, admire imperativeness and lean on contradiction. The expression of trusting simplicity in Marner's face, heightened by that absence of special observation, that defenceless, deer-like gaze which belongs to large prominent eyes, was strongly contrasted by the self-complacent suppression of inward triumph that lurked in the narrow slanting eyes and compressed lips of William Dane. One of the most frequent topics of conversation between the two friends was Assurance of salvation: Silas confessed that he could never arrive at anything higher than hope mingled with fear, and listened with longing wonder when William declared that he had possessed unshaken assurance ever since, in the period of his conversion, he had dreamed that he saw the words "calling and election sure" standing by themselves on a white page in the open Bible. Such colloquies have occupied many a pair of pale-faced weavers, whose unnurtured souls have been like young winged things, fluttering forsaken in the twilight.

It had seemed to the unsuspecting Silas that the friendship had suffered no chill even from his formation of another attachment of a closer kind. For some months he had been engaged to a young servant-woman, waiting only for a little increase to their mutual savings in order to their marriage; and it was a great delight to him that Sarah did not object to William's occasional presence in their Sunday interviews. It was at this point in their history that Silas's cataleptic fit occurred during the prayer-meeting; and amidst the various queries and expressions of interest addressed to him by his fellow-members, William's suggestion alone jarred with the general sympathy towards a brother thus singled out for special dealings. He observed that, to him, this trance looked more like a visitation of Satan than a proof of divine favour, and exhorted his friend to see that he hid no accursed thing within his soul. Silas, feeling bound to accept rebuke and admonition as a brotherly office, felt no resentment, but only pain, at his friend's doubts concerning him; and to this was soon added some anxiety at the perception that Sarah's manner towards him began to exhibit a strange fluctuation between an effort at an increased manifestation of regard and involuntary signs of shrinking and dislike. He asked her if she wished to break off their engagement; but she denied this: their engagement was known to the church, and had been recognized in the prayer-meetings; it could not be broken off without strict investigation, and Sarah could render no reason that would be sanctioned by the feeling of the community. At this time the senior deacon was taken dangerously ill, and, being a childless widower, he was tended night and day by some of the younger brethren or sisters. Silas frequently took his turn in the night-watching with William, the one relieving the other at two in the morning. The old man, contrary to expectation, seemed to be on the way to recovery, when one night Silas, sitting up by his bedside, observed that his usual audible breathing had ceased. The candle was burning low, and he had to lift it to see the patient's face distinctly. Examination convinced him that the deacon was dead — had been dead some time, for the limbs were rigid. Silas asked himself if he had been asleep, and looked at the clock: it was already four in the morning. How was it that William had not come? In much anxiety he went to seek for help, and soon there were several friends assembled in the house, the minister among them, while Silas went away to his work, wishing he could have met William to know the reason of his non-appearance. But at six o'clock, as he was thinking of going to seek his friend, William came, and with him the minister. They came to summon him to Lantern Yard, to meet the church members there; and to his inquiry concerning the cause of the summons the only reply was, "You will hear." Nothing further was said until Silas was seated in the vestry, in front of the minister, with the eyes of those who to him represented God's people fixed solemnly upon him. Then the minister, taking out a pocket-knife, showed it to Silas, and asked him if he knew where he had left that knife? Silas said, he did not know that he had left it anywhere out of his own pocket — but he was trembling at this strange interrogation. He was then exhorted not to hide his sin, but to confess and repent. The knife had been found in the bureau by the departed deacon's bedside — found in the place where the little bag of church money had lain, which the minister himself had seen the day before. Some hand had removed that bag; and whose hand could it be, if not that of the man to whom the knife belonged? For some time Silas was mute with astonishment: then he said, "God will clear me: I know nothing about the knife being there, or the money being gone. Search me and my dwelling; you will find nothing but three pound five of my own savings, which William Dane knows I have had these six months." At this William groaned, but the minister said, "The proof is heavy against you, brother Marner. The money was taken in the night last past, and no man was with our departed brother but you, for William Dane declares to us that he was hindered by sudden sickness from going to take his place as usual, and you yourself said that he had not come; and, moreover, you neglected the dead body."

"I must have slept," said Silas. Then, after a pause, he added, "Or I must have had another visitation like that which you have all seen me under, so that the thief must have come and gone while I was not in the body, but out of the body. But, I say again, search me and my dwelling, for I have been nowhere else."

The search was made, and it ended — in William Dane's finding the well-known bag, empty, tucked behind the chest of drawers in Silas's chamber! On this William exhorted his friend to confess, and not to hide his sin any longer. Silas turned a look of keen reproach on him, and said, "William, for nine years that we have gone in and out together, have you ever known me tell a lie? But God will clear me."

"Brother," said William, "how do I know what you may have done in the secret chambers of your heart, to give Satan an advantage over you?"

Silas was still looking at his friend. Suddenly a deep flush came over his face, and he was about to speak impetuously, when he seemed checked again by some inward shock, that sent the flush back and made him tremble. But at last he spoke feebly, looking at William.

"I remember now — the knife wasn't in my pocket."

William said, "I know nothing of what you mean." The other persons present, however, began to inquire where Silas meant to say that the knife was, but he would give no further explanation: he only said, "I am sore stricken; I can say nothing. God will clear me."

On their return to the vestry there was further deliberation. Any resort to legal measures for ascertaining the culprit was contrary to the principles of the church in Lantern Yard, according to which prosecution was forbidden to Christians, even had the case held less scandal to the community. But the members were bound to take other measures for finding out the truth, and they resolved on praying and drawing lots. This resolution can be a ground of surprise only to those who are unacquainted with that obscure religious life which has gone on in the alleys of our towns. Silas knelt with his brethren, relying on his own innocence being certified by immediate divine interference, but feeling that there was sorrow and mourning behind for him even then — that his trust in man had been cruelly bruised. *The lots declared that Silas Marner was guilty.* He was solemnly suspended from church-membership, and called upon to render up the stolen money: only on confession, as the sign of repentance, could he be received once more within the folds of the church. Marner listened in silence. At last, when everyone rose to depart, he went towards William Dane and said, in a voice shaken by agitation —

"The last time I remember using my knife, was when I took it out to cut a strap for you. I don't remember putting it in my pocket again. *You* stole the money, and you have woven a plot to lay the sin at my door. But you may prosper, for all that: there is no just God that governs the earth righteously, but a God of lies, that bears witness against the innocent."

There was a general shudder at this blasphemy.

William said meekly, "I leave our brethren to judge whether this is the voice of Satan or not. I can do nothing but pray for you, Silas."

Poor Marner went out with that despair in his soul — that shaken trust in God and man, which is little short of madness to a loving nature. In the bitterness of his wounded spirit, he said to himself, "*She* will cast me off too." And he reflected that, if she did not believe the testimony against him, her whole faith must be upset as his was. To people accustomed to reason about the forms in which their religious feeling has incorporated itself, it is difficult to enter into that simple, untaught state of mind in which the form and the feeling have never been severed by an act of reflection. We are apt to think it inevitable that a man in Marner's position should have begun to question the validity of an appeal to the divine judgment by drawing lots; but to him this would have been an effort of independent thought such as he had never known; and he must have made the effort at a moment when all his energies were turned into the anguish of disappointed faith. If there is an angel who records the sorrows of men as well as their sins, he knows how many and deep are the sorrows that spring from false ideas for which no man is culpable.

Marner went home, and for a whole day sat alone, stunned by despair, without any impulse to go to Sarah and attempt to win her belief in his innocence. The second day he took refuge from benumbing unbelief, by getting into his loom and working away as usual; and before many hours were past, the minister and one of the deacons came to him with the message from Sarah, that she held her engagement to him at an end. Silas received the message mutely, and then turned away from the messengers to work at his loom again. In little more than a month from that time, Sarah was married to William Dane; and not long afterwards it was known to the brethren in Lantern Yard that Silas Marner had departed from the town.[1]

1 George Eliot, *Silas Marner*, 1861, Chapter One. www.gutenberg.org/files/550/550-h/550-h.htm.

Daily Assignment

- Warm-up: Pets are our friends, and, in many ways, they have "human characteristics." But they are not human beings. Explain.
- Students will complete Concept Builder 1-B.
- Prayer journal.
- Students should outline all assigned essays for the week.

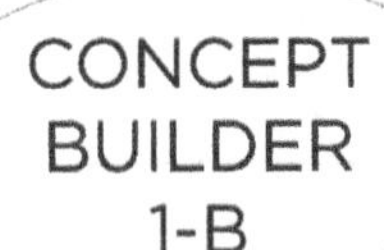

Writing Style

Compare and contrast the writing styles in the following passages:

A. There was a considerable difference between the ages of my parents, but this circumstance seemed to unite them only closer in bonds of devoted affection. There was a sense of justice in my father's upright mind which rendered it necessary that he should approve highly to love strongly. Perhaps during former years he had suffered from the late-discovered unworthiness of one beloved and so was disposed to set a greater value on tried worth. There was a show of gratitude and worship in his attachment to my mother, differing wholly from the doting fondness of age, for it was inspired by reverence for her virtues and a desire to be the means of, in some degree, recompensing her for the sorrows she had endured, but which gave inexpressible grace to his behaviour to her. Everything was made to yield to her wishes and her convenience. He strove to shelter her, as a fair exotic is sheltered by the gardener, from every rougher wind and to surround her with all that could tend to excite pleasurable emotion in her soft and benevolent mind. Her health, and even the tranquillity of her hitherto constant spirit, had been shaken by what she had gone through. During the two years that had elapsed previous to their marriage my father had gradually relinquished all his public functions; and immediately after their union they sought the pleasant climate of Italy, and the change of scene and interest attendant on a tour through that land of wonders, as a restorative for her weakened frame. (Mary Shelley, *Frankenstein*).

B. That was why he had shied in such panic. He had felt the give under his feet and heard the crackle of a snow-hidden ice skin. And to get his feet wet in such a temperature meant trouble and danger. At the very least it meant delay, for he would be forced to stop and build a fire, and under its protection to bare his feet while he dried his socks and moccasins. He stood and studied the creek bed and its banks, and decided that the flow of water came from the right. He reflected awhile, rubbing his nose and cheeks, then skirted to the left, stepping gingerly and testing the footing for each step. Once clear of the danger, he took a fresh chew of tobacco and swung along at his four-mile gait. (Jack London, "To Build a Fire")

Elements	Passage A	Passage B
Narration: Does the author let the reader see into everyone's mind? Give an example.	*Yes. Shelley reveals the characters' thoughts. "There was a sense of justice in my father's upright mind which rendered it necessary that he should approve highly to love strongly."*	*No. London merely allows the reader to see into one character's mind. "That was why he had shied in such panic. He had felt the give under his feet and heard the crackle of a snow-hidden ice skin."*
Diction: Does the author use complicated/big words? Give an example.	yes. "her health, and even the Tranquility of her hitherto Constant spirit"	no. "one clear of danger he took a fresh chew of..."
Imagery: Does the author use a lot of descriptive words to explain things? Give an example.	yes. "But this circumstense seemed to unite them only closer in bonds of devoted Affection	no. "He stood and studied the creek bed and it's banks"

Lesson 3

Sample Literary Analysis

The setting of a story or a play is as important as the characters, for the setting is what creates the "mood." In *Murder in the Cathedral*, T.S. Eliot uses a cathedral as his entire setting, and much to the advantage of the play, he never leaves it.

Thomas a'Beckett is an archbishop who steps out of line according to the king of the land. Therefore, he must die. Eliot uses the cathedral as a place of refuge, peril, and later, death. It is in the cathedral where the life of Thomas a'Beckett essentially begins and ends. The fact that he is an archbishop is also significant to the setting. Beckett is ordained in the cathedral; he preaches in the cathedral; he gives the sacraments in the cathedral. The cathedral is the central focus of his life. It is in the walls of the cathedral that God seems so present, but even there evil resides. Normally, the cathedral is safe, but in this play murder comes to the safe cathedral. Eliot is saying something about life.

Martyrdom of Saint Thomas Becket, Anonymous, c. 1250 (PD-Art).

Since people come here to worship and to pray, the chorus (who sings throughout the play) fits in wonderfully. The chorus is critically consequential to the development of the climax. It joins a'Beckett in the cathedral and ultimately the assassins — the knights — join the chorus, and chicanery results. It all happens in the cathedral. The archbishop, the chorus, the knights (who murder Thomas), and finally the cathedral become the closing scene of this brilliant play. It is in the cathedral that Thomas a'Beckett lives out his destiny. (Jessica Stobaugh)

Daily Assignment

- Warm-up: Have you ever lost a pet? How did he/she die? How did you feel?
- Students will complete a daily Concept Builder 1-C.
- Prayer journal.
- Students should write rough drafts of all assigned essays.

Building an Outline

Examine the setting in these two passages.

A. Southern Arkansas was a generous but exhausted land. Cotton grew to bountiful heights. Southwest winds permanently bent rice plants pregnant with pounds and pounds of offspring. Pecan trees cradled whole acres of antediluvian loam with their gigantic arms. Every spring, bayous and rivers deposited a rich delta gift along the banks of grateful farmland. It was a gift from Minnesota and Ohio — freely given by the ubiquitous Mississippi River. This was really an unselfish land, a land that seemed to give more than it took.

The house in which I now lived was a natural addition to this magnificent land. Built during the depression years of cheap labor, it reflected my grandparent's unbounded optimism. They had built it with a profitable business and Depression-priced labor. They shamelessly flaunted their prosperity in a culture that was painfully impoverished. No one seemed to mind. The South has always been kind to its elitists. They were a chosen people, or so they claimed with every offering of ebullience. No one questioned their credentials — especially when my grandmother imported bricks from New Orleans streets, painted wicker chairs from replete Havana shops, and crystal chandeliers from abandoned Liverpool mansions. I remember that the bricks surrounding our fireplace evoked a faint smell of horse manure every winter as we enjoyed our winter fires.

Where? Southern Arkansas

When? the Great Depression

Is the setting important? Why or why not? Yes because it helps us understand what it was like for them

B. In the later part of the 17th century, there lived a man of science — an eminent proficient in every branch of natural philosophy — who, not long before our story opens, had made experience of a spiritual affinity, more attractive than any chemical one. He had left his laboratory to the care of an assistant, cleared his fine countenance from the furnace-smoke, washed the stain of acids from his fingers, and persuaded a beautiful woman to become his wife. In those days, when the comparatively recent discovery of electricity, and other kindred mysteries of nature, seemed to open paths into the region of miracle, it was not unusual for the love of science to rival the love of woman, in its depth and absorbing energy. The higher intellect, the imagination, the spirit, and even the heart, might all find their congenial aliment in pursuits which, as some of their ardent votaries believed, would ascend from one step of powerful intelligence to another, until the philosopher should lay his hand on the secret of creative force, and perhaps make new worlds for himself. We know not whether Aylmer possessed this degree of faith in man's ultimate control over nature. He had devoted himself, however, too unreservedly to scientific studies, ever to be weaned from them by any second passion. His love for his young wife might prove the stronger of the two; but it could only be by intertwining itself with his love of science, and uniting the strength of the latter to its own. (Nathaniel Hawthorne, "The Birthmark")

Where? Laboratory

When? 17th century

Is the setting important? Why or why not? Yes because then we know what a lab can do

Grammar Review: Overview

Grammar Review concerns quality and substance, not content. It is, simply, the way you write. Traits of an effective style include: focus, concreteness, vitality, originality, grace, and commitment.

There are three elements of style that you will need to address:

- focus: awareness of audience/task; clear purpose.
- content: ideas are specific, relevant to focus, and fully developed.
- organization: there is a logical order of ideas.

Who is your audience? What is your task? How can you walk your reader to a point of enlightenment? Are you trying to entertain? To inform? Both? Your answers to these questions, and other stylistic questions, will both focus your paper and move your reader to a desired conclusion, or it will diffuse your paper and move your reader into a place of confusion. Is the focus clearly stated? To what audience is this essay written? Does it focus the reader or confuse the reader? Are your ideas relevant to focus and fully developed? Finally, is your paper logically organized?

Which of the following passages has the best "style"? Why?

A. Fishing in King Tut Lake was the manliest fishing possible. King Tut was no man-made lake with Augustine grass, manicured sea shores, and smooth, welcoming docks launching the angler into a viscous realm. King Tut, only a mile in length through a swamp, coiled like a horseshoe. It was difficult to know, at some places along its circumference, where the swamp ended and King Tut began.

Within its environs were a plethora of vicious water snakes, venomous moccasins — euphemistically called cottonmouths — and huge snapping turtles. The intrepid aggression of these wild reptiles was encouraged by the absence of human contact.

The most salient and intimidating feature of King Tut Lake, however, was huge cypress trees, some older than the Republic. Over the years, dry seasons had teased huge cypress knees out of the shallow transplanted bayou water, until, by 1965, the cypress trees squatted in the tepid lake, only a few years from being a swamp, like squatting sumo wrestlers. At five on this July evening in the middle of the 1960s my dad and I pushed our little 14-footer into mossy King Tut Lake. It felt a lot like the way the French explorer Marquette must have felt when he eased his canoe from the relative safety of backwater streams into the Mississippi River.

We were immediately attacked by a disoriented or terribly brave three- foot water snake that skillfully circled our john boat and then went in for the kill. For three successive attacks, the water snake bit our aluminum boat. I had been told that snakes do not bite in the water — but this one surely did. While I found the whole thing unnerving, my dad merely laughed. I lobbied strenuously to shoot the thing with the 22-caliber pistol in our boat, and my dad gently pushed the thing away with his paddle — even as the serpent continued to attack his paddle!

Finally, after the water snake was sufficiently satisfied that the big old floating monster in his lake was dead or knew his position in the cosmos or was not going to bother him again or whatever water snakes think when they attack big things, it withdrew with obvious satisfaction and quietly slid to the top of a cypress knee from which it unceremoniously drove away a snapping turtle and glared at us as we slid by in our boat.

B. King Tut was a pretty wild lake in south Arkansas. I can remember a time when a mean snake attacked our boat. My dad and I were fishing. The snake actually bit our boat! Wow was I scared!

Daily Assignment

- Warm-up: Buck feels great loyalty to Thornton. Loyalty is a powerful human action. Define loyalty and then describe a situation where you were loyal to someone (e.g., a friend) or something (e.g., a sports team). How did it feel to be loyal?
- Students will complete Concept Builder 1-D.
- Prayer journal.
- Review the assigned text. Keep vocabulary cards.
- This is the day that students should write, and then rewrite, the final drafts of their assigned essays.

Vocabulary

Define the following words (found in Jack London, *The Call of the Wild*) and use them in a sentence:

1. Lacerated
   Definition: to tear or make deep cuts in flesh.
   Sentence: "the point had lacerated his neck"
2. Primordial basic and fundimental
   Definition:
   Sentence: "The pimordial needs of the masses"
3. Wizened
   Definition: Shriveled or wrinkled with age
   Sentence: "a wizened, weather-beaten old man."
4. Disconsolate
   Definition: causing or showing a lack of comfort; cheerless
   Sentence: "he'd met the man's disconsolate widow"
5. Malingerer
   Definition: exaggerate or feign illness in order to escape duty or work
   Sentence: "the docter said my son was a malingerer
6. Bedlam
   Definition: a scene of uproar or confusion
   Sentence: "there was bedlam in the cartroom
7. Innocuously
   Definition: not harmful of offensive
   Sentence: "it was an innocuous question"
8. Importune
   Definition: Ask some one pressingly and persistently for or to do something
   Sentence: "If he were alive now, I should importune him with Questions

General Discussion — Worldviews

Chapter 2

First Thoughts

If you are a committed Christian believer, you will be challenged to analyze worldviews of individuals and institutions around you. You are inextricably tied to your culture, but that does not mean you can't be "in this culture" but not "of this culture." Furthermore, you will be asked to explain your own worldview and to defend it against all sorts of assaults. It is important that you pause and examine several worldviews that you will encounter. You also need to articulate your own worldview.

Chapter Learning Objectives

In chapter 2 we will write our own worldviews, and we will also analyze other worldviews in literature.

As a result of this chapter study, you will be able to . . .

1. Consider your own worldview.
2. Analyze other worldviews in literature.

Look Ahead for Friday

- Turn in a final copy of essay
- Take Weekly Test

Background

Throughout this course and your educational career, you will be challenged to analyze the worldviews of many writers. Jack London, for instance, has a worldview that is radically different from the worldview that you encounter in the Joseph story.

For now, though, it is important that you pause and examine several worldviews that you will encounter in literature and the arts. You will then need to articulate your own worldview.

Remember two things about worldviews:

- All parts of culture have a worldview.
- Not all worldviews are correct assessments of reality.

Two primary worldviews originated from Greek philosophers:

- Aristotle argued that the empirical world was primary.
- Plato argued that the metaphysical world was primary.

Aristotle, for instance, argues that reality is connected to epistemology, or knowledge. If one cannot measure something or duplicate something, then it is not real. Plato, on the other hand, clearly argues that reality is in the heavens and must be discovered by mankind. What happens on earth is most important to Aristotle; what happens in heaven is most important to Plato.

The *Star Wars* movies of the last century highlight this dialectic in bold relief: are virtues good because they are appreciated by the Jedi, or are they appreciated by the Jedi because they are good (Plato vs. Aristotle)? In fact, every worldview we encounter, every decision we make, is determined by how we answer this basic question: "What is most important: what God (metaphysics) says or what man (empiricism) says?"

Daily Assignment

- Warm-up: In the *Star Wars* movies, Ewoks enjoy the natural beauty of the forest. They are the most harmonious civilization in the whole *Star Wars* series. The Ewoks are fighting to protect the forest — not to support the revolution. What worldview do they represent?
- Students will complete Concept Builder 2-A.
- Prayer journal: Students are encouraged to write in their prayer journal every day.
- Students need to review their material for the next assignment
- Students should systematically review their vocabulary words daily.

Worldview in Art

Romanticism is a worldview that emphasizes the unusual and the subjective. Thus, romantic art is usually flamboyant and exaggerated. It is always full of bright colors and happy landscapes (e.g., water falls). Naturalism, on the other hand, emphasizes the macabre, the objective. It often portrays bleak, dreary, cold landscapes.

Draw a romantic sunset and a naturalistic sunset:

Romantic Sunset

Naturalistic Sunset

Lesson 2

Literary Analysis: Worldview

The following are seven worldviews found in art and literature:

1

Theism: God is personally involved with humankind. Theism argues that the universe is a purposive, divinely created entity. It argues that all human life is sacred and all persons are of equal dignity. They are, in other words, created in the image of God. History is linear and moves toward a final goal. Nature is controlled by God and is an orderly system. Humanity is neither the center of nature nor the universe, but is the steward of creation. Righteousness will triumph in a decisive conquest of evil. Earthly life does not exhaust human existence but looks ahead to the resurrection of the dead and to a final, comprehensive judgment of humanity (adapted from Carl F. H. Henry, *Toward a Recovery of Christian Belief*). This was the only viable world view until the Renaissance. Examples: Homer, Virgil, C. S. Lewis, A. J. Cronin, Tolkien.

2

Deism: God was present but is no longer present. The world is like a clock wound up by God many years ago, but He is now absent. The clock (i.e., the world) is present; God is absent. Still, though, Deism embraced a Judeo-Christian morality. God's absence, for instance, in no way mitigated His importance to original creation. He was also omnipotent but not omniscient. His absence was His decision. He was in no way forced to be absent from the world. He chose to assume that role so that Socratic empiricism and rationalism could reign as sovereign king. Speculative Theism replaced revelatory biblical Theism. Once the living God was abandoned, Jesus Christ and the Bible became cognitive orphans (Carl F. H. Henry). Examples: Ben Franklin, Thomas Jefferson.

3

Romanticism: Once Americans distanced themselves from the self-revealing God of the Old and New Testaments, they could not resist making further concessions to subjectivity. Romanticism, and its American version, Transcendentalism, posited that God was nature and "it" was good. The more natural things were, the better. Nature was inherently good. Nature alone was the ultimate reality. In other words, nature was the Romantic god. Man was essentially a complex animal, too complex to be controlled by absolute, codified truth (as one would find in the Bible). Human intuition replaced the Holy Spirit. Depending upon the demands on individual lives, truth and good were relative and changing. Romanticism, however, like Deism, had not completely abandoned Judeo-Christian morality. Truth and the good, although changing, were nonetheless relatively durable. Examples: James Fenimore Cooper, Goethe.

4

Naturalism: If God exists, He is pretty wimpish. Only the laws of nature have any force. God is either uninterested or downright mean. All reality was reducible to impersonal processes and energy events (Carl F. H. Henry). All life, including human life, was transient. Its final destination was death. Truth and good, therefore, were also transient. They were culture-conditioned distinctions that the human race projected upon the cosmos and upon history (Carl F. H. Henry). This maturation, as it were, of the human race, necessitated a deliberate rejection of all transcendentally final authority. Examples: Joseph Conrad, Stephen Crane.

5

Realism: Akin to Naturalism is Realism. Reality is, to a Realist, a world with no purpose, no meaning, no order. Realism insists that personality has no ultimate status in the universe, but is logically inconsistent when it affirms an ethically imperative social agenda congruent with universal human rights and dignity. Realism, then, throws around terms like "dignity" and "human rights" and "power." What Realists mean, however, is that these concepts are real when they fulfill a social agenda that enhances human dominance over the universal. Thus, Realism believes in a world where bad things happen all the time to good people. Why not? There is no God, no ontological controlling force for good. The world is a place where the only reality is that which we can experience, but it must be experience that we can measure or replicate. Certainly pain and misery fit that category. If an experience is a unique occurrence (e.g., a miracle) it is not real. Examples: Ernest Hemingway, F. Scott Fitzgerald.

6

Absurdism: A modern movement where there is neither a god nor any reason to have one. Everything is disorganized, and anarchy rules. There is a compete abandonment of explaining the cosmos and therefore an abandonment of being in relationship with the deity. It is not that Absurdists are unsure about who creates everything, or is in control of everything. Absurdists simply do not care one way or the other. Examples: John Barth, Kurt Vonnegut, Jr.

7

Existentialism: The submergence of God in overwhelming data and in experience is the first step toward putting God out to die. Truth is open to debate. Everything is relative. A very pessimistic view. Examples: Albert Camus, Franz Kafka, and Jean-Paul Sartre.

Daily Assignment

- Warm-up: Who is my hero/heroine? Why? What does your choice tell you about your world view?
- Students will complete Concept Builder 2-B.
- Prayer journal.
- Students should outline all assigned essays for the week.

Celebrity Worldviews

What worldview does each quote manifest? The definitions of these worldviews are found in Lesson 2.

A. Theism

B. Deism

C. Romanticism/Transcendentalism

D. Naturalism

E. Realism

F. Existentialism

G. Absurdism

__B__ **Kate Gosselin:** My kids are the reason I have always done everything. My kids are the reason I laid on bed rest for 30 entire weeks. My kids are the reason that I wrote the books and it's always about them. And, I know that it looks it's all about me all the time and whatever, but what you don't see is down deep inside it's a desperate desire to provide for my kids.

__A__ **Danny Gokey:** I get my strength from my faith in God. My goal is to be a Christian who does mainstream music. I want my music to reach out to the multitudes. I want to bring entertainment, but I want to bring encouragement and hope at the same time.

__E__ **Zac Efron:** I don't have a Twitter, a MySpace or a Facebook or anything like that. . . . I kind of value in people not knowing where I am or what I'm doing.

__D__ **Kara Dioguardi:** I'm one of those people who's pretty honest and kind of say what I feel. I think you're going to see me be nice at times, but I'm a little more hard on the contestants.

__G__ **David Cook:** Whenever I feel like I need to get my ego in check, I'll call my family.

__F__ **David Archuleta:** The fact that people were able to feel what I was trying to give off as I sing is one of the coolest and best feelings ever.

Lesson 3

Culture Wars: The Battle for Truth

Worldview Review

Christian Theism: Christian theism advances a worldview that there is an omnipotent God who has authored an inspired, authoritative work called the Bible, upon whose precepts mankind should base its society.

Deism: Deism advances a worldview that accepts the notion that there is an authoritative, inspired source from which mankind should base its society (i.e., the Bible). Likewise, the deist is certain that there was once an omnipotent God. However, once the world was created, that same omnipotent God chose to absent Himself from His creation. The world, then, is like a clock. It was once created by an intelligent process; however, now the Creator is absent, leaving mankind on its own to figure out how the clock works and to go on living.

Romanticism: A natural companion to deism was rationalism. Rationalism (e.g., John Locke's philosophy) invited the deist to see mankind as a "chalkboard" on which was written experience that ultimately created a personality. Thus, rationalists/deists were fond of speaking of "unalienable right" or "common sense." The romantic (in America the romantic would be called "the transcendentalist") took issue with deism and theism. To the romantic, nature was God. Nature — an undefined indigenous, omnipotent presence — was very good. Original sin was man's separation from nature. In fact, the degree to which mankind returned to nature would determine his goodness and effectiveness. Thus, a man like Henry David Thoreau lived a year on Walden Pond so that he could find his God. In *Deerslayer* by James Fenimore Cooper, the protagonist is safe while he is on a lake separated from evil mankind. Only when he participates in human society is he in trouble. The romantic was naturally suspicious of theism because theism appeared to be dogmatic and close-minded. The romantics had confessions, but they had no dogma. Deism also bothered the romantics. Romanticism emphasized the subjective; deism emphasized the objective. In the romantic novel *Frankenstein,* the deist/rationalist Dr. Frankenstein creates a monster. Dr. Frankenstein, with disastrous results, turns his back on the subjective and tries to use science to create life.

Naturalism: Naturalism was inclined to agree with romanticism's criticism of theism and deism but did not believe in a benevolent nature. In fact, nature, to the naturalist, was malevolent, mischievous, and unpredictable. Mankind, as it were, lost control of the universe, and the person who had control did not really care much for his creation. Theism, of course, was absurd. How could any sane person who experienced World War I believe in a loving, living God? Deism was equally wrong. There is no God — nature is unpredictable. Romanticism was on the right track but terribly naive. God and His creation were certainly not "good" in any sense of the word. Nature was evil. Naturalism embraced a concept of fate not dissimilar to that held by the Greeks. In Homer's *Iliad,* for instance, the characters were subject to uncontrolled fate and pernicious gods and goddesses who inflicted terrible and good things on mankind with no apparent design or reason. To the naturalist, God was at best absent or ineffective; at worst, he was malevolent.

Realism: Realism was philosophically akin to naturalism, which did not believe in God at all. In a sense, naturalism was a natural companion to realism. Realism was different from naturalism in degree, not in substance. Realism argued that if people were honest, they would admit that God is not present at all. If there were anything worth embracing, it was reality. Realism advanced an in-your-face view of life. Realists prided themselves in "telling it like it is." They entered the cosmic arena and let the chips fall where they may. They shared the same criticisms of views that the naturalists held.

Absurdism: Absurdism certainly believed that realism was on track. Where realism erred, however, was its propensity to see meaning in life. Mind you, the meaning was tied to things one could see and feel, not in things that were abstract or immutable, but the realist still sought some meaning in this life. The absurdist abandoned all hope of finding meaning in life and embraced a sort of nihilism. The absurdist was convinced that everything was meaningless and absurd. The subjectivity of a romantic was appealing to the absurdist. However, even that implied that something was transcendent — a desire — and the absurdist would have nothing to do with that. Billy Pilgrim, a protagonist in one of the absurdist Kurt Vonnegut Jr.'s novels, became "unhinged from time" and "wandered around in the cosmos." Things without meaning happened to him whose life had no meaning. Everything was absurd.

Existentialism: Existentialism stepped outside the debate of meaning altogether. Existentialists argued that the quest was futile. The only thing that mattered was subjective feeling. "Experience" was a God at whose feet the existentialist worshiped. Romanticism was on the right track in that it invited mankind to explore subjectivity. Where it erred was when it refused to give up the deity. Naturalism was an anomaly. It was too busy arguing with the cosmos to see that reality was in human desire, not in providence. The degree to which mankind was to discover and experience these desires determined the degree to which people participated in the divine.

Daily Assignment

- Warm-up: Describe an event or philosophy in current culture that is against the biblical worldview.
- Students will complete Concept Builder 2-C.
- Prayer journal.
- Students should write rough drafts of all assigned essays and speech.

Interaction with the World

Analyze the worldviews of *The Lion King* characters:

Character	Education	Religion	Relationships
Simba	*Taught by his father and Rafiki. He represents generations that precede him.*	*Simba is raised in the religion of his father.*	*Simba is influenced a great deal by relationships.*
Mufasa	Taught by Father	FAther	loyal
Scar	FAther	Revenge	Pride
Hyenas	SCAR	FOOD	Followers
Rafiki	Elders (?)	divination	leader
Pumba & Timon	life	hakna matata	Side kicks
Zazu	King / Life	FAther	(?)
Nala	King		Friend / wife

Character	Worldview
Simba	*Theism*
Mufasa	Deism
Scar	NAturalism
Hyenas	absurdism
Rafiki	Realism
Pumba & Timon	Exist
Zazu	Romantism
Nala	theism

Lesson 4

Grammar Review: Active/Passive Voice

Voice is that modification of the verb that shows whether the subject names the actor or the thing acted upon. The active voice shows that the subject names the actor. The passive voice shows that the subject names the thing acted upon.

The following are active voice sentences:

> The industrious bees gather honey from the flowers.
>
> The storm drove the vessel against the rock.

The following are passive voice sentences:

> Our words should be carefully chosen.
>
> The English were conquered by the Normans.

In any grammar text, check out these common stylistic problems: sentence variety, passive voice, too many qualifiers.

Compare the following:

A. The soldier was hit by the shrapnel.

B. The shrapnel hit the soldier.

Sentence A is passive voice, and sentence B is active voice. Typically, use of active voice verbs produces more effective writing.

Daily Assignment

- Warm-up: Describe one object that captures who you really are. Why did you choose that object?
- Students will complete Concept Builder 2-D.
- Prayer journal.
- Review the assigned text. Keep vocabulary cards.
- This is the day that students should write, and then rewrite, the final drafts of their assigned essay.

My Worldview

Write your worldview:

A. What is the priority of the spiritual, unseen, transcendent world?

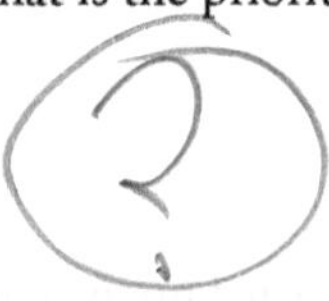

B. What is the essential uniqueness of humankind? Is there something different about people as compared to other living creatures? yes. We are different from Animals because we have souls they don't and we were made in Gods image.

C. What is the objective character of truth and goodness? Is there a right thing to do? Or are all decisions based on circumstances? God has allowed us to know right from wrong. And bible can help with knowing right from wrong too.

D. Pleasure — what do you really enjoy doing? Is it moral?

Nothing on this earth will last

E. Fate — what/who really determines your life? Chance? Circumstances? God?

God

F. Justice — what are the consequences of our actions? Is there some sort of judgment? Do bad people suffer? Why do good people suffer?

All people suffer because of sin.
yes there will be consequences

Narration — *The Call of the Wild* (Jack London)

Chapter 3

First Thoughts

The *narration* of a story is the way the author chooses to tell the story. An author intentionally uses different forms of narration, typically one of the following types. After this lesson, students should understand why an author chooses a particular narrative technique. They should also be able to write a literary analysis about the narration of any literary work.

Chapter Learning Objectives

In chapter 3 we will write our own worldviews, and we will also analyze other worldviews in literature.

As a result of this chapter study, you will be able to . . .

1. Define naturalism and discuss why it is not biblical.
2. Discuss the way females are presented in *The Call of the Wild.*

Look Ahead for Friday

- Turn in a final copy of essay
- Take Weekly Test

Literary Analysis: Narration

First-person Narrator: a character who refers to himself or herself using "I." The narrator is the protagonist (e.g., Huw in *How Green Was My Valley*) or a reliable participant in the story, perhaps a foil (e.g., the narrator in "The Fall of the House of Usher," by Edgar Allan Poe).

Second-person Narrator: addresses the reader and/or the main character as "you" (and may also use first-person narration, but not necessarily). Probably the rarest mode in literature (though quite common in song lyrics) is the second-person narrative mode, in which the narrator refers to one of the characters as "you," therefore making readers feel they are characters in the story. Besides the fact that second person is unacceptable in formal English fiction, and therefore gives the impression that the literary work is "cheap fiction," most authors much prefer using the similar, and far more acceptable, first-person narration. A.A. Milne, in *Winnie the Pooh*, uses both first and second person narration.

Third-person Narrator: not a character in the story; refers to the story's characters as "he" and "she." The author gives no insight into the mind of any character. This is probably the most common form of narration. This is the favorite narrative technique of American authors Stephen Crane (e.g., "Blue Hotel") and Herman Melville (e.g., *Billy Budd*).

Limited Omniscient Narrator: is only able to tell what one person is thinking or feeling. Normally, an author chooses one character from whose perspective he will tell the story. For example, Jack London, in *Call of the Wild*, tells his story from the perspective of Buck. However, London uses third person to tell the story, versus Anne Sewell's Black Beauty, where she tells the story from a horse's perspective but uses first person. Both are Limited Omniscient Narration but London uses third person; Sewell uses first person.

Omniscient Narrator: invites readers into the minds of all the characters. We know what everyone is thinking. Victor Hugo in his epic novels, e.g., *Les Miserables*, prefers this narrative technique.

Reliable Narrator: everything this narrator says is true, and the narrator knows everything that is necessary to the story. Reliability is a critical issue related to ethos. After all, if we cannot trust the narrator, we cannot be sure about anything else (e.g., plot). Authors normally choose reliable narrators. Edith Wharton, in her classic *Ethan Frome*, chooses a reliable stranger to tell her story rather than using a character in the story. This allows her to analyze each character dispassionately.

Unreliable Narrator: narrator may not know all the relevant information; may be intoxicated or mentally ill; may lie to the audience. Most critics consider Holden Caulfield in *Catcher in the Rye* to be unreliable. Likewise, the narrator in the short story "Yellow Wallpaper," by Charlotte Gilmore, is quite literally insane, so, naturally, the credibility of the narration is questionable.

Daily Assignment

- Warm-up: Pretend that you are a dog who is sleeping outside under a dripping faucet. What are you dreaming?
- Students will complete Concept Builder 3-A.
- Prayer journal: Students are encouraged to write in their prayer journal every day.
- Students need to review their material for the next assignment
- Students should systematically review their vocabulary words daily.

Creating Narration

Create your own narration. (Examples: **First-Person Narration:** I love soccer. **Omniscient Narration:** Mary and Sally thought, *I love soccer.* **Limited Omniscient Narration:** Mary thought, *I love soccer.* Sally said, "I love it, too." **Third-Person Objective:** Mary and Sally played soccer very well, and, by their actions, the reader might surmise that they loved soccer.)

A. First-Person Narration

I love to play my ukulele

B. Omniscient Narration

all the people in the room wondered what had happened

C. Limited Omniscient Narration

Kayla thought, I love ukulele Hannah said, "I love to hear you play the ukulele

D. Third-Person Objective Narration

Hannah and Kayla Run very well.

Lesson 2

Chapter 1: Into the Primitive

Old longings nomadic leap,
Chafing at custom's chain;
Again from its brumal sleep
Wakens the ferine strain.[1]

Buck did not read the newspapers, or he would have known that trouble was brewing, not alone for himself, but for every tidewater dog, strong of muscle and with warm, long hair, from Puget Sound to San Diego. Because men, groping in the Arctic darkness, had found a yellow metal, and because steamship and transportation companies were booming the find, thousands of men were rushing into the Northland. These men wanted dogs, and the dogs they wanted were heavy dogs, with strong muscles by which to toil, and furry coats to protect them from the frost.

Buck lived at a big house in the sun-kissed Santa Clara Valley. Judge Miller's place, it was called. It stood back from the road, half hidden among the trees, through which glimpses could be caught of the wide cool veranda that ran around its four sides. The house was approached by graveled driveways which wound about through wide-spreading lawns and under the interlacing boughs of tall poplars. At the rear, things were on even a more spacious scale than at the front. There were great stables, where a dozen grooms and boys held forth, rows of vine-clad servants' cottages, an endless and orderly array of outhouses, long grape arbors, green pastures, orchards, and berry patches. Then there was the pumping plant for the artesian well, and the big cement tank where Judge Miller's boys took their morning plunge and kept cool in the hot afternoon.

And over this great demesne Buck ruled. Here he was born, and here he had lived the four years of his life. It was true, there were other dogs, there could not but be other dogs on so vast a place, but they did not count. They came and went, resided in the populous kennels, or lived obscurely in the recesses of the house after the fashion of Toots, the Japanese pug, or Ysabel, the Mexican hairless — strange creatures that rarely put nose out of doors or set foot to ground. On the other hand, there were the fox terriers, a score of them at least, who yelped fearful promises at Toots and Ysabel looking out of the windows at them and protected by a legion of housemaids armed with brooms and mops.

But Buck was neither house-dog nor kennel-dog. The whole realm was his. He plunged into the swimming tank or went hunting with the Judge's sons; he escorted Mollie and Alice, the Judge's daughters, on long twilight or early morning rambles; on wintry nights he lay at the Judge's feet before the roaring library fire; he carried the Judge's grandsons on his back, or rolled them in the grass, and guarded their footsteps through wild adventures down to the fountain in the stable yard, and even beyond, where the paddocks were, and the berry patches. Among the terriers he stalked imperiously, and Toots and Ysabel he utterly ignored, for he was king over all creeping, crawling, flying things of Judge Miller's place, humans included.

His father, Elmo, a huge St. Bernard, had been the Judge's inseparable companion, and Buck bid fair to follow in the way of his father. He was not so large — he weighed only one hundred and forty pounds — for his mother, Shep, had been a Scotch shepherd dog. Nevertheless, one hundred and forty pounds, to which was added the dignity that comes of good living and universal respect, enabled him to carry himself in right royal fashion. During the four years since his puppyhood he had lived the life of a sated aristocrat; he had a fine pride in himself, was even a trifle egotistical, as country gentlemen sometimes become because of their insular situation. But he had saved himself by not becoming a mere pampered house-dog. Hunting and kindred outdoor delights had kept down the fat and hardened his muscles; and to him, as to the cold-tubing races, the love of water had been a tonic and a health preserver.

1 www.literature.org/authors/london-jack/the-call-of-the-wild/chapter-01.html.

Daily Assignment

- Warm-up: In what ways can instant messaging be harmful to writing?
- Students will complete Concept Builder 3-B.
- Prayer journal.
- Students should outline all assigned essays for the week.

Style

You are unjustly accused of participating in a fight. Write letters to three friends: a peer, your parents, and your pastor.

I. DEAR BEST FRIEND (A PEER), I hope that you will pray for me as I go through this trial. I know that you will believe me when I say that I had nothing to do with those bullies. Thank you for being such a good friend.

II. DEAR MOM AND DAD, I have been injustly accused of participating in a horrific fight between a group of bullies and innocent children. I am not sure what I should do because no body will believe me if I tell the truth.

III. DEAR PASTOR, What should I do when I'm falsly accused of doing something unGodly? please help me find Gods purpose in this. maybe even some bible references. Thank you.

Sample Essay: Narration

The following is a paper about narration in a book entitled *Ethan Frome* by Edith Wharton.

Narration in *Ethan Frome*

In her early 20th century novel *Ethan Frome*, Edith Wharton employed the narrative technique called limited omniscient. The story was retold through the narration of a young engineer, who in effect formed a sort of relationship with the indefinable Ethan Frome. Using this narration strategy allowed Wharton to bring the reader into the action but to do so at a safe distance.

One might wonder what Wharton's reasoning was in using an outsider to unveil her most outstanding novel. There was no relation between the older, crippled, stoic and somewhat bitter Frome, and the younger, vivacious stranger. Their relationship seemed contrived. Each, however, seemed to hold a sort of awe and respect for the other. This drew them together and added credibility to the engineer. He knew Frome because in some ways they were the same person, or, rather, the engineer was what Frome wanted to be but never could be.

At the same time, there is distance between Frome and the engineer. This makes the whole narration technique work — there is a sort of mutual obeisance that keeps Ethan, the engineer, and the reader at bay. We all speak to one another, but we keep our emotional distance. Ethan does not want to become too close to the engineer because it is too painful — he always wanted to be an engineer. The neutral commentator stays away from Ethan because he does not want to touch Ethan's pain. And the reader is invited to be a "naturalistic" audience; i.e., like nature, we are only tangentially involved in their pain. We observe from a distance. We, the reader, therefore, are not even tempted to indulge in the appearance of sentimentality. Narration made all this possible.

Wharton chose wisely. The engineer served to do more than just narrate; he is also a representation of what Frome could have been. If he had chosen not to return home when his father died, if he had chosen not to marry Zeena, Ethan could have fulfilled his dream of becoming an engineer and could have been successful and happy. Alas, he did not and so lived in sorrow and misery for the rest of his unhappy life, wretched and torn. As seen in chapter 8, "Confused motions of rebellion stormed in him. He was too young, too strong, and too full of the sap of living to submit so easily to the destruction of his hopes." Frome had a romantic side, a side that allowed him the pleasure of imagining life as an engineer, or as being out west with his beloved Matty, or as just being happy. The narration teased this out. A fitting example of this romantic Frome is in chapter 4 where Ethan envisions himself and Matty spending the evening together. "Like a married couple, he in his stocking feet smoking his pipe, she laughing and talking. . . ." Frome's sense of peace and happiness was a perfect example of his romantic character. Everything was grand and jovial; his cares and strivings were to the wind when he was alone with Matty Silver.

However, this romantic ideal was not to stay such for long because his world was caving in. His desires and hopes were not to be. And so," All the long misery of his baffled past, of his youth of failure, hardship and vain effort, rose up in his soul in bitterness and seemed to take shape before him in the woman (his wife Zeena) who at every turn had barred his way. She had taken everything else from him. Now she meant to take the one thing that made up for all the others." Which was Matty. Suddenly, the dreamy Frome became distraught and bitter.

Ethan represented Wharton's penchant toward naturalism. Simply put, naturalism is a worldview that posited that fate controls mankind. Naturalism emphasized the ordinary, the everyday. To Wharton, and to Frome by the end of the novel, if there were a God, he certainly was not a nice one. The effervescent hope of an adolescent Frome was replaced by an angry, unhappy, bitter man captured in a veritable hell with two broken bitter women.

Edith Wharton invites the reader into her naturalistic world by having us journey via flashback through the mind of the engineer and his friend Ethan Frome. We see the idealistic New Englander deteriorate into the trapped, wretched farmer whom we know as the indomitable Ethan Frome. As the reader sees this world unfold, he is led by the hand of an omniscient narrator through a naturalistic, hellish universe. (Jessica Stobaugh).

Daily Assignment

- Warm-up: Readers must judge the reliability of narrators. For example, the narrator in Edgar Allan Poe's short story "Tell Tale Heart" literarily is obviously insane as he tells the story! How reliable is that! How reliable a narrator is Buck in *The Call of the Wild*? What makes narration reliable? Unreliable?
- Students will complete a daily Concept Builder 3-C.
- Prayer journal.
- Students should write rough drafts of all assigned essays.

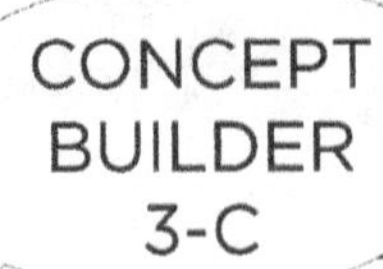

Naturalism in Art

A. Naturalism has realistic, often gross images.

B. Naturalism has many nature scenes but these scenes are dark, foggy, and dangerous.

C. Naturalism has a lot of confused, angry characters.

D. Naturalism creates a world where there is no God, no one in control, no benevolent force.

Rate this picture 1 (least) to 5 (greatest) in the categories above:

A. 1 2 3 4 5

B. 1 2 3 4 5

C. 1 2 3 4 5

D. 1 2 3 4 5

What is the most naturalistic characteristic of this painting? The setting

The Harvesters, by Pieter Brueghel the Elder, 1565 (PD-Art).

A. Naturalism has realistic, often gross images.

B. Naturalism has many nature scenes but these scenes are dark, foggy, and dangerous.

C. Naturalism has a lot of confused, angry characters.

D. Naturalism creates a world where there is no God, no one in control, no benevolent force.

Rate this picture 1 (least) to 5 (greatest) in the categories above:

A. 1 2 3 4 5

B. 1 2 3 4 5

C. 1 2 3 4 5

D. 1 2 3 4 5

Christ on the Sea of Galilee, by Eugène Delacroix, 1854 (PD-US).

What is the most naturalistic characteristic of this painting?

it's dark, foggy and dangerous

A. Naturalism has realistic, often gross images.

B. Naturalism has many nature scenes but these scenes are dark, foggy, and dangerous.

C. Naturalism has a lot of confused, angry characters.

D. Naturalism creates a world where there is no God, no one in control, no benevolent force.

Rate this picture 1 (least) to 5 (greatest) in the categories above:

A. 1 2 3 4 5

B. 1 2 3 4 5

C. 1 2 3 4 5

D. 1 2 3 4 5

What is the most naturalistic characteristic of this painting?

The Scream by Edvard Munch. Lithography, 1895 (PD-US).

Grammar Review: Spelling

By the time you are in middle school or high school, good spelling should be a given. However, to Albert Einstein, who could not spell well, and to many others, spelling is quite a chore. The following are several commonly misspelled words:

advice	affect	beginning
believe	benefit	criticize
despise	formerly	hypocrisy
led	marriage	privilege
receive	seize	separate
shepherd	siege	tragedy
tries	undoubtedly	until

Some Rules for Spelling[1]

Rule I — Final F, L, or S.

Monosyllables ending in *f, l*, or *s*, preceded by a single vowel, double the final consonant; as *staff, mill, pass — muff, knell, gloss — off, hiss, puss.*

Exceptions — The words *clef, if,* and *of,* are written with single *f*; and *as, gas, has, was, yes, his, is, this, us, pus,* and *thus,* with single *s*. So *bul,* for the flounder; *nul,* for *no,* in law; *sol,* for *sou* or *sun*; and *sal,* for *salt,* in chemistry, have but the single *l*.

OBS — Because *sal, salis,* in Latin, doubles not the *l*, the chemists write *salify, salifiable, salification, saliferous, saline, salinous, saliniform, salifying,* etc., with single *l*, contrary to Rule 3d. But in *gas* they ought to double the *s*; for this is a word of their own inventing. Neither have they any plea for allowing it to form *gases* and *gaseous* with the *s* still single; for so they make it violate two general rules at once. If the singular cannot now be written *gass*, the plural should nevertheless be *gasses*, and the adjective should be *gasseous*, according to Rule 3d.

Rule II — Other Finals.

Words ending in any other consonant than *f, l*, or *s*, do not double the final letter; as, *mob, nod, dog, sum, sun, cup, cur, cut, fix, whiz.*

Exceptions — We double the consonant in *abb, ebb, add, odd, egg, jagg, ragg, inn, err, burr, purr, butt, buzz, fuzz, yarr,* and some proper names. But we have also *ab* (*from*) and *ad* (*to*) for prefixes; and *jag, rag, in, bur,* and *but*, are other words that conform to the rule.

Rule III — Doubling.

Monosyllables, and words accented on the last syllable, when they end with a single consonant preceded by a single vowel, or by a vowel after *qu*, double their final consonant before an additional syllable that begins with a vowel: as,

1 Goold Brown, *The Grammar of English Grammars,* sixth edition (c. 1851), p. 247; www.gutenberg.org/cache/epub/11615/pg11615.html.

rob, robbed, robber; fop, foppish, foppery; squat, squatter, squatting; thin, thinner, thinnest; swim, swimmer, swimming; commit, committeth, committing, committed, committer, committees; acquit, acquittal, acquittance, acquitted, acquitting, acquitteth.

Exceptions

1. X final, being equivalent to *ks*, is never doubled: thus, from *mix*, we have *mixed, mixing*, and *mixer*.
2. When the derivative retains not the accent of the root, the final consonant is not always doubled: as, *prefer', pref'erence, pref'erable; refer', ref'erence, ref'erable*, or *refer'rible; infer', in'ference, in'ferable*, or*infer'rible; transfer'*, a *trans'fer, trans'ferable*, or*transfer'rible.*
3. But letters doubled in Latin, are usually doubled in English, without regard to accent, or to any other principle: as, Britain, *Britan'nic, Britannia*; appeal, *appel'lant*; argil, *argil'laus, argilla'ceous*; cavil, *cav'illous, cavilla'tion*; excel', *ex'cellent, ex'cellence*; inflame', *inflam'mable, inflamma'tion.*

Rule IV — No Doubling.

A final consonant, when it is not preceded by a single vowel, or when the accent is not on the last syllable, should remain single before an additional syllable: as, *toil, toiling; oil, oily; visit, visited; differ, differing; peril, perilous; viol, violist; real, realize, realist; dial, dialing, dialist; equal, equalize, equality; vitriol, vitriolic, vitriolate.*

Exceptions

1. The final *l* of words ending in *el*, must be doubled before another vowel, lest the power of the *e* be mistaken, and a syllable be lost: as, *travel, traveller; duel, duellist; revel, revelling; gravel, gravelly; marvel, marvellous.* Yet the word *parallel*, having three Ells already, conforms to the rule in forming its derivatives; as, *paralleling, paralleled*, and *unparalleled.*
2. Contrary to the preceding rule, the preterits, participles, and derivative nouns, of the few verbs ending in *al, il*, or *ol*, unaccented — namely, *equal, rival, vial, marshal, victual, cavil, pencil, carol, gambol*, and *pistol* — are usually allowed to double the *l*, though some dissent from the practice: as,*equalled, equalling; rivalled, rivalling; cavilled, cavilling, caviller; carolled, carolling, caroller.*
3. When *ly* follows *l*, we have two Ells of course, but in fact no doubling: as, *real, really; oral, orally; cruel, cruelly; civil, civilly; cool, coolly; wool, woolly.*
4. Compounds, though they often remove the principal accent from the point of duplication, always retain the double letter: as, *wit'snapper, kid'napper,114 grass'hopper, duck'-legged, spur'galled, hot'spurred, broad'-brimmed, hare'-lipped, half-witted.* So, *compromitted* and *manumitted*; but *benefited* is different.

Daily Assignment

- Warm-up: In first-person narration describe a memorable event (e.g., I went to the store and a man gave me a newspaper.); then, do the same thing in third-person objective narration (e.g., The man at the store gave the young person a newspaper.).
- Students will complete Concept Builder 3-D.
- Prayer journal.
- Review the assigned text. Keep vocabulary cards.
- This is the day that students should write, and then rewrite, the final drafts of their assigned essays.

Narration in Literature

Match the following narration type with the narration examples.

A. First-Person Narration

B. Omniscient Narration

C. Limited Omniscient Narration

D. Third-Person Objective Narration

___A___ Now this is the point. You fancy me mad. Madmen know nothing. But you should have seen me. You should have seen how wisely I proceeded — with what caution — with what foresight, with what dissimulation, I went to work! I was never kinder to the old man than during the whole week before I killed him. And every night about midnight I turned the latch of his door and opened it oh, so gently! And then, when I had made an opening sufficient for my head, I put in a dark lantern all closed, closed so that no light shone out, and then I thrust in my head. Oh, you would have laughed to see how cunningly I thrust it in! I moved it slowly, very, very slowly, so that I might not disturb the old man's sleep. (Edgar Allan Poe, "The Tell Tale Heart")

C
_____ The cold passed reluctantly from the earth, and the retiring fogs revealed an army stretched out on the hills, resting. As the landscape changed from brown to green, the army awakened, and began to tremble with eagerness at the noise of rumors. It cast its eyes upon the roads, which were growing from long troughs of liquid mud to proper thoroughfares. A river, amber-tinted in the shadow of its banks, purled at the army's feet; and at night, when the stream had become of a sorrowful blackness, one could see across it the red, eyelike gleam of hostile campfires set in the low brows of distant hills.

Once a certain tall soldier developed virtues and went resolutely to wash a shirt. He came flying back from a brook waving his garment bannerlike. He was swelled with a tale he had heard from a reliable friend, who had heard it from a truthful cavalryman, who had heard it from his trustworthy brother, one of the order — lies at division headquarters. He adopted the important air of a herald in red and gold. "We're goin' t' move t' morrah — sure," he said pompously to a group in the company street. "We're goin' 'way up the river, cut across, an' come around in behint 'em." (Stephen Crane, *The Red Badge of Courage*)

___D___ Scrooge knew he was dead? Of course he did. How could it be otherwise? Scrooge and he were partners for I don't know how many years. Scrooge was his sole executor, his sole administrator, his sole assign, his sole residuary legatee, his sole friend, and sole mourner. And even Scrooge was not so dreadfully cut up by the sad event, but that he was an excellent man of business on the very day of the funeral, and solemnised it with an undoubted bargain.

Scrooge never painted out Old Marley's name. There it stood, years afterwards, above the warehouse door: Scrooge and Marley. The firm was known as Scrooge and Marley. Sometimes people new to the business called Scrooge Scrooge, and sometimes Marley, but he answered to both names. It was all the same to him. (Charles Dickens, *A Christmas Carol*)

___B___ "This out of all will remain — They have lived and have tossed: So much of the game will be gain, Though the gold of the dice has been lost."

They limped painfully down the bank, and once the foremost of the two men staggered among the rough-strewn rocks. They were tired and weak, and their faces had the drawn expression of patience which comes of hardship long endured. They were heavily burdened with blanket packs which were strapped to their shoulders. Head-straps, passing across the forehead, helped support these packs. Each man carried a rifle. They walked in a stooped posture, the shoulders well forward, the head still farther forward, the eyes bent upon the ground.

"I wish we had just about two of them cartridges that's layin' in that cache of ourn," said the second man. His voice was utterly and drearily expressionless. He spoke without enthusiasm; and the first man, limping into the milky stream that foamed over the rocks, vouchsafed no reply. (Jack London, "The Love of Life")

Theme — *The Call of the Wild* (Jack London)

Chapter 4

First Thoughts

A theme is the central focus or concept the author is trying to reveal, to explore, to examine, not to be confused with a moral, or commentary it may imply. A recurring theme is a motif. Along with plot, character, setting, and style, theme is considered one of the fundamental components of fiction.

Chapter Learning Objectives

In chapter 4 we will understand the meaning of theme and discuss how it is used in literature.

As a result of this chapter study you will be able to . . .

1. Examine chapter 6, "The Love of Man," and discuss what biblical themes Buck exemplifies.
2. Evaluate how Christians should/can evaluate aberrant worldviews.

Look Ahead for Friday

- Turn in a final copy of essay
- Take Weekly Test

Lesson 1

Literary Analysis: Theme

The theme is the one-sentence major purpose of a literary piece, rarely stated but implied. It is the quintessential meaning of a literary work, the meaning of the work that will transcend time and location. The theme(s) invite(s) readers to return again and again to the work to experience anew the literary work. Settings, characters, and tones come and go, but themes remain forever. The theme is not a moral, which is a statement of the author's didactic purpose of his literary piece. A thesis statement is very similar to the theme.

In the following examples, which is a moral statement and which statement is a theme?

A. The protagonist discovers that while nature is beautiful, it can also be unforgiving and even brutal.

B. One should never take nature for granted — it may be beautiful, but it also is brutal.

A is a theme and B is a moral statement.

Daily Assignment

- Warm-up: Create a short story that has a theme of immutability (never growing old).
- Students will complete Concept Builder 4-A.
- Prayer journal: Students are encouraged to write in their prayer journal every day.
- Students need to review their material for the next assignment
- Students should systematically review their vocabulary words daily.

Theme Development

The theme is the central purpose of a literary piece. It is the central idea that an author wants to share with a reader. The author mostly uses the plot and characters to advance a theme.

In Jack London's *The Call of the Wild* an important theme is "survival of the fittest." Complete the chart below to show how London develops the theme. Find two other incidents from London's setting that advance this theme.

Setting Details	Resulting Character Trait
Buck is stolen and taken north.	*He grows hard and strong.*
buck stays with thorton	he learns to love and to have fun after traveling 3,000 miles
buck is sold to weird people who don't know what their doing	he grows near to death

Theme: Survival of the Fittest

The Gift of the Magi

Is there a moral or a theme in the following short story, "The Gift of the Magi," by O. Henry?

One dollar and eighty-seven cents. That was all. And sixty cents of it was in pennies. Pennies saved one and two at a time by bulldozing the grocer and the vegetable man and the butcher until one's cheeks burned with the silent imputation of parsimony that such close dealing implied. Three times Della counted it. One dollar and eighty-seven cents. And the next day would be Christmas.

There was clearly nothing to do but flop down on the shabby little couch and howl. So Della did it. Which instigates the moral reflection that life is made up of sobs, sniffles, and smiles, with sniffles predominating.

While the mistress of the home is gradually subsiding from the first stage to the second, take a look at the home. A furnished flat at $8 per week. It did not exactly beggar description, but it certainly had that word on the lookout for the mendicancy squad.

In the vestibule below was a letterbox into which no letter would go and an electric button from which no mortal finger could coax a ring. Also appertaining hereunto was a card bearing the name "Mr. James Dillingham Young."

The "Dillingham" had been flung to the breeze during a former period of prosperity when its possessor was being paid $30 per week. Now, when the income was shrunk to $20, though, they were thinking seriously of contracting to a modest and unassuming D. But whenever Mr. James Dillingham Young came home and reached his flat above, he was called "Jim" and greatly hugged by Mrs. James Dillingham Young, already introduced to you as Della. Which is all very good.

Della finished her cry and attended to her cheeks with the powder rag. She stood by the window and looked out dully at a gray cat walking a gray fence in a gray backyard. Tomorrow would be Christmas Day, and she had only $1.87 with which to buy Jim a present. She had been saving every penny she could for months, with this result. Twenty dollars a week doesn't go far. Expenses had been greater than she had calculated. They always are. Only $1.87 to buy a present for Jim. Her Jim. Many a happy hour she had spent planning for something nice for him. Something fine and rare and sterling — something just a little bit near to being worthy of the honor of being owned by Jim.

There was a pier glass between the windows of the room. Perhaps you have seen a pier glass in an $8 flat. A very thin and very agile person may, by observing his reflection in a rapid sequence of longitudinal strips, obtain a fairly accurate conception of his looks. Della, being slender, had mastered the art.

Suddenly she whirled from the window and stood before the glass. Her eyes were shining brilliantly, but her face had lost its color within twenty seconds. Rapidly she pulled down her hair and let it fall to its full length.

Now, there were two possessions of the James Dillingham Youngs in which they both took a mighty pride. One was Jim's gold watch that had been his father's and his grandfather's. The other was Della's hair. Had the queen of Sheba lived in the flat across the airshaft, Della would have let her hair hang out the window some day to dry just to depreciate Her Majesty's jewels and gifts. Had King Solomon been the janitor, with all his treasures piled up in the basement, Jim would have pulled out his watch every time he passed, just to see him pluck at his beard from envy.

So now Della's beautiful hair fell about her, rippling and shining like a cascade of brown waters. It reached below her knee and made itself almost a garment for her. And then she did it up again nervously and quickly. Once she faltered for a minute and stood still while a tear or two splashed on the worn red carpet.

On went her old brown jacket; on went her old brown hat. With a whirl of skirts and with the brilliant sparkle still in her eyes, she fluttered out the door and down the stairs to the street.

Where she stopped the sign read: "Mne. Sofronie. Hair Goods of All Kinds." One flight up Della ran, and collected herself, panting. Madame, large, too white, chilly, hardly looked the "Sofronie."

"Will you buy my hair?" asked Della.

"I buy hair," said Madame. "Take yer hat off and let's have a sight at the looks of it."

Down rippled the brown cascade.

"Twenty dollars," said Madame, lifting the mass with a practiced hand.

"Give it to me quick," said Della.

Oh, and the next two hours tripped by on rosy wings. Forget the hashed metaphor. She was ransacking the stores for Jim's present.

She found it at last. It surely had been made for Jim and no one else. There was no other like it in any of the stores, and she had turned all of them inside out. It was a platinum fob chain simple and chaste in design, properly proclaiming its value by substance alone and not by meretricious ornamentation — as all good things should do. It was even worthy of The Watch. As soon as she saw it, she knew that it must be Jim's. It was like him. Quietness and value — the description applied to both. Twenty-one dollars they took from her for it, and she hurried home with the 87 cents. With that chain on his watch Jim might be properly anxious about the time in any company. Grand as the watch was, he sometimes looked at it on the sly on account of the old leather strap that he used in place of a chain.

When Della reached home, her intoxication gave way a little to prudence and reason. She got out her curling irons and lighted the gas and went to work repairing the ravages made by generosity added to love. Which is always a tremendous task, dear friends — a mammoth task.

Within forty minutes her head was covered with tiny, close-lying curls that made her look wonderfully like a truant schoolboy. She looked at her reflection in the mirror long, carefully, and critically.

"If Jim doesn't kill me," she said to herself, "before he takes a second look at me, he'll say I look like a Coney Island chorus girl. But what could I do — oh! What could I do with a dollar and eighty-seven cents?"

At 7 o'clock the coffee was made and the frying pan was on the back of the stove, hot and ready to cook the chops.

Jim was never late. Della doubled the fob chain in her hand and sat on the corner of the table near the door that he always entered. Then she heard his step on the stair away down on the first flight, and she turned white for just a moment. She had a habit for saying a little silent prayer about the simplest everyday things, and now she whispered: "Please God, make him think I am still pretty."

The door opened and Jim stepped in and closed it. He looked thin and very serious. Poor fellow, he was only twenty-two — and to be burdened with a family! He needed a new overcoat and he was without gloves.

Jim stopped inside the door, as immovable as a setter at the scent of quail. His eyes were fixed upon Della, and there was an expression in them that she could not read, and it terrified her. It was not anger, nor surprise, nor disapproval, nor horror, nor any of the sentiments that she had been prepared for. He simply stared at her fixedly with that peculiar expression on his face.

Della wriggled off the table and went for him.

"Jim, darling," she cried, "don't look at me that way. I had my hair cut off and sold because I couldn't have lived through Christmas without giving you a present. It'll grow out again — you won't mind, will you? I just had to do it. My hair grows awfully fast. Say 'Merry Christmas!' Jim, and let's be happy. You don't know what a nice — what a beautiful, nice gift I've got for you."

"You've cut off your hair?" asked Jim, laboriously, as if he had not arrived at that patent fact yet even after the hardest mental labor.

"Cut it off and sold it," said Della. "Don't you like me just as well, anyhow? I'm me without my hair, ain't I?"

Jim looked about the room curiously.

"You say your hair is gone?" he said, with an air almost of idiocy.

"You needn't look for it," said Della. "It's sold, I tell you — sold hairs of my head that were numbered," she went on with sudden serious sweetness, "but nobody could ever count my love for you. Shall I put the chops on, Jim?"

Out of his trance Jim seemed quickly to wake. He enfolded his Della. For ten seconds let us regard with discreet scrutiny some inconsequential object in the other direction. Eight dollars a week or a million a year — what is the difference? A mathematician or a wit would give you the wrong answer. The magi brought valuable gifts, but that was not among them. This dark assertion will be illuminated later on.

Jim drew a package from his overcoat pocket and threw it upon the table.

"Don't make any mistake, Dell," he said, "about me. I don't think there's anything in the way of a haircut or a shave or a shampoo that could make me like my girl any less. But if you'll unwrap that package you may see why you had me going a while at first."

White fingers, and nimble, tore at the string and paper. And then an ecstatic scream of joy; and then, alas, a quick feminine change to hysterical tears and wails, necessitating the immediate employment of all the comforting powers of the lord of the flat.

For there lay The Combs — the set of combs, side and back, that Della had worshiped long in a Broadway window. Beautiful combs, pure tortoise shell, with jeweled rims—just the shade to wear in the beautiful vanished hair. They were expensive combs, she knew, and her heart had simply craved and yearned over them without the least hope of possession. And now, they were hers, but the tresses that should have adorned the coveted adornments were gone.

But she hugged them to her bosom, and at length she was able to look up with dim eyes and a smile and say: "My hair grows so fast, Jim!"

And then Della leaped up like a little singed cat and cried, "Oh, oh!"

Jim had not yet seen his beautiful present. She held it out to him eagerly upon her open palm. The dull precious metal seemed to flash with a reflection of her bright and ardent spirit.

"Isn't it a dandy, Jim? I hunted all over town to find it. You'll have to look at the time a hundred times a day now. Give me your watch. I want to see how it looks on it."

Instead of obeying, Jim tumbled down on the couch and put his hands under the back of his head and smiled.

"Dell," said he, "let's put our Christmas presents away and keep 'em a while. They're too nice to use just at present. I sold the watch to get the money to buy your combs. And now suppose you put the chops on."

The magi, as you know, were wise men — wonderfully wise men — who brought gifts to the Babe in the manger. They invented the art of giving Christmas presents. Being wise, their gifts were no doubt wise ones, possibly bearing the privilege of exchange in case of duplication. And here I have lamely related to you the uneventful chronicle of two foolish children in a flat who most unwisely sacrificed for each other the greatest treasures of their house. But in a last word to the wise of these days let it be said that of all who give gifts these two were the wisest. O all who give and receive gifts, such as they are wisest. Everywhere they are wisest. They are the magi.[1]

1 www.night.net/christmas/Gift-Magi.html.

Daily Assignment

- Warm-up: Describe one theme in the 23rd Psalm. Next, write a poem that exhibits the same theme.
- Students will complete Concept Builder 4-B.
- Prayer journal.
- Students should outline all assigned essays for the week.

Theme: protection and Mercy and Justice

Moral: to bring Justice

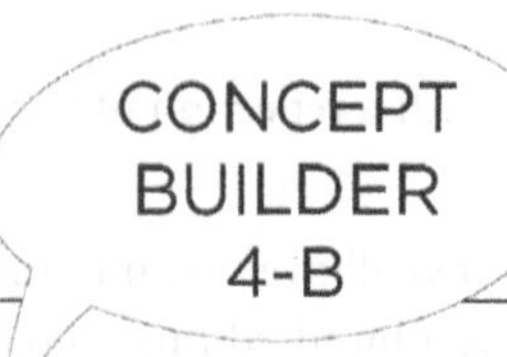

Theme vs. Moral

A theme is not a moral. A theme is a statement of purpose of the piece. A moral is a lesson learned in the piece. **Read to find the theme and the moral of this fable.**

"The Brave Quail"

(Adapted from the *Panchatantra* Indian folk tales)

In a forest near Varanasi, there once live some quails. The shady grove in which they nested was also the favorite grazing ground of a herd of elephants. The leader of the herd was a wise and just elephant, the Bodhisattva.

One day, one of the quails laid some eggs. "I hope my eggs will be safe till they are hatched," she said to the father quail.

"You will have to keep careful watch," replied the father quail. Soon after the fledglings were hatched, the elephant herd arrived.

"What shall I do?" cried the mother. "I can only fall at their feet and beg for protection."

"As the leader came close to her nest, the mother quail cried out, "Oh mighty elephant, my little ones are in danger. If your herd enters the grove, they will be trampled to death."

"Do not fear little one," said the elephant leader, "Your fledglings will not be harmed."

The kind elephant stood over the nest as the herd grazed. When the herd was leaving, the leader cautioned, "There is a rogue elephant who is wild and dangerous. He might soon be coming this way."

"What shall I do, I am so small and weak," said the helpless quail.

"All you can do is appeal to him for mercy," advised the good elephant and departed.

Before long the rogue elephant arrived. The mother wasted no time and ran to the rogue elephant, begging, "Oh powerful one! I beg of you, spare my young ones!"

"How dare you come in my way?" the rogue elephant replied and in no time destroyed the nest and killed the father.

"There! That is the end of your silly brood," the rogue elephant sneered.

The mother quail grieved over her family for a long time. She vowed to teach the rogue elephant a lesson. She thought long and hard and finally came up with a plan.

She went to her friend crow and narrated her sad tale. The crow was very sympathetic.

"The rogue must not go unpunished," the crow proclaimed and agreed to the mother quail's plan. The quail then went to her friend, the ant, and sought her help.

"I heard about your babies," the ant said. "I am deeply grieved. What can I do?" The quail told the ant her plan and the ant readily agreed.

The quail then went to the frog, her long-time friend, and narrated what happened. "I am trying to get my friends, the crow, the ant, and you to help me punish the spiteful elephant who killed my babies."

"You can count on me" said the frog and followed the quail.

The three friends then implemented the quail's plan. First, the crow darted at the elephant and plucked out the elephant's eyes. Then the ant quickly went and laid her eggs in the eye sockets. As the eggs hatched and the baby ants began biting, the elephant could not bear the pain any more and desperately searched for water to wash his eyes. As the elephant dashed around in pain, the frog croaked close to a steep precipice. The blind elephant followed the sound of the frog's croaking, thinking that water would be nearby.

Soon the elephant hurtled down to his death.

The three friends came together near the pond. "Thank you all for helping me to carry out my plan," the mother quail said. "Let this be a lesson to all that even the small and weak can join together to correct an injustice."

Sample Essay: Theme

Theme in *The Adventures of Huckleberry Finn*

On one level *Huckleberry Finn* is the story of a young, carefree teenager answering to no one except himself, but it is much more. It is a biting satire of the American penchant toward sentimental romanticism.

Like most late 19th-century Americans, Huck Finn is a young man on a journey. In the novel he escapes with his slave-friend Jim down the Mississippi River in search of freedom. As they journey, Huck, like most southerners of his age and setting, experiences some guilt — he is helping a slave escape. However, that guilt is mitigated by the feeling of satisfaction he experiences as he helps his friend escape. Huck, then, is on a journey of ambivalence. He is a pilgrim — not a wanderer. A pilgrim has a purpose and destination. A wanderer has neither. A pilgrim is never lost; a wanderer is always lost. This journey of Huck, then, is the quintessential American journey. (James P. Stobaugh).

Daily Assignment

- Warm-up: What is the theme of your apartment/house? Colonial? Modern? Next describe the theme of your room. Neat? Messy?
- Students will complete Concept Builder 4-C.
- Prayer journal.
- Students should write rough drafts of all assigned essays and speech.

CONCEPT BUILDER 4-C

Themes in Movies

The theme is the central purpose of an artistic piece. It is the central idea that an artist wants to share with his viewer.

What is the central theme of these movies:

A. *Chariots of Fire* ?

B. *Ben Hur* ?

C. *Pocahontas* To listen to your heart

D. *Bambi* to learn

E. *Snow White and the Seven Dwarfs* don't give in to temptation

Lesson 4

Grammar Review: Capitalization

Review capitalization rules.

The following is from a grammar book published in 1851: The Grammar of English Grammars.[1]

RULES FOR THE USE OF CAPITALS.

Rule I — Of Books

When particular books are mentioned by their names, the chief words in their titles begin with capitals, and the other letters are small; as,"Pope's Essay on Man" — "the Book of Common Prayer" — "the Scriptures of the Old and New Testaments."

Rule II — First Words

The first word of every distinct sentence, or of any clause separately numbered or paragraphed, should begin with a capital; as, "Rejoice evermore. Pray without ceasing. In every thing give thanks: for this is the will of God in Christ Jesus concerning you. Quench not the Spirit. Despise not prophesyings. Prove all things: hold fast that which is good." — *1 Thess.*, v, 16–21.

"14. He has given his assent to their acts of pretended legislation: 15. *For* quartering large bodies of armed troops among us: 16. *For* protecting them, by a mock trial, from punishment for murders: 17. *For* cutting off our trade with all parts of the world: 18. *For* imposing taxes on us without our consent:" etc. *Declaration of American Independence.*

Rule III — of the Deity

All names of the Deity, and sometimes their emphatic substitutes, should begin with capitals; as, "God, Jehovah, the Almighty, the Supreme Being, Divine Providence, the Messiah, the Comforter, the Father, the Son, the Holy Spirit, the Lord of Sabaoth."
"The hope of my spirit turns trembling to Thee." — *Moore.*

Rule IV — Proper Names

Proper names, of every description, should always begin with capitals; as, "Saul of Tarsus, Simon Peter, Judas Iscariot, England, London, the Strand,the Thames, the Pyrenees, the Vatican, the Greeks, the Argo and the Argonauts."

Rule V — of Titles

Titles of office or honour, and epithets of distinction, applied to persons, begin usually with capitals; as, "His Majesty William the Fourth, Chief Justice Marshall, Sir Matthew Hale, Dr. Johnson, the Rev. Dr. Chalmers, Lewis the Bold, Charles the Second, James the Less, St. Bartholomew, Pliny the Younger, Noah Webster, Jun., Esq."

1 Gould, *The Grammar of English Grammars*, p. 202–206; www.gutenberg.org/cache/epub/11615/pg11615.html.

Rule VI — One Capital

Those compound proper names which by analogy incline to a union of their parts without a hyphen, should be so written, and have but one capital: as, "Eastport, Eastville, Westborough, Westfield, Westtown, Whitehall, Whitechurch, Whitehaven, Whiteplains, Mountmellick, Mountpleasant, Germantown, Germanflats, Blackrock, Redhook, Kinderhook, Newfoundland, Statenland, Newcastle, Northcastle, Southbridge, Fairhaven, Dekalb, Deruyter, Lafayette, Macpherson."

Rule VII — Two Capitals

The compounding of a name under one capital should be avoided when the general analogy of other similar terms suggests a separation under two; as, "The chief mountains of Ross-shire are Ben Chat, *Benchasker*, Ben Golich, Ben Nore, Ben Foskarg, and Ben Wyvis." — *Glasgow Geog.*, Vol. ii, p. 311. Write *Ben Chasker.* So, when the word *East, West, North,* or *South,* as part of a name, denotes relative position, or when the word *New* distinguishes a place by contrast, we have generally separate words and two capitals; as, "East Greenwich, West Greenwich, North Bridgewater, South Bridgewater, New Jersey, New Hampshire."

Rule VIII — Compounds

When any adjective or common noun is made a distinct part of a compound proper name, it ought to begin with a capital; as, "The United States, the Argentine Republic, the Peak of Teneriffe, the Blue Ridge, the Little Pedee, Long Island, Jersey City, Lower Canada, Green Bay, Gretna Green, Land's End, the Gold Coast."

Rule IX — Apposition

When a common and a proper name are associated merely to explain each other, it is in general sufficient, if the proper name begin with a capital, and the appellative, with a small letter; as, "The prophet Elisha, Matthew the publican, the brook Cherith, the river Euphrates, the Ohio river, Warren county, Flatbush village, New York city."

Rule X — Personifications

The name of an object personified, when it conveys an idea strictly individual, should begin with a capital; as, "Upon this, *Fancy* began again to bestir herself."—*Addison*. "Come, gentle *Spring*, ethereal mildness, come." — *Thomson*.

Rule XI — Derivatives

Words derived from proper names, and having direct reference to particular persons, places, sects, or nations, should begin with capitals; as, "Platonic, Newtonian, Greek, or Grecian, Romish, or Roman, Italic, or Italian, German, or Germanic, Swedish, Turkish, Chinese, Genoese, French, Dutch, Scotch, Welsh:" so, perhaps, "to Platonize, Grecize, Romanize, Italicize, Latinize, or Frenchify."

Rule XII — Of I and O

The words *I* and *O* should always be capitals; as, "Praise the Lord, O Jerusalem; praise thy God, O Zion." — *Psalm* cxlvii. "O wretched man that I am!" — "For that which I do, I allow not: for what I would, that do I not; but what I hate, that do I." — *Rom.*, vii, 24 and 15.

Rule XIII — Of Poetry

Every line in poetry, except what is regarded as making but one verse with the line preceding, should begin with a capital; as, "Our sons their fathers' failing language see,

And such as Chaucer is, shall Dryden be." — *Pope.*

Of the exception, some editions of the Psalms in Metre are full of examples; as,

"Happy the man whose tender care

relieves the poor distress'd!

When troubles compass him around,

the Lord shall give him rest."

Psalms with Com. Prayer, N. Y., 1819, Ps. xli.

Rule XIV — Of Examples

The first word of a full example, of a distinct speech, or of a direct quotation, should begin with a capital; as, "Remember this maxim: 'Know thyself.' " — "Virgil says, 'Labour conquers all things.' " — "Jesus answered them, Is it not written in your law, I said, Ye are gods?" — *John*, x, 34. "Thou knowest the commandments, Do not commit adultery, Do not kill, Do not steal, Do not bear false witness, Honour thy father and thy mother." — *Luke*, xviii, 20.

Rule XV — Chief Words

Other words of particular importance, and such as denote the principal subjects treated of, may be distinguished by capitals; and names subscribed frequently have capitals throughout: as, "In its application to the Executive, with reference to the Legislative branch of the Government, the same rule of action should make the President ever anxious to avoid the exercise of any discretionary authority which can be regulated by Congress." — ANDREW JACKSON, 1835.

Rule XVI — Needless Capitals

Capitals are improper wherever there is not some special rule or reason for their use: a century ago books were disfigured by their frequency; as, "Many a Noble *Genius* is lost for want of Education. Which wou'd then be Much More Liberal. As it was when the *Church* Enjoy'd her Possessions. And *Learning* was, in the *Dark Ages*, Preserv'd almost only among the *Clergy*." — CHARLES LESLIE, 1700; *Divine Right of Tythes*, p. 228.

Daily Assignment

- Warm-up: Sing a few bars of a song you like to your pet, and then tell the reader what the theme of this song is. Why do you like it?
- Students will complete Concept Builder 4-D.
- Prayer journal.
- Review the assigned text. Keep vocabulary cards.
- This is the day that students should write, and then rewrite, the final drafts of their assigned essay.

CONCEPT BUILDER 4-D

Capitalization Review

Correct the following sentences:

1. Our company is called For Such A Time As This.

Our company is called for such a time as this.

2. "open the door now!" exclaimed the soldier.

"Open the door now!" Exclaimed the Solider

3. I visited the washington monument.

I visited the Washington Monument

4. The north defeated the south in the american civil war.

The North defeated the South in the American Civil War.

Characterization — *Joseph Narrative*

Chapter 5

First Thoughts

The Bible is the inspired, inerrant word of God. Additionally, it is a story of men and women struggling with everyday life. It is full of different types of literature, too. The following is a story, or narration, found in the first book of the Bible. Inspired by the Holy Spirit, Moses writes this wonderful story of forgiveness.

Chapter Learning Objectives

In chapter 5 we will understand the meaning of narrative and discuss how it is used in literature.

As a result of this chapter study you will be able to . . .

1. Write a list of all the wonderful characteristics Joseph manifests (e.g., steadfastness, forgiveness, etc.) and make a similar list of the characteristics that God manifests in the same story (e.g., mercy toward Joseph in prison).
2. Write a portion of the story of Joseph from the perspective of an Egyptian historian under the employment of Pharaoh. Next, write a portion of the story from the perspective of Joseph's half-brother Judah.

Look Ahead for Friday

- Turn in a final copy of essay
- Take Weekly Test

Lesson 1

Joseph Narrative

Joseph Narrative (Read Genesis 37, 39:1–8, 19–45:9)

Joseph fleeing from Potiphar's wife, by Philipp Veit, 1816/17 (PD-Art).

Daily Assignment

- Warm-up: Describe an antagonist in your life. How have you handled this person?
- Students will complete Concept Builder 5-A.
- Prayer journal: Students are encouraged to write in their prayer journal every day.
- Students need to review their material for the next assignment
- Students should systematically review their vocabulary words daily.

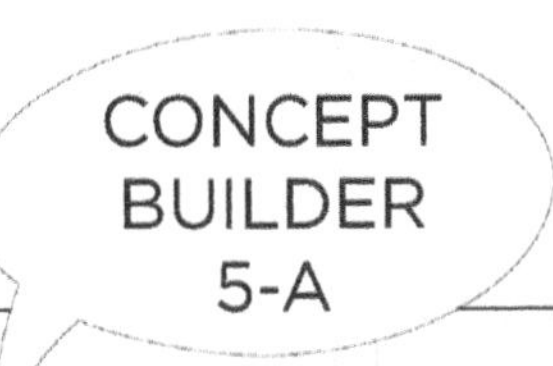

Active Reading

Read the Joseph narrative (Gen. 40ff)

What is the setting of this account?

egypt

Who is the protagonist?

Joseph

Who are some foils?

the King/servants

Who are the antagonists?

his brothers

How does Moses develop the protagonist?

through detailed description

Discuss some of the internal and external conflicts Joseph experiences.

hatred/fame

Imagine telling this story from Judah's perspective. How would it be different?

because he had hatred

Why doesn't Joseph punish his brothers?

because he forgave them

Why doesn't Joseph tell his brothers his true identity?

to see if they would repent

Literary Analysis: Characterization

Characterization is the technique a writer uses to help the reader know a person, or character, in the writing. Creating interesting, believable characters is at the heart of good writing. Often a reader will forget the plot of a book but still remember the characters. For instance, it is likely that most readers will forget the storyline in *The Empire Strikes Back*, but no one forgets Darth Vader. He is larger than the story itself!

An effective author invests a great deal of time making sure that the character is real. A character who does not exhibit human characteristics is ineffective. In fact, to be effective, even cartoon characters must exhibit real human characteristics.

An author develops four areas of characterization: physical appearance, actions, and attitudes of other characters toward the person, and a person's inner thoughts and feelings. Motivation is very important in character analysis. Does the writer convince the reader that the character is adequately motivated to exhibit the behavior he exhibits?

The main character is called the *protagonist*. An *antagonist* is the person with whom the main character has the most conflict. He is often the enemy of the main character (*protagonist*). In the Joseph story, Joseph's brothers are initially the antagonists, but, as the story unfolds, they become foils (below).

Characters who are introduced whose sole purpose is to develop the main character are called *foils*. The pharaoh is one of the primary foils in the Joseph story. Characters that appear in the story may perform actions, speak to other characters, be described by the narrator, or be remembered. Normally, an author uses foils and dialogue to develop the protagonist.

Conflict can occur within a character, too. This is called *internal conflict*. Uncle Tom in *Uncle Tom's Cabin* is torn internally between loyalty to his master and reaction to the inhumanity of chattel slavery. An *external conflict* is normally an obvious conflict between the protagonist and antagonist(s).

Daily Assignment

- Warm-up: Compare your family to a group of animals: who is who?
- Students will complete Concept Builder 5-B.
- Prayer journal.
- Students should outline all assigned essays for the week.

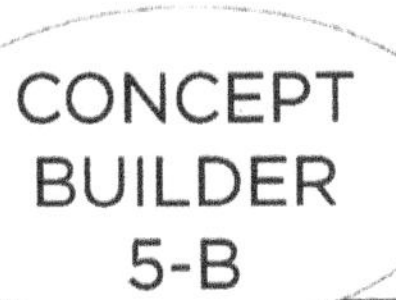

Characterization of Joseph – Part One

Draw and label eight of the most important events that formed the character Joseph.

Joseph's Dreams	Joseph's Robe
Joseph is sold	Potiphars wife
Joseph in prison	King's Dream interpreter
Joseph pharoah	Joseph forgives his brothers

Lesson 3

Characterization

The use of dialogue to develop a protagonist:

In this emotional passage, Moses is using dialogue to develop his protagonist, Joseph. It is a very economical and effective way to develop a character.

They said, "Sir, we really did come down here the first time only to buy food.

When we came to the place where we lodged for the night and opened our bags of grain, each one's money was at the top of his bag! It was the full amount of our money, and we have brought it back with us. We have brought additional money with us to buy food. We don't know who put our money in the bags."

Then the steward said, "May you be well. Don't be afraid. Your God and the God of your father must have put treasure in your bags. I received your money." Then he brought Simeon out to them.

The man brought the men into Joseph's house, gave them water to wash their feet, and got feed for their donkeys. Since the men had heard that they were going to eat a meal there, they prepared their gift for Joseph's arrival at noon. When Joseph came home, they brought him the gift they had carried into the house, and they bowed to the ground before him.

He asked if they were well, and he said, "How is your elderly father that you told me about? Is he still alive?"

They answered, "Your servant our father is well. He is still alive." And they bowed down to honor him.

When he looked up and saw his brother Benjamin, his mother's son, he asked, "Is this your youngest brother that you told me about?"

Then he said, "May God be gracious to you, my son." Joseph hurried out because he was overcome with emotion for his brother, and he was about to weep. He went into an inner room to weep.

Daily Assignment

- Warm-up: Who is your favorite movie actor? Movie actress? Why?
- Students will complete a daily Concept Builder 5-C.
- Prayer journal.
- Students should write rough drafts of all assigned essays.

Characterization of Joseph – Part Two

Characters are usually presented by description and through their actions, speech, and thoughts. **Choose one incident in the life of Joseph and show how Moses, the author, reveals Joseph's character.**

Joseph's Character Development

Actions	Dialogue	Thoughts
he interperates dreams for prisoners and later on for Pharoah	Genesis 40-41 ↑ the chapters	he wanted to get out of prison and he was able to predict things.

Result: he becomes Pharaoh

Sample Literary Analysis: Play Review

Play review of *I Remember Mama:*

I Remember Mama, by John Van Druten, adapted from Kathryn Forbes' book *Mama's Bank Account*, was first produced by Messrs. Richard Rodgers and Oscar Hammerstein II at the Shubert Theater, New Haven, Connecticut, on September 28, 1944, and subsequently at the Music Box Theater, New York City, on October 19, 1944.

I Remember Mama is the story of an immigrant family's struggle to make the American dream its own. The major conflict of this drama concerns Mama's money box. This money box is the place where Mama and her family deposit their dreams and take them out when they need to do so. For instance, when Nel wants to go to a private high school, the family takes money out of the box to make this dream possible. However, in order for there to be enough money in the box other members of the family have to deposit some of their dreams into the box. For instance, the two sisters agree to baby sit extra hours to help, and Papa gives up his tobacco. In the background is an imaginary bank account that assumes epic proportions throughout the play. When the family discovers that there is no bank account, that their riches can be found within their own hearts, within their family, they have finally found and owned the American dream. (Jessica Stobaugh)

Daily Assignment

- Warm-up: Who is your favorite relative? Describe him or her.
- Students will complete Concept Builder 5-D.
- Prayer journal.
- Review the assigned text. Keep vocabulary cards.
- This is the day that students should write, and then rewrite, the final drafts of their assigned essays.

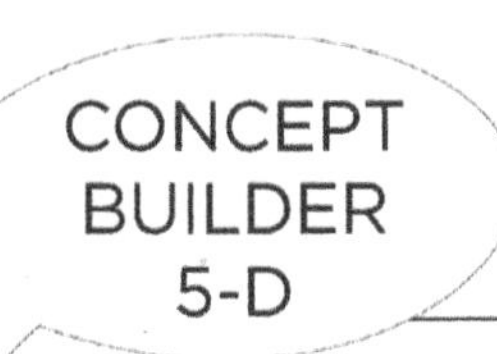

Characterization: Reaction of Others

Characters are developed by reactions of others to them.

Incident	Reactions by Family	Reactions by Egyptians	Reactions by God	Resulting Characteristic in Joseph
Joseph is sold into slavery.	Sadness and Quittiness	he's a miracle	this is my plan	diligence
Joseph refuses to disobey God with Potiphar's wife.	thought that he had attempted	Prison for him	Good Job Joseph!	Obedience
Joseph helps Pharaoh lead the nation in crisis.	I ♡ Him	We ♡ Him	he has Courage	Careness
Joseph has a reunion with his family.	Yah Joseph is back	Thank you Joseph	Joseph is Blessed	Forgiveness

Plot — *Joseph Narrative*

Chapter 6

First Thoughts

The plot includes the events of the story, in the order the story gives them. A typical plot has five parts: *Exposition, Rising Action, Crisis* or *Climax, Falling Action,* and *Resolution*. The plot is the story itself. A simple example is *Jack and the Bean Stalk.* which exhibits all the elements. First, we meet Jack and his family (exposition). Then we see a crisis coming — Jack is desperately poor (rising action). Next, we reach the climax — when the giant chases Jack to and then down the vine. Then we sense the action is falling (after the giant is dead) and there is a resolution (Jack and his family live happily ever after).

Chapter Learning Objectives

In chapter 6 we explore the literary device plot. We see how Moses develops the account of the life of Joseph.

As a result of this chapter study you will be able to . . .

1. Examine the account of how this biblical plot unfolded.
2. Develop and understand how plot moves a story from start to finish.

Look Ahead for Friday

- Turn in a final copy of essay
- Take Weekly Test

Play Review—Plot

Play Review of *I Remember Mama:*

The plot of *I Remember Mama* is predictable and therefore weak. In other words, there is nothing unique about the plot. How many plays have we read that have a child remembering his past? Too many! But this is no Huw remembering his Papa in *How Green Was My Valley*! There are no engaging plot twists like the surprising romance between Laurie and Amy in *Little Women*! But, in John Van Druten's defense, America at the end of World War II (when Mama appeared) was demanding a steady diet of nostalgia and sentimentality. With images of concentration camps and burning villages on countless movie screens, the last thing Americans wanted to see was realism! There is really no major crisis in the play. One wonders how Druten can maintain the viewer's interest over a two-hour period without one major death or life-threatening crisis!

As weak as the plot is, the characters are strong. Mama is a memorable and powerful character. Uncle Chris, too, with his extrovert personality, is one of the best, if not the best, developed characters in the play. Unfortunately, though, Katrin is predictable and at times whining. When Katrin finds out that she will receive Mama's brooch, she complains that it is an old thing and useless (Act 1). The reader grows tired of these trite, inane musings. The reader is hard pressed to find anything wrong with Katrin, if he stays only with the text. She is perfect! Katrin is no Laura Ingalls from *Little House on the Prairie* who unabashedly manifests such character flaws as selfishness and revenge. By the end of the play, the reader wonders if Katrin is a reliable narrator. Some characters, such as Mr. Hyde, are important for the plot, but disappear without any apparent reason. The reader is left hanging.

The setting occurs in early 20th century San Francisco. Early 20th-century San Francisco is an appropriate setting. The reader is impressed that the setting is not St. Paul, Minnesota, where there are millions of Norwegian immigrants. There are really very few in San Francisco, and this furthers the theme of an isolated American family pursuing the American dream.

In an age when American culture is falling apart so rapidly and completely, it is refreshing to read a play where a family is struggling to stay together and to make some dreams come true in the face of adversity. In a time when Americans are flocking to our version of entertainment, it is encouraging to see a family weeping when Mr. Hyde finishes *A Tale of Two Cities*. While the vision of this movie is not overtly Christian — no character finds fulfillment in his faith or in his church — it does celebrate and promote Judeo-Christian morality. While it does at times linger in mawkishness, the reader is grateful for the unapologetic promotion of honesty, intrepidness, and charity that *I Remember Mama* celebrates. (Jessica Stobaugh)

Daily Assignment

- Warm-up: Summarize your favorite novel, and state why you liked it so much. What is its climax?
- Students will complete Concept Builder 6-A.
- Prayer journal: Students are encouraged to write in their prayer journal every day.
- Students need to review their material for the next assignment
- Students should systematically review their vocabulary words daily.

Plot Practice

Discuss any book you have read, and identify the exposition (introductory information), rising action, climax, denouement (falling action), and resolution.

Exposition

little boy pip lives with his sister and brother in law and always goes to the grave yard to remember his parents. they are poor and the brother in law is a blacksmith

Rising Action

gets invited by miss havisham to play with her daughter Estella. After falling in love with her miss havisham sends him back home never to see her again

Climax

pip is all grown up and finds out that hes suddenly rich and moves to england. Finally gets to spend more time with Estella.

Denouement

miss havisham dies and Estella is on her own. After having her husband die as well. pip finds ? father and helps him escape inprisonment, then he dies. pip lost his fortune

Resolution

pip and Estella meet in a park and part their own ways as friends.

Lesson 2

Grammar Review: Commas

Rule 1

The members of a simple sentence should not, in general, be separated by a comma; as, "Every part of matter swarms with living creatures."

Exercises in Punctuation — Idleness is the great fomenter of all corruptions in the human heart. The friend of order has made half his way to virtue. All finery is a sign of littleness.

Rule 2

When a simple sentence is long, and the nominative is accompanied with an inseparable adjunct of importance, it may admit a comma immediately before the verb; as, "The good taste of the present age, has not allowed us to neglect the cultivation of the English language"; "Too many *of the pretended friendships of youth*, are mere combinations in pleasure."

Exercises — The indulgence of a harsh disposition is the introduction to future misery. To be totally indifferent to praise or censure is a real defect in character. The intermixture of evil in human society serves to exercise the suffering graces and virtues of the good.

Rule 3

When the connection of the different parts of a simple sentence is interrupted by an adjunct of importance, the adjunct must be distinguished by a comma before and after it; as, "His work is, *in many respects*, very imperfect. It is, *therefore*, not much approved." But when these interruptions are slight and unimportant, it is better to omit the comma; as, "Flattery is *certainly* pernicious;" "There is *surely* a pleasure in beneficence."

Exercises — Charity like the sun brightens all its objects. Gentleness is in truth the great avenue to mutual enjoyment. You too have your failings. Humility and knowledge with poor apparel excel pride and ignorance under costly attire. The best men often experience disappointments. Advice should be seasonably administered. No assumed behavior can always hide the real character.

Rule 4

The nominative case independent, and nouns in apposition, when accompanied with adjuncts, must be distinguished by commas; as, "My *son*, give me thy heart"; "Dear Sir, I write to express my gratitude for your many kindnesses"; "I am obliged to you, my *friends*, for your many favors"; "*Paul*, the *apostle*, of the Gentiles, was eminent for his zeal and knowledge"; "The *butterfly, child* of the summer, flutters in the sun."

But if *two* nouns in apposition are unattended with adjuncts, or if they form only a proper name, they should not be separated; as, "*Paul* the *apostle*, suffered martyrdom"; "The *statesman Jefferson*, wrote the declaration of Independence."

Exercises — Lord thou hast been our dwelling place in all generations. Continue my dear child to make virtue thy chief study. Canst thou expect thou betrayer of innocence to escape the hand of vengeance? Death the king of terrors chose a prime minister. Hope the balm of life sooths us under every misfortune. Confucius the great Chinese philosopher was eminently good as well as wise. The patriarch Joseph is an illustrious example of true piety.

Rule 5

The nominative case absolute and the infinitive mood absolute with their adjuncts, a participle with words depending on it, and, generally, any imperfect phrase that may be resolved into a simple sentence, must be separated from the rest of the sentence by commas; as, "*His father dying*, he succeeded to the estate"; "*To confess the truth*, I was in fault"; "The king, *approving the plan*, put it in execution"; "He, *having finished his academical course*, has returned home, *to prosecute his professional studies*."

Daily Assignment

- Warm-up: What part of your life would you change, if you could?
- Students will complete Concept Builder 6-B.
- Prayer journal.
- Students should outline all assigned essays for the week.

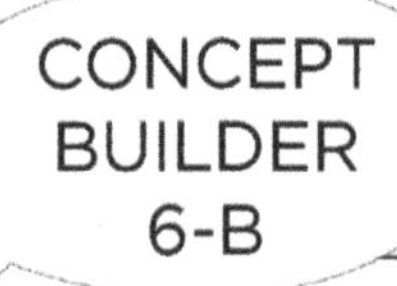

Plot Analysis of a Movie

Discuss any movie that you have seen and identify the exposition (introductory information), rising action, climax, denouement (falling action), and resolution.

Exposition

Elsa has magica powers. Anna is lonely
Parents die

Rising Action

Elsa's cornation Day | Anna falls in love with hans

Climax

Elsa runs away. Anna meets Kristoff and olaf

Denouement

Anna finds Elsa and she freezes Annas heart. then gets arrested

Resolution

Hans dumps anna while she's dying. Hans almost kills Elsa but anna saves her. Anna melts and they are happy.
The End

Plot: "The Frog-Prince"

One fine evening a young princess put on her bonnet and clogs, and went out to take a walk by herself in a wood; and when she came to a cool spring of water, that rose in the midst of it, she sat herself down to rest a while. Now she had a golden ball in her hand, which was her favourite plaything; and she was always tossing it up into the air, and catching it again as it fell. After a time she threw it up so high that she missed catching it as it fell; and the ball bounded away, and rolled along upon the ground, till at last it fell down into the spring. The princess looked into the spring after her ball, but it was very deep, so deep that she could not see the bottom of it. Then she began to bewail her loss, and said, "Alas! if I could only get my ball again, I would give all my fine clothes and jewels, and everything that I have in the world."

Action

Whilst she was speaking, a frog put its head out of the water, and said, "Princess, why do you weep so bitterly?" "Alas!" said she, "what can you do for me, you nasty frog? My golden ball has fallen into the spring." The frog said, "I want not your pearls, and jewels, and fine clothes; but if you will love me, and let me live with you and eat from off your golden plate, and sleep upon your bed, I will bring you your ball again." "What nonsense," thought the princess, "this silly frog is talking! He can never even get out of the spring to visit me, though he may be able to get my ball for me, and therefore I will tell him he shall have what he asks." So she said to the frog, "Well, if you will bring me my ball, I will do all you ask." Then the frog put his head down, and dived deep under the water; and after a little while he came up again, with the ball in his mouth, and threw it on the edge of the spring. As soon as the young princess saw her ball, she ran to pick it up; and she was so overjoyed to have it in her hand again, that she never thought of the frog, but ran home with it as fast as she could. The frog called after her, "Stay, princess, and take me with you as you said," But she did not stop to hear a word.

The next day, just as the princess had sat down to dinner, she heard a strange noise — tap, tap — plash, plash — as if something was coming up the marble staircase: and soon afterwards there was a gentle knock at the door, and a little voice cried out and said:

"Open the door, my princess dear,
Open the door to thy true love here!
And mind the words that thou and I said
By the fountain cool, in the greenwood shade."

Then the princess ran to the door and opened it, and there she saw the frog, whom she had quite forgotten. At this sight she was sadly frightened, and shutting the door as fast as she could came back to her seat. The king, her father, seeing that something had frightened her, asked her what was the matter. "There is a nasty frog," said she, "at the door, that lifted my ball for me out of the spring this morning: I told him that he should live with me here, thinking that he could never get out of the spring; but there he is at the door, and he wants to come in."

While she was speaking the frog knocked again at the door, and said:

"Open the door, my princess dear,
Open the door to thy true love here!
And mind the words that thou and I said
By the fountain cool, in the greenwood shade."

Then the king said to the young princess, "As you have given your word you must keep it; so go and let him in." She did so, and the frog hopped into the room, and then straight on — tap, tap — plash, plash — from the bottom of the room to the top, till he came up close to the table where the princess sat. "Pray lift me upon chair," said he to the princess, "and let me sit next to you." As soon as she had done this, the frog said, "Put your plate nearer to me, that I may eat out of it." This she did, and when he had eaten as much as he could, he said, "Now I am tired; carry me upstairs, and put me into your bed." And the princess, though very unwilling, took him up in her hand, and put him upon the pillow of her own bed, where he slept all night long. As soon as it was light he jumped up, hopped downstairs, and went out of the house. "Now, then," thought the princess, "at last he is gone, and I shall be troubled with him no more."

But she was mistaken; for when night came again she heard the same tapping at the door; and the frog came once more, and said:

"Open the door, my princess dear,
Open the door to thy true love here!
And mind the words that thou and I said
By the fountain cool, in the greenwood shade."

And when the princess opened the door the frog came in, and slept upon her pillow as before, till the morning broke. And the third night he did the same. But when the princess awoke on the following morning she was astonished to see, instead of the frog, a handsome prince, gazing on her with the most beautiful eyes she had ever seen, and standing at the head of her bed.

Climax

He told her that he had been enchanted by a spiteful fairy, who had changed him into a frog; and that he had been fated so to abide till some princess should take him out of the spring, and let him eat from her plate, and sleep upon her bed for three nights. "You," said the prince, "have broken his cruel charm, and now I have nothing to wish for but that you should go with me into my father's kingdom, where I will marry you, and love you as long as you live."

Falling Action

The young princess, you may be sure, was not long in saying "Yes" to all this; and as they spoke a gay coach drove up, with eight beautiful horses, decked with plumes of feathers and a golden harness; and behind the coach rode the prince's servant, faithful Heinrich, who had bewailed the misfortunes of his dear master during his enchantment so long and so bitterly, that his heart had well-nigh burst.

Denouement

They then took leave of the king, and got into the coach with eight horses, and all set out, full of joy and merriment, for the prince's kingdom, which they reached safely; and there they lived happily a great many years.[1]

1 The Brothers Grimm, *Grimm's Fairy Tales*, "The Frog-Prince," www.gutenberg.org/files/2591/2591-h/2591-h.htm#2H_4_0013.

Daily Assignment

- Warm-up: Summarize your favorite movie, and state why you liked it so much. What is its climax?
- Students will complete Concept Builder 6-C.
- Prayer journal.
- Students should write rough drafts of all assigned essays and speech.

Literary Plot

Match each component of this story with the literary component of the plot.

Summary of *The Runaway Bunny* by Margaret Wise Brown.

__C__ The little bunny finally understands that he cannot escape the pursuing love of his mother.

__D__ The little bunny happily accepts a carrot and decides to stay at home permanently.

__A__ The reader learns that the principal characters are a baby bunny and his mom. We also learn that the young bunny is planning to run away.

__B__ The little bunny begins to realize that he cannot run away from his mom.

__E__ The reader learns that no matter where the bunny runs, the mommy bunny pursues and catches him.

A. Exposition (introductory material)

B. Rising Action (unfolding action)

C. Climax (the most exciting part)

D. Denouement (the falling action)

E. Resolution (the conclusion)

Student Essay

Although not a characteristic book, the Joseph Narratives has the standard plot outline most all books bear. The Joseph Narratives has a certain event as the climax of the book and multiple occurrences as the rising actions. It also has the falling action that links the climax to the resolution. This story does not have an exposition, yet the multiple rising actions more than make up for it. Because of the complete plot outline, the Joseph Narratives parallel so closely to an actual book it could easily be made into a full-length novel in and of itself.

Joseph's revealing his identity to his brothers is most definitely the climax of the Joseph Narratives. All of the events that occur before that are part of the rising action. Although there is no exposition, there are enough events in the rising action to inform the reader of the characters and setting. The reader anticipates that a climax will take place after reading about Joseph's dreams concerning his brothers in Genesis 37:6–9. Events such as Joseph being sold into slavery, being condemned by Potiphar's wife, and interpreting the pharaoh's and his servants' dreams leave one predicting the climax. The climax is reached after the conversations Joseph has with his brothers, when Joseph explains that he is their dream-telling, long-lost brother.

The resolution finally occurs when all of Joseph's family is living together in Egypt. This is connected to the climax by the brothers going to tell their father that Joseph is alive. This connection is the falling action. Once they do this, the resolution is able to occur and the reader is delighted.

When reading the Joseph Narratives or any well-written novel, one will always discover a plot outline that will most definitely contain rising actions, a climax, falling actions, and a resolution. One reason the Joseph Narratives is such a fascinating story is because of the rising action. The multiple, miniature stories in the rising action not only lead the reader to the climax, but also make the Joseph Narratives suspenseful and intriguing. With the rising action and other parts of the plot outline, the Joseph Narratives has become one of the most well known stories in the Bible. (Claire)

Daily Assignment

- Warm-up: Everyone has a story. Share one of the saddest parts of your story. Did this event occur in the rising action or falling action in your life?
- Students will complete Concept Builder 6-D.
- Prayer journal.
- Review the assigned text. Keep vocabulary cards.
- This is the day that students should write, and then rewrite, the final drafts of their assigned essay.

test — Essay on plot due Friday 9/29

CONCEPT BUILDER 6-D

Completing a Story

Complete this story by filling in the plot in your own words.

EXPOSITION (INTRODUCTORY INFORMATION)

September 11, 1975, was a particularly warm, promising day even in the South where fall oftentimes is lost between tepid, late summer afternoons and frosty winter mornings. My heart was beaming too, for on this day I was to begin a two-day trip to Boston, where within the month I was to begin my seminary studies.

RISING ACTION on our way we were robbed and was left to fend for ourselves. after four days with no food or water we made it to boston. I was able to get a loan from the bank to help pay for rent at our hotel. I was also able to get my beautiful car back. Oh what a babe! then we were of the Seminary college.

CLIMAX we got to our classroom and had to explain why we were two days late. so the teacher decided to make us take a surprise test. thankfully I had studied hard before we got here. once he had graded it he said, "to be frank I don't think you will belong her at all! You know absolutly nothing!" as I looked down at my paper a big red F- punched me in the stomach and made me sick.

FALLING ACTION

But I never forgot this bridge, because against its rain-wasted side, my poor compact car crumbled like a cheap, flimsy pop can. At the same time, my dreams were similarly shattered. Before that day was to end I was to experience horror as I had never known. Besides breaking my hand in two places, I had a severed right foot, compound multiple fractures in my right femur, and a painful fractured right hip. And, by the time this ordeal ended, I had decided to forget the ministry. I had no intentions of trusting my life to a God who would throw me against the side of that concrete bridge on Highway 1. It ~~would take me another half a decade to finally finish my seminary work.~~

RESOLUTION Oh boy am I happy! yes after I thought that God didn't care he turned everything around and now I have be highly requested to join the Seminary College! And I am all healed and married with a child on the way. God is good all the time and all the time GOD is good.

Tone: Humor — *The Adventures of Tom Sawyer* (Mark Twain)

Chapter 7

First Thoughts

Perhaps no book captures the American idea of boyhood more than this novel. Partly autobiographical — Twain grew up on the Mississippi River — this book transcends its time and location. Not counting *The Gilded Age*, which was co-authored with Charles Dudley Warner, *The Adventures of Tom Sawyer* was Mark Twain's first novel. By the time Mark Twain died, it had become an American classic, and it remains perhaps the best loved of all his books among general readers.

Chapter Learning Objectives

In chapter 7 we explore the tone of Mark Twain's novel, and we analyze the way he creates humor.

As a result of this chapter study you will be able to . . .

1. Discuss when/if a lie is acceptable.
2. Chapter 8 in Tom Sawyer is a parody of a romantic novel. Explain.

Look Ahead for Friday

- Turn in a final copy of essay
- Take Weekly Test

Lesson 1

Literary Analysis: Humor/Tone

Tone or mood is the "feeling" a literary work evokes in the reader. What mood is evoked in the following short story, "The Fall of the House of Usher," by Edgar Allan Poe?

During the whole of a dull, dark, and soundless day in the autumn of the year, when the clouds hung oppressively low in the heavens, had been passing alone, on horseback, through a singularly dreary tract of country; and at length found myself, as the shades of the evening drew on, within view of the melancholy House of Usher. I know not how it was — but, with the first glimpse of the building, a sense of insufferable gloom pervaded my spirit. I say insufferable; for the feeling was unrelieved by any of that half-pleasurable, because poetic, sentiment, with which the mind usually receives even the sternest natural images of the desolate or terrible. I looked upon the scene before me — upon the mere house, and the simple landscape features of the domain — upon the bleak walls — upon the vacant eye-like windows — upon a few rank sedges — and upon a few white trunks of decayed trees — with an utter depression of soul which I can compare to no earthly sensation more properly than to the after-dream of the reveler upon opium — the bitter lapse into everyday life — the hideous dropping off of the reveler upon opium — the bitter lapse into everyday life — the hideous dropping off of the veil. There was an iciness, a sinking, a sickening of the heart — an unredeemed dreariness of thought which no goading of the imagination could torture into aught of the sublime. What was it — I paused to think — what was it that so unnerved me in the contemplation of the House of Usher? It was a mystery all insoluble; nor could I grapple with the shadowy fancies that crowded upon me as I pondered. I was forced to fall back upon the unsatisfactory conclusion, that while, beyond doubt, there are combinations of very simple natural objects which have the power of thus affecting us, still the analysis of this power lies among considerations beyond our depth.

It was possible, I reflected, that a mere different arrangement of the particulars of the scene, of the details of the picture, would be sufficient to modify, or perhaps to annihilate its capacity for sorrowful impression; and, acting upon this idea, I reined my horse to the precipitous brink of a black and lurid tarn that lay in unruffled lustre by the dwelling, and gazed down — but with a shudder even more thrilling than before — upon the remodeled and inverted images of the gray sedge, and the ghastly tree-stems, and the vacant and eye-like windows.[1]

1 www.classicreaader.com.

Daily Assignment

- Warm-up: Describe someone who is really funny — who makes you laugh. What makes that person funny?
- Students will complete Concept Builder 7-A.
- Prayer journal: Students are encouraged to write in their prayer journal every day.
- Students need to review their material for the next assignment
- Students should systematically review their vocabulary words daily.

Tone

Tone is the feeling that a writer creates for the reader. He/she uses several techniques. Use the chart below to identify the principal mood Twain creates and to list the different elements he uses to create that mood/tone.

Mood:

ELEMENT	EXAMPLE
Figurative Language	"Well, I lay if i get a hold of you I'll
Imagery	he wondered if she would pity him if she knew
Descriptions	they were her state pair, and were buit for style not service
Dialogue	in an instant both boys were rolling and tumbling in the dirt.
Sound Devices (slang, et al.)	"I Ain't affraid."
Situational Irony (humorous situations)	Tom runs away and jumps over fence it's funny.

Lesson 2

Humor from *The Adventures of Tom Sawyer*[1]

"TOM!"

No answer.

"TOM!"

No answer.

"What's gone with that boy, I wonder? You TOM!"

No answer.

The old lady pulled her spectacles down and looked over them about the room; then she put them up and looked out under them. She seldom or never looked through them for so small a thing as a boy; they were her state pair, the pride of her heart, and were built for "style," not service — she could have seen through a pair of stove lids just as well. She looked perplexed for a moment, and then said, not fiercely, but still loud enough for the furniture to hear:

"Well, I lay if I get hold of you I'll —"

She did not finish, for by this time she was bending down and punching under the bed with the broom, and so she needed breath to punctuate the punches with. She resurrected nothing but the cat.

"I never did see the beat of that boy!"

She went to the open door and stood in it and looked out among the tomato vines and "jimpson" weeds that constituted the garden. No Tom. So she lifted up her voice at an angle calculated for distance and shouted:

"Y-o-u-u Tom!"

There was a slight noise behind her and she turned just in time to seize a small boy by the slack of his roundabout and arrest his flight.

"There! I might 'a' thought of that closet. What you been doing in there?"

"Nothing."

"Nothing! Look at your hands. And look at your mouth. What is that truck?"

"I don't know, aunt."

"Well, I know. It's jam—that's what it is. Forty times I've said if you didn't let that jam alone I'd skin you. Hand me that switch."

The switch hovered in the air — the peril was desperate —

"My! Look behind you, aunt!"

The old lady whirled round, and snatched her skirts out of danger. The lad fled on the instant, scrambled up the high board fence, and disappeared over it.

His aunt Polly stood surprised a moment, and then broke into a gentle laugh.

"Hang the boy, can't I never learn anything? Ain't he played me tricks enough like that for me to be looking out for him by this time?"[1] But old fools is the biggest fools there is. Can't learn an old dog new tricks, as the saying is. But my goodness, he never plays them alike, two days, and how is a body to know what's coming? He 'pears to know just how long he can torment me before I get my dander up, and he knows if he can make out to put me off for a minute or make me laugh, it's all down again and I can't hit him a lick. I ain't doing my duty by that boy, and that's the Lord's truth, goodness knows. Spare the rod and spile the child, as the Good Book says. I'm a laying up sin and suffering for us both, I know. He's full of the Old Scratch, but laws-a-me! he's my own dead sister's boy, poor thing, and I ain't got the heart to lash him, somehow. Every time I let him off, my conscience does hurt me so, and every time I hit him my old heart most breaks. Well-a-well, man that is born of woman is of few days and full of trouble, as the Scripture says, and I reckon it's so. He'll play hookey this evening… I'll just be obleeged to make him work, tomorrow, to punish him. It's mighty hard to make him work Saturdays, when all the boys is having holiday, but he hates work more than he hates anything else, and I've got to do some of my duty by him, or I'll be the ruination of the child."

1 http://wyllie.lib.virginia.edu:8086/perl/toccer-new?id=Twa2Tom.sgm&images=images/modeng&data=texts/english/modeng/paresed&tag=public&part=1.

Tom did play hookey, and he had a very good time. He got back home barely in season to help Jim, the small colored boy, saw next-day's wood and split the kindlings before supper — at least he was there in time to tell his adventures to Jim while Jim did three-fourths of the work. Tom's younger brother (or rather half-brother) Sid was already through with his part of the work (picking up chips), for he was a quiet boy, and had no adventurous, troublesome ways.

While Tom was eating his supper, and stealing sugar as opportunity offered, Aunt Polly asked him questions that were full of guile, and very deep — for she wanted to trap him into damaging revealments. Like many other simple-hearted souls, it was her pet vanity to believe she was endowed with a talent for dark and mysterious diplomacy, and she loved to contemplate her most transparent devices as marvels of low cunning. Said she:

"Tom, it was middling warm in school, warn't it?" "Yes'm."

"Powerful warm, warn't it?" "Yes'm."

"Didn't you want to go in a-swimming, Tom?"

A bit of a scare shot through Tom — a touch of uncomfortable suspicion. He searched Aunt Polly's face, but it told him nothing. So he said:

"No'm — well, not very much."

The old lady reached out her hand and felt Tom's shirt, and said:

"But you ain't too warm now, though." And it flattered her to reflect that she had discovered that the shirt was dry without anybody knowing that that was what she had in her mind. But in spite of her, Tom knew where the wind lay, now. So he forestalled what might be the next move:

"Some of us pumped on our heads — mine's damp yet. See?"

Aunt Polly was vexed to think she had overlooked that bit of circumstantial evidence, and missed a trick. Then she had a new inspiration:

"Tom, you didn't have to undo your shirt collar where I sewed it, to pump on your head, did you? Unbutton your jacket!"

The trouble vanished out of Tom's face. He opened his jacket. His shirt collar was securely sewed.

"Bother! Well, go 'long with you. I'd made sure you'd played hookey and been a-swimming. But I forgive ye, Tom. I reckon you're a kind of a singed cat, as the saying is — better'n you look. This time."

She was half sorry her sagacity had miscarried, and half glad that Tom had stumbled into obedient conduct for once. But Sidney said:

"Well, now, if I didn't think you sewed his collar with white thread, but it's black."

"Why, I did sew it with white!

Tom!"

But Tom did not wait for the rest.

Daily Assignment

- Warm-up: Describe your favorite comedian. Why do you like him/her?
- Students will complete Concept Builder 7-B.
- Prayer journal.
- Students should outline all assigned essays for the week.

Active Reading

Read the excerpt from chapter one in *Tom Sawyer* by Mark Twain, and then answer the following questions:

Why does Twain begin his book with so much dialogue?

as a hook. to trap the audience with ceriosity.

Who is the protagonist?

Aunt Polly and Tom Sawyer

What is the narrative technique?

Third-person

From the first page or two, what can you infer about Tom Sawyer's personality?

Scandalist, trouble maker, trickster

Lesson 3

Sample Essay: Tone in *The Screwtape Letters*

Tone is very important to the book *The Screwtape Letters*. C.S. Lewis is using the devil and his nephew Wormwood to tell the Christian community important truths. He wants Christians to laugh at themselves so that they can learn something. In a way, C.S. Lewis is writing what Shakespeare wrote in one of his soliloquies: "O what fools we mortals be" (from Hamlet).

"I (Screwtape) once had a patient, a sound atheist, who used to read in the British Museum. One day, as he sat reading, I saw his mind beginning to go the wrong way. The enemy (God) of course was at his elbow in an instant." In these letters that are written by C.S. Lewis, Screwtape (the devil) is writing a series of letters to his dear nephew Wormwood. Lewis begins by using understatement. The person is a sound atheist. Next, Screwtape ends by poking fun at Christians.

"Before I knew where I was I saw my twenty years' work beginning to totter. If I had lost my head and begun to attempt a defense by argument, I should have been undone. But I was not such a fool. I struck instantly at the part of the man which I had best under my control, and suggested that it was just about time to have some lunch. The Enemy presumably made the counter suggestion (you know how one cannot quite overhear what He says to them?) that this was more important than lunch. At least I think that this must have been his line, for when I said, 'Quite, in fact much too important to tackle at the end of a morning,' the patient brightened up quite considerably; and by the time I had added, 'much better to come back after lunch and go into with a fresh mind,' he was already half way to the front door."[1]

In this passage, Lewis takes an ordinary event — eating — and shows how Satan uses it to capture Christians. It appears funny because something pretty innocent becomes something questionable for Christians.

C.S. Lewis puts forth truth by writing these hilarious letters about how Satan can so easily entangle people into doing stupid things that logically make no sense. (Timothy Stobaugh)

1 www.biblestudyinfo.com.

Daily Assignment

- Warm-up: Tell your favorite joke. Analyze why it is humorous.
- Students will complete Concept Builder 7-C.
- Prayer journal.
- Students should write rough drafts of all assigned essays and speech.

Changing the Tone

Tone or Mood is the feeling that a writer creates for the reader. He/she often uses the plot to develop the mood. For instance, change the following incident into a sad/serious incident.

"TOM!"

No answer.

"TOM!"

No answer.

"What's gone with that boy, I wonder? You TOM!" No answer.

The old lady pulled her spectacles down and looked over them about the room; then she put them up and looked out under them. She seldom or never looked through them for so small a thing as a boy; they were her state pair, the pride of her heart, and were built for "style," not service — she could have seen through a pair of stove-lids just as well. She looked perplexed for a moment, and then said, not fiercely, but still loud enough for the furniture to hear:

"Well, I lay if I get hold of you I'll —"

She did not finish, for by this time she was bending down and punching under the bed with the broom, and so she needed breath to punctuate the punches with. She resurrected nothing but the cat.

"I never did see the beat of that boy!"

She went to the open door and stood in it and looked out among the tomato vines and "jimpson" weeds that constituted the garden. No Tom. So she lifted up her voice at an angle calculated for distance and shouted:

"Y-o-u-u Tom!"

There was a slight noise behind her and she turned just in time to seize a small boy by the slack of his roundabout and arrest his flight.

"There! I might 'a' thought of that closet. What you been doing in there?" "Nothing."

"Nothing! Look at your hands. And look at your mouth. What is that truck?" "I don't know, aunt."

"Well, I know. It's jam — that's what it is. Forty times I've said if you didn't let that jam alone I'd skin you. Hand me that switch."

The switch hovered in the air — the peril was desperate — "My! Look behind you, aunt!"

The old lady whirled round, and snatched her skirts out of danger. The lad fled on the instant, scrambled up the high board-fence, and disappeared over it.

His aunt Polly stood surprised a moment, and then broke into a gentle laugh.

"TOM!"
No answer
"TOM!"
No answer
"What's gone with that boy I wonder? You Tom!" No answer
The old lady was frightened for she could not find her beloved tom. Just then a knaw was outside the door. The old lady opened it to find an officer standing tall and saluting.
"how can I help ye, officer?"
"I'm afraid I have some horrific news for you" Replied the officer. "Tom Sawyer had been playing near the river with a friend and of course boys will be boys, they started to playfully tackle when Tom's friend pushed him near the river, and he slipped, causing him to fall in and hit his head on a boulder. I am sorry for your lose mame". As he left, the old lady sobbed. Tom was her only child. how would she be able to move on?

Grammar Review: Commas

Rule 6

A compound sentence must be resolved into simple ones by placing commas between its members; as, "The decay, the waste, and the dissolution of a plant, may affect our spirits, and suggest a train of serious reflections."

Three or more nouns, verbs, adjectives, participles, or adverbs, connected by conjunctions, expressed or understood, must be separated by commas; as, "The husband, wife, and children, suffered extremely"; "In a letter, we may advise, exhort, comfort, request, and discuss"; "David was a brave, wise, and pious man"; "A man, fearing, serving, and loving his Creator, lives for a noble purpose"; "Success generally depends on acting prudently, steadily, and vigorously, in what we undertake."

Two or more nouns, verbs, adjectives, participles, or adverbs, occurring in the same construction, with their conjunctions understood, must be separated by commas; as, "Reason, virtue, answer one great aim"; "Virtue supports in adversity, moderates in prosperity"; "Plain, honest truth, needs no artificial covering"; "We are fearfully, wonderfully framed."

Exercises — We have no reason to complain of the lot of man nor of the mutability of the world. Sensuality contaminates the body depresses the understanding deadens the moral feelings of the heart and degrades man from his rank in creation.

Self-conceit presumption and obstinacy blast the prospects of many a youth. He is alternately supported by his father his uncle and his elder brother. The man of virtue and honor will be trusted relied upon and esteemed. Conscious guilt renders one mean-spirited timorous and base. An upright mind will never be at a loss to discern what is just and true lovely honest and of good report. Habits of reading writing and thinking are the indispensable qualifications of a good student. The great business of life is to be employed in doing justly loving mercy and talking humbly with our Creator. To live soberly righteously and piously comprehends the whole of our duty.

In our health life possessions connexions pleasures there are causes of decay imperceptibly working. Deliberate slowly execute promptly. An idle trifling society is near akin to such as is corrupting. This unhappy person had been seriously affectionately admonished but in vain.

Rule 7

Comparative sentences whose members are short, and sentences connected with relative pronouns the meaning of whose antecedents is restricted or limited to a particular sense, should not be separated by a comma; as, "Wisdom is better than riches"; "No preacher is so successful as thee"; "He accepted *what* I had rejected"; "Self-denial is the *sacrifice which* virtue must make"; "Subtract from many modern poets *all that* may be found in Shakespeare, and trash will remain"; "Give it to the *man whom* you most esteem." In this last example, the assertion is not of "man in general," but of "the man whom you most esteem."

But when the antecedent is used in a general sense, a comma is properly inserted before the relative; as, "*Man, who* is born of a woman, is of few days and full of trouble"; "There is no *charm* in the female sex, *which* can supply the place of virtue."

This rule is equally applicable to constructions in which the relative is understood; as, "Value duly the privileges you enjoy;" that is, "privileges *which* you enjoy."

Exercises — How much better it is to get wisdom than gold! The friendships of the world can exist no longer than interest cements them. Eat what is set before you. They who excite envy will easily incur censure. A man who is of a detracting spirit will misconstrue the most innocent words that can be put together. Many of the evils which occasion our complaints of the world are wholly imaginary.

The gentle mind is like the smooth stream which reflects every object in its just proportion and in its fairest colors. In that unaffected civility which springs from a gentle mind there is an incomparable charm. The Lord whom I serve is eternal. This is the man we saw yesterday.

Rule 8

When two words of the same sort, are connected by a conjunction expressed, they must not be separated; as, "Libertines call religion, bigotry *or* superstition"; "True worth is modest *and* retired"; "The study of natural history, expands *and* elevates the mind"; "Some men sin deliberately and presumptuously." When words are connected in pairs, the pairs only should be separated; as, "There is a natural difference between merit *and* demerit, virtue *and* vice, wisdom and folly;" "Whether we eat or drink, labor or sleep, we should be temperate."

But if the parts connected by a conjunction are not short, they may be separated by a comma; as, "Romances may be said to be miserable rhapsodies, *or* dangerous incentives to evil."

Exercises — Idleness brings forward and nourishes many bad passions. True friendship will at all times avoid a rough or careless behavior. Health and peace a moderate fortune and a few friends sum up all the undoubted articles of temporal felicity. Truth is fair and artless simple and sincere uniform and consistent. Intemperance destroys the strength of our bodies and the vigor of our minds.

Rule 9

Where the verb of a simple member is understood, a comma may, in some instances, be inserted; as, "From law arises security; from security, curiosity; from curiosity, knowledge." But in others, it is better to omit the comma; "No station is so high, no power so great, no character so unblemished, as to exempt men from the attacks of rashness, malice, and envy."

Exercises — As a companion he was severe and satirical; as a friend captious and dangerous. If the spring put forth no blossoms in summer there will be no beauty and in autumn no fruit. So if youth be trifled away without improvement manhood will be contemptible and old age miserable.

Rule 10

When a simple member stands as the object of a preceding verb, and its verb may be changed into the infinitive mood, the comma is generally omitted; as, "I suppose *he is at rest*"; changed, "I suppose *him to be at rest.*"

But when the verb to be is followed by a verb in the infinitive mood, which, by transposition, may be made the nominative case to it, the verb to be is generally separated from the infinitive by a comma; as, "The most obvious remedy is, to withdraw from all associations with bad men"; "The first and most obvious remedy against the infection, is, to withdraw from all associations with bad men."[1]

Exercises — They believed he was dead. He did not know that I was the man. I knew she was still alive. The greatest misery is to be condemned by our own hearts. The greatest misery that we can endure is to be condemned by our own hearts.

1 Ibid.

Daily Assignment

- Warm-up: Describe an incident that would be humorous to one person and not to someone else.
- Students will complete Concept Builder 7-D.
- Prayer journal.
- Review the assigned text. Keep vocabulary cards.
- This is the day that students should write, and then rewrite, the final drafts of their assigned essay.

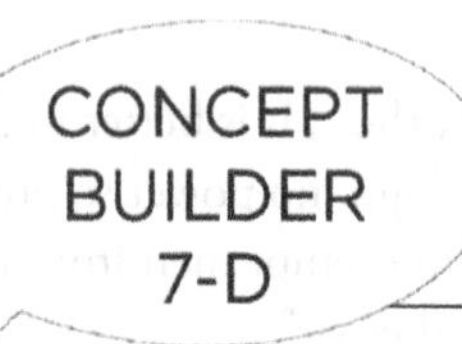

The Author's Voice

Literary critics sometimes refer to mood as an "author's voice." Voice is a way an author allows a reader to discern the human personalities in the author's work. For example, if I wanted to show the reader that a character was a teenager I could have the character say, "Hey, dude, what is happening man?"

Complete the following diagram, considering how Twain develops voice. Write your responses on top of the circles.

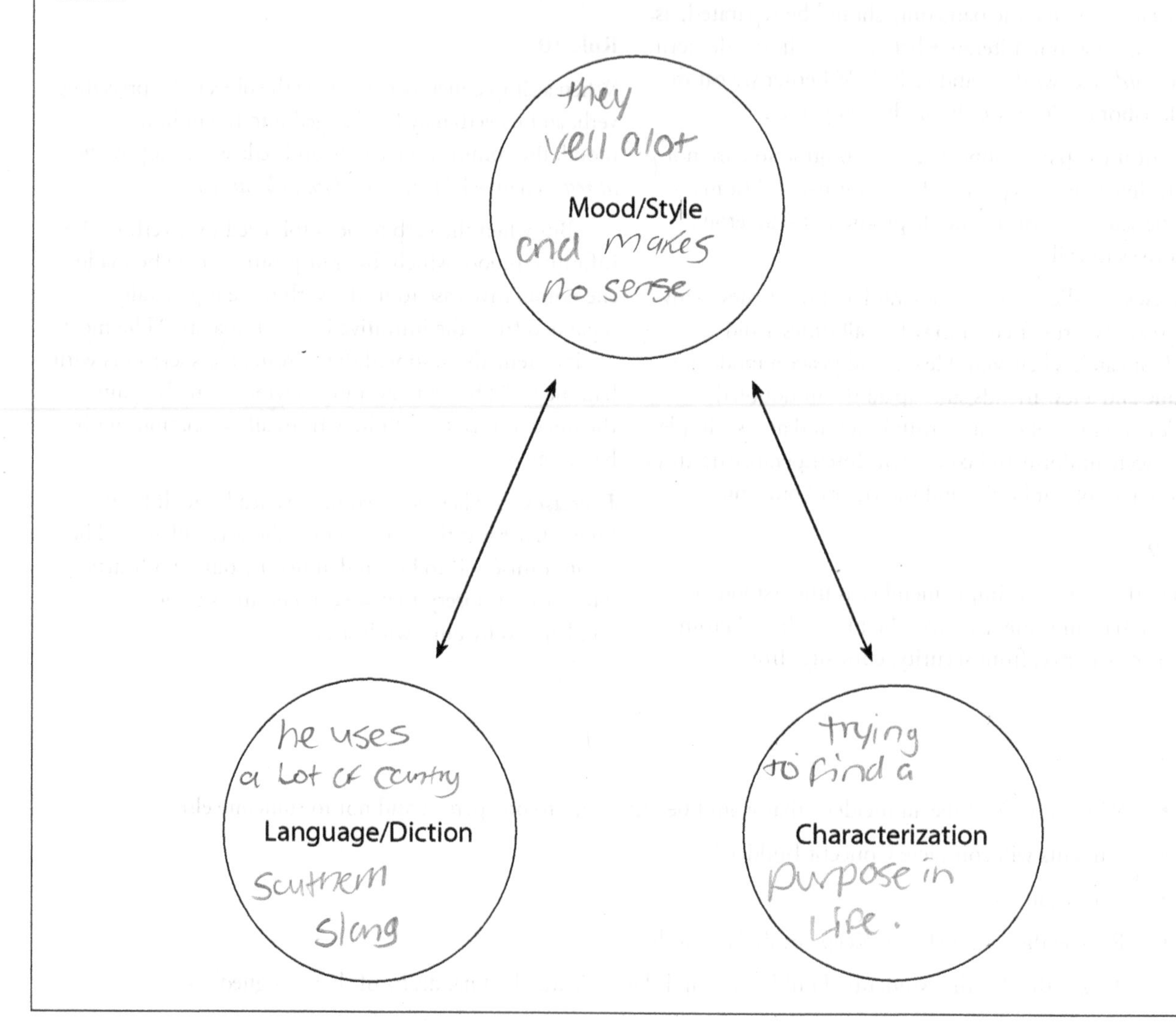

Allegory — *Idylls of the King* (Alfred Lord Tennyson)

Chapter 8

First Thoughts

You will recognize immediately the storyline in *Idylls of the King*. This book, which is really a very long, narrative poem, is another version of the King Arthur legend. Yes, you will recognize King Arthur, Guinevere, Sir Lancelot, and the other knights of the Round Table. The poem is hard to read at times, but it is worth the effort. Alfred Lord Tennyson is one of the best English poets of the Victorian Age.

Chapter Learning Objectives

In chapter 8 we analyze the use of allegory in *Idylls of the King*.

As a result of this chapter study you will be able to . . .

1. Discuss symbolism in *Idylls of the King*.
2. Analyze Tennyson's faith journey.
3. Evaluate Tennyson's view of heaven.

Look Ahead for Friday

- Turn in a final copy of essay
- Take Weekly Test

Lesson 1

Literary Analysis: Allegory

After our first reading of *Idylls*, most of us think it is only a tale of knights and fair maidens and adventure, but there is much more to it. It is full of *symbolism* and *allegory*. An allegory is a story that symbolizes something other than what it really is. It has a person, place, event, and/or object that has a meaning in itself but suggests other emotional meanings as well. Some scholars, for instance, have suggested that the snakelike river surrounding Castle Perilous represents time. The river has three loops that represent three stages of life — youth, middle-age, and old age. The three knights at the crossings personify the temptations at all stages of life.

Perhaps the most famous example of symbolism occurs in the American novel *The Scarlet Letter* by Nathaniel Hawthorne. In the scene that follows in the next lesson, Hester Prynne, the protagonist, is publicly humiliated for committing adultery. She is standing in front of the old Puritan jail in which she has been held. She has embroidered on her dress a beautiful scarlet *A*.

Daily Assignment

- Warm-up: What is your favorite book? Why?
- Students will complete Concept Builder 8-A.
- Prayer journal: Students are encouraged to write in their prayer journal every day.
- Students need to review their material for the next assignment
- Students should systematically review their vocabulary words daily.

Active Reading

Read this excerpt of *Idylls of the King* by Lord Alfred Tennyson, and answer the following questions.

The Coming of Arthur
Leodogran, the King of Cameliard,

Had one fair daughter, and none other child;
And she was the fairest of all flesh on earth,
Guinevere, and in her his one delight.

For many a petty king ere Arthur came
Ruled in this isle, and ever waging war
Each upon other, wasted all the land;
And still from time to time the heathen host
Swarmed overseas, and harried what was left.
And so there grew great tracts of wilderness,
Wherein the beast was ever more and more,
But man was less and less, till Arthur came.

For first Aurelius lived and fought and died,
And after him King Uther fought and died,
But either failed to make the kingdom one.
And after these King Arthur for a space,
And through the puissance of his Table Round,
Drew all their petty princedoms under him.
Their king and head, and made a realm, and reigned.

And thus the land of Cameliard was waste,
Thick with wet woods, and many a beast therein,
And none or few to scare or chase the beast;
So that wild dog, and wolf and boar and bear
Came night and day, and rooted in the fields,
And wallowed in the gardens of the King.
And ever and anon the wolf would steal
The children and devour, but now and then,
Her own brood lost or dead, lent her fierce teat
To human sucklings; and the children, housed
In her foul den, there at their meat would growl,
And mock their foster mother on four feet,
Till, straightened, they grew up to wolf-like men,
Worse than the wolves. And King Leodogran
Groaned for the Roman legions here again,
And Csar's eagle: then his brother king,
Urien, assailed him: last a heathen horde,
Reddening the sun with smoke and earth with blood,
And on the spike that split the mother's heart
Spitting the child, brake on him, till, amazed,
He knew not whither he should turn for aid.

1. Describe King Arthur. Who does he symbolize?

Wasteful

2. What is the narrative point of view? Why do you think Tennyson chose this point of view?

to help us understand what he's feeling.

3. What is the setting? Is it important? In other words, could this story happen anywhere?

Cameliard
yes it's impatent
yes it ceuld but only with this King

Lesson 2

Allegory in *The Scarlet Letter*

When the young woman — the mother of this child — stood fully revealed before the crowd, it seemed to be her first impulse to clasp the infant closely to her bosom; not so much by an impulse of motherly affection, as that she might thereby conceal a certain token, which was wrought or fastened into her dress. In a moment, however, wisely judging that one token of her shame would but poorly serve to hide another, she took the baby on her arm, and with a burning blush, and yet a haughty smile, and a glance that would not be abashed, looked around at her townspeople and neighbors. On the breast of her gown, in fine red cloth, surrounded with an elaborate embroidery and fantastic flourishes of gold thread, appeared the letter A. It was so artistically done, and with so much fertility and gorgeous luxuriance of fancy, that it had all the effect of a last and fitting decoration to the apparel which she wore, and which was of a splendour in accordance with the taste of the age, but greatly beyond what was allowed by the sumptuary regulations of the colony.

The young woman was tall, with a figure of perfect elegance on a large scale. She had dark and abundant hair, so glossy that it threw off the sunshine with a gleam; and a face which, besides being beautiful from regularity of feature and richness of complexion, had the impressiveness belonging to a marked brow and deep black eyes. She was ladylike, too, after the manner of the feminine gentility of those days; characterized by a certain state and dignity, rather than by the delicate, evanescent, and indescribable grace which is now recognized as its indication. And never had Hester Prynne appeared more ladylike, in the antique interpretation of the term, than as she issued from the prison. Those who had before known her, and had expected to behold her dimmed and obscured by a disastrous cloud, were astonished, and even startled, to perceive how her beauty shone out, and made a halo of the misfortune and ignominy in which she was enveloped. It may be true that, to a sensitive observer, there was something exquisitely painful in it. Her attire, which indeed, she had wrought for the occasion in prison, and had modeled much after her own fancy, seemed to express the attitude of her spirit, the desperate recklessness of her mood, by its wild and picturesque peculiarity. But the point which drew all eyes, and, as it were, transfigured the wearer — so that both men and women who had been familiarly acquainted with Hester Prynne were now impressed as if they beheld her for the first time — was that scarlet letter, so fantastically embroidered and illuminated upon her bosom. It had the effect of a spell, taking her out of the ordinary relations with humanity, and enclosing her in a sphere by herself (Nathaniel Hawthorne, *The Scarlet Letter*).[1]

1 www.classicreader.com/read.php/sid.1bookid.69/sec.2/

Daily Assignment

- Warm-up: What is your favorite car? Why?
- Students will complete Concept Builder 8-B.
- Prayer journal.
- Students should outline all assigned essays for the week.

Allegory in *Idylls of the King*

An allegory is full of symbolism. Note the symbols *in Idylls of the King*.

Character	What he/she represents
King Arthur	good. trying to keep the evil out and the hardships of being a king
Mordred	evil, Revenge all because of an event or person maybe even because of want.
Ivanhoe	loyalty & friendship. trust
Guinevere	a supportive wife. love and true relationships

Lesson 3

Characterization

Typically, the paragraph is the unit of choice for composition writing. Limit one topic to each paragraph.

In fact, the paragraph is so useful that, after completing a thorough outline, a skillful writer will write one large paragraph and then, if needed, subdivide that paragraph into several others. Depending on the number of topics, the composition may include several paragraphs.

The proper construction of paragraphs is also of great importance. The following rules[2] will serve as guides for paragraphing. They should be learned and the pupil should be drilled in their application.

1. A sentence which continues the topic of the sentence that precedes it rather than introduces a new topic should never begin a paragraph.
2. Each paragraph should possess a single central topic to which all the statements in the paragraph should relate. The introduction of a single statement not so related to the central topic violates the unity.
3. A sentence or short passage may be detached from the paragraph to which it properly belongs if the writer wishes particularly to emphasize it.
4. For ease in reading, a passage that exceeds three hundred words in length may be broken into two paragraphs, even though no new topic has been developed.
5. Any digression from the central topic, or any change in the viewpoint in considering the central topic, demands a new paragraph.
6. Coherence in a paragraph requires a natural and logical order of development.
7. Smoothness of diction in a paragraph calls for the intelligent use of proper connective words between closely related sentences. A common fault, however, is the incorrect use of such words as and or but between sentences which are not closely related.
8. In developing the paragraph, emphasis is secured by a careful consideration of the relative values of the ideas expressed, giving to each idea space proportionate to its importance to the whole. This secures the proper climax.
9. The paragraph, like the composition itself, should possess clearness, unity, coherence, and emphasis. It is a group of related sentences developing a central topic. Its length depends upon the length of the composition and upon the number of topics to be discussed.

2 Frederick W. Hamilton, *Word Study and English Grammar, A Primer of Information about Words, Their Relations, and Their Uses* (Chicago, IL: The Committee on Education United Typothetae of America, 1918), p. 22.

Daily Assignment

- Warm-up: What do you want to do/be when you grow up? Why?
- Students will complete a daily Concept Builder 8-C.
- Prayer journal.
- Students should write rough drafts of all assigned essays.

Paragraphs

One of the central components of prose selection is the paragraph. It does not matter how long a paragraph is. Length is not important as long as the paragraph contains a sentence or sentences unified around one central, controlling idea.

Circle the problem with this paragraph and rewrite it correctly.

Huckleberry Finn was one of the earliest novels where the issue of motivation and self are paramount. We have come a long way, baby! Kenneth J. Gergen in his book *The Saturated Self: Dilemmas of Identity in Contemporary Life* (HarperCollins, 1991) argues that self-motivation has appeared at the end of this century as a sort of selfishness that is very destructive to Christianity. Huck Finn also has a mean dad. As Huckleberry regularly relativizes his situation on the banks of the Mississippi, likewise Christians are making their faith into another relative system of truth. Jesus Christ is the way, and the truth, and the life! There is no other! The fact is, most people may not care if Jesus Christ is your Lord and Savior. But let me warn you: the moment you say that He is the only Savior — the only Way, the only Truth, and the only Life — then people will be bothered. So the task before you in the next century is not only to preach that Jesus Christ is Lord but to preach that He is the only Lord. Stand tall and strong, Saint! Do not equivocate on this point! If you think that is something you should read *Tom Sawyer*!

---

huckleberry finn was one of the eariest novels where the issue of motivation and self are paramant. we have come a long way baby! Huck Finn also has a mean dad. As huckleberry regulaty relativizes his situation on the banks of the mississippi, likewise christians are making their faith into another relative system of truth. . . . . ect.

Student Essay: Excalibur

In the passages of Alfred Lord Tennyson's allegorical epic, *The Idylls of the King*, the author tells of the rise of the "great king, Arthur," and his eventual downfall at the hands of the heathen leader Mordred. However, the story's literal meaning is not the extent of its significance, its incidents not wholly tied to its narrative. Rather, the book employs symbolic writing in order to add a religious and moral depth to the legend of King Arthur.

There are numerous examples of symbolism in these passages, but the most prominent (and perhaps the most lauded) symbol is the sword Excalibur. Arthur's sword, symbol of divine kingship, is as much a character in the legend as any human or supernatural being. Excalibur is a symbol of the responsibility of power. One side of Arthur's sword is engraved, "In the oldest tongue of all this world/ 'Take me,' but turn the blade and ye shall see/ And written in the speech ye speak yourself/ 'Cast me away!'" In an earlier chapter of the book, Tennyson describes Arthur's face as sad as he receives the sword, though Merlin counsels, "'Take thou and strike! The time to cast away/ Is yet far-off.'" From the very words etched on the sword, it is immediately seen that the very nature of kingship is cyclical. "Take me" becomes a call to arms for Arthur. By grasping the sword, Arthur accepts responsibility that leadership entails, his sadness an acknowledgement that his power will inevitably wane.

But Excalibur is also a weapon, and therefore there must be an opponent for it to be used. Arthur finds it when he and Merlin go riding to a lake. Here they "see an arm clothed in white samite, rising from the water and holding a sword." Presently a damsel rides rapidly toward them, and at Merlin's bidding dismounts and walks with dry feet over the water. She takes the sword, the arm vanishes, and the damsel brings the coveted weapon back to Arthur. Here is seen the co-mingling of Christian and pagan motifs, the Christ-like walking on water with the fairy quality of Excalibur and the mythic making of a king. Yet Excalibur is still a weapon. The Lady of the Lake (the arm risen from the water) represents the Church, the virgin bride of Christ, and thus the sword she offers is a spiritual weapon, as well as a physical one. During his reign, Arthur battled the enemies of Christendom, but after he slayed Mordred, his time was done, the "Cast me away!" written on his sword now came to pass, for in the place he was going, there was no need of weapons.

Tennyson crafted this masterful work in the hopes that he might create an ideal in the minds of his readers by setting a moral and behavioral code of conduct. The standards of King Arthur's Knights were not merely a way to tell how *they* acted but rather to erect an image of how he believed his *readers* should act, and he does this subtly, leading by examples. Tennyson himself wrote, "I tried in my *Idylls* to teach men the need of an ideal — a moralistic, Victorian standard of proper conduct." (Joseph)

Daily Assignment

- Warm-up: If you could be in one movie, what movie would that be? Which character would you be?
- Students will complete Concept Builder 8-D.
- Prayer journal.
- Review the assigned text. Keep vocabulary cards.
- This is the day that students should write, and then rewrite, the final drafts of their assigned essays.

Poetic Devices

Alliteration is the repetition of consonant sounds at the beginning of words.

Assonance is the repetition of vowel sounds.

Consonance is the repetition of consonant sounds in the middle and at the end of words.

Repetition is the recurrence of words and phrases.

Show examples of each below, in your own words.

Poetic Devices	Examples
Alliteration	Gun, Gum, Game
Assonance	Wow, bow, sow
Consonance	Sand, fund, drowned
Repetition	I love you, I love you, I love you.

Characterization — *Idylls of the King* (Alfred Lord Tennyson)

Chapter 9

First Thoughts

Idylls of the King, published between 1856 and 1885, is a cycle of 12 narrative poems by the English poet Alfred, Lord Tennyson. The character Arthur attempts and fails to ameliorate mankind and create a perfect kingdom, from his coming to power to his death at the hands of the traitor Mordred. Tennyson uses several characters to develop this mysterious, mythical figure. The failure of Arthur to raise others to the same level as himself ultimately presages a tragic ending.

Chapter Learning Objectives

In chapter 9 we examine Tennyson's characters, who so effectively develop the character of Arthur.

As a result of this chapter study you will be able to . . .

1. Compare and contrast Guinevere and Elaine, and, finally, discuss the wonderful foil Lancelot.
2. Compare and contrast King Arthur with King David. Consider their strengths and weaknesses and kinds of leadership.
3. Describe the historical King Arthur and how his story evolved over time.

Look Ahead for Friday

- Turn in a final copy of essay
- Take Weekly Test

Sample Essay: Characterization

There are two ways an author can develop a character:

- Omniscient narration: The author literally tells the audience what a character is like.
- The audience must infer for themselves what the character is like through the character's thoughts, actions, and interaction with other characters.

There is by definition only one main character, or protagonist. Foils are used to develop the protagonist. An enemy of the protagonist is an antagonist foil.

The following is a characterization of a child's family:

My mother and father are more alike than they are different. However, their differences are very interesting.

What are the similarities and differences between my mom and my dad? They both have a strong relationship with Jesus Christ. They understand and agree that family life is important. Their goal in life is to raise up world changers for Christ. They strive to please the Lord in all they do. Many times they stumble; many times they fall short. However, they always start fresh.

At first glance, they are so similar that one finds very few real differences. Mom and Dad both rule our family (under the Lordship of Christ). However, in our family, Mom is an important person to convince! She is a powerful force in the house. When a decision is made, Mom always has major input into that decision. Her authority, though, is more subtle than Dad's but is evident in all aspects of family life. She is an omnipresent part of the family!

Dad, on the other hand, is an entirely different book. He is more outgoing and round. He knows everything about anything. If one has a question about Plato or baseball, ask him! He is a fun-loving sort of person. However, he is more easily persuaded to a position than Mom — especially when his daughters ask him!

All in all, Mom and Dad are very similar, with only a few insignificant differences. (Jessica Stobaugh)

Daily Assignment

- Warm-up: Often God uses an antagonist in our lives to make us more like Him. Describe such a situation in your own life.
- Students will complete Concept Builder 9-A.
- Prayer journal: Students are encouraged to write in their prayer journal every day.
- Students need to review their material for the next assignment
- Students should systematically review their vocabulary words daily.

Characterization of Arthur

Tennyson uses narration, character reaction, and the setting to develop Arthur. Note the narration and character reaction in a summary as was done with the setting.

Setting	And thus the land of Cameliard was waste, Thick with wet woods, and many a beast therein,/ And none or few to scare or chase the beast; So that wild dog, and wolf and boar and bear Came night and day, and rooted in the fields, And wallowed in the gardens of the King.	*The land was in chaos until Arthur came and brought order.*
Narration	And Arthur, passing thence to battle, felt Travail, and throes and agonies of the life, Desiring to be joined with Guinevere; And thinking as he rode, "Her father said That there between the man and beast they die. Shall I not lift her from this land of beasts Up to my throne, and side by side with me?"	Omniscient Narrator
Character Reaction	And Arthur yet had done no deed of arms, But heard the call, and came: and Guinevere Stood by the castle walls to watch him pass;	Felt special

Lesson 2

Characterization of Animals

One can characterize animals, too. Normally an author does this by giving an animal human characteristics (i.e., personification). Anne Sewell's *Black Beauty* tells her story from the perspective of a horse. The plot, theme, setting, narration, and tone are dependent upon the character/protagonist Black Beauty, a black stallion. The following is chapter 1, "My Early Home," *Black Beauty*.

Black Beauty: The Autobiography of a Horse
by Anna Sewell

The first place that I can well remember was a large pleasant meadow with a pond of clear water in it. Some shady trees leaned over it, and rushes and water-lilies grew at the deep end. Over the hedge on one side we looked into a plowed field, and on the other we looked over a gate at our master's house, which stood by the roadside; at the top of the meadow was a grove of fir trees, and at the bottom a running brook overhung by a steep bank.

While I was young I lived upon my mother's milk, as I could not eat grass. In the daytime I ran by her side, and at night I lay down close by her. When it was hot we used to stand by the pond in the shade of the trees, and when it was cold we had a nice warm shed near the grove.

As soon as I was old enough to eat grass my mother used to go out to work in the daytime, and come back in the evening.

There were six young colts in the meadow besides me; they were older than I was; some were nearly as large as grown-up horses. I used to run with them, and had great fun; we used to gallop all together round and round the field as hard as we could go. Sometimes we had rather rough play, for they would frequently bite and kick as well as gallop.

One day, when there was a good deal of kicking, my mother whinnied to me to come to her, and then she said:

"I wish you to pay attention to what I am going to say to you. The colts who live here are very good colts, but they are cart-horse colts, and of course they have not learned manners. You have been well-bred and well-born; your father has a great name in these parts, and your grandfather won the cup two years at the Newmarket races; your grand-mother had the sweetest temper of any horse I ever knew, and I think you have never seen me kick or bite. I hope you will grow up gentle and good, and never learn bad ways; do your work with a good will, lift your feet up well when you trot, and never bite or kick even in play."

I have never forgotten my mother's advice; I knew she was a wise old horse, and our master thought a great deal of her. Her name was Duchess, but he often called her Pet.

Our master was a good, kind man. He gave us good food, good lodging, and kind words; he spoke as kindly to us as he did to his little children. We were all fond of him, and my mother loved him very much. When she saw him at the gate she would neigh with joy, and trot up to him. He would pat and stroke her and say, "Well, old Pet, and how is your little Darkie?" I was a dull black, so he called me Darkie; then he would give me a piece of bread, which was very good, and sometimes he brought a carrot for my mother. All the horses would come to him, but I think we were his favorites. My mother always took him to the town on a market day in a light gig.

There was a plowboy, Dick, who sometimes came into our field to pluck blackberries from the hedge. When he had eaten all he wanted he would have what he called fun with the colts, throwing stones and sticks at them to make them gallop. We did not much mind him, for we could gallop off; but sometimes a stone would hit and hurt us.

One day he was at this game, and did not know that the master was in the next field; but he was there, watching what was going on; over the hedge he jumped in a snap, and catching Dick by the arm, he gave him such a box on the ear as made him roar with the pain and surprise. As soon as we saw the master we trotted up nearer to see what went on.

"Bad boy!" he said, "bad boy! to chase the colts. This is not the first time, nor the second, but it shall be the last. There — take your money and go home; I shall not want you on my farm again." So we never saw Dick any more. Old Daniel, the man who looked after the horses, was just as gentle as our master, so we were well off.

Daily Assignment

- Warm-up: Describe the most abhorrent (i.e., the worst) villain you known.
- Students will complete Concept Builder 9-B.
- Prayer journal.
- Students should outline all assigned essays for the week.

Epic Poetry

Epic poetry is poetry that celebrates the exploits of a national figure. It is often meant to be sung. Identify the **antagonist** (opponent of the protagonist) and **crisis** in this epic poem.

"Casey at the Bat" by Ernest Lawrence Thayer

Taken from the *San Francisco Examiner* — June 3, 1888

The outlook wasn't brilliant for the Mudville nine that day;
The score stood four to two, with but one inning more to play,
And then when Cooney died at first, and Barrows did the same,
A pall-like silence fell upon the patrons of the game.

A straggling few got up to go in deep despair. The rest
Clung to that hope which springs eternal in the human breast;
They thought, "If only Casey could but get a whack at that —
We'd put up even money now, with Casey at the bat."

But Flynn preceded Casey, as did also Jimmy Blake,
And the former was a hoodoo, while the latter was a cake;
So upon that stricken multitude grim melancholy sat;
For there seemed but little chance of Casey getting to the bat.

But Flynn let drive a single, to the wonderment of all,
And Blake, the much despised, tore the cover off the ball;
And when the dust had lifted, and men saw what had occurred,
There was Jimmy safe at second and Flynn a-hugging third.

Then from five thousand throats and more there rose a lusty yell;
It rumbled through the valley, it rattled in the dell;
It pounded on the mountain and recoiled upon the flat,
For Casey, mighty Casey, was advancing to the bat.

There was ease in Casey's manner as he stepped into his place;
There was pride in Casey's bearing and a smile lit Casey's face.
And when, responding to the cheers, he lightly doffed his hat,
No stranger in the crowd could doubt 'twas Casey at the bat.

Ten thousand eyes were on him as he rubbed his hands with dirt.
Five thousand tongues applauded when he wiped them on his shirt.
Then while the writhing pitcher ground the ball into his hip,
Defiance flashed in Casey's eye, a sneer curled Casey's lip.

And now the leather-covered sphere came hurtling through the air, And Casey stood a-watching it in haughty grandeur there.
Close by the sturdy batsman the ball unheeded sped —
"That ain't my style," said Casey. "Strike one!" the umpire said.

From the benches, black with people, there went up a muffled roar, Like the beating of the storm-waves on a stern and distant shore; "Kill him! Kill the umpire!" shouted some one on the stand;
And it's likely they'd have killed him had not Casey raised his hand.

With a smile of Christian charity great Casey's visage shone;
He stilled the rising tumult; he bade the game go on;
He signaled to the pitcher, and once more the dun sphere flew;
But Casey still ignored it, and the umpire said "Strike two!"

"Fraud!" cried the maddened thousands, and echo answered "Fraud!" But one scornful look from Casey and the audience was awed.
They saw his face grow stern and cold, they saw his muscles strain, And they knew that Casey wouldn't let that ball go by again.

The sneer has fled from Casey's lip, the teeth are clenched in hate;
He pounds with cruel violence his bat upon the plate.
And now the pitcher holds the ball, and now he lets it go,
And now the air is shattered by the force of Casey's blow.

Oh, somewhere in this favored land the sun is shining bright,
The band is playing somewhere, and somewhere hearts are light,
And somewhere men are laughing, and little children shout;
But there is no joy in Mudville — mighty Casey has struck out.

Protagonist	Antagonist	Crisis
Casey	the pitcher	getting 2 strikes

Lesson 3

Grammar Review: Paragraphs

Typically, begin a paragraph with a topic sentence. In some instances the paragraph may have the topic sentence at the end of the paragraph. Such paragraphs inevitably begin with a quote or rhetorical question.

What does it mean to write and speak effectively? One can send a photograph of a thing, or send a CD with music describing the thing, or paint a picture of the thing and communicate well enough, but this is not rhetoric. Rhetoric is a discipline that demands that the reader dutifully follow laws of grammar, logic, and communication to explain and to describe the thing. Rhetoric, simply, is the ability to communicate effectively through the written and spoken word. Written and spoken are the crucial concepts of understanding rhetoric.

Daily Assignment

- Warm-up: Compare yourself to one of the characters in *Idylls Of The King*. Why did you choose that person?
- Students will complete Concept Builder 9-C.
- Prayer journal.
- Students should write rough drafts of all assigned essays and speech.

Epic Heroes

Epic heroes are larger than life.

Underline words that describe Arthur.

Brave	Tentative	Cowardly	Honest	Loyal	Strong
Aggressive	Handsome	Smart	Immoral	Sensitive	Weak
Humble	Selfish	Selfless	Unpredictable	Overconfident	Outgoing

Underline words that describe Casey.

Brave	Tentative	Cowardly	Honest	Loyal	Strong
Aggressive	Handsome	Smart	Immoral	Sensitive	Weak
Humble	Selfish	Selfless	Unpredictable	Overconfident	Outgoing

Underline words that describe Samson (in the Bible).

Brave	Tentative	Cowardly	Honest	Loyal	Strong
Aggressive	Handsome	Smart	Immoral	Sensitive	Weak
Humble	Selfish	Selfless	Unpredictable	Overconfident	Outgoing

Student Essay

Opposites in *Idylls of the King*

Idylls of the King, by Alfred Lord Tennyson, is a poem about the King Arthur legend set in Europe during the Middle Ages. In his poem, Tennyson creates strong contrasts between two sets of characters, Arthur/Lancelot and Elaine/Guinevere, so that they seem nearly polar opposite in multiple ways.

The first example of almost polar opposites is King Arthur and his favorite knight/best friend, Lancelot. At the start of the poem, they pledge to be friends:

> "Sir and my liege," he cried, "the fire of God descends upon thee in the battlefield. I know thee for my King!" Arthur answers: "Man's word is God in man; let chance what will, I trust thee to the death." (The Coming of Arthur).

There, striking differences begin. King Arthur is described as "The truthful king" (The Round Table), and called many times "our good king" and "the good king" (The Round Table).

In stark contrast, Arthur's best friend Lancelot is deceptive:

> "Not long thereafter from the city gates issued Sir Lancelot riding airily, warm with a gracious parting from the Queen (King Arthur's wife) . . ." (The Round Table).

In so deceiving Arthur, Lancelot is breaking his knightly code, unlike Arthur, who keeps to his kingly duties. Truthful, King Arthur is a good king who is loved by his people, while Lancelot betrays not only his best friend's trust but his knightly code of conduct. They are opposites.

Another instance of strong contrast in characters in Idylls of the King is King Arthur's wife Guinevere and "the lily maid of Astolat," named Elaine. Entrusted with Lancelot's shield, "Do me this grace, my child, to have my shield in keeping till I come," Elaine dutifully and faithfully guards it, even making it "A case of silk."

> "High in her chamber up a tower to the east guarded the sacred shield of Lancelot.. . . He left it with her, when he rode . . ." (Lancelot and Elaine).

Elaine is faithful and guards the shield placed in her care.

Unfaithful, the king's wife, Guinevere, is not trustworthy, allowing her affair with Lancelot to continue, even though she knows it is unwise.

> "The Queen looked hard upon her lover, he on her; and each foresaw the dolorous day to be. . . ."

The queen even goes so far as to accuse Lancelot of cheating on her when he gives attention to Elaine:

> "What are these? Diamonds for me! they had been thrice their worth being your gift, had you not lost your own. to loyal hearts the value of all gifts Must vary as the giver's. Not for me! For her! for your new fancy."

The inverse of Elaine, Guinevere is unfaithful to Arthur, while Elaine is true to her duties.

While Arthur is truthful, Lancelot is deceptive; while Guinevere is unfaithful to Arthur, Elaine is faithful to that which was entrusted to her. In *Idylls of the King*, Tennyson creates contrasting characters. (JB)

Daily Assignment

- Warm-up: Discuss two to three foils in your life. Why have these people been so vital to your development?
- Students will complete Concept Builder 9-D.
- Prayer journal.
- Review the assigned text. Keep vocabulary cards.
- This is the day that students should write, and then rewrite, the final drafts of their assigned essay.

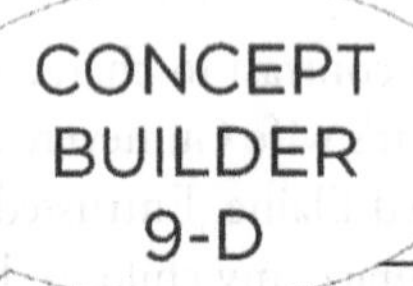

Epic Hero Exploits

Inevitably epic heroes conquer hardships, slay dragons, and accomplish heroic deeds. In fact, every hero has to overcome one or two obstacles or he/she will not be great.

List the obstacles that face these heroes.

Hero/Heroine	Obstacles He/She Faces
King Arthur	*Mordred and other enemies.*
Spider-Man	
Queen Esther	
My Mom	
My Dad	
A Friend	

Plot — *Treasure Island* (Robert Louis Stevenson)

Chapter 10

First Thoughts

Stevenson wrote *Treasure Island* for his stepson in 1881. He said, "If this doesn't fetch the kids, why, they have gone rotten since my day." It's a tale of pirates, a treasure map, a mutiny, and a one-legged sea cook. *Treasure Island* remains one of literature's best-loved adventure stories. The heroes and villains of the classic tale — Long John Silver, Jim Hawkins, Dr. Livesey, Billy Bones, Squire Trelawney, and Ben Gunn — are some of the most famous characters in American literature. In short, this novel is a must-read for every American youth!

Chapter Learning Objectives

In chapter 10 we analyze one of the premier adventure novels in the English language.

As a result of this chapter study you will be able to . . .

1. Evaluate the just or unjust reward that Long John Silver receives.
2. Discuss the excessive use of coincidence in this novel.

Look Ahead for Friday

- Turn in a final copy of essay
- Take Weekly Test

Lesson 1

Literary Analysis: Plot

The plot is the pattern of incidents that make up a story. It includes the events of the story in the order the story gives them. A typical plot has five parts: Exposition, Rising Action, Crisis or Climax, Falling Action, and Resolution. Crisis or Climax is the moment or event in the plot in which the conflict is most directly addressed: the main character "wins" or "loses"; the secret is revealed. After the climax, the denouement or falling action occurs.

As a result of this lesson, you should understand how an author develops plot.

Consider the following essay on the plot of the popular movie *Chariots of Fire.*

Chariots of Fire, produced by David Puttman (*Midnight Express, The Killing Fields*, and *The Mission*), is the true story of Eric Liddell and Harold Abrahams. While it is the story of how two famous athletes overcome overwhelming odds to win the 1924 Olympics, the story is more complicated than that. It is a human drama of epic proportions — the Christian-principled Liddell choosing to lose one great race to win the more important race of life and the choleric, slightly neurotic Abrahams who overcomes ethnic prejudice to become the fastest man in the world and a symbol of the enlightened 1920s.

The plot develops very well and cannot be discussed separately from the characters. We see the story through a flashback of a foil named Aubry. Aubry seems to be a particularly appropriate narrator because he is close to both principal characters — Liddell and Abrahams — and because he is sanguine, calm, and almost too good to be true. The viewer feels secure in his hands, even though he never won a race. There clearly is a climax and rapid falling action. Eric Liddell defies king and country to honor God, and Harold Abrahams defies societal prejudice and his own fears to honor human will and perseverance. The first is a cosmological victory; the second an existential one. However, they are equally epic in proportion. This is the story of two men, Abrahams the Jew and Liddell the Christian, who fight for their heritage and pride. Abrahams runs as a weapon against prejudice. Liddell runs to honor his God by exhibiting a gift — being fast — that God gives him. The viewer feels both inspired and satisfied.

The setting is in the 1920s between the two World Wars. The 1920s is a time of transition. The first counter culture is appearing. This generation that has experienced the carnage of World War I is not prepared to accept without question the morality and institution of their elders. Abrahams rebels against this authority by defying religious taboos. "I am an Englishman!" Abrahams often says. Liddell also defies this authority in favor of a more important authority. He openly, but respectfully, defies the king of England in a scene at the end of the movie. He refuses to race on Sunday because it violates his conscience and his Bible. The setting is important, then, and is clearly portrayed in the uniforms and songs of the era.

Chariots of Fire, named for the chariot of fire that took the prophet Elijah to heaven, is a unique movie for this time because it celebrates a man who stands up for his principles and his God. In their own way, Liddell and Abrahams are prophets of their time, showing their generation, and ours, a better way to live. (Timothy Stobaugh)

Daily Assignment

- Warm-up: If your life were a "novel," where would the climax occur? Describe this incident.
- Students will complete Concept Builder 10-A.
- Prayer journal: Students are encouraged to write in their prayer journal every day.
- Students need to review their material for the next assignment
- Students should systematically review their vocabulary words daily.

Active Reading

As you read, use the following marks to help you better interact with the text.

I - This is important. **?** - This is not clear to me. **J** - Interesting point

Stevenson does not give the reader the name of this strange visitor (until later). Why?

Imagery is a word that describes descriptions that authors use to bring their subject alive.

Circle three examples. Make vocabulary cards for the underlined words.

Treasure Island **by Robert Louis Stevenson**
Chapter 1 — "The Old Sea-dog at the Admiral Benbow"

The Old Sea-dog at the Admiral Benbow SQUIRE TRELAWNEY, Dr. Livesey, and the rest of these gentlemen having asked me to write down the whole particulars about Treasure Island, from the beginning to the end, keeping nothing back but the bearings of the island, and that only because there is still treasure not yet lifted, I take up my pen in the year of grace 17__ and go back to the time when my father kept the Admiral Benbow inn and the brown old seaman with the sabre cut first took up his lodging under our roof.

"I remember him as if it were yesterday, as he came plodding to the inn door." I remember him as if it were yesterday, as he came plodding to the inn door, his sea-chest following behind him in a hand-barrow — a tall, strong, heavy, nut-brown man, his tarry pigtail falling over the shoulder of his soiled blue coat, his hands ragged and scarred, with black, broken nails, and the sabre cut across one cheek, a dirty, livid white. I remember him looking round the cover and whistling to himself as he did so, and then breaking out in that old sea-song that he sang so often afterwards: "Fifteen men on the dead man's chest — Yo-ho-ho, and a bottle of rum!" in the high, old tottering voice that seemed to have been tuned and broken at the capstan bars. Then he rapped on the door with a bit of stick like a handspike that he carried, and when my father appeared, called roughly for a glass of rum. This, when it was brought to him, he drank slowly, like a connoisseur, lingering on the taste and still looking about him at the cliffs and up at our signboard.

"This is a handy cove," says he at length; "and a pleasant sittyated grog-shop. Much company, mate?" My father told him no, very little company, the more was the pity.

"Well, then," said he, "this is the berth for me. Here you, matey," he cried to the man who trundled the barrow; "bring up alongside and help up my chest. I'll stay here a bit," he continued. "I'm a plain man; rum and bacon and eggs is what I want, and that head up there for to watch ships off. What you mought call me? You mought call me captain. Oh, I see what you're at — there"; and he threw down three or four gold pieces on the threshold.

"You can tell me when I've worked through that," says he, looking as fierce as a commander.

And indeed bad as his clothes were and coarsely as he spoke, he had none of the appearance of a man who sailed before the mast, but seemed like a mate or skipper accustomed to be obeyed or to strike. The man who came with the barrow told us the mail had set him down the morning before at the Royal George, that he had inquired what inns there were along the coast, and hearing ours well spoken of, I suppose, and described as lonely, had chosen it from the others for his place of residence. And that was all we could learn of our guest.

He was a very silent man by custom. All day he hung round the cove or upon the cliffs with a brass telescope; all evening he sat in a corner of the parlour next the fire and drank rum and water very strong. Mostly he would not speak when spoken to, only look up sudden and fierce and blow through his nose like a fog-horn; and we and the people who came about our house soon learned to let him be. Every day when he came back from his stroll he would ask if any seafaring men had gone by along the road. At first we thought it was the want of company of his own kind that made him ask this question, but at last we began to see he was desirous to avoid them.

Lesson 2

Grammar Review: Write In Positive Terms

Effective writers write in positive — not negative terms. For instance, *I was sick yesterday* is a better sentence than *I was not feeling very well yesterday. The man was dishonest* is a better sentence than *The man was not honest.* Generally speaking, in writing, shorter is better, but practice with complex sentences is certainly commendable for maturing writers.

Daily Assignment

- Warm-up: Write a story that begins with the following passage . Be sure you include exposition, rising action, a climax, denouement (falling action), and resolution. My mother's father, James Jesse Bayne — I call him Big Daddy — ran away from his two-room, Louisiana pine barren home when he was eight. For the next seven years he lived in woods and swamps in the wild Delta bottoms. Living on the outskirts of early 20th-century poor southern towns, he experienced poverty that was sublime in its intensity. Southern cuisine and lifestyle were the epitome of conservation and economy.

  Practically nothing was discarded from any animal: intestines, gizzards, stomachs — it all was eaten. There was precious little left for hoboes like Big Daddy, who was forced to eat crawdads and red-bellied brim. There is not much that was big about Big Daddy. At 16 his blond — almost white — hair and blue-eyes oversaw a body that was not symmetrical. For instance, his left arm was at least two inches longer than his right.
- Students will complete Concept Builder 10-B.
- Prayer journal.
- Students should outline all assigned essays for the week.

Conflicts in the Plot

Conflict is a struggle between opposing forces that moves the plot. Usually these opposing forces are manifested in characters. Compete the following in regard to plot and characters.

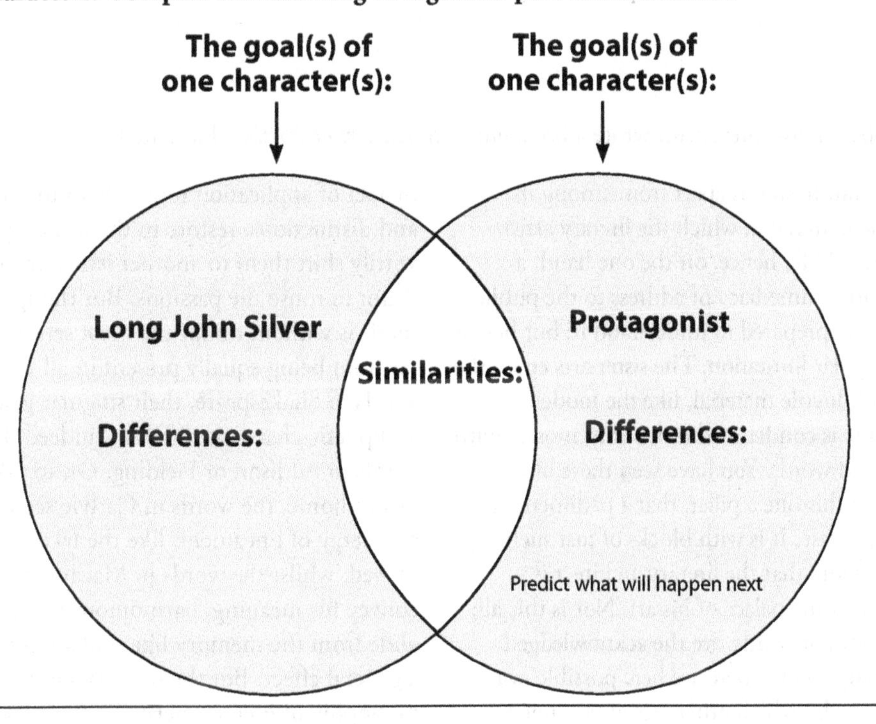

Lesson 3

Choice of Words

In 1905, Robert Louis Stevenson wrote a book entitled *The Art of Writing*. He stated:

> The art of literature stands apart from among its sisters, because the material in which the literary artist works is the dialect of life; hence, on the one hand, a strange freshness and immediacy of address to the public mind, which is ready prepared to understand it; but hence, on the other, a singular limitation. The sister arts enjoy the use of a plastic and ductile material, like the modeller's clay; literature alone is condemned to work in mosaic with finite and quite rigid words. You have seen these blocks, dear to the nursery: this one a pillar, that a pediment, a third a window or a vase. It is with blocks of just such arbitrary size and figure that the literary architect is condemned to design the palace of his art. Nor is this all; for since these blocks, or words, are the acknowledged currency of our daily affairs, there are here possible none of those suppressions by which other arts obtain relief, continuity, and vigour: no hieroglyphic touch, no smoothed impasto, no inscrutable shadow, as in painting; no blank wall, as in architecture; but every word, phrase, sentence, and paragraph must move in a logical progression, and convey a definite conventional import.
>
> Now the first merit which attracts in the pages of a good writer, or the talk of a brilliant conversationalist, is the apt choice and contrast of the words employed. It is, indeed, a strange art to take these blocks, rudely conceived for the purpose of the market or the bar, and by tact of application touch them to the finest meanings and distinctions, restore to them their primal energy, wittily shift them to another issue, or make of them a drum to rouse the passions. But though this form of merit is without doubt the most sensible and seizing, it is far from being equally present in all writers. The effect of words in Shakespeare, their singular justice, significance, and poetic charm, is different, indeed, from the effect of words in Addison or Fielding. Or, to take an example nearer home, the words in Carlyle seem electrified into an energy of lineament, like the faces of men furiously moved; whilst the words in Macaulay, apt enough to convey his meaning, harmonious enough in sound, yet glide from the memory like undistinguished elements in a general effect. But the first class of writers have no monopoly of literary merit. There is a sense in which Addison is superior to Carlyle; a sense in which Cicero is better than Tacitus, in which Voltaire excels Montaigne: it certainly lies not in the choice of words; it lies not in the interest or value of the matter; it lies not in force of intellect, of poetry, or of humour. The three first are but infants to the three second; and yet each, in a particular point of literary art, excels his superior in the whole. What is that point?[1]

1 Robert Louis Stevenson, *The Art of Writing*, transcribed from the 1905 Chatto & Windus edition by David Price, www.gutenberg.org/dirs/etext96/artow10h.htm.

Daily Assignment

- Warm-up: Draw a picture then write a story that is based on your picture. Be sure you include exposition, rising action, a climax, denouement (falling action), and resolution.
- Students will complete a daily Concept Builder 10-C.
- Prayer journal.
- Students should write rough drafts of all assigned essays.

Sequencing the Plot — Part 1

The sequence is the order of events in a plot. It is never coincidental; every author has a purpose in sequencing his events. **Number the events as they occur in the book.**

______ An old drunken seaman named Billy Bones becomes a long-term lodger at the Admiral Benbow Inn.

______ After several other events, the treasure is divided among Trelawney and his loyal men, including Jim and Ben Gunn, and they return to England, leaving the surviving pirates marooned on the island. Silver escapes with the help of the fearful Ben Gunn and a small part of the treasure.

______ Hiding in the woods, Jim sees Silver murder Tom, a crewman loyal to Smollett. Running for his life, he encounters Ben Gunn, another ex-crewman of Flint's who has been marooned three years on the island, but who treats Jim kindly in return for a chance of getting back to civilization.

______ In the meanwhile, Trelawney, Livesey, and their men surprise and overpower the few pirates left aboard the Hispaniola. They row to shore and move into an abandoned, fortified stockade on the island, where they are soon joined by Jim Hawkins, having left Ben Gunn behind.

______ Jim Hawkins comes to the house of local landlord Squire Trelawney and his mother's friend and patron Dr. Livesey. Together, they examine the oilskin packet, which contains a logbook detailing the treasure looted during Captain Flint's career, and a detailed map of an island, with the location of Flint's treasure caches marked on it. Squire Trelawney immediately plans to outfit a sailing vessel to hunt the treasure down, with the help of Dr. Livesey and Jim. Livesey warns Trelawney to be silent about their objective.

______ Despite Captain Smollett's misgivings about the mission and Silver's hand-picked crew, the *Hispaniola* sets sail.

______ Jim and his mother open Bones's sea chest to collect the amount due for Bones's room and board, but before they can count out the money due them, they hear pirates approaching the inn and are forced to flee and hide, Jim taking with him a mysterious oilskin packet from the chest.

______ When they reach Treasure Island, the bulk of Silver's men go ashore immediately. Although Jim is not yet aware of this, Silver's men have given him the black spot and demanded to seize the treasure immediately, discarding Silver's own more careful plan to postpone any open mutiny or violence until after the treasure is safely aboard.

______ Jim lands with Silver's men, but runs away from them almost as soon as he is ashore.

______ During the night, Jim sneaks out of the stockade, takes Ben Gunn's coracle, and approaches the *Hispaniola* under cover of darkness. He cuts the ship's anchor cable, setting her adrift and out of reach of the pirates on shore. After daybreak, he manages to approach the schooner again and board her.

http://en.wikipedia.org/wiki/Treasure_Island

Lesson 4

How *Treasure Island* Was Written

It was far indeed from being my first book, for I am not a novelist alone. But I am well aware that my paymaster, the Great Public, regards what else I have written with indifference, if not aversion; if it call upon me at all, it calls on me in the familiar and indelible character; and when I am asked to talk of my first book, no question in the world but what is meant is my first novel.

Sooner or later, somehow, anyhow, I was bound to write a novel. It seems vain to ask why. Men are born with various manias: from my earliest childhood, it was mine to make a plaything of imaginary series of events; and as soon as I was able to write, I became a good friend to the paper-makers. Reams upon reams must have gone to the making of :Rathillet," "The Pentland Rising," "The King's Pardon" (otherwise "Park Whitehead"), "Edward Daven," "A Country Dance," and "A Vendetta in the West"; and it is consolatory to remember that these reams are now all ashes, and have been received again into the soil. I have named but a few of my ill-fated efforts, only such indeed as came to a fair bulk ere they were desisted from; and even so they cover a long vista of years. "Rathillet" was attempted before fifteen, "The Vendetta" at twenty-nine, and the succession of defeats lasted unbroken till I was thirty-one. By that time, I had written little books and little essays and short stories; and had got patted on the back and paid for them - though not enough to live upon. I had quite a reputation, I was the successful man; I passed my days in toil, the futility of which would sometimes make my cheek to burn - that I should spend a man's energy upon this business, and yet could not earn a livelihood: and still there shone ahead of me an unattained ideal: although I had attempted the thing with vigour not less than ten or twelve times, I had not yet written a novel. All — all my pretty ones — had gone for a little, and then stopped inexorably like a schoolboy's watch. I might be compared to a cricketer of many years' standing who should never have made a run. Anybody can write a short story — a bad one, I mean — who has industry and paper and time enough; but not every one may hope to write even a bad novel. It is the length that kills.

The accepted novelist may take his novel up and put it down, spend days upon it in vain, and write not any more than he makes haste to blot. Not so the beginner. Human nature has certain rights; instinct — the instinct of self-preservation — forbids that any man (cheered and supported by the consciousness of no previous victory) should endure the miseries of unsuccessful literary toil beyond a period to be measured in weeks. There must be something for hope to feed upon. The beginner must have a slant of wind, a lucky vein must be running, he must be in one of those hours when the words come and the phrases balance of themselves — even to begin. And having begun, what a dread looking forward is that until the book shall be accomplished! For so long a time, the slant is to continue unchanged, the vein to keep running, for so long a time you must keep at command the same quality of style: for so long a time your puppets are to be always vital, always consistent, always vigorous! I remember I used to look, in those days, upon every three-volume novel with a sort of veneration, as a feat — not possibly of literature — but at least of physical and moral endurance and the courage of Ajax.

In the fated year I came to live with my father and mother at Kinnaird, above Pitlochry. Then I walked on the red moors and by the side of the golden burn; the rude, pure air of our mountains inspirited, if it did not inspire us, and my wife and I projected a joint volume of logic stories, for which she wrote "The Shadow on the Bed," and I turned out "Thrawn Janet," and a first draft of "The Merry Men." I love my native air, but it does not love me; and the end of this delightful period was a cold, a fly-blister, and a migration by Strathairdle and Glenshee to the Castleton of Braemar.

There it blew a good deal and rained in a proportion; my native air was more unkind than man's ingratitude, and I must consent to pass a good deal of my time between four walls in a house lugubriously known as the Late Miss McGregor's Cottage. And now admire the finger of predestination. There was a schoolboy in the Late Miss McGregor's Cottage, home from the holidays, and much in want of "something craggy to break his mind upon." He had no thought of literature; it was the art of Raphael that received his fleeting suffrages; and with the aid of pen and ink and a shilling box of water colours, he had soon turned one of the rooms into a picture gallery. My more immediate duty towards the gallery was to be showman; but I would sometimes unbend a little, join the artist (so to speak) at the easel, and pass the afternoon with him in a generous emulation, making coloured drawings. On one of these occasions, I made the map of an island; it was elaborately and (I thought) beautifully coloured; the shape of it took my fancy beyond expression; it contained harbours that pleased me like sonnets; and with the unconsciousness of the predestined, I ticketed my performance "Treasure Island." I am told there are people who do not care for maps, and find it hard to believe. The names, the shapes of the woodlands, the courses of the roads and rivers, the prehistoric footsteps of man still distinctly traceable up hill and down dale, the mills and the ruins, the ponds and the ferries, perhaps the *Standing Stone* or the *Druidic Circle* on the heath; here is an inexhaustible fund of interest for any man with eyes to see or twopence-worth of imagination to understand with! No child but must remember laying his head in the grass, staring into the infinitesimal forest and seeing it grow populous with fairy armies.

Somewhat in this way, as I paused upon my map of "Treasure Island," the future character of the book began to appear there visibly among imaginary woods; and their brown faces and bright weapons peeped out upon me from unexpected quarters, as they passed to and fro, fighting and hunting treasure, on these few square inches of a flat projection. The next thing I knew I had some papers before me and was writing out a list of chapters. How often have I done so, and the thing gone no further! But there seemed elements of success about this enterprise. It was to be a story for boys; no need of psychology or fine writing; and I had a boy at hand to be a touchstone. Women were excluded. I was unable to handle a brig (which the *Hispaniola* should have been), but I thought I could make shift to sail her as a schooner without public shame. And then I had an idea for John Silver from which I promised myself funds of entertainment; to take an admired friend of mine (whom the reader very likely knows and admires as much as I do), to deprive him of all his finer qualities and higher graces of temperament, to leave him with nothing but his strength, his courage, his quickness, and his magnificent geniality, and to try to express these in terms of the culture of a raw tarpaulin. Such psychical surgery is, I think, a common way of "making character"; perhaps it is, indeed, the only way. We can put in the quaint figure that spoke a hundred words with us yesterday by the wayside; but do we know him? Our friend, with his infinite variety and flexibility, we know — but can we put him in? Upon the first, we must engraft secondary and imaginary qualities, possibly all wrong; from the second, knife in hand, we must cut away and deduct the needless arborescence of his nature, but the trunk and the few branches that remain we may at least be fairly sure of.

On a chill September morning, by the cheek of a brisk fire, and the rain drumming on the window, I began *The Sea Cook*, for that was the original title. I have begun (and finished) a number of other books, but I cannot remember to have sat down to one of them with more complacency. It is not to be wondered at, for stolen waters are proverbially sweet. I am now upon a painful chapter. No doubt the parrot once belonged to Robinson Crusoe. No doubt the skeleton is conveyed from Poe. I think little of these, they are trifles and details; and no man can hope to have a monopoly of skeletons or make a corner in talking birds. The stockade, I am told, is from *Masterman Ready*. It may be, I care not a jot. These useful writers had fulfilled the poet's saying: departing, they had left behind them Footprints on the sands of time, Footprints which perhaps another — and I was the other! It is my debt to Washington Irving that exercises my conscience, and justly so, for I believe plagiarism was rarely carried farther. I chanced to pick up the *Tales of a Traveller* some years ago with a view to an anthology of prose narrative, and the book flew up and struck me: Billy Bones, his chest, the company in the parlour, the whole inner spirit, and a good deal of the material detail of my first chapters — all were there, all were the property of Washington Irving. But I had no guess of it then as I sat writing by the fireside, in what seemed the spring-tides of a somewhat pedestrian inspiration; nor yet day by day, after lunch, as I read aloud my morning's work to the family. It seemed to me original as sin; it seemed to belong to me like my right eye. I had counted on one boy, I found I had two in my audience. My father caught fire at once with all the romance and childishness of his original nature. His own stories, that every night of his life he put himself to sleep with, dealt perpetually with ships, roadside inns, robbers, old sailors, and commercial travellers before the era of steam. He never finished one of these romances; the lucky man did not require to! But in *Treasure Island* he recognised something kindred to his own imagination; it was his kind of picturesque; and he not only heard with delight the daily chapter, but set himself acting to collaborate. When the time came for Billy Bones's chest to be ransacked, he must have passed the better part of a day preparing, on the back of a legal envelope, an inventory of its contents, which I exactly followed; and the name of "Flint's old ship" — the *Walrus* — was given at his particular request. And now who should come dropping in, *ex machinâ*, but Dr. Japp, like the disguised prince who is to bring down the curtain upon peace and happiness in the last act; for he carried in his pocket, not a horn or a talisman, but a publisher had, in fact, been charged by my old friend, Mr. Henderson, to unearth new writers for *Young Folks*. Even the ruthlessness of a united family recoiled before the extreme measure of inflicting on our guest the mutilated members of *The Sea Cook*; at the same time, we would by no means stop our readings; and accordingly the tale was begun again at the beginning, and solemnly re-delivered for the benefit of Dr. Japp. From that moment on, I have thought highly of his critical faculty; for when he left us, he carried away the manuscript in his portmanteau.

Here, then, was everything to keep me up, sympathy, help, and now a positive engagement. I had chosen besides a very easy style. Compare it with the almost contemporary "Merry Men," one reader may prefer the one style, one the other — 'tis an affair of character, perhaps of mood; but no expert can fail to see that the one is much more difficult, and the other much easier to maintain. It seems as though a full-grown experienced man of letters might engage to turn out *Treasure Island* at so many pages a day, and keep his pipe alight. But alas! this was not my case. Fifteen days I stuck to it, and turned out fifteen chapters; and then, in the early paragraphs of the sixteenth, ignominiously lost hold. My mouth was empty; there was not one word of *Treasure Island* in my bosom; and here were the proofs of the beginning already waiting me at the "Hand and Spear"! Then I corrected them, living for the most part alone, walking on the heath at Weybridge in dewy autumn mornings, a good deal pleased with what I had done, and more appalled than I can depict to you in words at what remained for me to do. I was thirty-one; I was the head of a family; I had lost my health; I had never yet paid my way, never yet made £200 a year; my father had quite recently bought back and cancelled a book that was judged a failure: was this to be another and last fiasco? I was indeed very close on despair; but I shut my mouth hard, and during the journey to Davos, where I was to pass the winter, had the resolution to think of other things and bury myself in the novels of M. de Boisgobey. Arrived at my destination, down I sat one morning to the unfinished tale; and behold! it flowed from me like small talk; and in a second tide of delighted industry, and again at a rate of a chapter a day, I finished *Treasure Island*. It had to be transcribed almost exactly; my wife was ill; the schoolboy remained alone of the faithful; and John Addington Symonds (to whom I timidly mentioned what I was engaged on) looked on me askance. He was at that time very eager I should write on the characters of Theophrastus: so far out may be the judgments of the wisest men. But Symonds (to be sure) was scarce the confidant to go to for sympathy on a boy's story. He was large-minded; "a full man," if there was one; but the very name of my enterprise would suggest to him only capitulations of sincerity and solecisms of style. Well! he was not far wrong.

Treasure Island — it was Mr. Henderson who deleted the first title, *The Sea Cook* — appeared duly in the story paper, where it figured in the ignoble midst, without woodcuts, and attracted not the least attention. I did not care. I liked the tale myself, for much the same reason as my father liked the beginning: it was my kind of picturesque. I was not a little proud of John Silver, also; and to this day rather admire that smooth and formidable adventurer. What was infinitely more exhilarating, I had passed a landmark; I had finished a tale, and written "The End" upon my manuscript, as I had not done since "The Pentland Rising," when I was a boy of sixteen not yet at college. In truth it was so by a set of lucky accidents; had not Dr. Japp come on his visit, had not the tale flowed from me with singular case, it must have been laid aside like its predecessors, and found a circuitous and unlamented way to the fire. Purists may suggest it would have been better so. I am not of that mind. The tale seems to have given much pleasure, and it brought (or, was the means of bringing) fire and food and wine to a deserving family in which I took an interest. I need scarcely say I mean my own.

But the adventures of *Treasure Island* are not yet quite at an end. I had written it up to the map. The map was the chief part of my plot. For instance, I had called an islet "Skeleton Island," not knowing what I meant, seeking only for the immediate picturesque, and it was to justify this name that I broke into the gallery of Mr. Poe and stole Flint's pointer. And in the same way, it was because I had made two harbours that the *Hispaniola* was sent on her wanderings with Israel Hands. The time came when it was decided to republish, and I sent in my manuscript, and the map along with it, to Messrs. Cassell. The proofs came, they were corrected, but I heard nothing of the map. I wrote and asked; was told it had never been received, and sat aghast. It is one thing to draw a map at random, set a scale in one corner of it at a venture, and write up a story to the measurements. It is quite another to have to examine a whole book, make an inventory of all the allusions contained in it, and with a pair of compasses, painfully design a map to suit the data. I did it; and the map was drawn again in my father's office, with embellishments of blowing whales and sailing ships, and my father himself brought into service a knack he had of various writing, and elaborately *forged* the signature of Captain Flint, and the sailing directions of Billy Bones. But somehow it was never *Treasure Island* to me.

I have said the map was the most of the plot. I might almost say it was the whole. A few reminiscences of Poe, Defoe, and Washington Irving, a copy of Johnson's *Buccaneers*, the name of the Dead Man's Chest from Kingsley's *At Last*, some recollections of canoeing on the high seas, and the map itself, with its infinite, eloquent suggestion, made up the whole of my materials. It is, perhaps, not often that a map figures so largely in a tale, yet it is always important. The author must know his countryside, whether real or imaginary, like his hand; the distances, the points of the compass, the place of the sun's rising, the behaviour of the moon, should all be beyond cavil. And how troublesome the moon is! I have come to grief over the moon in *Prince Otto*, and so soon as that was pointed out to me, adopted a precaution which I recommend to other men - I never write now without an almanack. With an almanack, and the map of the country, and the plan of every house, either actually plotted on paper or already and immediately apprehended in the mind, a man may hope to avoid some of the grossest possible blunders. With the map before him, he will scarce allow the sun to set in the east, as it does in *The Antiquary*. With the almanack at hand, he will scarce allow two horsemen, journeying on the most urgent affair, to employ six days, from three of the Monday morning till late in the Saturday night, upon a journey of, say, ninety or a hundred miles, and before the week is out, and still on the same nags, to cover fifty in one day, as may be read at length in the inimitable novel of *Rob Roy*. And it is certainly well, though far from necessary, to avoid such "croppers." But it is my contention — my superstition, if you like — that who is faithful to his map, and consults it, and draws from it his inspiration, daily and hourly, gains positive support, and not mere negative immunity from accident. The tale has a root there; it grows in that soil; it has a spine of its own behind the words. Better if the country be real, and he has walked every foot of it and knows every milestone. But even with imaginary places, he will do well in the beginning to provide a map; as he studies it, relations will appear that he had not thought upon; he will discover obvious, though unsuspected, short-cuts and footprints for his messengers; and even when a map is not all the plot, as it was in *Treasure Island*, it will be found to be a mine of suggestion.[2]

2 Robert Louis Stevenson. *The Art of Writing*. Transcribed from the 1905 Chatto & Windus edition by David Price, http://www.gutenberg.org/dirs/etext96/artow10h.htm.

Daily Assignment

- Warm-up: Look back at the rising action in your personal story. Discuss ways that God watched over you and therefore was a part of this rising action.
- Students will complete Concept Builder 10-D.
- Prayer journal.
- Review the assigned text. Keep vocabulary cards.
- This is the day that students should write, and then rewrite, the final drafts of their assigned essays.

Sequencing the Plot — Part 2

The sequence is the order of events in a plot. It is never coincidental — every author has a purpose in sequencing his events. Look at the sequence of events as they emerge in *Treasure Island.* **Now, put the different components in the plot: Rising, Action, Exposition, Climax, Falling Action (Denouement), Resolution.**

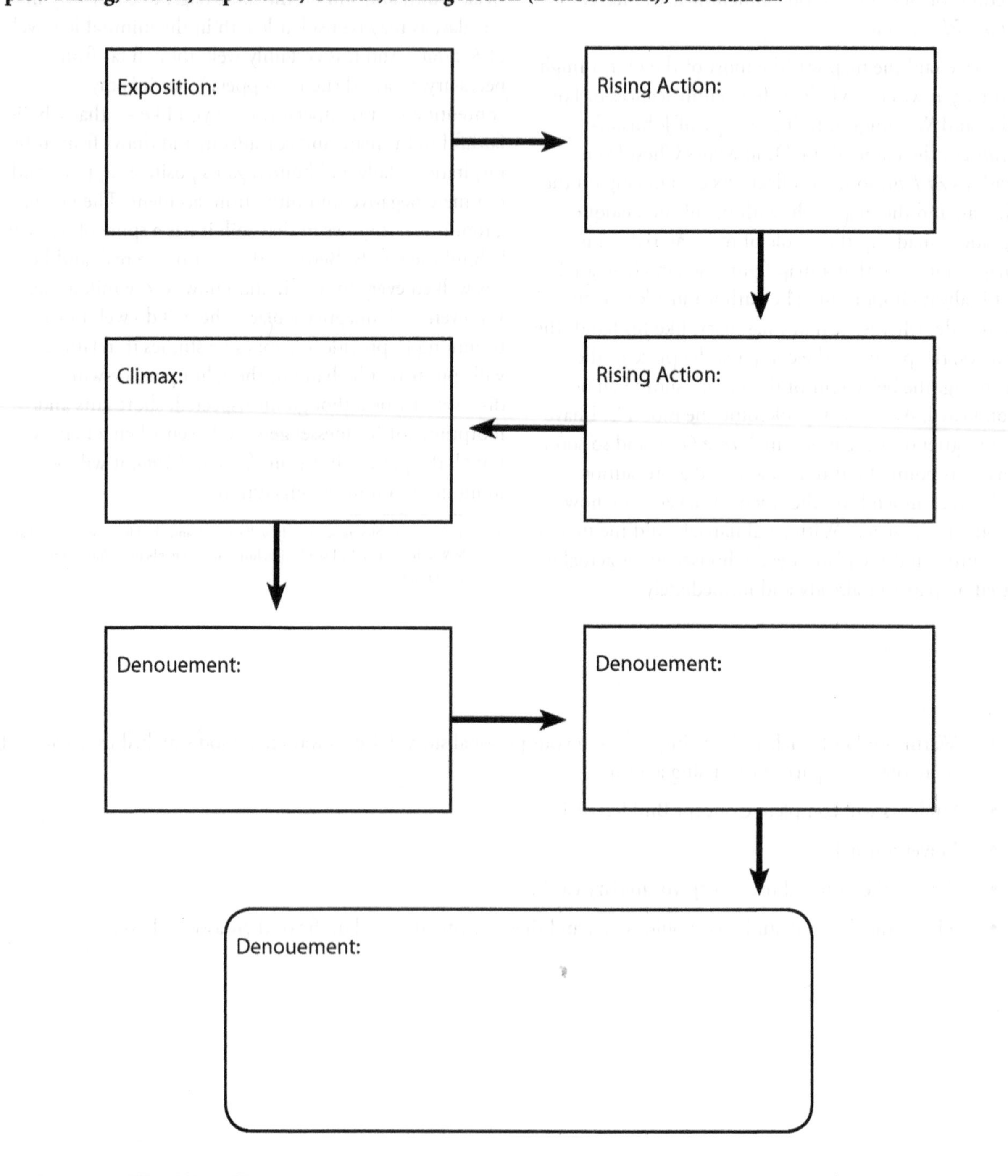

Suspense — *Treasure Island* (Robert Louis Stevenson)

Chapter 11

First Thoughts

Perhaps no book has more adventure tales than Stevenson's *Treasure Island.* It is full of suspense. Readers are often sitting on the edge of their seats! The tone of a literary piece is the mood or feeling that it evokes in the reader. One important tone or mood is suspense.

Chapter Learning Objectives

In chapter 11 we will analyze how Stevenson produces suspense in Treasure Island.

As a result of this chapter study you will be able to . . .

1. Determine how Stevenson creates suspense in *Treasure Island.*
2. Analyze the worldview of *Treasure Island.*
3. Compare and contrast the way suspense is created in *Treasure Island* with the way suspense is created in *Kidnapped.*

Look Ahead for Friday

- Turn in a final copy of essay
- Take Weekly Test

Lesson 1

Literary Example of Suspense

How does author Stephen Crane build suspense in *The Red Badge of Courage* (Ch. 5) below?

There were moments of waiting. The youth thought of the village street at home before the arrival of the circus parade on a day in the spring. He remembered how he had stood, a small, thrillful boy, prepared to follow the dingy lady upon the white horse, or the band in its faded chariot. He saw the yellow road, the lines of expectant people, and the sober houses. He particularly remembered an old fellow who used to sit upon a cracker box in front of the store and feign to despise such exhibitions. A thousand details of color and form surged in his mind.

The old fellow upon the cracker box appeared in middle prominence.

Someone cried, "Here they come!"

There was rustling and muttering among the men.

They displayed a feverish desire to have every possible cartridge ready to their hands. The boxes were pulled around into various positions, and adjusted with great care. It was as if seven hundred new bonnets were being tried on. The tall soldier, having prepared his rifle, produced a red handkerchief of some kind. He was engaged in knitting it about his throat with exquisite attention to its position, when the cry was repeated up and down the line in a muffled roar of sound.

"Here they come! Here they come!" Gun locks clicked.

Across the smoke infested fields came a brown swarm of running men who were giving shrill yells. They came on, stooping and swinging their rifles at all angles. A flag, tilted forward, sped near the front.

As he caught sight of them the youth was momentarily startled by a thought that perhaps his gun was not loaded. He stood trying to rally his faltering intellect so that he might recollect the moment when he had loaded, but he could not.

A hatless general pulled his dripping horse to a stand near the colonel of the 304th. He shook his fist in the other's face. "You've got to hold'em back!" he shouted, savagely; "you've got to hold'em back!"

In his agitation the colonel began to stammer. "A all r right, General, all right, by Gawd! We we'll do our — we-we'll d-d-do — do our best, General." The general made a passionate gesture and galloped away. The colonel, perchance to relieve his feelings, began to scold like a wet parrot. The youth, turning swiftly to make sure that the rear was unmolested, saw the commander regarding his men in a highly regretful manner, as if he regretted above everything his association with them.

The man at the youth's elbow was mumbling, as if to himself: "Oh, we're in for it now! Oh, we're in for it now!"

The captain of the company had been pacing excitedly to and fro in the rear. He coaxed in schoolmistress fashion, as to a congregation of boys with primers. His talk was an endless repetition. "Reserve your fire, boys — don't shoot till I tell you — save your fire — wait till they get close up — don't be fools —."

Perspiration streamed down the youth's face, which was soiled like that of a weeping urchin. He frequently, with a nervous movement, wiped his eyes with his coat sleeve. His mouth was still a little ways open.

He got the one glance at the foe swarming field in front of him, and instantly ceased to debate the question of his piece being loaded. Before he was ready to begin — before he had announced to himself that he was about to fight — he threw the obedient, well balanced rifle into position and fired a first wild shot. Directly he was working at his weapon like an automatic affair.

He suddenly lost concern for himself, and forgot to look at a menacing fate. He became not a man but a member. He felt that something of which he was a part — a regiment, an army, a cause, or a country — was in a crisis. He was welded into a common personality which was dominated by a single desire. For some moments he could not flee no more than a little finger can commit a revolution from a hand.

If he had thought the regiment was about to be annihilated perhaps he could have amputated himself from it. But its noise gave him assurance. The regiment was like a firework that, once ignited, proceeds superior to circumstances until its blazing vitality fades. It wheezed and banged with a mighty power. He pictured the ground before it as strewn with the discomfited.

There was a consciousness always of the presence of his comrades about him. He felt the subtle battle brotherhood more potent even than the cause for which they were fighting. It was a mysterious fraternity born of the smoke and danger of death.

He was at a task. He was like a carpenter who has made many boxes, making still another box, only there was furious haste in his movements. He, in his thought, was careering off in other places, even as the carpenter who as he works whistles and thinks of his friend or his enemy, his home or a saloon. And these jolted dreams were never perfect to him afterward, but remained a mass of blurred shapes.

Presently he began to feel the effects of the war atmosphere — a blistering sweat, a sensation that his eyeballs were about to crack like hot stones. A burning roar filled his ears.

Following this came a red rage. He developed the acute exasperation of a pestered animal, a well meaning cow worried by dogs. He had a mad feeling against his rifle, which could only be used against one life at a time. He wished to rush forward and strangle with his fingers. He craved a power that would enable him to make a world sweeping gesture and brush all back. His impotency appeared to him, and made his rage into that of a driven beast.

Buried in the smoke of many rifles his anger was directed not so much against the men whom he knew were rushing toward him as against the swirling battle phantoms which were choking him, stuffing their smoke robes down his parched throat. He fought frantically for respite for his senses, for air, as a babe being smothered attacks the deadly blankets.

There was a blare of heated rage mingled with a certain expression of intentness on all faces. Many of the men were making low toned noises with their mouths, and these subdued cheers, snarls, imprecations, prayers, made a wild, barbaric song that went as an undercurrent of sound, strange and chantlike with the resounding chords of the war march. The man at the youth's elbow was babbling. In it there was something soft and tender like the monologue of a babe. The tall soldier was swearing in a loud voice. From his lips came a black procession of curious oaths. All of a sudden another broke out in a querulous way like a man who has mislaid his hat. "Well, why don't they support us? Why don't they send supports? Do they think —."

The youth in his battle sleep heard this as one who dozes hears.

There was a singular absence of heroic poses. The men bending and surging in their haste and rage were in every impossible attitude. The steel ramrods clanked and clanged with incessant din as the men pounded them furiously into the hot rifle barrels. The flaps of the cartridge boxes were all unfastened and bobbed idiotically with each movement. The rifles, once loaded, were jerked to the shoulder and fired without apparent aim into the smoke or at one of the blurred and shifting forms which upon the field before the regiment had been — growing larger and larger like puppets under a magician's hand.

The officers, at their intervals, rearward, neglected to stand in picturesque attitudes. They were bobbing to and fro roaring directions and encouragements. The dimensions of their howls were extraordinary. They expended their lungs with prodigal wills. And often they nearly stood upon their heads in their anxiety to observe the enemy on the other side of the tumbling smoke.

The lieutenant of the youth's company had encountered a soldier who had fled screaming at the first volley of his comrades. Behind the lines these two were acting a little isolated scene. The man was blubbering and staring with sheep like eyes at the lieutenant, who had seized him by the collar and was pummeling him. He drove him back into the ranks with many blows. The soldier went mechanically, dully, with his animal like eyes upon the officer. Perhaps there was to him a divinity expressed in the voice of the other — stern, hard, with no reflection of fear in it. He tried to reload his gun, but his shaking hands prevented. The lieutenant was obliged to assist him.

The men dropped here and there like bundles.

The captain of the youth's company had been killed in an early part of the action. His body lay stretched out in the position of a tired man resting, but upon his face there was an astonished and sorrowful look, as if he thought some friend had done him an ill turn. The babbling man was grazed by a shot that made the blood stream widely down his face. He clapped both hands to his head. "Oh!" he said, and ran. Another grunted suddenly as if he had been struck by a club in the stomach. He sat down and gazed ruefully. In his eyes there was mute, indefinite reproach. Farther up the line a man, standing behind a tree, had had his knee joint splintered by a ball. Immediately he had dropped his rifle and gripped the tree with both arms. And there he remained, clinging desperately and crying for assistance that he might withdraw his hold upon the tree.

At last an exultant yell went along the quivering line. The firing dwindled from an uproar to a last vindictive popping. As the smoke slowly eddied away, the youth saw that the charge had been repulsed. The enemy were scattered into reluctant groups. He saw a man climb to the top of the fence, straddle the rail, and fire a parting shot. The waves had receded, leaving bits of dark debris upon the ground.

Some in the regiment began to whoop frenziedly. Many were silent. Apparently they were trying to contemplate themselves.

After the fever had left his veins, the youth thought that at last he was going to suffocate. He became aware of the foul atmosphere in which he had been struggling. He was grimy and dripping like a laborer in a foundry. He grasped his canteen and took a long swallow of the warmed water.

A sentence with variations went up and down the line. "Well, we've helt'em back. We've helt'em back; derned if we haven't." The men said it blissfully, leering at each other with dirty smiles.

The youth turned to look behind him and off to the right and off to the left. He experienced the joy of a man who at last finds leisure in which to look about him.

Under foot there were a few ghastly forms motionless. They lay twisted in fantastic contortions. Arms were bent and heads were turned in incredible ways. It seemed that the dead men must have fallen from some great height to get into such positions. They looked to be dumped out upon the ground from the sky.

From a position in the rear of the grove a battery was throwing shells over it. The flash of the guns startled the youth at first. He thought they were aimed directly at him. Through the trees he watched the black figures of the gunners as they worked swiftly and intently. Their labor seemed a complicated thing. He wondered how they could remember its formula in the midst of confusion.

The guns squatted in a row like savage chiefs. They argued with abrupt violence. It was a grim pow-wow. Their busy servants ran hither and thither.

A small procession of wounded men was going drearily toward the rear. It was a flow of blood from the torn body of the brigade.

To the right and to the left were the dark lines of other troops. Far in front he thought he could see lighter masses protruding in points from the forest. They were suggestive of unnumbered thousands.

Once he saw a tiny battery go dashing along the line of the horizon. The tiny riders were beating the tiny horses.

From a sloping hill came the sound of cheerings and clashes. Smoke welled slowly through the leaves.

Batteries were speaking with thunderous oratorical effort. Here and there were flags, the red in the stripes dominating. They splashed bits of warm color upon the dark lines of troops.

The youth felt the old thrill at the sight of the emblem. They were like beautiful birds strangely undaunted in a storm.

As he listened to the din from the hillside, to a deep pulsating thunder that came from afar to the left, and to the lesser clamors which came from many directions, it occurred to him that they were fighting, too, over there, and over there, and over there. Heretofore he had supposed that all the battle was directly under his nose.

As he gazed around him the youth felt a flash of astonishment at the blue, pure sky and the sun gleaming on the trees and fields. It was surprising that Nature had gone tranquilly on with her golden process in the midst of so much devilment.[1]

1 Stephen Crane, *The Red Badge of Courage*, chapter 5; www.gutenberg.org/files/73/73-h/73-h.htm.

Daily Assignment

- Warm-up: When is fear OK? And when is fear bad? What is the difference between fear and suspense?
- Students will complete Concept Builder 11-A.
- Prayer journal: Students are encouraged to write in their prayer journal every day.
- Students need to review their material for the next assignment
- Students should systematically review their vocabulary words daily.

Suspense

Draw a suspenseful picture of a stormy day. Then draw a warm, happy picture of a stormy day.

Suspenseful Picture	Happy Picture

Lesson 2

Grammar Review: Possessives

A. Typically, the writer should form the possessive singular of nouns with an apostrophe and an s ('s).

The house's door

The phone's cord

B. This is true no matter what the ending might be. For example,

James's book

Roberta's bicycle

C. Exceptions include the possessive *Jesus' teachings* and *Moses' laws*. To decrease confusion the writer might instead say

The teachings of Jesus

The law of Moses.

D. Possessive words such as *hers, its, oneself, theirs*, and *yours* require no apostrophe.

The book is hers for the asking.

The trees are theirs.

Daily Assignment

- Warm-up: Describe a suspenseful book you read. What made it suspenseful?
- Students will complete Concept Builder 11-B.
- Prayer journal.
- Students should outline all assigned essays for the week.

Suspense 1

Show how Stevenson builds suspense in the first few chapters of his book using different literary elements. Fill in the circles with incidents from the story.

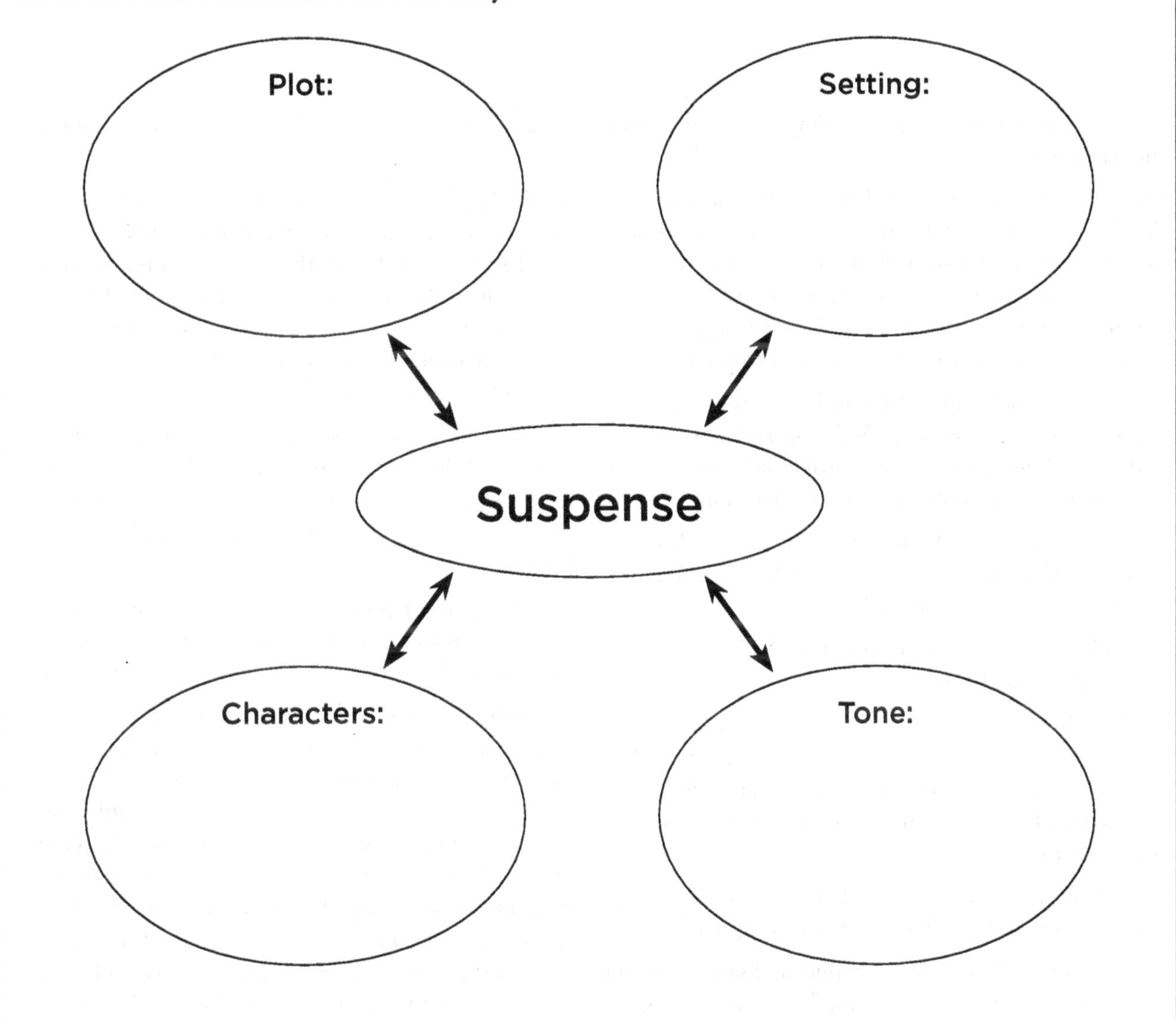

Lesson 3

Suspense in "Riki Tiki Tavi" by Rudyard Kipling

In this short story by Rudyard Kipling a heroic mongoose named Riki Tiki Tavi confronts a snake intent on killing a human family:

Teddy and his mother and father were there at early breakfast; but Rikki-tikki saw that they were not eating anything. They sat stone-still, and their faces were white. Nagaina was coiled up on the matting by Teddy's chair, within easy striking distance of Teddy's bare leg, and she was swaying to and fro singing a song of triumph.

"Son of the big man that killed Nag," she hissed, "stay still. I am not ready yet. Wait a little. Keep very still, all you three. If you move I strike, and if you do not move I strike. Oh, foolish people, who killed my Nag!"

Teddy's eyes were fixed on his father, and all his father could do was to whisper, "Sit still, Teddy. You mustn't move. Teddy, keep still."

Then Rikki-tikki came up and cried: "Turn round, Nagaina; turn and fight!"

"All in good time," said she, without moving her eyes. "I will settle my account with you presently. Look at your friends, Rikki-tikki. They are still and white; they are afraid. They dare not move, and if you come a step nearer I strike."

"Look at your eggs," said Rikki-tikki, "in the melon-bed near the wall. Go and look, Nagaina."

The big snake turned half round, and saw the egg on the verandah. "Ah-h! Give it to me," she said.

Rikki-tikki put his paws one on each side of the egg, and his eyes were blood-red. "What price for a snake's egg? For a young cobra? For a young king-cobra? For the last — the very last of the brood? The ants are eating all the others down by the melon-bed."

Nagaina spun clear round, forgetting everything for the sake of the one egg; and Rikki-tikki saw Teddy's father shoot out a big hand, catch Teddy by the shoulder, and drag him across the little table with the tea-cups, safe and out of reach of Nagaina.

"Tricked! Tricked! Tricked! Rikk-tck-tck!" chuckled Rikki-tikki. "The boy is safe, and it was I — I — I that caught Nag by the hood last night in the bathroom." Then he began to jump up and down, all four feet together, his head close to the floor. "He threw me to and fro, but he could not shake me off. He was dead before the big man blew him in two. I did it. Rikki-tikki-tck-tck! Come then, Nagaina. Come and fight with me. You shall not be a widow long."

Nagaina saw that she had lost her chance of killing Teddy, and the egg lay between Rikki-tikki's paws. "Give me the egg, Rikki-tikki. Give me the last of my eggs, and I will go away and never come back," she said, lowering her hood.

"Yes, you will go away, and you will never come back; for you will go to the rubbish-heap with Nag. Fight, widow! The big man has gone for his gun! Fight!"

Rikki-tikki was bounding all round Nagaina, keeping just out of reach of her stroke, his little eyes like hot coals. Nagaina gathered herself together, and flung out at him. Rikki-tikki jumped up and backward. Again and again and again she struck, and each time her head came with a whack on the matting of the verandah, and she gathered herself together like a watch-spring. Then Rikki-tikki danced in a circle to get behind her, and Nagaina spun round to keep her head to his head, so that the rustle of her tail on the matting sounded like dry leaves blown along by the wind.

He had forgotten the egg. It still lay on the verandah, and Nagaina came nearer and nearer to it, till at last, while Rikki-tikki was drawing breath, she caught it in her mouth, turned to the verandah steps and flew like an arrow down the path, with Rikki-tikki behind her. When the cobra runs for her life, she goes like a whip-lash flicked across a horse's neck.

Rikki-tikki knew that he must catch her, or all the trouble would begin again. She headed straight for the long grass by the thorn-bush, and as he was running Rikki-tikki heard Darzee still singing his foolish little song of triumph. But Darzee's wife was wiser. She flew off her nest as Nagaina came along and flapped her wings about Nagaina's head. If Darzee had helped they might have turned her; but Nagaina only lowered her hood and went on. Still, the instant's delay brought Rikki-tikki up to her, and as she plunged into the rat-hole where she and Nag used to live, his little white teeth were clenched on her tail, and he went down with her — and very few mongooses, however wise and old they may be, care to follow a cobra into its hole. It was dark in the hole; and Rikki-tikki never knew when it might open out and give Nagaina room to turn and strike at him. He held on savagely, and struck out his feet to act as brakes on the dark slope of the hot, moist earth.

Then the grass by the mouth of the hole stopped waving, and Darzee said: "It is all over with Rikki-tikki! We must sing his death-song. Valiant Rikki-tikki is dead! For Nagaina will surely kill him underground."

So he sang a very mournful song that he made up on the spur of the minute, and just as he got to the most touching part the grass quivered again, and Rikki-tikki, covered with dirt, dragged himself out of the hole leg by leg, licking his whiskers. Darzee stopped with a little shout. Rikki-tikki shook some of the dust out of his fur and sneezed. "It is all over," he said. "The widow will never come out again." And the red ants that live between the grass stems heard him, and began to troop down one after another to see if he had spoken the truth.

Rikki-tikki curled himself up in the grass and slept where he was — slept and slept till it was late in the afternoon, for he had done a hard day's work.

"Now," he said, when he awoke, "I will go back to the house. Tell the Coppersmith, Darzee, and he will tell the garden that Nagaina is dead."

The Coppersmith is a bird who makes a noise exactly like the beating of a little hammer on a copper pot; and the reason he is always making it is because he is the town-crier to every Indian garden, and tells all the news to everybody who cares to listen. As Rikki-tikki went up the path, he heard his "attention" notes like a tiny dinner-gong; and then the steady "Ding-dong-lock! Nag is dead — dong! Nagaina is dead! Ding-dong-tock!" That set all the birds in the garden singing, and the frogs croaking; for Nag and Nagaina used to eat frogs as well as little birds.

When Rikki got to the house, Teddy and Teddy's mother (she looked very white still, for she had been fainting) and Teddy's father came out and almost cried over him; and that night he ate all that was given him till he could I eat no more, and went to bed on Teddy's shoulder, where Teddy's mother saw him when she came to look late at night.

"He saved our lives and Teddy's life," she said to her husband. "Just think, he saved all our lives."

Rikki-tikki woke up with a jump, for all the mongooses are light sleepers.

"Oh, it's you," said he. "What are you bothering for? All the cobras are dead; and if they weren't, I'm here."

Rikki-tikki had a right to be proud of himself; but he did not grow too proud, and he kept that garden as a mongoose should keep it, with tooth and jump and spring and bite, till never a cobra dared show its head inside the walls.[2]

2 Rudyard Kipling, "Riki Tiki Tavi," Selections from the Books of Rudyard Kipling (London: MacMillan and Co., 1923); www.gutenberg.org/cache/epub/16578/pg16578.html.

Daily Assignment

- Warm-up: Describe a suspenseful movie. What made it suspenseful?
- Students will complete a daily Concept Builder 11-C.
- Prayer journal.
- Students should write rough drafts of all assigned essays.

Suspense 2

Show how Stevenson builds suspense in the first few chapters of *Treasure Island.* Fill in the boxes with incidents from the book.

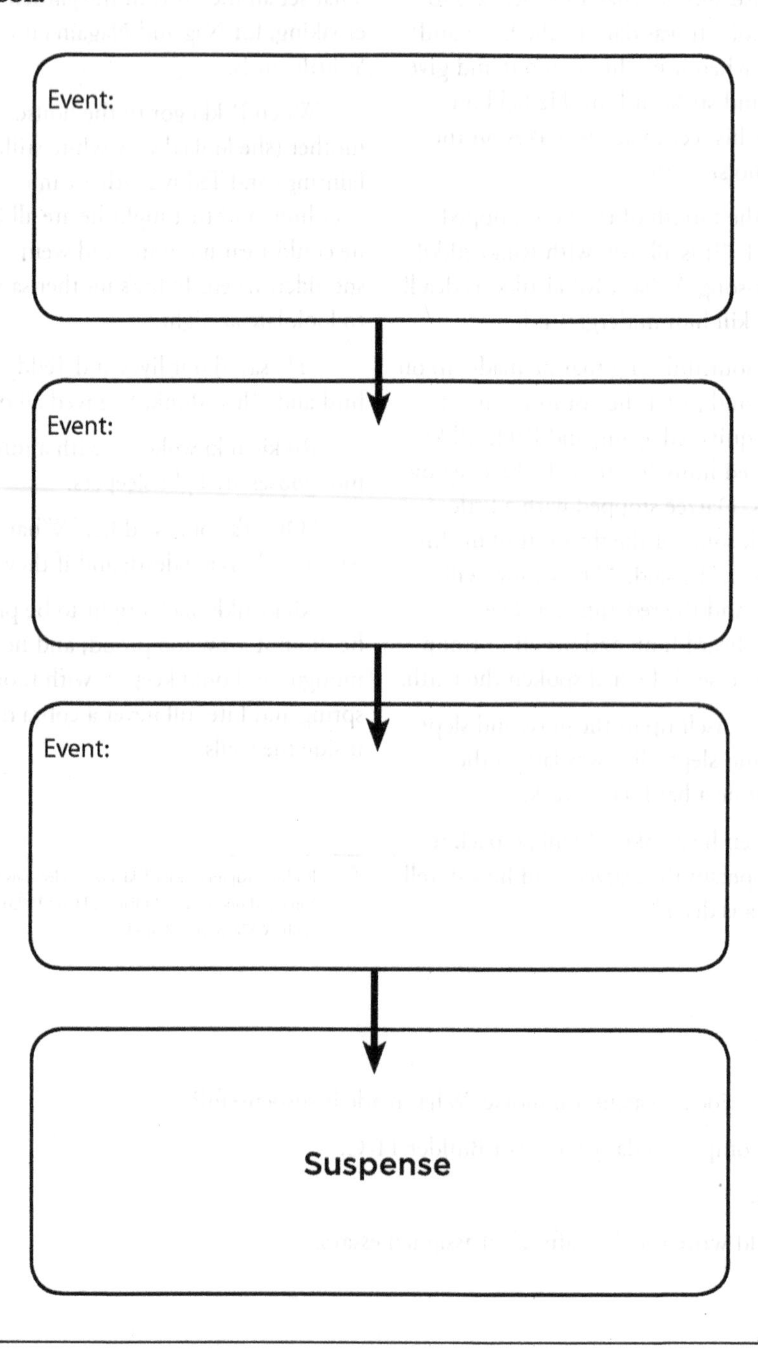

Student Essay

Suspense versus fear. Fear brings screams and sometimes tears, while suspense provides thrilling, sitting-on-the-edge-of-your-seat excitement or anxiety. Robert Louis Stevenson uses suspense in his epic novel *Treasure Island.* A particular instance of this is found within the first chapter of the book, when character introduction occurs and the foundation of the plot is laid out.

Chapter 1 is opened by Jim Hawkins, the main character and narrator, who welcomes a strange guest at Jim's family's inn. Throughout the next few paragraphs, the reader learns that this is not some random eerie person, but a character hiding something: "All day he hung around the cove, or upon the cliffs, with a brass telescope; all evening he sat in a corner of the parlor next the fire, and drank rum and water very strong." Thus, suspense begins to build. Who is this man? What is he hiding? What is he looking for? These questions constantly run through the reader's mind whilst reading this first chapter.

As if a mysterious old pirate hiding something was not enough, Stevenson reveals that the "Captain" is seemingly waiting for a man with a wooden leg. "He took [Jim] aside one day and told [him] to keep a 'weather-eye out for a seafaring man with one leg.' " Suspense is revealed through this by creating more questions and uncertainty in the reader's mind. Is this man bad? Good? A long-lost friend? So throughout the first chapter suspense is built, making the reader continue to read in order to find out what happens.

The final part of chapter 1 ends with a confrontation between the captain and the doctor. The captain, used to getting what he wants from people, is astounded when the doctor disregards his demand for silence, "slapping his hand upon the table before him." As the rest of the pub goes silent, the doctor continues to carry on. The captain, enraged, "sprang to his feet, drew and opened a sailor's clasp-knife, and, balancing it open on the palm of his hand, threatened to pin [the doctor] to the wall." However, the man remains nonplussed. Furthermore, the doctor speaks to the captain like a child, threatening to turn him in if there are any complaints against him. Surprisingly, in his drunken state, the captain obeys, and "kept his peace that evening, and for many evenings to come." Thus, suspense is somewhat relieved, although the questions still linger. The reader becomes less worried about the captain, because, now, somebody can put him in his place. However, the suspense is still there, in the back of the reader's mind.

Throughout the first chapter of Robert Louis Stevenson's novel, *Treasure Island*, suspense is built and relieved. In one exciting chapter, suspense climbs to a peak with strange new characters, and drops only a little with the bravery of the kind but firm doctor. Stevenson creates this suspense by planting unanswered questions in the reader's mind. As a result, the reader is captivated and feels as if he cannot stop reading until he knows the outcome. (Sheridan)

Daily Assignment

- Warm-up: What makes certain animals scary? Like a cobra? Or a raven? Describe the scariest animal you know.
- Students will complete Concept Builder 11-D.
- Prayer journal.
- Review the assigned text. Keep vocabulary cards.
- This is the day that students should write, and then rewrite, the final drafts of their assigned essays.

Predicting and Foreshadowing

Most authors are quite intentional about the way they structure their literary piece. A clever reader, however, will discern the outcome/resolution long before the literary piece ends. Find as many hints as possible in *Treasure Island* (if possible, before you finish reading it) and offer an informed prediction.

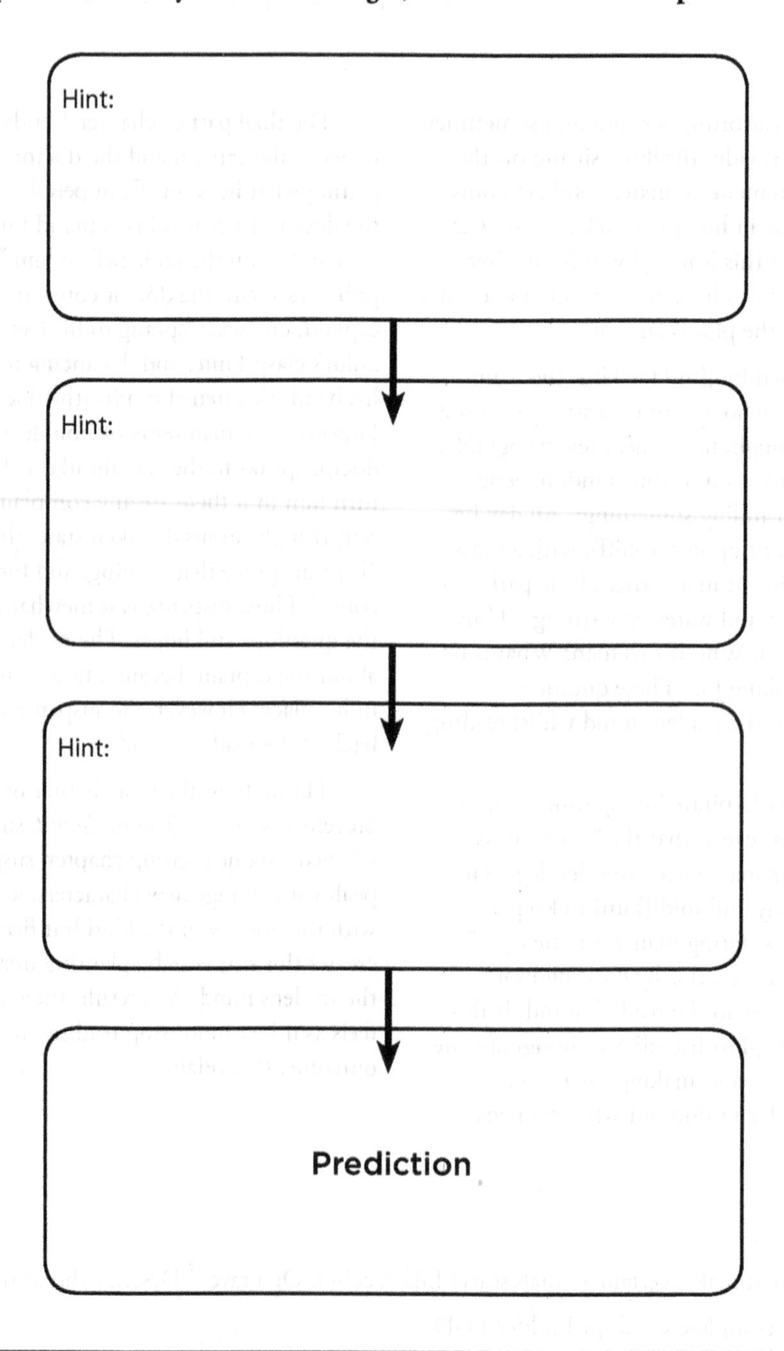

Narration - *How Green Was My Valley* (Richard Llewellyn)

Chapter 12

First Thoughts

This unpretentious novel is the story of Huw Morgan, a Welsh boy growing up in the coal fields. Tragedy, humor, courage, and strength permeate this remarkable novel. Richard Llewellyn's 1939 international best-selling novel *How Green Was My Valley* stands the test of time as a literary classic. Set in a Welsh coal mining village in the last quarter of the 19th century, its themes of spiritual honesty opposed to physical yearning and bondage are developed in a language that combines Fitzgerald's richness and Steinbeck's clarity. The author delights readers with incisive ways of observing everyday life that make them seem timeless. This characteristic helps make a writing transcend generations.

Chapter Learning Objectives

In chapter 12 we will analyze narration and the way it is used in *How Green Was My Valley*.

As a result of this chapter study you will be able to . . .

1. Closely examine Huw's family and discuss how the family members exhibit Judeo-Christian characteristics toward one another.
2. Analyze how the pastor foil functions.

Look Ahead for Friday

- Turn in a final copy of essay
- Take Weekly Test

Lesson 1

Literary Analysis: Narration

Narration is the way an author tells his story. In *How Green Was My Valley* the author uses first person (I) as the literary narrative technique. In fact, the entire novel is a first-person flashback. The narrator is remembering past events and relating them to the reader in the present.

One of the most famous first-person narrative flashbacks occurs in a short story, "The Tell-Tale Heart," by Edgar Allan Poe.

True! Nervous, very, very dreadfully nervous I had been and am; but why will you say that I am mad? The disease had sharpened my senses, not destroyed, not dulled them. Above all was the sense of hearing acute. I heard all things in the heaven and in the earth. I heard many things in hell. How then am I mad? Hearken! and observe how healthily, how calmly, I can tell you the whole story.

It is impossible to say how first the idea entered my brain, but, once conceived, it haunted me day and night. Object there was none. Passion there was none. I loved the old man. He had never wronged me. He had never given me insult. For his gold I had no desire. I think it was his eye! Yes, it was this! One of his eyes resembled that of a vulture — a pale blue eye with a film over it. Whenever it fell upon me my blood ran cold, and so by degrees, very gradually, I made up my mind to take the life of the old man, and thus rid myself of the eye for ever.

Now this is the point. You fancy me mad. Madmen know nothing. But you should have seen me. You should have seen how wisely I proceeded — with what caution — with what foresight, with what dissimulation, I went to work! I was never kinder to the old man than during the whole week before I killed him. And every night about midnight I turned the latch of his door and opened it oh, so gently! And then, when I had made an opening sufficient for my head, I put in a dark lantern all closed, closed so that no light shone out, and then I thrust in my head. Oh, you would have laughed to see how cunningly I thrust it in! I moved it slowly, very, very slowly, so that I might not disturb the old man's sleep. It took me an hour to place my whole head within the opening so far that I could see him as he lay upon his bed. Ha! would a madman have been so wise as this? And then when my head was well in the room I undid the lantern cautiously — oh, so cautiously — cautiously (for the hinges creaked), I undid it just so much that a single thin ray fell upon the vulture eye. And this I did for seven long nights, every night just at midnight, but I found the eye always closed, and so it was impossible to do the work, for it was not the old man who vexed me but his Evil Eye. And every morning, when the day broke, I went boldly into the chamber and spoke courageously to him, calling him by name in a hearty tone, and inquiring how he had passed the night. So you see he would have been a very profound old man, indeed, to suspect that every night, just at twelve, I looked in upon him while he slept.

Upon the eighth night I was more than usually cautious in opening the door. A watch's minute hand moves more quickly than did mine. Never before that night had I felt the extent of my own powers, of my sagacity. I could scarcely contain my feelings of triumph. To think that there I was opening the door little by little, and he not even to dream of my secret deeds or thoughts. I fairly chuckled at the idea, and perhaps he heard me, for he moved on the bed suddenly as if startled. Now you may think that I drew back — but no. His room was as black as pitch with the thick darkness (for the shutters were close fastened through fear of robbers), and so I knew that he could not see the opening of the door, and I kept pushing it on steadily, steadily.

I had my head in, and was about to open the lantern, when my thumb slipped upon the tin fastening, and the old man sprang up in the bed, crying out, "Who's there?"

I kept quite still and said nothing. For a whole hour I did not move a muscle, and in the meantime I did not hear him lie down. He was still sitting up in the bed, listening; just as I have done night after night hearkening to the death watches in the wall.

Presently, I heard a slight groan, and I knew it was the groan of mortal terror. It was not a groan of pain or of grief — oh, no! It was the low stifled sound that arises from the bottom of the soul when overcharged with awe. I knew the sound well. Many a night, just at midnight, when all the world slept, it has welled up from my own bosom, deepening, with its dreadful echo, the terrors that distracted me.[1]

1 http://xroads.virginia.edu/~hyper/poe/telltale.html.

Daily Assignment

- Warm-up: Describe your earliest memory. How reliable is this memory?
- Students will complete Concept Builder 12-A.
- Prayer journal: Students are encouraged to write in their prayer journal every day.
- Students need to review their material for the next assignment
- Students should systematically review their vocabulary words daily.

Elements of a Story

Analyze the following elements of the novel *How Green Was My Valley*.

Elements	Yes/No	Because . . .
Characters Do the characters seem real?		
Narration Is Huw a credible narrator?		
Setting Is the setting important? Does it seem real?		
Plot Does the story flow logically? Does it flow well?		
Theme Is there a theme?		

Lesson 2

Sample Essay: Narration

At times it is difficult to know who the narrator is! Such is the case with the Anglo-Saxon poem "The Seafarer." In this poem the narrator is discussing the good things and bad things about life. The question readers ask is, "Is this poem a dialogue between two speakers or a monologue in a speaker's own mind?"

The Seafarer

This tale is true, and mine. It tells
How the sea took me, swept me back
And forth in sorrow and fear and pain,
Showed me suffering in a hundred ships,
In a thousand ports, and in me. It tells
Of smashing surf when I sweated in the cold
Of an anxious watch, perched in the bow
As it dashed under cliffs. My feet were cast
In icy bands, bound with frost,
With frozen chains, and hardship groaned
Around my heart. Hunger tore
At my sea-weary soul. No man sheltered
On the quiet fairness of earth can feel
how wretched I was, drifting through winter
On an ice-cold sea, whirled in sorrow,
Alone in a world blown clear of love,
Hung with icicles. The hail storms flew.

The Anglo-Saxon poem, "The Seafarer," is supposed by some to be a monologue in the speaker's mind. Nevertheless, others make the assumption that there are two narrators to this epic poem. Perhaps there are not two narrators but two "voices" coming from one person, the seaman or seafarer. He speaks in two different voices, or tones, rather. The narrator alternates somewhat frequently between these two tones. The first tone that he uses in the poem is one of melancholy and despair. Very much unlike it is the second, a tone of hope and thankfulness. He gives references to God with gratitude. It is debatable whether the seafarer is having an argument with himself in his own mind or if he is looking back as an old man in remembrance of his past sailing life. Or perhaps he is telling a story.

At the beginning of "The Seafarer," the speaker begins by explaining the cruel life of a sailor. He tells of his sorrow and suffering. "With frozen chains, and hardship groaned / Around my heart. Hunger tore / At my sea-weary soul." Later on, he complains of the things he is tired of seeing versus the things he longs to see: "The song of the swan / Might serve for pleasure, the cry of the sea-fowl / The death-noise of birds instead of laughter, / The mewing of gulls instead of mead."

Then he switches voices or tones. It is assumable that the same person is speaking because there is no break in his thought.

"Frost bound the earth and hail would fall, / The coldest seeds. And how my heart / Would begin to beat, knowing once more / The salt waves tossing and the towering sea / The time for journeys would come and my soul / Called me eagerly out, sent me over."

He quickly changes from shuddering in the remembrance of the horrible dangers of the sea, to describing how his soul is called out to sea. The speaker is not contradicting himself, but rather he is simply adding on to his earlier thoughts. Perhaps he is wrestling with the pros and cons of his sailing life. Or maybe he is telling a story. He transfers back and forth between the joys and sorrows of being a seafarer.

Another way that we can interpret the fact that there is only one speaker is that in another changing of the voices, he says, "As the paths of exile stretch endlessly on? / And yet my heart wanders away, / My soul roams with the sea, the whales' / Home, wandering to the widest corners / Of the world, returning ravenous with desire." When the speaker said, "And yet my heart," that contributes the information that most likely the next few lines are also his own thought. The next few lines are about his love of sailing.

All in all, "The Seafarer" is probably a monologue in the sailor's mind. As said before, perhaps the narrator is wrestling with the pros and cons of his sailing life. Or he is telling a story. This poem might also be an old sailor's analysis of his past life on the sea. Regardless of the situation in which he is speaking, it is apparent that he uses two voices. One is of melancholy and despair, while the other can be described by hopefulness and thankfulness. We can assume there is one narrator because of the various situations in which there could be one speaker. Another reason is the flow of the poem. There is not what appears to be a break in thought, but rather his thoughts build upon each other. The wording that the sailor uses while transitioning gives a reason to believe that the whole poem is from a single individual's standpoint. The complexity of the human mind allows the narrator to possess two voices. (Sophia)

Daily Assignment

- Warm-up: Using metaphors and words that a four-year-old will understand, explain how rain clouds are formed.
- Students will complete Concept Builder 12-B.
- Prayer journal.
- Students should outline all assigned essays for the week.

Forming Conclusions

Analyze the conclusion of the novel *How Green Was My Valley*.

Elements	Yes/No	Because . . .
In spite of the fact that his hometown can be ugly and brutal, Huw obviously loves his hometown.		
Huw is in a loving, supportive family.		
The coal mine brings both life and death to Huw's community.		
While Huw is not overtly a Christian, his actions and attitudes clearly show that he is a theist (or someone who acts out of a moral code).		

Lesson 3

Grammar Review: Parallelism

Formal writing demands similarity in form. Parallel construction requires that expressions of similar content and function should be comparable (parallel). Consider the following:

The American, the German, Italian, and Russian all fought over the last piece of cake. (incorrect)

The American, the German, the Italian, and the Russian all fought over the last piece of cake. (correct)

Playing baseball is considerably different from the game of soccer. (incorrect)

Playing baseball is considerably different from playing soccer. (correct)

The game of baseball is considerably different from the game of soccer. (correct)

Daily Assignment

- Warm-up: Describe a relative or friend who has been very important to your formation as a person.
- Students will complete a daily Concept Builder 12-C.
- Prayer journal.
- Students should write rough drafts of all assigned essays.

CONCEPT BUILDER 12-C

Generalizations

To make a generalization about a literary work is to form an analytical opinion based upon facts and observations in the story. **What generalizations from *How Green Was My Valley* can you conclude from the following facts/observations?**

Facts/Observations	Generalization
Huw remembers father and brothers when they came home from the mines on Saturday night.	
Facts/Observations There was trouble brewing at the mines. The men talked of unions and organizing, and the owners were angry.	Generalization
Facts/Observations When he learned that his brother Ivor was to marry, he was sorry to lose his brother; but from the first moment Huw saw Ivor's Bronwen, he loved her.	Generalization

Generalization
Huw loved his father a great deal.

Student Essay

Reliable Narration in *How Green Was My Valley*

How Green Was My Valley, by Richard Llewellyn, is the story of a young Welsh boy named Huw Morgan growing up in a coal mining village during the reign of Queen Victoria. Told in a series of flashbacks by the protagonist himself, the reader is assured of Huw's credibility as a narrator because of his objective account of his life, feelings, and interactions with others and the large amount of clear detail he gives.

Credibility is defined as "the quality or power of inspiring belief." One way Huw inspires belief in the reader is through his objective, unbiased narration of events and his reaction to them. One example of his fact-based narration is his telling of the time he hit his teacher and his varying feelings afterward:

> A left to the chin, and O, the joy to feel your fist bounce solidly on the flesh you hate, and the look of startled pain in hated eyes, a right to the wind, and a left and right to the head to put him down again, just as Mr. Motshill came through the door. Strange how in one minute you will be hot to fight and certain of the justness of your wrong, and the next, sick, and ready to fall in the dust with shame. . . . "I have been sent from school, Mama," I said, in no voice at all. . . . "Did you give him a good kick?" Mama asked me. . . . I could have carried fifty shelves on my little fingers, so good did I feel. But Mr. Gruffydd had other notions about it. . . . Slink from the little house I did, and up the hill, and slunk round our back, and in, to sit in the darkness on the covered engine, and see Mr. Gruffydd again, and hear his voice, and with every word to writhe."

The way Huw matter-of-factly states what occurred and his different feelings of shame and pride indicates that he is a reliable narrator. Huw's reliability as a narrator is also evident in the way he gives excellent detail in a very clear, precise way.

> I looked up in the darkening sky and saw the big winding wheel chopping the light with its spokes as it slowed down, and swung to stop. I heard the clatter of the last lamps and the rattle of the last brass checks as the men handed them in, and their boots heavy in the dust going farther and farther from my hearing, and the voice of a myriad of rats, having happiness in the black waters of the empty pit, rose up to seep aside all other sounds, and terror found me."

The narrator's clear diction and rich details also point to his trustworthiness. Huw, in a distinct and clear manner, describes his life in lush detail, indicating that he is accurately remembering real events in his life.

Thus, in *How Green Was My Valley*, Huw Morgan is a reliable narrator because of his objective and detailed account of his life. (JB)

Daily Assignment

- Warm-up: Describe the place you want to live in the future. Why do you choose this place?
- Students will complete Concept Builder 12-D.
- Prayer journal.
- Review the assigned text. Keep vocabulary cards.
- This is the day that students should write, and then rewrite, the final drafts of their assigned essays.

Narrative Techniques

Analyze the narrative technique of the novel *How Green Was My Valley,* as well as the use of other narrative techniques in books you have read.

Narrative Technique	Advantage/Disadvantage	Example
First Person Narration: The narrator tells the story.	The reader is drawn into the character and into the story very quickly. The narrator can use dialogue to reveal the character's thoughts. This is a way to have the reader feel empathy toward one particular character. First-person narration is also a great way to exhibit colloquial language in order to produce humor (e.g., *The Adventures of Tom Sawyer* by Mark Twain). One obvious disadvantage is that the narrator must be reliable, or the reader will question the veracity of the narrator's story (e.g., *A Separate Peace* by John Knowles) Huw is a pretty reliable first-person narrator: "Strange that the mind will forget so much of what only this moment has passed, and yet hold clear and bright the memory of what happened years ago; of men and women long since dead." — Huw Morgan, *How Green Was My Valley*	I really enjoyed hitting the baseball. After I hit the ball, it flew to Mark. (The reader is invited into the mind of the narrator, who is telling the story in first person.)
Omniscient Narration: The author uses all the characters to tell the story.		
Limited Omniscient Narration: The author uses one or two characters to tell the story.		
Third Person Objective: The author (not the narrator) tells the story.		

Theme — *Alice in Wonderland* (Lewis Carroll)

Chapter 13

First Thoughts

Walt Disney returned the precocious Alice to the American psyche in the 1960s, but he hardly did Carroll's brilliant fantasy justice. On one level, *Alice in Wonderland* is a children's story; on another level it is a scathing criticism of Victorian England. As you read Carroll's novel, try to read it at both levels.

Chapter Learning Objectives

In chapter 13 we will analyze themes in *Alice in Wonderland.*

As a result of this chapter study you will be able to . . .

1. Some define maturity as learning to delay gratification. Using this definition, find biblical characters who were mature and immature.
2. Find examples of puns and other word plays in *Alice in Wonderland* and explain why Carroll uses them in his book.

Look Ahead for Friday

- Turn in a final copy of essay
- Take Weekly Test

Literary Analysis: Theme

As you know, the theme is the central idea of a literary piece, that enduring truth/opinion that transcends time and setting. The following essay explores the powerful theme of *enduring racism*.

Sample Essay: Theme

She was my 21st client. An overall-clad toddler was attached to one hand, and a mini-cart was in the other. This middle-aged, slightly overweight black woman seemed ordinary enough as she requested a bag of groceries from my Pittsburgh church's cooperative emergency food pantry (operated by 40 churches). I was one of the afternoon volunteers entrusted with this duty.

"Hello," I offered without looking up from my work pad. "My name is Jim."

Number 21 replied with a quiet, defeated, "Viola."

Unusual name, I thought. I once knew a Viola. Thirty years ago, in Arkansas, my family subcontracted most of our game cleaning to a thin, tobacco-chewing woman whose granddaughter was named Viola.

Viola's claim to fame was her gift: she could clean, dress, and fillet largemouth bass faster than any person alive. Her hands moved like wild birds.

Her gift generally unappreciated, Viola now lived in poverty in one of the worst sections of Pittsburgh. Twenty years ago Viola lived with her grandmother every summer and fall. Her grandmother's house was a plyboard shack, absent of indoor plumbing or electricity. Viola had never ridden in a car, never been ten miles from where she lived, and had no hope of doing either in her lifetime. She ate cornbread, mustard greens with a little lard, and great northern beans. She had never visited a dentist or a medical doctor, and she never would. Her world was full of poverty, hopelessness, and despair. And danger — her brother was one of the last lynching victims of the Ku Klux Klan.

Viola's shy grandmother affectionately called Viola "Grandbaby." Every summer Grandbaby visited her grandmother, and for six days a week she chopped Old Man Smith's cotton. With expertise and enthusiasm unmatched anywhere in Desha County, Arkansas, young Viola single-handedly massacred whole acres of crabgrass that threatened the young cotton. With her six-foot hoe, she effectively equalized the equation. And she was also one of the fastest pickers. Not as much of a phenomenon with a cotton bag as she was with a cotton hoe, Viola was still quite competent. My Uncle Sammy Smith knew he owed his cotton-growing success to a wiry little chopper from Marianna, Arkansas, who happened to visit her fish-cleaning grandmother every summer.

"Viola. That's V-I-O-L-A," said the woman sitting in front of me. "Do you have any ground meat today?"

I was lost in a remembered cotton field.

This woman in front of me, number 21, was my Old Man Smith's cotton chopper.

For the next 20 minutes Viola, with great reticence, and I shared our stories.

With great hope, Viola, her husband, and two children migrated to Pittsburgh — the Promised Land — in the late fifties. Immediately, her husband found a job in the J&L Steel Mill. Settling in the lower hill, in spite of an inadequate educational system and occasional acts of prejudice, life was better than in Marianne, Arkansas. But since her husband had a low-skill job and in spite of the fact that he belonged to the union, J&L laid off Viola's husband in a late sixties' recession. Later, when the Civic Arena was built, they were forced to move to public housing in the East End Garfield section of Pittsburgh. Then her husband disappeared. The child's father, Viola's new boyfriend, was with her now.

Perhaps the most tragic consequence of slavery was the forcible breakup of slave families by the sale of individual members. Nearly one-sixth of adult Mississippi former slaves studied in 1864–65 had been forcibly separated from a spouse. By the time Viola struggled to survive on the East End of Pittsburgh, nothing much seemed to have changed. (James P. Stobaugh)

Daily Assignment

- Warm-up: If you were directing a movie about Alice, what major actress would you have play Alice? Why did you make this choice?
- Students will complete Concept Builder 13-A.
- Prayer journal: Students are encouraged to write in their prayer journal every day.
- Students need to review their material for the next assignment
- Students should systematically review their vocabulary words daily.

Active Reading

Read chapter 1 of *Alice in Wonderland* ("Down the Rabbit-Hole") by Lewis Carroll, and then answer the following questions.

1. What is the narrative technique? What advantages does this offer Carroll?

2. Who is the protagonist? How is she created?

3. What is the setting? Is it believable?

4. Give two examples of imagery.

   a.

   b.

5. Even though this is a fantasy, can you identify with Alice?

Lesson 2

Sample Essay: Theme

Consider the following essay on one theme in Ernest Hemingway's *A Farewell To Arms*.

A Farewell to Arms has a very naturalistic worldview. Naturalism as a worldview includes a fear of nature, yet nature is powerful — it controls everything. Since nature is not controlled by a loving God, naturalism inherently creates fearful cynicism. The theme, then, of this cynical book is naturalistic. Hemingway argues that one should live for the moment. As Catherine says when asked what her religion is, "Henry is my religion." Later, when confronted with childbirth and perhaps death, Catherine changes her mind and says, "I have no religion." Confusion, contradiction, cynicism, and hopelessness are hallmarks of this book. Hemingway is convinced that there is no transcendent value to life; there is no reason to embrace anything but the pleasure — or pain — of every single moment.

Hemingway has departed considerably from the romantic Ralph Waldo Emerson. Emerson was very positive toward nature. For example, in his poem "Days," Emerson writes, "I in my pleached garden watched the pomp/Forgot my morning hostility" and shows his positive attitude toward nature. His garden helps him overcome his human hostility. Compare this vision to Hemingway's character Henry, leaving the hospital after his friend dies: "After a while I went out and left the hospital and walked back to the hotel in the rain." What a hopeless view of life.

Hemingway needed the joy of the Lord in his heart. John 14:6 says, "I am the way, the truth, and the life." First John 3:1 says, "How great a love the Father has given us." And finally, John 3:16 says, "For God loved the world in this way: He gave His One and Only Son. . . ." If Hemingway's vision had not been clouded by naturalism, perhaps he could have seen all this very clearly. Perhaps he could have seen that there is a purpose to life because God loves us all. (Jessica Stobaugh)

Daily Assignment

- Warm-up: Alice is on a great adventure. What is the best adventure you have had?
- Students will complete Concept Builder 13-B.
- Prayer journal.
- Students should outline all assigned essays for the week.

Elements of a Story

Analyze the following elements of the novel *Alice in Wonderland.*

Elements	Yes/No	Because . . .
Characters Do the characters seem real?		
Narration Is the narration credible (reliable, believable)?		
Setting Is the setting important? Does it seem real?		
Plot Does the story flow logically? Does it flow well?		
Theme Is there a theme?		

Lesson 3

Grammar Review: Keep Related Words Together

Generally speaking, subjects and verbs should not be separated by phrases or clauses that could be placed at the beginning of the sentence.

Julius Caesar, in his final years, abandoned the republic form of government and formed a dictatorship. (Interrupts the flow of reading.)

In his final years, Julius Caesar abandoned the republic form of government and formed a dictatorship. (Is a better sentence.)

Daily Assignment

- Warm-up: If you were directing a movie about Alice, what person in your family would you have play Alice? Why did you make this choice?
- Students will complete a daily Concept Builder 13-C.
- Prayer journal.
- Students should write rough drafts of all assigned essays.

CONCEPT BUILDER 13-C

Characters: Static or Dynamic?

A static character stays the same. A dynamic character changes. Does Alice change? How?

Character	Alice	Queen
Protagonist, antagonist, foil		
Static or dynamic?		
If the character changes, how?		
Why does he/she change?		

Student Essay

A theme is an idea or point that an author shows throughout a book. It can be something the author wants us to learn, or simply a subject. The challenge of facing new people with different ideas is a theme in *Alice in Wonderland.* This can be very difficult, and Alice ends up confused or frustrated a great deal of the time. This is so because Alice, the protagonist, falls into a world where everybody and everything is different from what she knows.

When Alice confronts the March Hare and the Mad Hatter, she is presented with people very unlike herself.

> "Your hair wants cutting," said the Hatter. He had been looking at Alice for some time with great curiosity, and this was his first speech. "You should learn not to make personal remarks," Alice said with some severity: "it's very rude."

The theme is exemplified because the Hare and the Hatter are some of the strange people that Alice meets. The Hatter says something that Alice considers rude and she must decide how to deal with it. This goes on continually in the chapter.

The theme weaves itself into the book later on in the chapter when Alice is once again confronted.

> "Take some more tea," the March Hare said to Alice, very earnestly. "I've had nothing yet," Alice replied in an offended tone: "So I can't take more." "You mean you can't take less," said the Hatter: "It's very easy to take more than nothing." "Nobody asked your opinion," said Alice. "Who's making personal remarks now?" the Hatter asked triumphantly. Alice did not quite know what to say to this: so she helped herself to some tea and bread-and-butter. . . .

Alice's reaction and difficulty understanding the Hatter's ideas about taking more than nothing are another example of the theme of dealing with new people and different ideas. Alice believes that you can't take more when you haven't had anything, but the Hatter believes that you simply can't take less. This idea is confusing to Alice, and she eventually leaves the tea party. Later, when Alice meets the queen she is introduced to a very different form of ideas.

The Queen of Wonderland is a violent and strange character. This mix is very harsh compared with what Alice is accustomed to.

> All the time they were playing, the Queen never left off quarreling with the other players, and shouting "Off with his head!" or "Off with her head!" Those whom she sentenced were taken into custody by the soldiers, who of course had to leave off being arches to do this, so that, by the end of the half hour or so, there were no arches left, and all the players, except the King, the Queen, and Alice, were in custody and under sentence of execution.

Alice is afraid of the queen and her ideas about execution and its importance. The reader sympathizes with Alice and in this example the theme is clearly illustrated. The queen is the person with different ideas — cruel ideas — and Alice finds it a great challenge to be with her.

Alice in Wonderland's theme is about the challenge of dealing with new people and ideas. Alice has a hard time with the people's ideas and personalities, and this theme is strong throughout the entire book. (Ian)

Daily Assignment

- Warm-up: What has been the hardest thing about growing up?
- Students will complete Concept Builder 13-D.
- Prayer journal.
- Review the assigned text. Keep vocabulary cards.
- This is the day that students should write, and then rewrite, the final drafts of their assigned essays.

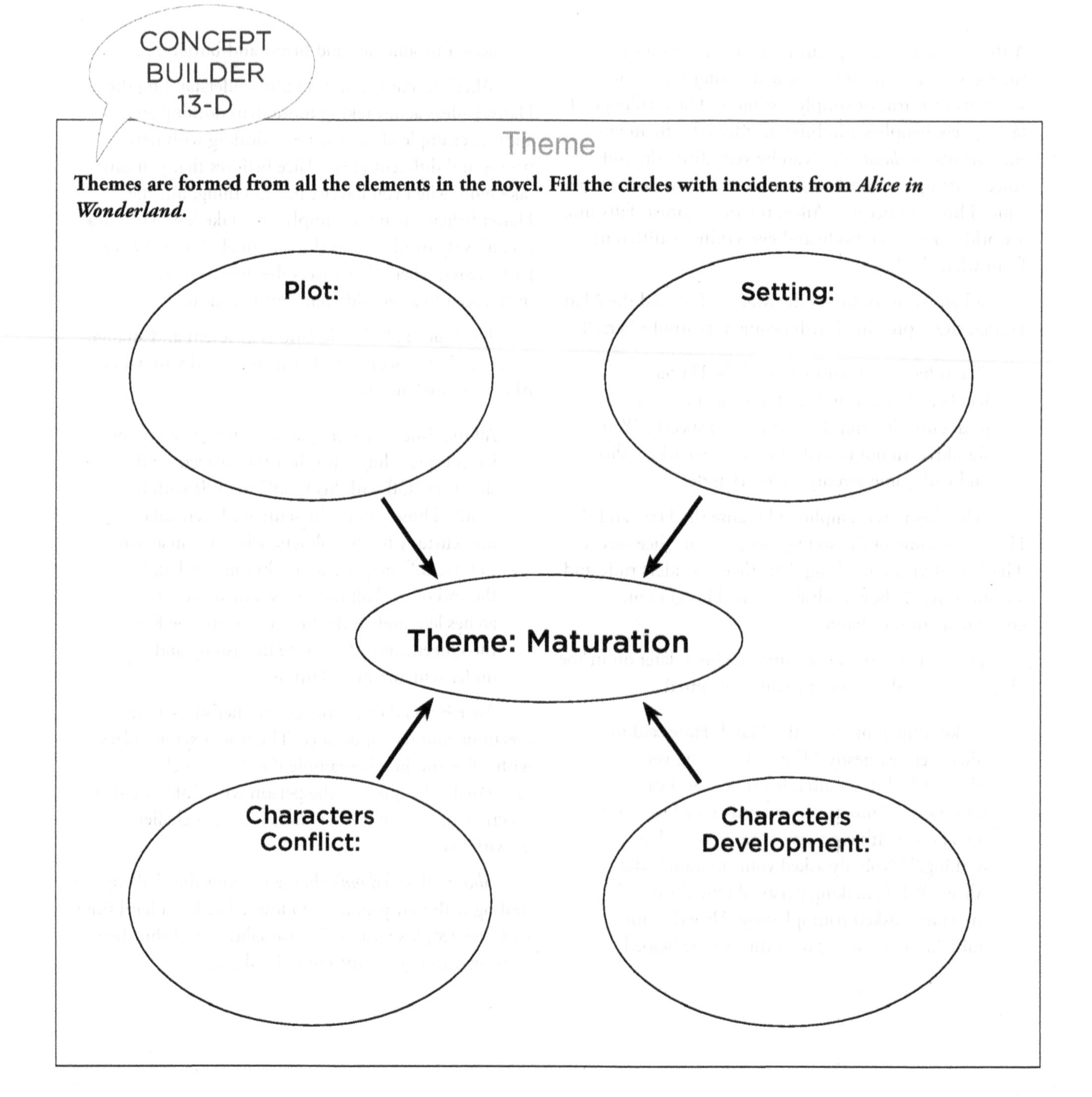

Parody - *Alice in Wonderland* (Lewis Carroll)

Chapter 14

First Thoughts

Amadeus, a movie based on a Broadway play about the famous composer Mozart, takes parody to new heights. A parody pokes fun at society and/or individuals in society. In this case, Mozart constantly pokes fun at Salieri, who is jealous of Mozart's genius and is offended by his coarseness and superficiality. Frustrated by his own mediocrity, Salieri tries to thwart Amadeus's career, but only succeeds in destroying himself. Some parodies are quite sobering. *The Floating Opera* (1956), John Barth's parody of modern life, invites the reader to seriously consider whether life has any meaning at all (Barth advances the worldview called absurdism). Entire books are parodies (e.g., *Don Quixote*, Cervantes, and *Alice in Wonderland*, Lewis Carroll).

Chapter Learning Objectives

In chapter 14 we will analyze the use of parody in *Alice in Wonderland.*

As a result of this chapter study you will be able to . . .

1. Explore what the Bible has to say about morality.
2. Compare George Orwell's *Animal Farm* with *Alice in Wonderland.*

Look Ahead for Friday

- Turn in a final copy of essay
- Take Weekly Test

Lesson 1

Literary Analysis: Parody

A parody is a literary work imitating another in order to make a point. In form and substance, *Alice in Wonderland* pokes fun at Victorian English political writings and social morality. In a previous generation, Jonathan Swift did the same thing in his book called *Gulliver's Travels*. Like *Alice in Wonderland*, on one level *Gulliver's Travels* is a children's story. On another level, *Gulliver's Travels* attacks contemporary politicians. Swift pokes fun at the hypocrisy of English leaders at this time. Eventually, parody utilizes satire. With the desire to ameliorate and to inform, satire uses irony and understatement to ridicule people and institutions.

The White Rabbit, illustration by John Tenniel for *Alice's Adventures in Wonderland/Chapter 1,* 1865 (PD-US).

Daily Assignment

- Warm-up: What actress would you choose to play the Queen of Hearts?
- Students will complete Concept Builder 14-A.
- Prayer journal: Students are encouraged to write in their prayer journal every day.
- Students need to review their material for the next assignment
- Students should systematically review their vocabulary words daily.

Characterization

Characterization is the way an author develops a character in his literary work. Offer evidence from the text to show how Carroll develops Alice as a character.

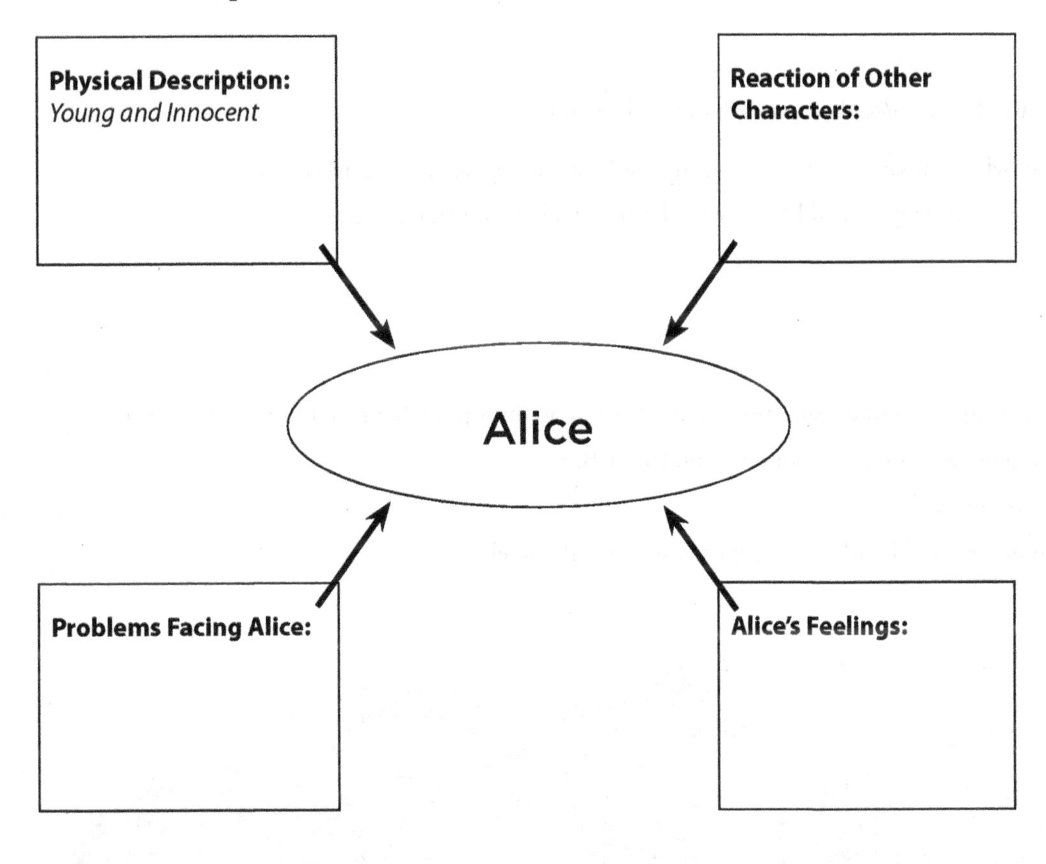

Lesson 2

Grammar Review: Irregardless

There is no word *irregardless.* The writer must use the word *regardless.*

Irregardless of what you say, I intend to serve the Lord with all my heart. (incorrect)

Regardless of what you say, I intend to serve the Lord with all my heart. (correct)

Daily Assignment

- Warm-up: Describe a situation when someone inappropriately made fun of someone else.
- Students will complete Concept Builder 14-B.
- Prayer journal.
- Students should outline all assigned essays for the week.

The Cheshire Cat, illustration by John Tenniel for *Alice's Adventures in Wonderland*/Chapter 6, 1865 (PD-US).

Episodes

This novel is episodic — Carroll takes the reader from episode to episode. As Alice wanders in her imaginary world, she learns new lessons that help her develop as a character. Normally, this development occurs as she experiences internal conflict. **Complete this chart.**

Elements	Internal Conflict	Outcome/Behavioral Change
Alice is bored with sitting on the riverbank with her sister, who is reading a book. Suddenly she sees a white rabbit, wearing a coat and carrying a watch, run past, lamenting running late. She follows it down a rabbit hole and falls very slowly down a tunnel lined with curious objects.	She feels confusion and fear.	Alice begins her long road to maturity.
Alice finds a box under the table in which there is a cake with the words "EAT ME" on it. She eats it and the cake makes Alice grow so tall that her head hits the ceiling. She cries.		
The Cheshire Cat appears in a tree, directing her to the March Hare's house.		

Lesson 3

An Example of Parody

Bill the Lizard

It was the White Rabbit, trotting slowly back again, and looking anxiously about as it went, as if it had lost something; and she heard it muttering to itself "The Duchess! The Duchess! Oh my dear paws! Oh my fur and whiskers! She'll get me executed, as sure as ferrets are ferrets! Where CAN I have dropped them, I wonder?" Alice guessed in a moment that it was looking for the fan and the pair of white kid gloves, and she very good-naturedly began hunting about for them, but they were nowhere to be seen — everything seemed to have changed since her swim in the pool, and the great hall, with the glass table and the little door, had vanished completely.

Very soon the Rabbit noticed Alice, as she went hunting about, and called out to her in an angry tone, "Why, Mary Ann, what ARE you doing out here? Run home this moment, and fetch me a pair of gloves and a fan! Quick, now!" And Alice was so much frightened that she ran off at once in the direction it pointed to, without trying to explain the mistake it had made.

"He took me for his housemaid," she said to herself as she ran. "How surprised he'll be when he finds out who I am! But I'd better take him his fan and gloves — that is, if I can find them." As she said this, she came upon a neat little house, on the door of which was a bright brass plate with the name "W. RABBIT" engraved upon it. She went in without knocking, and hurried upstairs, in great fear lest she should meet the real Mary Ann, and be turned out of the house before she had found the fan and gloves.

"How queer it seems," Alice said to herself, "to be going messages for a rabbit! I suppose Dinah'll be sending me on messages next!" And she began fancying the sort of thing that would happen: "Miss Alice! Come here directly, and get ready for your walk!" "Coming in a minute, nurse! But I've got to see that the mouse doesn't get out." "Only I don't think," Alice went on, "that they'd let Dinah stop in the house if it began ordering people about like that!"

By this time she had found her way into a tidy little room with a table in the window, and on it (as she had hoped) a fan and two or three pairs of tiny white kid gloves: she took up the fan and a pair of the gloves, and was just going to leave the room, when her eye fell upon a little bottle that stood near the looking-glass. There was no label this time with the words "DRINK ME," but nevertheless she uncorked it and put it to her lips. "I know SOMETHING interesting is sure to happen," she said to herself, "whenever I eat or drink anything; so I'll just see what this bottle does. I do hope it'll make me grow large again, for really I'm quite tired of being such a tiny little thing!"

It did so indeed, and much sooner than she had expected: before she had drunk half the bottle, she found her head pressing against the ceiling, and had to stoop to save her neck from being broken. She hastily put down the bottle, saying to herself "That's quite enough — I hope I shan't grow any more — As it is, I can't get out at the door — I do wish I hadn't drunk quite so much!"

Alas! it was too late to wish that! She went on growing, and growing, and very soon had to kneel down on the floor: in another minute there was not even room for this, and she tried the effect of lying down with one elbow against the door, and the other arm curled round her head. Still she went on growing, and, as a last resource, she put one arm out of the window, and one foot up the chimney, and said to herself "Now I can do no more, whatever happens. What WILL become of me?"

Luckily for Alice, the little magic bottle had now had its full effect, and she grew no larger: still it was very uncomfortable, and, as there seemed to be no sort of chance of her ever getting out of the room again, no wonder she felt unhappy.

"It was much pleasanter at home," thought poor Alice, "when one wasn't always growing larger and smaller, and being ordered about by mice and rabbits. I almost wish I hadn't gone down that rabbit-hole — and yet — and yet — It's rather curious, you know, this sort of life! I do wonder what CAN have happened to me! When I used to read fairy-tales, I fancied that kind of thing never happened, and now here I am in the middle of one! There ought to be a book written about me, that there ought! And when I grow up, I'll write one — but I'm grown up now," she added in a sorrowful tone; "at least there's no room to grow up any more HERE."

"But then," thought Alice, "shall I NEVER get any older than I am now? That'll be a comfort, one way — never to be an old woman — but then — always to have lessons to learn! Oh, I shouldn't like THAT!"

"Oh, you foolish Alice!" she answered herself. "How can you learn lessons in here? Why, there's hardly room for YOU, and no room at all for any lesson-books!"

And so she went on, taking first one side and then the other, and making quite a conversation of it altogether; but after a few minutes she heard a voice outside, and stopped to listen.

"Mary Ann! Mary Ann!" said the voice. "Fetch me my gloves this moment!" Then came a little pattering of feet on the stairs. Alice knew it was the Rabbit coming to look for her, and she trembled till she shook the house, quite forgetting that she was now about a thousand times as large as the Rabbit, and had no reason to be afraid of it.

Presently the Rabbit came up to the door, and tried to open it; but, as the door opened inwards, and Alice's elbow was pressed hard against it, that attempt proved a failure. Alice heard it say to itself "Then I'll go round and get in at the window."

"THAT you won't" thought Alice, and, after waiting till she fancied she heard the Rabbit just under the window, she suddenly spread out her hand, and made a snatch in the air. She did not get hold of anything, but she heard a little shriek and a fall, and a crash of broken glass, from which she concluded that it was just possible it had fallen into a cucumber-frame, or something of the sort.

Next came an angry voice — the Rabbit's — "Pat! Pat! Where are you?" And then a voice she had never heard before, "Sure then I'm here! Digging for apples, yer honour!"

"Digging for apples, indeed!" said the Rabbit angrily. "Here! Come and help me out of THIS!" (Sounds of more broken glass.)

"Now tell me, Pat, what's that in the window?"

"Sure, it's an arm, yer honour!" (He pronounced it "arrum.")

"An arm, you goose! Who ever saw one that size? Why, it fills the whole window!"

"Sure, it does, yer honour: but it's an arm for all that."

"Well, it's got no business there, at any rate: go and take it away!"

There was a long silence after this, and Alice could only hear whispers now and then; such as, "Sure, I don't like it, yer honour, at all, at all!" "Do as I tell you, you coward!" and at last she spread out her hand again, and made another snatch in the air. This time there were TWO little shrieks, and more sounds of broken glass. "What a number of cucumber-frames there must be!" thought Alice. "I wonder what they'll do next! As for pulling me out of the window, I only wish they COULD! I'm sure I don't want to stay in here any longer!"

She waited for some time without hearing anything more: at last came a rumbling of little cartwheels, and the sound of a good many voices all talking together: she made out the words: "Where's the other ladder? — Why, I hadn't to bring but one; Bill's got the other — Bill! fetch it here, lad! — Here, put 'em up at this corner — No, tie 'em together first — they don't reach half high enough yet — Oh! they'll do well enough; don't be particular — Here, Bill! catch hold of this rope — Will the roof bear? — Mind that loose slate — Oh, it's coming down! Heads below!" (a loud crash) — "Now, who did that? — It was Bill, I fancy — Who's to go down the chimney? — Nay, I shan't! YOU do it! — That I won't, then! — Bill's to go down — Here, Bill! the master says you're to go down the chimney!"

"Oh! So Bill's got to come down the chimney, has he?" said Alice to herself. "Shy, they seem to put everything upon Bill! I wouldn't be in Bill's place for a good deal: this fireplace is narrow, to be sure; but I THINK I can kick a little!"

She drew her foot as far down the chimney as she could, and waited till she heard a little animal (she couldn't guess of what sort it was) scratching and scrambling about in the chimney close above her: then, saying to herself "This is Bill," she gave one sharp kick, and waited to see what would happen next.

The first thing she heard was a general chorus of "There goes Bill!" then the Rabbit's voice along — "Catch him, you by the hedge!" then silence, and then another confusion of voices — "Hold up his head — Brandy now — Don't choke him — How was it, old fellow? What happened to you? Tell us all about it!"

Last came a little feeble, squeaking voice, ("That's Bill," thought Alice,) "Well, I hardly know — No more, thank ye; I'm better now — but I'm a deal too flustered to tell you — all I know is, something comes at me like a Jack-in-the-box, and up I goes like a sky-rocket!"

"So you did, old fellow!" said the others.

"We must burn the house down!" said the Rabbit's voice; and Alice called out as loud as she could, "If you do. I'll set Dinah at you!"

There was a dead silence instantly, and Alice thought to herself, "I wonder what they WILL do next! If they had any sense, they'd take the roof off." After a minute or two, they began moving about again, and Alice heard the Rabbit say, "A barrowful will do, to begin with."

"A barrowful of WHAT?" thought Alice; but she had not long to doubt, for the next moment a shower of little pebbles came rattling in at the window, and some of them hit her in the face. "I'll put a stop to this," she said to herself, and shouted out, "You'd better not do that again!" which produced another dead silence.

Alice noticed with some surprise that the pebbles were all turning into little cakes as they lay on the floor, and a bright idea came into her head. "If I eat one of these cakes," she thought, "it's sure to make SOME change in my size; and as it can't possibly make me larger, it must make me smaller, I suppose."

So she swallowed one of the cakes, and was delighted to find that she began shrinking directly. As soon as she was small enough to get through the door, she ran out of the house, and found quite a crowd of little animals and birds waiting outside. The poor little Lizard, Bill, was in the middle, being held up by two guinea-pigs, who were giving it something out of a bottle. They all made a rush at Alice the moment she appeared; but she ran off as hard as she could, and soon found herself safe in a thick wood.

"The first thing I've got to do," said Alice to herself, as she wandered about in the wood, "is to grow to my right size again; and the second thing is to find my way into that lovely garden. I think that will be the best plan."

It sounded an excellent plan, no doubt, and very neatly and simply arranged; the only difficulty was, that she had not the smallest idea how to set about it; and while she was peering about anxiously among the trees, a little sharp bark just over her head made her look up in a great hurry.

An enormous puppy was looking down at her with large round eyes, and feebly stretching out one paw, trying to touch her. "Poor little thing!" said Alice, in a coaxing tone, and she tried hard to whistle to it; but she was terribly frightened all the time at the thought that it might be hungry, in which case it would be very likely to eat her up in spite of all her coaxing.

Hardly knowing what she did, she picked up a little bit of stick, and held it out to the puppy; whereupon the puppy jumped into the air off all its feet at once, with a yelp of delight, and rushed at the stick, and made believe to worry it; then Alice dodged behind a great thistle, to keep herself from being run over; and the moment she appeared on the other side, the puppy made another rush at the stick, and tumbled head over heels in its hurry to get hold of it; then Alice, thinking it was very like having a game of play with a cart-horse, and expecting every moment to be trampled under its feet, ran round the thistle again; then the puppy began a series of short charges at the stick, running a very little way forwards each time and a long way back, and barking hoarsely all the while, till at last it sat down a good way off, panting, with its tongue hanging out of its mouth, and its great eyes half shut.

This seemed to Alice a good opportunity for making her escape; so she set off at once, and ran till she was quite tired and out of breath, and till the puppy's bark sounded quite faint in the distance.

"And yet what a dear little puppy it was!" said Alice, as she leant against a buttercup to rest herself, and fanned herself with one of the leaves: "I should have liked teaching it tricks very much, if — if I'd only been the right size to do it! Oh dear! I'd nearly forgotten that I've got to grow up again! Let me see — how IS it to be managed? I suppose I ought to eat or drink something or other; but the great question is, what?"

The great question certainly was, what? Alice looked all round her at the flowers and the blades of grass, but she did not see anything that looked like the right thing to eat or drink under the circumstances. There was a large mushroom growing near her, about the same height as herself; and when she had looked under it, and on both sides of it, and behind it, it occurred to her that she might as well look and see what was on the top of it.

She stretched herself up on tiptoe, and peeped over the edge of the mushroom, and her eyes immediately met those of a large caterpillar, that was sitting on the top with its arms folded, quietly smoking a long hookah, and taking not the smallest notice of her or of anything else.[1]

1 Lewis Carroll, *Alice's Adventures in Wonderland*, chapter 4; www.literaturepage.com/read/aliceinwonderland.html

Daily Assignment

- Warm-up: Contrast the *The Chronicles of Narnia* and *Alice in Wonderland.* How is the fantasy component different?
- Students will complete a daily Concept Builder 14-C.
- Prayer journal.
- Students should write rough drafts of all assigned essays.

Parody

A parody pokes fun at an individual, institution, or society at large. In this case, Carroll is poking fun at Victorian England.

Complete the following chart.

Incident/Elements	Textual Evidence
Bill the Lizard may be a play on the name of Benjamin Disraeli.	This occurs when Alice is stuck in one of the rooms of the White Rabbit's house.
Victorian children were expected to behave at all times. As Marjorie and C.H.B. Quennell point out in their book A History of Everyday Things in England, "In practice this meant that instant obedience to every order, respectful manners and punctuality were expected as a matter of course from every member of the family. Argument and 'answering back' were never permitted, and indeed, they were seldom attempted" (103). Many of the rules put before Victorian children must have seemed somewhat arbitrary.	
The Queen of Hearts is presumptuous and dangerous and represents Queen Victoria.	
Parodies of Victorian songs/poems.	
The Lobster Quadrille that Alice encounters is a parody of the quadrille, a dance that was used to open nearly every fashionable ball at the time that Alice's adventures was written and published.	

Student Essay

Although Lewis Carroll's *Alice in Wonderland* is a child's fantasy, it is also a clever parody of Victorian England's way of life. Lewis focuses on Victorian schooling, morals, and royalty with quick wit and audacity.

All throughout the book, Alice is always reciting long, boring poems to strict animals that resemble Victorian school teachers. This is a direct mockery of the way Victorian schooling was done. Students were taught the three R's, reading, wRiting, and aRithmetic, ("Reeling, Writhing . . . the different branches of Arithmetic — Ambition, Distraction, Uglification, and Derision") through repetition. Carroll emphasizes the dry nature of such schooling. When a wet Alice and various creatures are trying to figure out the best and quickest method to get dry, one authoritative and strict mouse begins telling a long history lesson as it was "the driest thing she knew." In other scenes, Alice is seen reciting *How Doth the Little Crocodile*, a popular school poem, many times. These kinds of poems often times emphasized some kind of moral the student was suppose to observe less some drastic evil befell them. "She had read several nice little histories about children who had got burnt, and eaten up by wild beasts and other unpleasant things, all because they would not remember the simple rules their friends had taught them . . . such as, that a read-hot poker will burn you if you hold it too long."

Morals were a huge component of Victorian life. Under Queen Victoria, the image of strong morality, and the strong Anglican Church, there was a moral for everything. From the tea table to courting, there was a code of conduct for every action imaginable. In Alice in Wonderland, Carroll mocked these morals and personified them in the Duchess. "You're thinking about something, my dear, and that makes you forget to talk. I can't tell you just now what the moral of that is, but I shall remember it in a bit." After every remark that Alice makes, the Duchess quickly tags a moral onto it, for she firmly believed that "everything's got a moral, if only you can find it." These morals are always shown as complicated and nonsensical, "and the moral of that is "Be what you would seem to be" — or if you'd like it put more simply — "Never imagine yourself not to be otherwise than what it might appear to others that what you were or might have been was not otherwise than what you had been would have appeared to them to be otherwise."

Victorians were obliged to obey these rigid moral standards that ruled society, and failure to do so removed one from genteel society. Furthermore, Victorian society had a low tolerance of crime, and suspects of crimes were quickly cut down. Carroll audaciously mocks the Victorian justice system and even Queen Victoria, herself, who is caricatured as the Queen of Hearts who is shown as short-tempered, critical, and cruel. "The Queen had only one way of settling all difficulties, great or small. 'Off with his head!' she said." The Queen of Hearts ordered extreme punishments for every mistake and wrongdoing; if someone missed their turn in a game, they were beheaded; if the Queen simply became annoyed, the unfortunate victim was beheaded. When discussing with the king and executioner the best method of executing the Cheshire cat, who at the time was a floating head, Carroll writes, "The Queen's argument was, that if something wasn't done about it in less than no time she'd have everybody executed, all round." England's judicial system is further mocked in chapter 11, "Who Stole the Tarts?" The King of Hearts served as the judge in a trial of a condemned knave and showed the same sense of judgment as his wife, " 'Give your evidence,' said the King; 'and don't be nervous, or I'll have you executed on the spot.' " The jurors were shown as stupid people who could hardly remember their names, much less follow the trial. " 'Write that down,' the King said to the jury, and the jury eagerly wrote down all three dates on their slates, and then added them up, and reduced the answer to shillings and pence." As a finishing touch to the parody of the English justice system, Carroll gibes this system with this: " 'No, no!' said the Queen. "'Sentence first — verdict afterwards.'"

Using the backdrop of a child's fantasy story, Lewis Carroll created a sharp, pointed parody of Victorian life, behind the veil of humor and wit in *Alice in Wonderland*. (Daphnide)

Daily Assignment

- Warm-up: Did you like *Alice In Wonderland*? Why or why not?
- Students will complete Concept Builder 14-D.
- Prayer journal.
- Review the assigned text. Keep vocabulary cards.
- This is the day that students should write, and then rewrite, the final drafts of their assigned essays.

CONCEPT BUILDER 14-D

Setting

The setting is very important to this novel. Fill in the empty circles with supporting details from the text.

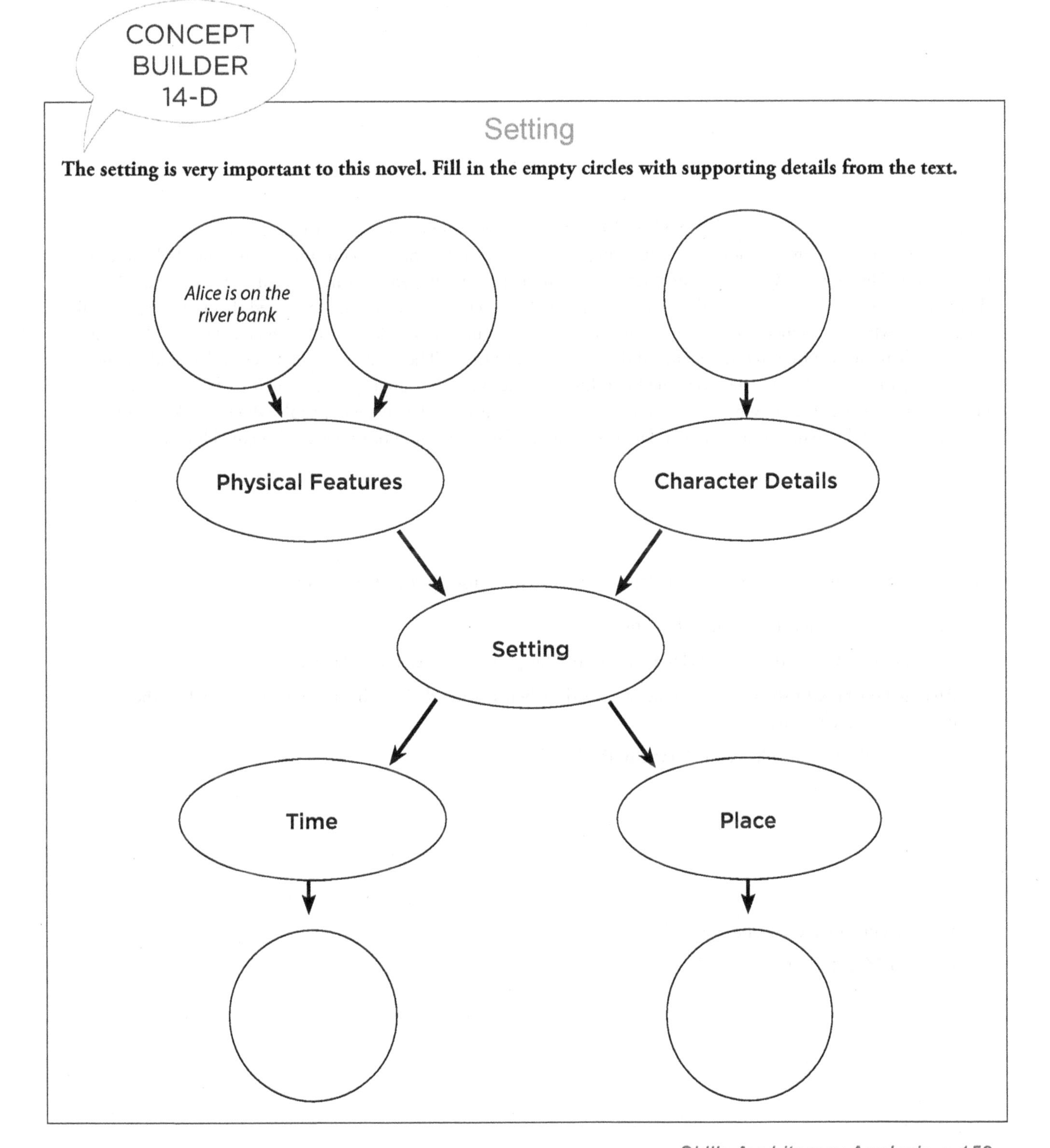

Dialogue — "Oracle of the Dog" (G.K. Chesterton)

Chapter 15

First Thoughts

If C.S. Lewis were the greatest apologist of the 20th century, G.K. Chesterton was perhaps the greatest of the 19th century. He was also a great fiction writer, an example of a sonorous marriage of consummate writing skill and pious Christianity. The task that Chesterton undertook — to influence and hopefully convert secular culture through skillful art — is one that belongs to this generation more than ever. Chesterton once lamented that Christians are like Englishmen who visit France. These Englishmen, Chesterton argued, spoke slowly and with elucidation. They were shocked when they realized that the French did not understand them. The French would never understand English — no matter how slowly and effectively the Englishmen spoke. The only language the French understood was French. Likewise, Christians, Chesterton continued, spoke in Christian language to people who didn't know the language. Until Christians speak in secular language, the secular world will not understand them. Think about it.

Chapter Learning Objectives

In chapter 15 we will analyze the use of dialogue in G.K. Chesterton's "The Oracle of the Dog."

As a result of this chapter study you will be able to . . .

1. Ascertain how Chesterton uses dialogue to advance his plot and develop his characters.
2. Analyze how far Christians can go to be "accepted," when sharing their faith with unbelievers, before they compromise their witness
3. Find examples of coincidence in "Oracle of the Dog."

Look Ahead for Friday

- Turn in a final copy of essay
- Take Weekly Test

Lesson 1

Literary Analysis: Dialogue

Dialogue is used by a writer to advance the plot and to develop characters. Examine the following dialogue and reflect on how it accomplishes the above two goals.

Dialogue:

Mom's malady, however, was already fatal. Her stamina and obstinacy propelled her forward for almost a year, but the carcinoma had already ambushed her. No one could tell, though, because she was in such great health. "My health," my mother ironically said with a shrug, "killed me."

By the time our family surgeon and good friend Dr. Johnny Joe Jones, one of Dr. Donahue's cardinals, called the Hogs with mom one last time before she went into the operating room and opened her up with his scalpel, mom was mellifluent with metastatic carcinoma.

Dr. Johnny Joe was the best surgeon in Arkansas. There was one — Dr. Robert P. Howell — who was as good, but it was rumored that he was a Unitarian. Besides, he enjoyed Jack Daniels too much. That was okay if one sought his services on a Wednesday. He was sober on Wednesdays out of respect for his Assembly of God mother who always went to church on Wednesdays. And it was Thursday.

Trained in Houston, Texas — the medical school mecca of the South — everyone wanted a doctor trained in Houston — he must be good if he was from Houston — Dr. Johnny Joe was a brilliant, skilled surgeon. He had assisted in the first heart transplant attempt (the patient died) in Arkansas. He was also a Presbyterian. Everyone knew that the best doctors were Presbyterians who went to medical schools in Houston. In spite of one nasty habit — Dr. Johnny Joe chewed Red Chief Tobacco during surgery — he was much sought after. "Wipe my mouth, nurse," Dr. Johnny Joe said.

Dr. Jones loved the Razorbacks. When he had to miss the game he nonetheless kept the radio blaring in the operating room. Once, while removing Mrs. Nickle's appendix, Texas intercepted a pass and ran back for a touchdown. Reacting to this tragedy, Dr. Jones' scalpel cut out Mrs. Nickle's appendix and spleen. No one blamed him.

Daily Assignment

- Warm-up: Try to persuade your parents to allow you to attend a church party that ends beyond your curfew.
- Students will complete Concept Builder 15-A.
- Prayer journal: Students are encouraged to write in their prayer journal every day.
- Students need to review their material for the next assignment
- Students should systematically review their vocabulary words daily.

Dialogue

Dialogue is used by a writer to advance the plot and to develop characters. Read this excerpt from *The Red Badge of Courage* (chapter 1) by Steven Crane, and then answer the following questions.

The cold passed reluctantly from the earth, and the retiring fogs revealed an army stretched out on the hills, resting. As the landscape changed from brown to green, the army awakened, and began to tremble with eagerness at the noise of rumors. It cast its eyes upon the roads, which were growing from long troughs of liquid mud to proper thoroughfares. A river, amber-tinted in the shadow of its banks, purled at the army's feet; and at night, when the stream had become of a sorrowful blackness, one could see across it the red, eyelike gleam of hostile camp-fires set in the low brows of distant hills.

Once a certain tall soldier developed virtues and went resolutely to wash a shirt. He came flying back from a brook waving his garment bannerlike. He was swelled with a tale he had heard from a reliable friend, who had heard it from a truthful cavalryman, who had heard it from his trustworthy brother, one of the orderlies at division headquarters. He adopted the important air of a herald in red and gold.

"We're goin' t' move t'morrah — sure," he said pompously to a group in the company street. "We're goin' 'way up the river, cut across, an' come around in behint 'em."

To his attentive audience he drew a loud and elaborate plan of a very brilliant campaign. When he had finished, the blue-clothed men scattered into small arguing groups between the rows of squat brown huts.

A negro teamster who had been dancing upon a cracker box with the hilarious encouragement of two score soldiers was deserted. He sat mournfully down. Smoke drifted lazily from a multitude of quaint chimneys.

"It's a lie! that's all it is — a thunderin' lie!" said another private loudly. His smooth face was flushed, and his hands were thrust sulkily into his trouser's pockets. He took the matter as an affront to him. "I don't believe the derned old army's ever going to move. We're set. I've got ready to move eight times in the last two weeks, and we ain't moved yet."

The tall soldier felt called upon to defend the truth of a rumor he himself had introduced. He and the loud one came near to fighting over it.

A corporal began to swear before the assemblage. He had just put a costly board floor in his house, he said. During the early spring he had refrained from adding extensively to the comfort of his environment because he had felt that the army might start on the march at any moment. Of late, however, he had been impressed that they were in a sort of eternal camp.

Many of the men engaged in a spirited debate. One outlined in a peculiarly lucid manner all the plans of the commanding general. He was opposed by men who advocated that there were other plans of campaign. They clamored at each other, numbers making futile bids for the popular attention. Meanwhile, the soldier who had fetched the rumor bustled about with much importance. He was continually assailed by questions.

"What's up, Jim?" "Th'army's goin' t' move."

"Ah, what yeh talkin' about? How yeh know it is?"

"Well, yeh kin b'lieve me er not, jest as yeh like. I don't care a hang."

1. How does the dialogue advance the plot?

2. What is the narrative point of view? Why does Crane choose this approach?

Lesson 2

"The Oracle of the Dog"

"Yes," said Father Brown, "I always like a dog, so long as he isn't spelt backwards." Those who are quick in talking are not always quick in listening. Sometimes even their brilliancy produces a sort of stupidity. Father Brown's friend and companion was a young man with a stream of ideas and stories, an enthusiastic young man named Fiennes, with eager blue eyes and blond hair that seemed to be brushed back, not merely with a hair-brush but with the wind of the world as he rushed through it. But he stopped in the torrent of his talk in a momentary bewilderment before he saw the priest's very simple meaning.

"You mean that people make too much of them?" he said. "Well, I don't know. They're marvelous creatures. Sometimes I think they know a lot more than we do."

Father Brown said nothing but continued to stroke the head of the big retriever in a half-abstracted but apparently soothing fashion.

"Why," said Fiennes, warming again to his monologue, "there was a dog in the case I've come to see you about; what they call the 'Invisible Murder Case,' you know. It's a strange story, but from my point of view the dog is about the strangest thing in it. Of course, there's the mystery of the crime itself, and how old Druce can have been killed by somebody else when he was all alone in the summer-house —"

The hand stroking of the dog stopped for a moment in its rhythmic movement; and Father Brown said calmly, "Oh, it was a summer-house, was it? "

"I thought you'd read all about it in the papers," answered Fiennes. "Stop a minute; I believe I've got a cutting that will give you all the particulars." He produced a strip of newspaper from his pocket and handed it to the priest, who began to read it, holding it close to his blinking eyes with one hand while the other continued its half-conscious caresses of the dog. It looked like the parable of a man not letting his right hand know what his left hand did.

"Many mystery stories, about men murdered behind locked doors and windows, and murderers escaping without means of entrance and exit, have come true in the course of the extraordinary events at Cranston on the coast of Yorkshire, where Colonel Druce was found stabbed from behind by a dagger that has entirely disappeared from the scene, and apparently even from the neighborhood.

"The summer-house in which he died was indeed accessible at one entrance, the ordinary doorway which looked down the central walk of the garden towards the house. But by a combination of events almost to be called a coincidence, it appears that both the path and the entrance were watched during the crucial time, and there is a chain of witnesses who confirm each other. The summer-house stands at the extreme end of the garden, where there is no exit or entrance of any kind. The central garden path is a lane between two ranks of tall delphiniums, planted so close that any stray step off the path would leave its traces; and both path and plants run right up to the very mouth of the summer-house, so that no straying from that straight path could fail to be observed, and no other mode of entrance can be imagined.

"Patrick Floyd, secretary of the murdered man, testified that he had been in a position to overlook the whole garden from the time when Colonel Druce last appeared alive in the doorway to the time when he was found dead; as he, Floyd, had been on the top of a step-ladder clipping the garden hedge. Janet Druce, the dead man's daughter, confirmed this, saying that she had sat on the terrace of the house throughout that time and had seen Floyd at his work. Touching some part of the time, this is again supported by Donald Druce, her brother, who overlooked the garden standing at his bedroom window in his dressing-gown, for he had risen late. Lastly the account is consistent with that given by Dr. Valentine, a neighbor, who called for a time to talk with Miss Druce on the terrace, and by the Colonel's solicitor, Mr. Aubrey Traill, who was apparently the last to see the murdered man alive — presumably with the exception of the murderer.

"All are agreed that the course of events was as follows: about half-past three in the afternoon, Miss Druce went down the path to ask her father when he would like tea; but he said he did not want any and was waiting to see Traill, his lawyer, who was to be sent to him in the summer-house. The girl then came away and met Traill coming down the path; she directed to her father and he went in as directed. About half an hour afterwards he came out again, the Colonel coming with him to the door and showing himself to all appearance in health and even high spirits. He had been somewhat annoyed earlier in the day by his son's irregular hours, but seemed to recover his temper in a perfectly normal fashion, and had been rather markedly genial in receiving other visitors, including two of his nephews who came over for the day. But as these were out walking during the whole period of the tragedy, they had no evidence to give. It is said, indeed, that the Colonel was not on very good terms with Dr. Valentine, but that gentleman only had a brief interview with the daughter of the house, to whom he was supposed to be paying serious attentions.

"Traill, the solicitor, says he left the Colonel entirely alone in the summer-house, and this is confirmed by Floyd's bird's-eye view of the garden, which showed nobody else passing the only entrance. Ten minutes later Miss Druce again went down the garden and had not reached the end of the path, when she saw her father, who was conspicuous by his white linen coat, lying in a heap on the floor. She uttered a scream which brought others to the spot, and on entering the place they found the Colonel lying dead beside his basket-chair, which was also upset. Dr. Valentine, who was still in the immediate neighborhood, testified that the wound was made by some sort of stiletto, entering under the shoulder-blade and piercing the heart. The police have searched the neighborhood for such a weapon, but no trace of it can be found."

"So Colonel Druce wore a white coat, did he?" said Father Brown as he put down the paper.

"Trick he learnt in the tropics," replied Fiennes with some wonder. "He'd had some queer adventures there, by his own account; and I fancy his dislike of Valentine was connected with the doctor coming from the tropics, too. But it's all an infernal puzzle. The account there is pretty accurate; I didn't see the tragedy, in the sense of the discovery; I was out walking with the young nephews and the dog — the dog I wanted to tell you about. But I saw the stage set for it as described: the straight lane between the blue flowers right up to the dark entrance, and the lawyer going down it in his blacks and his silk hat, and the red head of the secretary showing high above the green hedge as he worked on it with his shears. Nobody could have mistaken that red head at any distance; and if people say they saw it there all the time, you may be sure they did. This red-haired secretary Floyd is quite a character; a breathless, bounding sort of fellow, always doing everybody's work as he was doing the gardener's. I think he is an American; he's certainly got the American view of life; what they call the viewpoint, bless 'em."

"What about the lawyer?" asked Father Brown.

There was a silence and then Fiennes spoke quite slowly for him. "Traill struck me as a singular man. In his fine black clothes he was almost foppish, yet you can hardly call him fashionable. For he wore a pair of long, luxuriant black whiskers such as haven't been seen since Victorian times. He had rather a fine grave face and a fine grave manner, but every now and then he seemed to remember to smile. And when he showed his white teeth he seemed to lose a little of his dignity and there was something faintly fawning about him. It may have been only embarrassment, for he would also fidget with his cravat and his tie-pin, which were at once handsome and unusual, like himself. If I could think of anybody—but what's the good, when the whole thing's impossible? Nobody knows who did it. Nobody knows how it could be done. At least there's only one exception I'd make, and that's why I really mentioned the whole thing. The dog knows."

Father Brown sighed and then said absently: "You were there as a friend of young Donald, weren't you? He didn't go on your walk with you?"

"No," replied Fiennes smiling. "The young scoundrel had gone to bed that morning and got up that afternoon. I went with his cousins, two young officers from India, and our conversation was trivial enough. I remember the elder, whose name I think is Herbert Druce and who is an authority on horse-breeding, talked about nothing but a mare he had bought and the moral character of the man who sold her — while his brother Harry seemed to be brooding on his bad luck at Monte Carlo. I only mention it to show you, in the light of what happened on our walk, that there was nothing psychic about us. The dog was the only mystic in our company."

"What sort of a dog was he?" asked the priest.

"Same breed as that one," answered Fiennes. "That's what started me off on the story, your saying you didn't believe in believing in a dog. He's a big black retriever named Nox, and a suggestive name too; for I think what he did a darker mystery than the murder. You know Druce's house and garden are by the sea; we walked about a mile from it along the sands and then turned back, going the other way. We passed a rather curious rock called the Rock of Fortune, famous in the neighborhood because it's one of those examples of one stone barely balanced on another, so that a touch would knock it over. It is not really very high, but the hanging outline of it makes it look a little wild and sinister; at least it made it look so to me, for I don't imagine my jolly young companions were afflicted with the picturesque. But it may be that I was beginning to feel an atmosphere; for just then the question arose of whether it was time to go back to tea, and even then I think I had a premonition that time counted for a good deal in the business. Neither Herbert Druce nor I had a watch, so we called out to his brother, who was some paces behind, having stopped to light his pipe under the hedge. Hence it happened that he shouted out the hour, which was twenty past four, in his big voice through the growing twilight; and somehow the loudness of it made it sound like the proclamation of something tremendous. His unconsciousness seemed to make it all the more so; but that was always the way with omens; and particular ticks of the clock were really very ominous things that afternoon. According to Dr. Valentine's testimony, poor Druce had actually died just about half-past four.

"Well, they said we needn't go home for ten minutes, and we walked a little farther along the sands, doing nothing in particular — throwing stones for the dog and throwing sticks into the sea for him to swim after. But to me the twilight seemed to grow oddly oppressive and the very shadow of the top-heavy Rock of Fortune lay on me like a load. And then the curious thing happened. Nox had just brought back Herbert's walking-stick out of the sea and his brother had thrown his in also. The dog swam out again, but just about what must have been the stroke of the half-hour, he stopped swimming. He came back again on to the shore and stood in front of us. Then he suddenly threw up his head and sent up a howl or wail of woe, if ever I heard one in the world.

"'What the devil's the matter with the dog?' asked Herbert; but none of us could answer. There was a long silence after the brute's wailing and whining died away on the desolate shore; and then the silence was broken. As I live, it was broken by a faint and far-off shriek, like the shriek of a woman from beyond the hedges inland. We didn't know what it was then; but we knew afterwards. It was the cry the girl gave when she first saw the body of her father."

"You went back, I suppose," said Father Brown patiently. "What happened then?"

"I'll tell you what happened then," said Fiennes with a grim emphasis. "When we got back into that garden the first thing we saw was Traill the lawyer; I can see him now with his black hat and black whiskers relieved against the perspective of the blue flowers stretching down to the summer-house, with the sunset and the strange outline of the Rock of Fortune in the distance. His face and figure were in shadow against the sunset; but I swear the white teeth were showing in his head and he was smiling.

"The moment Nox saw that man, the dog dashed forward and stood in the middle of the path barking at him madly, murderously, volleying out curses that were almost verbal in their dreadful distinctness of hatred. And the man doubled up and fled along the path between the flowers."

Father Brown sprang to his feet with a startling impatience. "So the dog denounced him, did he?" he cried. "The oracle of the dog condemned him. Did you see what birds were flying, and are you sure whether they were on the right hand or the left? Did you consult the augurs about the sacrifices? Surely you didn't omit to cut open the dog and examine his entrails. That is the sort of scientific test you heathen humanitarians seem to trust when you are thinking of taking away the life and honor of a man."

Fiennes sat gaping for an instant before he found breath to say, "Why, what's the matter with you? What have I done now?"

A sort of anxiety came back into the priest's eyes — the anxiety of a man who has run against a post in the dark and wonders for a moment whether he has hurt it.

"I'm most awfully sorry," he said with sincere distress. "I beg your pardon for being so rude; pray forgive me."

Fiennes looked at him curiously. "I sometimes think you are more of a mystery than any of the mysteries," he said. "But anyhow, if you don't believe in the mystery of the dog, at least you can't get over the mystery of the man. You can't deny that at the very moment when the beast came back from the sea and bellowed, his master's soul was driven out of his body by the blow of some unseen power that no mortal man can trace or even imagine. And as for the lawyer, I don't go only by the dog; there are other curious details too. He struck me as a smooth, smiling, equivocal sort of person; and one of his tricks seemed like a sort of hint. You know the doctor and the police were on the spot very quickly; Valentine was brought back when walking away from the house, and he telephoned instantly. That, with the secluded house, small numbers, and enclosed space, made it pretty possible to search everybody who could have been near; and everybody was thoroughly searched — for a weapon. The whole house, garden, and shore were combed for a weapon. The disappearance of the dagger is almost as crazy as the disappearance of the man."

"The disappearance of the dagger," said Father Brown, nodding. He seemed to have become suddenly attentive.

"Well," continued Fiennes, "I told you that man Traill had a trick of fidgeting with his tie and tie-pin — especially his tie-pin. His pin, like himself, was at once showy and old-fashioned. It had one of those stones with concentric colored rings that look like an eye; and his own concentration on it got on my nerves, as if he had been a Cyclops with one eye in the middle of his body. But the pin was not only large but long; and it occurred to me that his anxiety about its adjustment was because it was even longer than it looked; as long as a stiletto in fact."

Father Brown nodded thoughtfully. "Was any other instrument ever suggested?" he asked.

"There was another suggestion," answered Fiennes, "from one of the young Druces — the cousins, I mean. Neither Herbert nor Harry Druce would have struck one at first as likely to be of assistance in scientific detection; but while Herbert was really the traditional type of heavy Dragoon, caring for nothing but horses and being an ornament to the Horse Guards, his younger brother Harry had been in the Indian Police and knew something about such things. Indeed in his own way he was quite clever; and I rather fancy he had been too clever; I mean he had left the police through breaking some red-tape regulations and taking some sort of risk and responsibility of his own. Anyhow, he was in some sense a detective out of work, and threw himself into this business with more than the ardor of an amateur. And it was with him that I had an argument about the weapon — an argument that led to something new. It began by his countering my description of the dog barking at Traill; and he said that a dog at his worst didn't bark, but growled."

"He was quite right there," observed the priest.

"This young fellow went on to say that, if it came to that, he'd heard Nox growling at other people before then; and among others at Floyd the secretary. I retorted that his own argument answered itself; for the crime couldn't be brought home to two or three people, and least of all to Floyd, who was as innocent as a harum-scarum schoolboy, and had been seen by everybody all the time perched above the garden hedge with his fan of red hair as conspicuous as a scarlet cuckatoo. 'I know there's difficulties anyhow,' said my colleague, 'but I wish you'd come with me down the garden a minute. I want to show you something I don't think anyone else has seen.' This was on the very day of the discovery, and the garden was just as it had been: the step-ladder was still standing by the hedge, and just under the hedge my guide stooped and disentangled something from the deep grass. It was the shears used for clipping the hedge, and on the point of one of them was a smear of blood."

There was a short silence, and then Father Brown said suddenly, "What was the lawyer there for?"

"He told us the Colonel sent for him to alter his will," answered Fiennes. "And, by the way, there was another thing about the business of the will that I ought to mention. You see, the will wasn't actually signed in the summer-house that afternoon."

"I suppose not," said Father Brown; "there would have to be two witnesses."

"The lawyer actually came down the day before and it was signed then; but he was sent for again next day because the old man had a doubt about one of the witnesses and had to be reassured."

"Who were the witnesses?" asked Father Brown.

"That's just the point," replied his informant eagerly, "the witnesses were Floyd the secretary and this Dr. Valentine, the foreign sort of surgeon or whatever he is; and the two have a quarrel. Now I'm bound to say that the secretary is something of a busybody. He's one of those hot and headlong people whose warmth of temperament has unfortunately turned mostly to pugnacity and bristling suspicion; to distrusting people instead of to trusting them. That sort of red-haired red-hot fellow is always either universally credulous or universally incredulous; and sometimes both. He was not only a Jack of all trades, but he knew better than all tradesmen. He not only knew everything, but he warned everybody against everybody. All that must be taken into account in his suspicions about Valentine; but in that particular case there seems to have been something behind it. He said the name of Valentine was not really Valentine. He said he had seen him elsewhere known by the name of De Villon. He said it would invalidate the will; of course he was kind enough to explain to the lawyer what the law was on that point. They were both in a frightful wax."

Father Brown laughed. "People often are when they are to witness a will," he said, "for one thing, it means that they can't have any legacy under it. But what did Dr. Valentine say? No doubt the universal secretary knew more about the doctor's name than the doctor did. But even the doctor might have some information about his own name."

Fiennes paused a moment before he replied.

"Dr. Valentine took it in a curious way. Dr. Valentine is a curious man. His appearance is rather striking but very foreign. He is young but wears a beard cut square; and his face is very pale, dreadfully pale and dreadfully serious. His eyes have a sort of ache in them, as if he ought to wear glasses or had given himself a headache with thinking; but he is quite handsome and always very formally dressed, with a top hat and a dark coat and a little red rosette. His manner is rather cold and haughty, and he has a way of staring at you which is very disconcerting. When thus charged with having changed his name, he merely stared like a sphinx and then said with a little laugh that he supposed Americans had no names to change. At that I think the Colonel also got into a fuss and said all sorts of angry things to the doctor; all the more angry because of the doctor's pretensions to a future place in his family. But I shouldn't have thought much of that but for a few words that I happened to hear later, early in the afternoon of the tragedy. I don't want to make a lot of them, for they weren't the sort of words on which one, would like, in the ordinary way, to play the eavesdropper. As I was passing out towards the front gate with my two companions and the dog, I heard voices which told me that Dr. Valentine and Miss Druce had withdrawn for a moment into the shadow of the house, in an angle behind a row of flowering plants, and were talking to each other in passionate whisperings — sometimes almost like hissings; for it was something of a lovers' quarrel as well as a lovers' tryst. Nobody repeats the sort of things they said for the most part; but in an unfortunate business like this I'm bound to say that there was repeated more than once a phrase about killing somebody. In fact, the girl seemed to be begging him not to kill somebody, or saying that no provocation could justify killing anybody; which seems an unusual sort of talk to address to a gentleman who has dropped in to tea."

"Do you know," asked the priest, "whether Dr. Valentine seemed to be very angry after the scene with the secretary and the Colonel — I mean about witnessing the will?"

"By all accounts," replied the other, "he wasn't half so angry as the secretary was. It was the secretary who went away raging after witnessing the will."

"And now," said Father Brown, "what about the will itself?"

"The Colonel was a very wealthy man, and his will was important. Traill wouldn't tell us the alteration at that stage, but I have since heard, only this morning in fact, that most of the money was transferred from the son to the daughter. I told you that Druce was wild with my friend Donald over his dissipated hours."

"The question of motive has been rather overshadowed by the question of method," observed Father Brown thoughtfully. "At that moment, apparently, Miss Druce was the immediate gainer by the death."

...What a cold-blooded way of talking," cried Fiennes, staring at him. "You don't really mean to hint that she —"

"Is she going to marry that Dr. Valentine?" asked the other.

"Some people are against it," answered his friend. "But he is liked and respected in the place and is a skilled and devoted surgeon."

"So devoted a surgeon," said Father Brown, "that he had surgical instruments with him when he went to call on the young lady at tea-time. For he must have used a lancet or something, and he never seems to have gone home."

Fiennes sprang to his feet and looked at him in a heat of inquiry. "You suggest he might have used the very same lancet —"

Father Brown shook his head. "All these suggestions are fancies just now," he said. "The problem is not who did it or what did it, but how it was done. We might find many men and even many tools — pins and shears and lancets. But how did a man get into the room? How did even a pin get into it?"

He was staring reflectively at the ceiling as he, spoke, but as he said the last words his eye cocked in an alert fashion as if he had suddenly seen a curious fly on the ceiling.

"Well, what would you do about it?" asked the young man. "You have a lot of experience, what would you advise now?"

"I'm afraid I'm not much use," said Father Brown with a sigh. "I can't suggest very much without having ever been near the place or the people. For the moment you can only go on with local inquiries. I gather that your friend from the Indian Police is more or less in charge of your inquiry down there. I should run down and see how he is getting on. See what he's been doing in the way of amateur detection. There may be news already."

As his guests, the biped and the quadruped, disappeared, Father Brown took up his pen and went back to his interrupted occupation of planning a course of lectures on the Encyclical Rerum Novarum. The subject was a large one and he had to recast it more than once, so that he was somewhat similarly employed some two days later when the big black dog again came bounding into the room and sprawled all over him with enthusiasm and excitement. The master who followed the dog shared the excitement if not the enthusiasm. He had been excited in a less pleasant fashion, for his blue eyes seemed to start from his head and his eager face was even a little pale.

"You told me," he said abruptly and without preface, "to find out what Harry Druce was doing. Do you know what he's done?"

The priest did not reply, and the young man went on in jerky tones:

"I'll tell you what he's done. He's killed himself."

Father Brown's lips moved only faintly, and there was nothing practical about what he was saying — nothing that had anything to do with this story or this world.

"You give me the creeps sometimes," said Fiennes. "Did you — did you expect this?"

"I thought it possible," said Father Brown; "that was why I asked you to go and see what he was doing. I hoped you might not be too late."

"It was I who found him," said Fiennes rather huskily. "It was the ugliest and most uncanny thing I ever knew. I went down that old garden again and I knew there was something new and unnatural about it besides the murder. The flowers still tossed about in blue masses on each side of the black entrance into the old gray summer-house; but to me the blue flowers looked like blue devils dancing before some dark cavern of the underworld. I looked all around; everything seemed to be in its ordinary place. But the queer notion grew on me that there was something wrong with the very shape of the sky. And then I saw what it was. The Rock of Fortune always rose in the background beyond the garden hedge and against the sea. And the Rock of Fortune was gone."

Father Brown had lifted his head and was listening intently.

"It was as if a mountain had walked away out of a landscape or a moon fallen from the sky; though I knew, of course, that a touch at any time would have tipped the thing over. Something possessed me and I rushed down that garden path like the wind and went crashing through that hedge as if it were a spider's web. It was a thin hedge really, though its undisturbed trimness had made it serve all the purposes of a wall. On the shore I found the loose rock fallen from its pedestal; and poor Harry Druce lay like a wreck underneath it. One arm was thrown round it in a sort of embrace as if he had pulled it down on himself; and on the broad brown sands beside it, in large crazy lettering, he had scrawled the words, "The Rock of Fortune falls on the Fool.""

"It was the Colonel's will that did that," observed Father Brown. "The young man had staked everything on profiting himself by Donald's disgrace, especially when his uncle sent for him on the same day as the lawyer, and welcomed him with so much warmth. Otherwise he was done; he'd lost his police job; he was beggared at Monte Carlo. And he killed himself when he found he'd killed his kinsman for nothing."

"Here, stop a minute!" cried the staring Fiennes. "You're going too fast for me."

"Talking about the will, by the way," continued Father Brown calmly, "before I forget it, or we go on to bigger things, there was a simple explanation, I think, of all that business about the doctor's name. I rather fancy I have heard both names before somewhere. The doctor is really a French nobleman with the title of the Marquis de Villon. But he is also an ardent Republican and has abandoned his title and fallen back on the forgotten family surname. 'With your Citizen Riquetti you have puzzled Europe for ten days.'"

"What is that?" asked the young man blankly.

"Never mind," said the priest. "Nine times out of ten it is a rascally thing to change one's name; but this was a piece of fine fanaticism. That's the point of his sarcasm about Americans having no names — that is, no titles. Now in England the Marquis of Hartington is never called Mr. Hartington; but in France the Marquis de Villon is called M. de Villon. So it might well look like a change of name. As for the talk about killing, I fancy that also was a point of French etiquette. The doctor was talking about challenging Floyd to a duel, and the girl was trying to dissuade him."

"Oh, I see," cried Fiennes slowly. "Now I understand what she meant."

"And what is that about?" asked his companion, smiling.

"Well," said the young man, "it was something that happened to me just before I found that poor fellow's body; only the catastrophe drove it out of my head. I suppose it's hard to remember a little romantic idyll when you've just come on top of a tragedy. But as I went down the lanes leading to the Colonel's old place, I met his daughter walking with Dr. Valentine. She was in mourning of course, and he always wore black as if he were going to a funeral; but I can't say that their faces were very funereal. Never have I seen two people looking in their own way more respectably radiant and cheerful. They stopped and saluted me and then she told me they were married and living in a little house on the outskirts of the town, where the doctor was continuing his practise. This rather surprised me, because I knew that her old father's will had left her his property; and I hinted at it delicately by saying I was going along to her father's old place and had half expected to meet her there. But she only laughed and said, "Oh, we've given up all that. My husband doesn't like heiresses." And I discovered with some astonishment they really had insisted on restoring the property to poor Donald; so I hope he's had a healthy shock and will treat it sensibly. There was never much really the matter with him; he was very young and his father was not very wise. But it was in connection with that that she said something I didn't understand at the time; but now I'm sure it must be as you say. She said with a sort of sudden and splendid arrogance that was entirely altruistic:

"'I hope it'll stop that red-haired fool from fussing any more about the will. Does he think my husband, who has given up a crest and a coronet as old as the Crusades for his principles, would kill an old man in a summer-house for a legacy like that?' Then she laughed again and said, 'My husband isn't killing anybody except in the way of business. Why, he didn't even ask his friends to call on the secretary.' Now, of course, I see what she meant."

"I see part of what she meant, of course," said Father Brown. "What did she mean exactly by the secretary fussing about the will?"

Fiennes smiled as he answered. "I wish you knew the secretary, Father Brown. It would be a joy to you to watch him make things hum, as he calls it. He made the house of mourning hum. He filled the funeral with all the snap and zip of the brightest sporting event. There was no holding him, after something had really happened. I've told you how he used to oversee the gardener as he did the garden, and how he instructed the lawyer in the law. Needless to say, he also instructed the surgeon in the practise of surgery; and as the surgeon was Dr. Valentine, you may be sure it ended in accusing him of something worse than bad surgery. The secretary got it fixed in his red head that the doctor had committed the crime; and when the police arrived he was perfectly sublime. Need I say that he became on the spot the greatest of all amateur detectives? Sherlock Holmes never towered over Scotland Yard with more Titanic intellectual pride and scorn than Colonel Druce's private secretary over the police investigating Colonel Druce's death. I tell you it was a joy to see him. He strode about with an abstracted air, tossing his scarlet crest of hair and giving curt impatient replies. Of course it was his demeanor during these days that made Druce's daughter so wild with him. Of course he had a theory. It's just the sort of theory a man would have in a book; and Floyd is the sort of man who ought to be in a book. He'd be better fun and less bother in a book."

"What was his theory?" asked the other.

"Oh, it was full of pep," replied Fiennes gloomily. "It would have been glorious copy if it could have held together for ten minutes longer. He said the Colonel was still alive when they found him in the summer-house and the doctor killed him with the surgical instrument on pretense of cutting the clothes."

"I see," said the priest. "I suppose he was lying flat on his face on the mud floor as a form of siesta."

"It's wonderful what hustle will do," continued his informant. "I believe Floyd would have got his great theory into the papers at any rate, and perhaps had the doctor arrested, when all these things were blown sky high as if by dynamite by the discovery of that dead body lying under the Rock of Fortune. And that's what we come back to after all. I suppose the suicide is almost a confession. But nobody will ever know the whole story."

There was a silence, and then the priest said modestly, "I rather think I know the whole story."

Fiennes stared. "But look here," he cried, "how do you come to know the whole story, or to be sure it's the true story? You've been sitting here a hundred miles away writing a sermon; do you mean to tell me you really know what happened already? If you've really come to the end, where in the world do you begin? What started you off with your own story?"

Father Brown jumped up with a very unusual excitement and his first exclamation was like an explosion.

"The dog!" he cried. "The dog, of course! You had the whole story in your hands in the business of the dog on the beach, if you'd only noticed the dog properly."

Fiennes stared still more. "But you told me before that my feelings about the dog were all nonsense, and the dog had nothing to do with it."

"The dog had everything to do with it," said Father Brown, "as you'd have found out if you'd only treated the dog as a dog and not as God Almighty judging the souls of men."

He paused in an embarrassed way for a moment, and then said, with a rather pathetic air of apology:

"The truth is, I happen to be awfully fond of dogs. And it seemed to me that in all this lurid halo of dog superstitions nobody was really thinking about the poor dog at all. To begin with a small point, about his barking at the lawyer or growling at the secretary. You asked how I could guess things a hundred miles away; but honestly it's mostly to your credit, for you described people so well that I know the types. A man like Traill who frowns usually and smiles suddenly, a man who fiddles with things, especially at his throat, is a nervous, easily embarrassed man. I shouldn't wonder if Floyd, the efficient secretary, is nervy and jumpy too; those Yankee hustlers often are. Otherwise he wouldn't have cut his fingers on the shears and dropped them when he heard Janet Druce scream.

"Now dogs hate nervous people. I don't know whether they make the dog nervous too; or whether, being after all a brute, he is a bit of bully; or whether his canine vanity (which is colossal) is simply offended at not being liked. But anyhow there was nothing in poor Nox protesting against those people, except that he disliked them for being afraid of him. Now I know you're awfully clever, and nobody of sense sneers at cleverness. But I sometimes fancy, for instance, that you are too clever to understand animals. Sometimes you are too clever to understand men, especially when they act almost as simply as animals. Animals are very literal; they live in a world of truisms. Take this case; a dog barks at a man and a man runs away from a dog. Now you do not seem to be quite simple enough to see the fact; that the dog barked because he disliked the man and the man fled because he was frightened of the dog. They had no other motives and they needed none. But you must read psychological mysteries into it and suppose the dog had super-normal vision, and was a mysterious mouthpiece of doom. You must suppose the man was running away, not from the dog but from the hangman. And yet, if you come to think of it, all this deeper psychology is exceedingly improbable. If the dog really could completely and consciously realize the murderer of his master, he wouldn't stand yapping as he might at a curate at a tea-party; he's much more likely to fly at his throat. And on the other hand, do you really think a man who had hardened his heart to murder an old friend and then walk about smiling at the old friend's family, under the eyes of his old friend's daughter and postmortem doctor — do you think a man like that would be doubled up by mere remorse because a dog barked? He might feel the tragic irony of it; it might shake his soul, like any other tragic trifle. But he wouldn't rush madly the length of a garden to escape from the only witness whom he knew to be unable to talk. People have a panic like that when they are frightened, not of tragic ironies, but of teeth. The whole thing is simpler than you can understand.

"But when we come to that business by the seashore, things are much more interesting. As you stated then, they were much more puzzling. I didn't understand that tale of the dog going in and out of the water; it didn't seem to me a doggy thing to do. If Nox had been very much upset about something else, he might possibly have refused to go after the stick at all. He'd probably go off nosing in whatever direction he suspected the mischief. But when once a dog is actually chasing a thing, a stone or a stick or a rabbit, my experience is that he won't stop for anything but the most peremptory command, and not always for that. That he should turn around because his mood changed seems to me unthinkable."

"But he did turn around," insisted Fiennes, "and came back without the stick."

"He came back without the stick for the best reason in the world," replied the priest. "He came back because he couldn't find it. He whined because he couldn't find it. That's the sort of thing a dog really does whine about. A dog is a devil of a ritualist. He is as particular about the precise routine of a game as a child about the precise repetition of a fairy-tale. In this case something had gone wrong with the game. He came back to complain seriously of the conduct of the stick. Never had such a thing happened before. Never had an eminent and distinguished dog been so treated by a rotten old walking-stick."

"Why, what had the walking-stick done?" inquired the young man.

"It had sunk," said Father Brown.

Fiennes said nothing, but continued to stare, and it was the priest who continued:

"It had sunk because it was not really a stick, but a rod of steel with a very thin shell of cane and a sharp point. In other words, it was a sword-stick. I suppose a murderer never got rid of a bloody weapon so oddly and yet so naturally as by throwing it into the sea for a retriever."

"I begin to see what you mean," admitted Fiennes; "but even if a sword-stick was used, I have no guess of how it was used."

"I had a sort of guess," said Father Brown, "right at the beginning when you said the word summer-house. And another when you said that Druce wore a white coat. As long as everybody was looking for a short dagger, nobody thought of it; but if we admit a rather long blade like a rapier, it's not so impossible." He was leaning back, looking at the ceiling, and began like one going back to his own first thoughts and fundamentals.

"All that discussion about detective stories like the Yellow Room, about a man found dead in sealed chambers which no one could enter, does not apply to the present case, because it is a summer-house. When we talk of a Yellow Room, or any room, we imply walls that are really homogeneous and impenetrable. But a summer-house is not made like that; it is often made, as it was in this case, of closely interlaced but still separate boughs and strips of wood, in which there are chinks here and there. There was one of them just behind Druce's back as he sat in his chair up against the wall. But just as the room was a summer-house, so the chair was a basket-chair. That also was a lattice of loopholes. Lastly, the summer-house was close up under the hedge; and you have just told me that it was really a thin hedge. A man standing outside it could easily see, amid a network of twigs and branches and canes, one white spot of the Colonel's coat as plain as the white of a target.

"Now, you left the geography a little vague; but it was possible to put two and two together. You said the Rock of Fortune was not really high; but you also said it could be seen dominating the garden like a mountain-peak. In other words, it was very near the end of the garden, though your walk had taken you a long way round to it. Also, it isn't likely the young lady really howled so as to be heard half a mile. She gave an ordinary involuntary cry, and yet you heard it on the shore. And among other interesting things that you told me, may I remind you that you said Harry Druce had fallen behind to light his pipe under a hedge."

Fiennes shuddered slightly. "You mean he drew his blade there and sent it through the hedge at the white spot. But surely it was a very odd chance and a very sudden choice. Besides, he couldn't be certain the old man's money had passed to him, and as a fact it hadn't."

Father Brown's face became animated.

"You misunderstand the man's character," he said, as if he himself had known the man all his life. "A curious but not unknown type of character. If he had really known the money would come to him, I seriously believe he wouldn't have done it. He would have seen it as the dirty thing it was."

"Isn't that rather paradoxical?" asked the other.

"This man was a gambler," said the priest, "and a man in disgrace for having taken risks and anticipated orders. It was probably for something pretty unscrupulous, for every imperial police is more like a Russian secret police than we like to think. But he had gone beyond the line and failed. Now, the temptation of that type of man is to do a mad thing precisely because the risk will be wonderful in retrospect. He wants to say, 'Nobody but I could have seized that chance or seen that it was then or never. What a wild and wonderful guess it was, when I put all those things together; Donald in disgrace; and the lawyer being sent for; and Herbert and I sent for at the same time — and then nothing more but the way the old man grinned at me and shook hands. Anybody would say I was mad to risk it; but that is how fortunes are made, by the man mad enough to have a little foresight.' In short, it is the vanity of guessing. It is the megalomania of the gambler. The more incongruous the coincidence, the more instantaneous the decision, the more likely he is to snatch the chance. The accident, the very triviality, of the white speck and the hole in the hedge intoxicated him like a vision of the world's desire. Nobody clever enough to see such a combination of accidents could be cowardly enough not to use them! That is how the devil talks to the gambler. But the devil himself would hardly have induced that unhappy man to go down in a dull, deliberate way and kill an old uncle from whom he'd always had expectations. It would be too respectable."

He paused a moment; and then went on with a certain quiet emphasis.

"And now try to call up the scene, even as you saw it yourself. As he stood there, dizzy with his diabolical opportunity, he looked up and saw that strange outline that might have been the image of his own tottering soul; the one great crag poised perilously on the other like a pyramid on its point and remembered that it was called the Rock of Fortune. Can you guess how such a man at such a moment would read such a signal? I think it strung him up to action and even to vigilance.

He who would be a tower must not fear to be a toppling tower. Anyhow, he acted; his next difficulty was to cover his tracks. To be found with a sword-stick, let alone a blood-stained sword-stick, would be fatal in the search that was certain to follow. If he left it anywhere, it would be found and probably traced. Even if he threw it into the sea the action might be noticed, and thought noticeable — unless indeed he could think of some more natural way of covering the action. As you know, he did think of one, and a very good one. Being the only one of you with a watch, he told you it was not yet time to return, strolled a little farther and started the game of throwing in sticks for the retriever. But how his eyes must have rolled darkly over all that desolate seashore before they alighted on the dog!"

Fiennes nodded, gazing thoughtfully into space. His mind seemed to have drifted back to a less practical part of the narrative.

"It's queer," he said, "that the dog really was in the story after all."

"The dog could almost have told you the story, if he could talk," said the priest. "All I complain of is that because he couldn't talk, you made up his story for him, and made him talk with the tongues of men and angels. It's part of something I've noticed more and more in the modern world, appearing in all sorts of newspaper rumors and conversational catch-words; something that's arbitrary without being authoritative. People readily swallow the untested claims of this, that, or the other. It's drowning all your old rationalism and skepticism, it's coming in like a sea; and the name of it is superstition." He stood up abruptly, his face heavy with a sort of frown, and went on talking almost as if he were alone. "It's the first effect of not believing in God that you lose your common sense, and can't see things as they are. Anything that anybody talks about, and says there's a good deal in it, extends itself indefinitely like a vista in a nightmare. And a dog is an omen and a cat is a mystery and a pig is a mascot and a beetle is a scarab, calling up all the menagerie of polytheism from Egypt and old India; Dog Anubis and great green-eyed Pasht and all the holy howling Bulls of Bashan; reeling back to the bestial gods of the beginning, escaping into elephants and snakes and crocodiles; and all because you are frightened of four words: 'He was made Man.'"

The young man got up with a little embarrassment, almost as if he had overheard a soliloquy. He called to the dog and left the room with vague but breezy farewells. But he had to call the dog twice, for the dog had remained behind quite motionless for a moment, looking up steadily at Father Brown as the wolf looked at St. Francis.[1]

1 http://etext.lib.virginia.edu//toc/modeng/public/CheOrac.html.

Daily Assignment

- Warm-up: Imagine what a dog would say as he waits for his master to take him for a walk.
- Students will complete Concept Builder 15-B.
- Prayer journal.
- Students should outline all assigned essays for the week.

Visualizing

Descriptions in "The Oracle of the Dog" help the readers visualize the action as it unfolds in the plot. While there is very little action, the reader is asked to follow very closely the resolution of the mystery. Detail what the plot is. Next, what is the plot? Where does the action occur? What are some of the actions that are occurring?

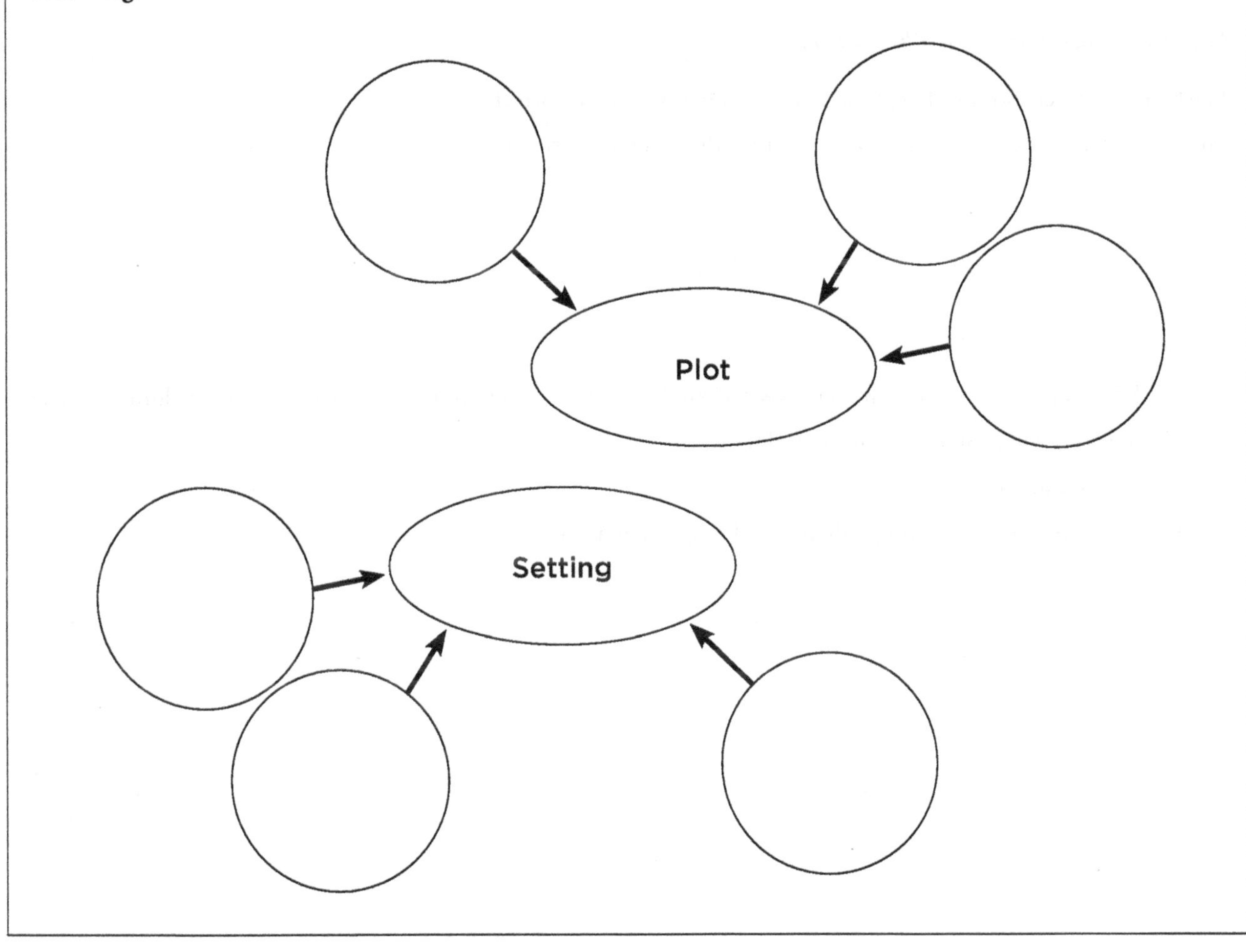

Lesson 3

Grammar Review: Different From

Always use *different from* not *different than.*

The Christians were not much *different than* the other people. (incorrect)
The Christians were not much *different from* the other people. (correct)

Daily Assignment

- Warm-up: Write a conversation between a grandfather and his grandson about what they will do during the day.
- Students will complete Concept Builder 15-C.
- Prayer journal.
- Students should write rough drafts of all assigned essays and speech.

Dialogue: Develop the Characters

Dialogue is used by a writer to advance the plot and to develop characters. Read this excerpt from *The Adventures of Tom Sawyer* (chapter 1) by Mark Twain, and then answer the following questions.

While Tom was eating his supper, and stealing sugar as opportunity offered, Aunt Polly asked him questions that were full of guile, and very deep -- for she wanted to trap him into damaging revealments.

Like many other simple-hearted souls, it was her pet vanity to believe she was endowed with a talent for dark and mysterious diplomacy, and she loved to contemplate her most transparent devices as marvels of low cunning. Said she:

"Tom, it was middling warm in school, warn't it?" "Yes'm."

"Powerful warm, warn't it?" "Yes'm."

"Didn't you want to go in a-swimming, Tom?"

A bit of a scare shot through Tom — a touch of uncomfortable suspicion. He searched Aunt Polly's face, but it told him nothing. So he said: "No'm — well, not very much."

The old lady reached out her hand and felt Tom's shirt, and said: "But you ain't too warm now, though." And it flattered her to reflect that she had discovered that the shirt was dry without anybody knowing that that was what she had in her mind. But in spite of her, Tom knew where the wind lay, now. So he forestalled what might be the next move:

"Some of us pumped on our heads — mine's damp yet. See?"

Aunt Polly was vexed to think she had overlooked that bit of circumstantial evidence, and missed a trick. Then she had a new inspiration: "Tom, you didn't have to undo your shirt collar where I sewed it, to pump on your head, did you? Unbutton your jacket!"

The trouble vanished out of Tom's face. He opened his jacket. His shirt collar was securely sewed. "Bother! Well, go 'long with you. I'd made sure you'd played hookey and been a-swimming. But I forgive ye, Tom. I reckon you're a kind of a singed cat, as the saying is — better'n you look. This time."

She was half sorry her sagacity had miscarried, and half glad that Tom had stumbled into obedient conduct for once.

1. What does this dialogue tell you about Tom?

2. What does the dialogue tell you about Aunt Polly?

Student Essay

Dialogue, as used in "The Oracle of the Dog" drives the story forward and advances its characters. In the story, Father Brown (the protagonist) is talking to a young man named Fiennes. They are talking about a recent murder and the mystery that surrounds it. The dialogue between them subtly reveals to the reader important facts and develops the two characters.

As Father Brown and Fiennes walk, Father Brown gets impatient with young Fiennes for his belief that the dog anticipated the murder. "The moment Nox saw that man, the dog dashed forward and stood in the middle of the path barking at him madly, murderously, volleying out curses that were almost verbal in their dreadful distinctness of hatred. And the man doubled up and fled along the path between the flowers." Father Brown sprang to his feet with a starting impatience. "So the dog denounced him, did he?" he cried. "The oracle of the dog condemned him. Did you see what birds were flying, and are you sure whether they were on the right hand or the left?" In this example Fiennes is developed through his dialogue as a superstitious man who believes that the oracle of the dog predicted who executed the murder. Father Brown is shown as a character with little patience for foolish ideas (although he later apologizes for his outburst) and who believes that a logical explanation can be found. The way the characters talk to each other greatly affects the way the reader interprets their personalities. However, more is developed through dialogue than simply the characters.

As the men continue to talk, the dialogue drives the story forward. (Fiennes is talking)

> There was a dog in the case I've come to see you about; what they call the Invisible Murder Case, you know. It's a strange story, but from my point of view the dog is about the strangest thing in it. Of course, there's the crime itself, and how old Druce can have been killed by somebody else when he was all alone in the summer house. . . ." The hand stroking of the dog stopped for a moment in its rhythmic movement; and Father Brown said calmly, "Oh, it was a summer-house was it?"

In this short example, the dialogue reveals multiple things about the story that drive it forward. The first of these is that the story is about a murder case. The second is that Druce was killed when he was alone, an important detail later on in the story. The final point, that acts mainly as character development, is that Fiennes is very interested in the case. Fiennes acts as the reader's chief plot developer throughout the story. The dialogue between Fiennes and Father Brown cleverly develops the story.

Dialogue is the chief method by which the characters are developed and the story driven forward in "The Oracle of the Dog." As Father Brown and Fiennes converse, their characters and the plot is cleverly revealed to the reader. (Ian)

Daily Assignment

- Warm-up: Write an imaginary conversation that a three- and four-year-old might have about Sunday School.
- Students will complete Concept Builder 15-D.
- Prayer journal.
- Review the assigned text. Keep vocabulary cards.
- This is the day that students should write, and then rewrite, the final drafts of their assigned essay.

Dialogue: Develop the Characters

Dialogue is used by a writer to advance the plot and to develop characters. Read this excerpt from *The Time Machine* (chapter 3) by H.G. Wells, and then answer the following question.

"I told some of you last Thursday of the principles of the Time Machine, and showed you the actual thing itself, incomplete in the workshop. There it is now, a little travel-worn, truly; and one of the ivory bars is cracked, and a brass rail bent; but the rest of it's sound enough. I expected to finish it on Friday, but on Friday, when the putting together was nearly done, I found that one of the nickel bars was exactly one inch too short, and this I had to get remade; so that the thing was not complete until this morning. It was at ten o'clock to-day that the first of all Time Machines began its career. I gave it a last tap, tried all the screws again, put one more drop of oil on the quartz rod, and sat myself in the saddle. I suppose a suicide who holds a pistol to his skull feels much the same wonder at what will come next as I felt then. I took the starting lever in one hand and the stopping one in the other, pressed the first, and almost immediately the second. I seemed to reel; I felt a nightmare sensation of falling; and, looking round, I saw the laboratory exactly as before. Had anything happened? For a moment I suspected that my intellect had tricked me. Then I noted the clock. A moment before, as it seemed, it had stood at a minute or so past ten; now it was nearly half-past three!

"I drew a breath, set my teeth, gripped the starting lever with both hands, and went off with a thud. The laboratory got hazy and went dark. Mrs. Watchett came in and walked, apparently without seeing me, towards the garden door. I suppose it took her a minute or so to traverse the place, but to me she seemed to shoot across the room like a rocket. I pressed the lever over to its extreme position. The night came like the turning out of a lamp, and in another moment came tomorrow. The laboratory grew faint and hazy, then fainter and ever fainter. Tomorrow night came black, then day again, night again, day again, faster and faster still. An eddying murmur filled my ears, and a strange, dumb confusedness descended on my mind.

"I am afraid I cannot convey the peculiar sensations of time travelling. They are excessively unpleasant. There is a feeling exactly like that one has upon a switchback — of a helpless headlong motion! I felt the same horrible anticipation, too, of an imminent smash. As I put on pace, night followed day like the flapping of a black wing.

Wells tries his best to capture the mixture of feelings the Time Traveler experiences. Discuss some of these feelings.

Humor — *The Screwtape Letters* (C.S. Lewis)

Chapter 16

First Thoughts

The Screwtape Letters is fiction, but it seems very real. The issues confronted in this book occur in everyday lives. The book contains 31 letters from Screwtape, the devil, to his nephew, Wormwood, a young demon. Screwtape is writing friendly advice to his nephew concerning how to obtain the soul of a young man.

Chapter Learning Objectives

In chapter 16 we will analyze the way C.S. Lewis develops humor in *The Screwtape Letters.*

As a result of this chapter study you will be able to . . .

1. Understand the difference between humor and satire.
2. Compare a passage from *The Voyage of the Dawn Treader* (Narnia Chronicles by C.S. Lewis) to John 14:1–7.
3. Discuss how a Christian believer overcomes and resists evil temptations.

Look Ahead for Friday

- Turn in a final copy of essay
- Take Weekly Test

Lesson 1

Sample Essay: Humor

The following essay illustrates how an author uses humor to discuss a very serious subject.

Tony kicks the snow into the gutter at Friendship and Roup. It isn't apparent to the casual observer, but his right shoe is an air-cushioned name-brand sneaker with an optimistic green vertical racing stripe running along each side. His left shoe is a less spectacular no-name sneaker with faded baby blue spots — obviously two sizes too large and a female shoe. In spite of the fact that he only has one air-cushioned shoe — the other one had been stolen at the local cooperative shelter last July — Tony is very proud of his name-brand sneaker.

The name-brand sneaker is a wistful memory of a life he has had to abandon. It is the last vestige of a capitalistic economy that he unceremoniously abandoned — along with his wife and two children — ten years ago. Losing his electrical engineering job to an ambitious Harvard M.B.A., Tony proudly declined less prestigious and financially rewarding demotions and resigned from his job. His wife was worried . . . but the Commonwealth of Pennsylvania agreed that he was worthy of unemployment. So between unemployment and the IRA the family hardly suffered at all. And for the next 52 weeks, Tony with rancorous glee with his fancy pen signed his unemployment checks and hung around the house.

Everyone was surprised when things deteriorated so rapidly. Tony was used to being in control, but now he was losing it. At first, as if he were designing a new electrical circuit, Tony looked for want ads in the daily paper. Nothing fit his qualifications. Then, he played the lottery and began drinking. It was surprising how little time it took Tony to lose all remaining vestiges of Middle Class America. He lost his 486 Digital Lap Top; then he lost his home; then he lost his family . . . and he was on the street.

Ellen, Tony's wife, was only mildly concerned at first. After all, he more or less had been looking around for a new job. And Ellen was made of sensible stuff. She stuck by her man. The unemployment checks were humbling but tolerable. Welfare was acceptable, too. Even when Tony began to drink a little she stood beside Tony. And she began to teach again. They needed the money. But now the children were alone. And Tony left them. And then she had asked him to go.

It was that awful look in his eyes. Somewhere, some place Tony had given up. And he was embarrassing Ellen. And Tony knew it and hated knowing it. He moved out onto the street. A lost soul. Many times Ellen had seen Tony peer into the surrealistic late night hue of his Digital Lap Top. With his persevering gaze and anxious tongue protruding from the right side of his mouth, Tony appeared invulnerable. Her conquering hero; her provider. Now though, his eyes were dulled from all the broken places life had taken him. (James P. Stobaugh)

Daily Assignment

- Warm-up: What is the primary challenge you face as you grow in Christ?
- Students will complete Concept Builder 16-A.
- Prayer journal: Students are encouraged to write in their prayer journal every day.
- Students need to review their material for the next assignment
- Students should systematically review their vocabulary words daily.

Humor

Read the text below and answer the following questions.

My mother, who walked three miles a day and regularly ate chicken gizzards fried in old lard, shrugged her shoulders and forgot about the whole thing. In fact, even after Geritol and BC Powders failed, she refused to visit her doctor. To question a doctor-friend's diagnosis was worse than a serious illness — it was downright unfriendly, something my mother manifestly refused to be. With confident sanguineness, old Dr. E.P. Donahue, throat reflector protruding from his head, oversized Masonic ring protruding from his left middle finger, pronounced Mom to be in remarkably good health. Dr. Donahue, who had delivered all three of Mom's boys, was infallible. The medical "pope," as it were, whose edicts, once promulgated, were infallible.

Mom's malady, however, was already fatal. Her stamina and obstinacy propelled her forward for almost a year, but the carcinoma had already ambushed her. No one could tell, though, because she was in such great health. Like a beautiful stallion whose robustness and wholesomeness camouflaged its metastasis malevolent concealed interior. "My health," my mother ironically said with a shrug, "killed me."

By the time our family surgeon and good friend Dr. Johnny Joe Jones, one of Dr. Donahue's colleagues, called the Hogs with mom one last time — Woeee Pigs! Soeeee! — before she went into the operating room and opened her up with his scalpel, Mom was mellifluent with metastatic carcinoma.

Dr. Johnny Joe was the best surgeon in Arkansas. There was one — Dr. Robert P. Howell — who was as good but it was rumored that he was a Unitarian. Besides, he enjoyed Jack Daniels too much. That was OK if one sought his services on a Wednesday. He was sober on Wednesdays out of respect for his Assembly of God mother who always went to church on Wednesdays. And it was Thursday. No one could trust a sober Unitarian anyway.

Trained in Houston, Texas — the medical school Mecca of the South — everyone wanted a doctor trained in Houston — he must be good if he was from Houston — Dr. Johnny Joe was a brilliant, skilled surgeon. He had assisted in the first heart transplant attempt (the patient died) in Arkansas. He was also a Presbyterian.

Everyone knew that the best doctors were Presbyterians who went to medical school in Houston. In spite of one nasty habit — Dr. Johnny Joe chewed Red Chief Tobacco during surgery — he was much sought after. "Wipe my mouth, nurse," Dr. Johnny Joe often said.

Dr. Jones loved the Razorbacks. When he had to miss the game he nonetheless kept the radio blaring in the operating room. Once, while removing Mrs. Nickle's appendix, Texas intercepted a pass and ran back for a touchdown. Reacting to this tragedy, Dr. Jones' scalpel accidently cut out Mrs. Nickle's appendix and spleen. No one blamed him. Texas won the game.

No, my mother was fortunate to have him. He was pretty busy, but since he was a good friend of my mother's old neighbor Josephine Mae Stuart, he agreed to take my mom's case.

1. How is characterization used to develop humor?

2. How is plot used to develop humor?

Lesson 2

Grammar Review: Colloquialisms

Typically, colloquialisms and slang expressions should not be used in formal papers; however, if they are, the writer should not draw attention to them. To do so, implies elitism.

The general urged his troops to "fish or cut bait." (incorrect)

The general urged his troops to fish or cut bait. (correct)

Daily Assignment

- Warm-up: Recite any grammatical "rules" that you have memorized.
- Students will complete Concept Builder 16-B.
- Prayer journal.
- Students should outline all assigned essays for the week.

Humor: Dramatic Irony

Dramatic irony occurs when a reader has special knowledge that the characters do not have. Circle examples of dramatic irony in the text below.

In the summer of 1965 I was 12 years old. On this particular morning my family was asleep. It was 6:30 a.m. when I stepped into our back yard.

The doughty St. Augustine grass irritated my virgin feet too long the captive of black Keds. The uninvited crabgrass surreptitiously invading our lawn, unobserved by our 68-year-old caretaker Aubry, vexing my feet, reminded me that neither I nor the crab grass belonged here this morning. This lawn belonged to my paternal grandmother, whom I cautiously called Mammaw, for she resented being called anything that remotely betrayed her caducity. My cousins called her Granny, but this cognomen was even more unappreciated.

Nonetheless, she was my grandmother and I had to call her something. Thus I tried my best to lay claim to my grandmother by calling her Mammaw, but I knew that she really belonged to an era and could never really belong to one little boy, no matter how congenital and fervent his claim was. The rest of the white world called her Helen while the African-American world called her Mrs. Helen. I don't think I ever heard her called Mrs. Parris (our last name).

I was Parris Stevens, named after my grandmother, Helen Parris Stevens, and I devoutly desired to be just like her — but who in Back Gate didn't?

I never knew what to call her. The fact is, 68 but young far beyond her years, Helen simply never told me what to call her. She was so ubiquitous it was our duty to ascertain the finest name we could and then call her that.

While she never dyed her hair — she cared little what people thought of her appearance or age — Helen was immutable. And she knew it. She loved pretentious gardens and immaculate lawns.

Monday through Friday, Aubry rode his bicycle to our property to care for Helen's lawn and flower garden. Today I would hug Aubry and call him friend. Then, he was another "colored" man, a man with no last name, under the employment of my moneyed family for wages that were scandalously low.

A southern garden was both afflicted and blessed by a ten-month growing season. It was constantly battling interloping Johnson grass and ravenous rodents. As a result, while northern flowers, shrubs, and perennials sported vivid colors and vigorous stems vitalized by cool summer evenings and short growing seasons, southern Arkansas begonias and roses had to endure endlessly long, hot summer days. Their paleness was the result of too much sun, not too little. However, commitment to task assured ardent redolence if not inspired accretion.

1. The main character is Mammaw. Yet, she is not even present! How is this dramatic irony?

2. The garden is compared to the author's grandmother. Why is this humorous?

Grammar Review: Different From

From The Archives: Original 1943 Screwtape Letters Review — "Religion: Sermons in Reverse"

The sharpest religio-psychological writer of the season is an elderly devil named Screwtape, whose letters of instruction have somehow fallen into the hands of C.S. Lewis, Fellow of Oxford's Magdalen College. (Writes Mr. Lewis in the preface to *The Screwtape Letters*: "I have no intention of explaining how. . . .")

In a series of Chesterfieldian letters, written from the cozy depths of Hell, Screwtape advises his inexperienced nephew Wormwood on the best means of eternally damning the soul of his "patient." The "patient," a young Englishman who is never named, "backslides" into religion, is "rescued" by life among clever agnostics, regains his faith, does his duty in London's air raids, and is snatched into salvation by a bomb.

Sectarian Fiends. Screwtape and his deputy are strictly Church-of-England fiends, in seeming agreement with God (called The Enemy) on sexual ethics, the nature of time, the unimportance of worldly goods, and almost everything else except Love and Free Will.

Screwtape writes with the sly temperateness of wisdom and of age: "Doubtless, like all young tempters, you are anxious to be able to report spectacular wickedness. But do remember, the only thing that matters is the extent to which you separate the man from the Enemy. It does not matter haw small the sins are, provided that their cumulative effect is to edge the man away from the Light and out into the Nothing. Murder is no better than cards if cards can do the trick. In deed the safest road to Hell is the gradual one — the gentle slope, soft underfoot, without sudden turnings, without mile stones, without signposts. . . ."

An enormous help in the devil's sleight of hand is the present vogue of The Historical Point of View. "The Enemy loves platitudes. Of a proposed course of action He wants men, so far as I can see, to ask very simple questions; is it righteous? is it prudent? is it possible? Now if we can keep men asking 'Is it in accordance with the general movement of our time? Is it progressive or reactionary? Is this the way that History is going?' they will neglect the relevant questions."

The Value of Time. Wormwood, a youngster full of a youngster's appetites, is beside himself with joy as the war intensifies. His uncle, snarling at "your readiness to forget the main point in your immediate enjoyment of human suffering," warns him: "I sometimes wonder if you young fiends ... are not in some danger of becoming infected by the sentiments and values of the humans among whom you work. They, of course, do tend to regard death as the prime evil and survival as the greatest good. But that is because we have taught them to do so. . . .

"You should be guarding him like the apple of your eye. If he dies now, you lose him. If he survives the war, there is always hope. . . . The long, dull monotonous years of middle-aged prosperity or middle-aged adversity are excellent campaigning weather. . . ..."[1]

1 http://calledtomission-nathandavidt.blogspot.com/2012/04/from-archives-original-1943-screwtape.html.

Daily Assignment

- Warm-up: Is there really a devil? How do you know?
- Students will complete Concept Builder 16-C.
- Prayer journal.
- Students should write rough drafts of all assigned essays and speech.

Humor: Situational Irony

Situational irony occurs when a character (or the reader) is surprised by what happens. Answer the questions below and explain why this situation is so ironical/humorous.

My mother grew up 10 or 12 blocks from Wolchanskies. Big Daddy's house was only a little bit better than a shack. Born in a rambling clapboard house next to the city sewage, Mom always understood limitation and constraint. Her home sat on buckshot clay that cracked and buckled every summer. The smell of feces and mildew intensified every hot summer afternoon. Behind her house was a wood-lot too often the victim of unscrupulous foresters. Enchanted trails and moss-covered paths that would pique the imagination of most children were compromised in my mother's forest by young locust trees unimpeded by shade and larger competition. Sunlight was everywhere abundant. Since there was no reason to grow up and clasp sunlight, the young trees grew out and selfishly deprived all the pretty things in the forest of light and life.

The forest was hardly a forest at all — it was a tangle of bush-size trees — and since it was warm and dry enough on the western edge, cane rattlers loved to slither in the shadows of the deadly Arkansas summer sun. On the eastern edge, joining the sewage reservoir, moccasins hissed warnings at mockingbirds, snapping turtles, and inquisitive little girls. My mother learned very early the advantages of limitation and constraint. She learned to measure each step carefully, always looking at what was in front of her. Controlling, as much as possible, where her next step would land.

Not all snakes were my mother's enemies. One huge, black and red king snake named Uncle Roy, lived under the old piano. Actually the piano didn't carry a tune at all. Big Momma kept it around to house Uncle Roy. An aggressive king snake brought all sorts of advantages to my mother's family — mice were noticeably absent. And no moccasin would dare bare his fangs!

Enjoying the only cool place in Big Momma's house, occasionally Uncle Roy slept behind the family toilet during the inferno Arkansas summers. This very nearly was his undoing, however. Once, when Big Daddy was enjoying a respite and the latest Back Corner Times, Uncle Roy affectionately licked Big Daddy's right achilles' tendon.

Such unfeigned, if unsolicited affection was too much even for Big Daddy, Uncle Roy's most fervent supporter. While his admiration for Uncle Roy's rodent vinery skills were second to none, he could not tolerate this violation of his most private savoir faire. Saltating with no thought of modesty, Big Daddy, in all his sartorial splendor, quickly hopped out of the bathroom into the dining room where the whole family was gathered for supper. Then, with his pin-striped railroad overalls around his legs, he ignobly fell to the ground with his uncovered derriere signaling his unconditional surrender to man and to reptile alike. Uncle Roy coyly retreated behind an old ceramic garbage can.

With surprisingly little remorse, Big Daddy banned Uncle Roy not only from the bathroom but also from the house.

1. What is the narrative technique?

2. How does the author create humor using a snake?

3. Is the reader surprised by what happens? Is Big Daddy? Big Momma? Why? What is the outcome?

Student Essay

Humor in The Screwtape Letters

C.S. Lewis's *The Screwtape Letters* engages his readers with its humorous portrayal of saturnine topics while still evoking an appreciation of the truths presented.

A series of letters from an experienced devil to his nephew instructing him in the arts of temptation, Lewis's theme in itself is enough to amuse his readers, who, with the rest of mankind, share a paradoxical interest in demonic subjects as evidenced by the variety of books, etc., written on such a theme. However, Lewis's book has a stronger claim to truth and approbation than others, such as Dante's *Inferno*, in that it presents its subjects in a perfect balance of satire, humor, and reality. Unlike the *Inferno* with its graphic allegory of hell, Lewis's book is not meant to inspire horror of the demonic and a keen sense of the punishment of sin, but rather to reveal to his readers the reality of demons and their roles in human life through a gentle use of satire and humor. Although *The Screwtape Letters* portrays Screwtape and his nephew in a mildly satirical light, the work is far from flippant or profane. Instead, his presentation aids his aim of revealing to the believer the schemes of the devil. Not only does he give his audience a more insightful view of sin and temptation, he also assists them in grasping a more complete comprehension of spiritual truths through his humorous portrayal of diabolical operations:

> The truth is, I slipped by mere carelessness into saying that the Enemy really loves the humans. That, of course, is an impossibility. He is one being; they are distinct from Him. Their good cannot be His. All His talk about Love must be a disguise for something else — He must have some real motive for creating them and taking so much trouble about them. The reason one comes to talk as if He really had this impossible Love is our utter failure to find out that real motive. What does He stand to make out of them? That is the insoluble question.

In this passage, Lewis throws his devils in a satirical light. Lewis's portrayal of the diabolical puzzlement of God's love for mankind causes the reader not only to chuckle at what appears to be a manifest concept but also to stop and wonder at the magnanimous enormity of that love to utterly undeserving subjects.

This mildly satirical view pervades his book and heightens the humor that Lewis creates to connect to his readers. There is something inexplicably hilarious in his unique approach to giving his readers a "behind-the-scenes" view of the devil's temptation of humans. A fuller understanding is thus reached of the daily struggle to overcome sin while also allowing his audience to laugh at themselves. As in the following passage, Lewis, through this humor, strikes his readers with a sudden realization of the lucrative behavior of man and hell's active, though unnoticed, management:

> The use of Fashions in thought is to distract the attention of men from their real dangers. We direct the fashionable of each generation against those vices of which it is least in danger and fix its approval on the virtue nearest to that vice which we are trying to make endemic. The game is to have them all running around with fire extinguishers whenever there is a flood, and all crowding to that side of the boat which is already nearly gunwale under. Thus we make it fashionable to expose the dangers of enthusiasm at the very moment when they are all really becoming worldly and lukewarm; a century later, when we are really making them all Byronic and drunk with emotion, the fashionable outcry is directed against the dangers of the mere "understanding." Cruel ages are put on their guard against Sentimentality, feckless and idle ones against Respectability, lecherous ones against Puritanism; and whenever all men are really hastening to be slaves or tyrants, we make Liberalism the prime bogey.

Here Screwtape is expounding to his nephew, Wormwood, one of the many "successful" tactics employed on the unsuspecting and foolish human race. Lewis realized that such humor was one of the best ways to convey truths about temptation and the devil to his readers who were more likely to read and appreciate a book poking fun at evil and themselves than a book warning them of demons and exorting them to Beware.

Nevertheless, Lewis manages to accomplish both. In using a humorous twist on a serious and unwelcoming topic, he grasps and engages the attention of a wider audience while still leaving them with a sobering reflection of the reality of the truths he cleverly incorporates into his book. (Emily)

Daily Assignment

- Warm-up: What is the most effective way to overcome sin?
- Students will complete Concept Builder 16-D.
- Prayer journal.
- Review the assigned text. Keep vocabulary cards.
- This is the day that students should write, and then rewrite, the final drafts of their assigned essay.

Humor: Exaggeration & Personification

Technically speaking, humor is a cognitive (of the mind) experience that produces laughter. It comes in many different forms. The following is a humorous poem. **The poet Charles Simic creates humor by exaggeration and by personification. Give at least one example of each from this poem.**

The Spoon

An old spoon
Bent, gouged
Polished to an evil
Glitter.
It has bitten
Into my life —
This kennel-bone
Sucked thin.
Now, it is a living
Thing: ready
To scratch a name
On a prison wall —
Ready to be passed on
To the little one
Just barely
Beginning to walk.

Exaggeration	
Personification	

Tone: Propaganda — *Uncle Tom's Cabin* (Harriet Beecher Stowe)

Chapter 17

First Thoughts

Isabella Jones Beecher gave her sister-in-law Harriet Beecher Stowe the idea to write *Uncle Tom's Cabin.* Isabella was outraged by Congress' decision to pass the Fugitive Slave Law (1850) that gave southern slave owners the right to reclaim runaway slaves in northern states. It was bad enough that Southerners participated in slavery, but now they were forcing Northerners to participate, too. Thinking about what she could do to protest this new outrage, Isabella Beecher sent a letter to her sister-in-law, Harriet Beecher Stowe, a housewife with six children who occasionally wrote for magazines. "If I could use a pen as you can," she wrote, "I would write something that would make this whole nation feel what an accursed thing slavery is." As Charles Stowe tells the story, his mother read the letter aloud to her children in their parlor in Brunswick, Maine. She rose from her chair and "with an expression on her face that stamped itself on the mind of her child, said: "I will write something. I will if I live." The "something" was *Uncle Tom's Cabin.* The book inspired the north and inflamed the south. Abraham Lincoln once claimed that Stowe and her little book did more to cause the Civil War than any other single person or thing.

Chapter Learning Objectives

In chapter 17 we will examine the use of tone in Harriet Beecher Stowe's *Uncle Tom's Cabin.*

As a result of this chapter study you will be able to . . .

1. Analyze the use of propaganda in *Uncle Tom's Cabin.*
2. Use arguments that Harriet Beecher Stowe advances in *Uncle Tom's Cabin.* After reading it, summarize Pastor Freeman's main arguments and, using Scripture, write a rebuttal.
3. Evaluate arguments offered by Stowe concerning the emancipation of slaves.

Look Ahead for Friday

- Turn in a final copy of essay
- Take Weekly Test

Lesson 1

Propaganda (Student Essay)

Uncle Tom's Cabin is a fictional novel, but it is also propaganda. Propaganda is the systematic and purposeful advancement of an ideological or political agenda. Since German Nazis abused the concept so badly in World War II, propaganda has a pejorative connotation. That was not always the case. Previous to World War II, propaganda often referred to revival campaigns!

The following is an essay that reflects the prejudice of the writer. He clearly does not find Bonnie and Clyde to be the onerous individuals that others did. That makes this piece propaganda — promotion of particular ideas, doctrines, practices, etc., to further his cause or to damage an opposing one.

The Story of Bonnie and Clyde by the notorious gangster Bonnie Parker of the Bonnie and Clyde Gang exhibits the sort of confidence held by most criminals in the early 1930s — for good reason too, because crime was epidemic. In the 1930s, crime was very high in Minnesota, Iowa, Wisconsin, Missouri, Illinois, Indiana, Ohio, and Michigan. Famous gangsters included John Dillinger, Baby Face Nelson, Machine Gun Kelly, Bonnie and Clyde, Pretty Boy Floyd, and Al Capone. They roamed freely and terrorized America. Yet, many wonder how they were so successful.

All the gangsters were successful because of three main reasons. One, there was not enough police staff. Two, the gangsters had better weapons and cars than the police staff. Third, America loved to drink alcohol, so the bootleggers could get away with murder (literally). They provided a product that America dearly wanted, and Americans tolerated all sorts of criminal activity to make sure they got it.

The Indiana State Police had only 41 members, including clerks and typists. How could less than 41 police cover all of Indiana? With crime rising, the police were badly outnumbered. It took America a long time to start building police stations. In fact, New York had over a half million people before it got a permanent police in 1853, Boston about 175,000 in 1859, and Philadelphia about 250,000 in 1856. Crime rates were not much better in the 1930s. It was very easy for a criminal to walk down the street and steal any car or rob any store with no fear of being caught.

Besides the problem of not having enough manpower, the police did not have weapons or cars as sophisticated as the gangsters had. Weapons were not hard to obtain for such gangsters as Dillinger; he would just steal them from the police. At times he would have up to three or four submachine guns in one car. Gangsters also had connections for making their cars bulletproof. None of the police cars were bulletproof. Another problem was that the American people sometimes supported the gangsters.

In the 1920s, drinking alcohol was prevalent, but Congress passed a prohibition law that made alcohol illegal. Bootleggers sprang up in every city across America. During Prohibition, alcoholic consumption declined overall, but many Americans consumed more than they did before or after Prohibition, simply because it was forbidden. The smuggling of illegal alcohol became big business dominated by ethnic groups who rose to the entrepreneurial occasion in the American spirit of free enterprise. It was at this time that one such group, the Sicilian Mafia, became most powerful of all, gaining much attention in the movies and newspapers.

In the 1930s, for the last time in American history, American law enforcement officials were outgunned, out-manned, and out-smarted by criminals. This situation was to change with the creation of the FBI and the growth of such other organizations as state police, but for this time at least, John Dillinger and his cronies ruled the roadways. (Peter Stobaugh)

Daily Assignment

- Warm-up: Harriet Beecher Stowe argued persuasively, but some argue, dishonestly to advance her position. Does a just cause justify "stretching the truth"?
- Students will complete Concept Builder 17-A.
- Prayer journal: Students are encouraged to write in their prayer journal every day.
- Students need to review their material for the next assignment
- Students should systematically review their vocabulary words daily.

Humor

Read chapter 1 ("In Which the Reader Is Introduced to a Man of Humanity") from *Uncle Tom's Cabin* by H.B. Stowe, and then answer the following questions.

1. Describe Mr. Shelby. Is he the protagonist? Or Uncle Tom?

2. Some African-Americans have been offended by the Uncle Tom character. They argue that he is more of an unflattering stereotype than a real person. What do you think?

3. Eliza is a powerful woman in American literature. She was willing to break the law to keep her family together. What are your feelings about that?

Lesson 2

Grammar Review: Misused Words

After all is always two words — not *afterall.*

There is no such word as *alright.* The correct word is *all right.*

Avoid using *and/or* in a formal paper.

The word *but* should rarely, if ever, begin a sentence. *But* is a coordinating conjunction, used with a comma to connect two sentences. (Example: Stowe effectively wrote about slavery, but her book is considered highly controversial by many.) *But* is never used in the construction"doubt but that" or "cannot help but."

Daily Assignment

- Warm-up: What would you do if you were Arthur Shelby? Did he do the right thing?
- Students will complete Concept Builder 17-B.
- Prayer journal.
- Students should outline all assigned essays for the week.

Character Conflict

***Uncle Tom's Cabin* is full of colorful characters with all sorts of conflict. Describe the ones listed below.**

Character	Conflict	Internal/External	Result
Little Eva	Uncle Tom is sold and placed on a riverboat, which sets sail down the Mississippi River. While on board, Tom meets and befriends a young white girl named Eva. When Eva falls into the river, Tom saves her. In gratitude, Eva's father, Augustine St. Clare, buys Tom from the slave trader and takes him with the family to their home in New Orleans. During this time, Tom and Eva begin to relate to one another because of their mutual Christian faith.	Little Eva is conflicted about Uncle Tom's loss of his family but very glad that he is her property/ friend (internal conflict).	Eventually Eva understands the evils of slavery, and, after her untimely death, Uncle Tom is freed. However, this changes later and he is sold to the villainous Simon Legree.
Uncle Tom			
Eliza Harris			
Simon Legree			
Arthur Shelby			

Lesson 3

On the Influence of *Uncle Tom's Cabin*

This novel by Harriet Beecher Stowe was one of the greatest successes of American publishing history as well as one of the most influential books — immediately influential, at any rate — that have ever appeared in the United States. A year after its publication on March 20, 1852, it had sold 305,000 copies in America and something like two million and a half copies in English and in translation all over the world. . . . Yet, in the period after the war, the novel's popularity steadily declined. . . . Up to the time when it was reprinted, in 1948, in the Modern Library Series, it was actually unavailable except at secondhand.

What were the reasons for this eclipse? It is often assumed in the United States that Uncle Tom was a mere propaganda novel which disappeared when it had accomplished its purpose and did not, on its merits, deserve to live. Yet it continued to be read in Europe, and, up to the great Revolution, at any rate, it was a popular book in Russia. If we come to Uncle Tom for the first time today, we are likely . . . to conclude that the postwar neglect of it has been due to the strained situation between the North and the South. . . . It was still possible at the beginning of this century for a South Carolina teacher to make his pupils hold up their right hands and swear that they would never read Uncle Tom. Both sides, after the terrible years of the war, were glad to disregard the famous novel. . . . [B]y the early nineteen-hundreds few young people had any at all clear idea of what Uncle Tom's Cabin contained. One could in fact grow up in the United States without ever having seen a copy. — Edmund Wilson[1]

1 Edmund Wilson, *Patriotic Gore* (New York: W.W. Norton, 1962), p. 5; books.google.com/books?isbn=0393312569.

Daily Assignment

- Warm-up: Many of us feel that some legal issues are immoral (i.e., against God's laws). How does one disobey civil laws in a way that honors God?
- Students will complete Concept Builder 17-C.
- Prayer journal.
- Students should write rough drafts of all assigned essays and speech.

Persuasion

***Uncle Tom's Cabin* is a great classic — well written and one of a kind. But it is also trying to convince people to support a political position (i.e., anti-slavery). Discuss how Stowe does this by presenting a problem, complicating matters, and offering an outcome.**

Problem

A slaveholder has to solve a problem: he needs money so he has to sell some slaves. This problem becomes an opportunity for Stowe to show her readers how harmful slavery is both to the slaves and to the slave owners.

Complicating Matters

Outcome

Critics Corner

It is interesting to consider one more aspect of Mrs. Stowe's novel, the method she used to solve the problem of writing about a black man at all. Apart from her lively procession of field-hands, house n*****s, Chloe, Topsy, etc. — who are the stock, lovable figures presenting no problem — she has only three other Negroes in the book. . . . Two of them may be dismissed immediately, since we have only the author's word that they are Negro and they are, in all other respects, as white as she can make them. . . . The figure from whom the novel takes its name, Uncle Tom, who is a figure of controversy yet, is black, wooly-haired, illiterate; and he is phenomenally forbearing. He has to be; he is black, and only through his forbearance can he survive or triumph. . . . The virtuous rage of Mrs. Stowe is motivated by . . . a panic of being hurled into the flames, of being caught in traffic with the devil. . . . Here, black equates with evil and white with grace . . . if she could not cast out the blacks . . . she could not embrace them either without purifying them of sin . . . Tom, therefore, her only black man, has been robbed of his humanity and divested of his sex.

— James Baldwin, "Everybody's Protest Novel," *Partisan Review*, June 16, 1949[1]

UNCLE TOM'S CABIN: ON THE CHARACTERS

Out of a background of undistinguished narrative, inelegantly and carelessly written, the characters leap into being with a vitality that is all the more striking for the ineptitude of the prose that presents them. These characters —like those of Dickens, at least in his early phase — express themselves a good deal better than the author expresses herself. The Shelbys and George Harris and Eliza and Aunt Chloe and Uncle Tom project themselves out of the void. They come before us arguing and struggling like real people who cannot be quiet.

— Edmund Wilson, *Patriotic Gore*[2]

UNCLE TOM'S CABIN: ON LITERARY MERITS

We may think of the book as a fantastic, even fanatic representation of Southern life, memorable more for its emotional oversimplification of the complexities of the slave system than for artistry or insight.

— Alice Crozier, *The Novels of Harriet Beecher Stowe*[3]

1 James Baldwin, "Everybody's Protest Novel," quoted in Harriet Beecher Stowe's *Uncle Tom's Cabin* by Elsa Dixier (Hauppauge, NY: Barron's Educational Series, Inc., 1985)p, 51; *books.google.com/books?isbn=0195166957.*

2 Wilson, *Patriotic Gore*, p. 5.

3 Alice Crozier, *The Novels of Harriet Beecher Stowe* (New York: Oxford University Press, 1969), p. 3.

Daily Assignment

- Warm-up: Can a powerless victim really be guilty of prejudice? For instance, could Eliza be prejudiced against white people? Explain your answer.
- Students will complete Concept Builder 17-D.
- Prayer journal.
- Review the assigned text. Keep vocabulary cards.
- This is the day that students should write, and then rewrite, the final drafts of their assigned essay.

Persuasive Technique

Examine the following from *Uncle Tom's Cabin* and complete the examples from each.

Persuasive Techniques		Example
Plot	Separating slave families did happen; however, it was not common.	Shelby has to sell Uncle Tom and Harry.
Character(s)	Almost all characters are stereotypes or stock characters (i.e., they represent a type rather than an individual).	
Setting	The South is a perfect setting to make a political statement about slavery.	

Allegory — *Uncle Tom's Cabin* (Harriet Beecher Stowe)

Chapter 18

First Thoughts

Uncle Tom is more than propaganda — it is a religious tract. Harriet Beecher Stowe, a very committed Christian herself, sought to share the gospel with unbelievers. As a matter of fact, some scholars argue that she is more concerned about conversion than abolition. In that sense, this piece of fiction is allegorical, or symbolizes something.

Chapter Learning Objectives

In chapter 18 we will examine the use of allegory in Harriet Beecher Stowe's *Uncle Tom's Cabin*.

As a result of this chapter study you will be able to . . .

1. Discuss the use of allegory in *Uncle Tom's Cabin*. Discuss how Stowe symbolizes the Christian motifs of journey, entrance into the promised land, sin, and others.
2. Evaluate Stowe's mixture of evangelism and social justice.
3. Compare and contrast this novel with John Bunyan's *Pilgrim's Progress*.

Look Ahead for Friday

- Turn in a final copy of essay
- Take Weekly Test

Lesson 1

Allegory

Allegory, or symbolism, a sort of extended metaphor where dissimilar things are compared, is a central part of our lives. When we are grouchy we symbolize ourselves as "bears." When we are passive we symbolize ourselves as "sheep."

Allegory has enriched world literature. Whether it was the ancient Anglo-Saxon poet who wrote "The Seafarer" or George Orwell in *Animal Farm* who subtly castigated communism, allegory has been used by authors to enrich, to inspire, to challenge. Allegory is, as it were, one of the most fruitful forms of rhetorical interpretation. It invites the reader to compare the familiar with the unfamiliar, and in the process to gain insightful understandings. Allegory is at the intersection of life and insight. Leo Tolstoy wrote, "Happiness is an allegory, unhappiness a story."

Suggested Literary Works with Allegory

Adams, Richard, *Watership Down*

Alighieri, Dante, *The Divine Comedy*

Bunyan, John, *Pilgrim's Progress*

Cervantes, *Don Quixote*

Conrad, Joseph, *Heart of Darkness*

Goldman, William, *Lord of the Flies*

Hawthorne, Nathaniel, *The House of the Seven Gables*

Hawthorne, Nathaniel, *The Scarlet Letter*

Irving, Washington, "The Devil and Tom Walker"

Lewis, C.S., *The Chronicles of Narnia*

London, Jack, *The Call of the Wild*

London, Jack, *The Sea Wolf*

Orwell, George, *Animal Farm*

Plato, "The Allegory of the Cave," in *The Republic*

Poe, Edgar Allan, "The Fall of the House of Usher"

Spenser, Edmund, "The Faerie Queen"

Stevenson, Robert Louis, *Dr. Jekyll and Mr. Hyde*

Stowe, Harriet Beecher Stowe, *Uncle Tom's Cabin*

Tennyson, Alfred Lord, "The Idylls of the King"

Tolkien, J.R.R., *The Hobbit*

Tolkien, J.R.R., *The Lord of the Rings Trilogy*

Daily Assignment

- Warm-up: Forgiveness is important, but how do we forgive someone but at the same time hold him/her accountable for his/her bad choices?
- Students will complete Concept Builder 18-A.
- Prayer journal: Students are encouraged to write in their prayer journal every day.
- Students need to review their material for the next assignment
- Students should systematically review their vocabulary words daily.

Brochure to Represent My Life

Create a brochure to represent your life.

The Story of My Life . . . Describe two or three incidents that made you the person you are.

Discuss what you value more than anything. Why?

Lesson 2

Uncle Tom's Cabin: On the Meaning of Little Eva

Stowe intended Little Eva's patient and protracted death as an exemplum of religious faith. . . . Yet her religious significance comes not only from her own extreme religiosity but also from the protective veneration it arouses in the other characters in the book, and presumably in her readers. . . . It is important to note that Little Eva doesn't actually convert anyone. Her sainthood is there to precipitate our nostalgia and our narcissism. We are meant to bestow on her that fondness we reserve for the contemplation of our own softer emotions. If "camp" is art that is too excessive to be taken seriously, art that courts our "tenderness," then Little Eva suggests Christianity beginning to function as camp. Her only real demand on her readers is for self-indulgence.

Stowe's infantile heroine anticipates that exaltation of the average which is the trademark of mass culture. Vastly superior as she is to most of her offspring, she is nonetheless the childish predecessor of Miss America, of "Teen Angel," of the ubiquitous, everyday, wonderful girl about whom thousands of popular songs and movies have been made.[1]

— Ann Douglas, *The Feminization of American Culture*, 1977

1 Ann Douglas, *The Feminization of American Culture*, 1977; www.pinkmonkey.com/booknotes/barrons/uncltom5.asp.

Daily Assignment

- Warm-up: Forgiveness is central to our mental health. Describe an incident where you forgave someone who did not deserve to be forgiven or who never asked to be forgiven.
- Students will complete Concept Builder 18-B.
- Prayer journal.
- Students should outline all assigned essays for the week.

A Book to Represent My Life

Complete this one-page cover of a book that represents your life.

A five-word title for my life is . . .

____

A symbol for my life is . . .

A one-sentence summary of the purpose of my life . . .

____

Lesson 3

Grammar Review: Misused Words

Can means *able*. *May* means *permission*.

I *can* do the work. *May* I leave now?

Effect is a noun; *affect* is a verb.

What is the *effect*? Will it *affect* the outcome?

In formal writing, *shall* is used for first person future tense. *Will* for second and third case future tense.

I *shall* finish the book. We *will* finish this book.

Daily Assignment

- Warm-up: There is a theory that says we mature as we learn to accept necessary suffering. Describe one incident of necessary suffering that helped you grow in Christ.
- Students will complete a daily Concept Builder 18-C.
- Prayer journal.
- Students should write rough drafts of all assigned essays.

Biblical Symbolism

***Uncle Tom's Cabin* is full of biblical symbolism. Give examples of each of these.**

Biblical Story	*Uncle Tom* Allegory
The Exodus Narrative: Let my People Go!	*Eliza seeks to escape to the Promised Land to find freedom and succor.*
The Exodus Narrative: Fleeing from Pharaoh!	
The Good Samaritan	

Student Essay

Allegory of Sin

In addition to her abolitionist views, Harriet Beecher Stowe, being a committed Christian, sought to spread the gospel. Stowe writes her novel not only as a work of propaganda for the anti-movement but also a religious tract introducing Christian themes. Consequently, the story of *Uncle Tom's Cabin* is comparable to the Christian's experiences with sin. Such is an underlying and recurring motif as Stowe uses allegory to present Christian themes.

Harriet Beecher Stowe primarily uses the plot of the novel in communicating the effects of sin. Bondage is the main condition all slaves undergo. Similarly, sin is essentially a bondage, an eternal separation from God. The state of freedom is comparable to the eternal salvation that Christ offers. Stowe writes the novel with two main centers of focus — Eliza as well as Tom. Although these two people are not described as sinful people, the bondage through which they go is analogous to sin.

Stowe continues the allegorical sense of sin through each character's struggle for freedom and to escape bondage. In Eliza's case, her decision to run away is decisive and immediate. In fact, such a decision is introduced in only the fifth chapter. Such an act demonstrates one type of Christian. Such Christian quickly flees from sin, disallowing further evil to enter the heart. He accepts Christ as his Savior, and his bondage is forever lifted. As the plot continues, more analogies can be made. As Eliza flees through the wilderness, her journey is laden with perils. Such coincides with the temptations and trials of the world young Christians face. The young Christian must struggle to avoid falling back into the bondage of sin. Such is the similar circumstance Eliza faces as she continually is forced to flee from her pursuers. Soon, she does reach the end of her journey and arrives safely in Canada, signifying the final stability a faithful Christian has.

The story of Tom's bondage differs much from that of Eliza's. Tom frequently switches masters, never making a concerted effort to become free. Tom does not push for his freedom but instead he waits for freedom to be bestowed onto him. This eventually does occur when St. Clare offers to free him. Likewise, the stubborn human refuses to admit his wrongdoing, only hoping he will be saved by other means. Such human does not make a purposeful effort to rid himself from sin. Tom continues in bondage as he becomes the slave of Legree. Here, Tom withstands the agnostic beliefs of Cassy as well as the hopeless mentality of his fellow slaves. Such a person withstands the world and avoids the snares of sin, but he does not act to repent nor believe in Jesus for salvation. When Tom dies, it symbolizes the eternal death, eternal separation from God in hell.

Utilizing allegory to communicate the Christian motif of sin, Stowe allows the reader to read *Uncle Tom's Cabin* at two levels. The plot effectively describes one's experience with sin, and two main approaches in response to the gift of salvation. Such is represented through the characters of Tom and Eliza. (Daniel)

Daily Assignment

- Warm-up: There is a theory that says we mature as persons as we face and overcome obstacles. Describe one obstacle you have faced and how it helped you grow as a person.
- Students will complete Concept Builder 18-D.
- Prayer journal.
- Review the assigned text. Keep vocabulary cards.
- This is the day that students should write, and then rewrite, the final drafts of their assigned essays.

Character: Change & Motivation

Complete the chart below.

Character	Eliza	Uncle Tom	Little Eva
Protagonist (or one of the main characters), Antagonist, Foil	Protagonist	Foil	Foil
Dynamic (changes)/ Static (stays the same)			
Motivation(s)			

Character Development — *Anne Frank: The Diary of a Young Girl* (Anne Frank)

Chapter 19

First Thoughts

Anne Frank's diary is one of the most famous non-fiction novels ever written. Born on June 12, 1929, Anne Frank was a German-Jewish teenager who went into hiding during the Nazi occupation of the Netherlands. In spite of the fact that Anne's father was a World War I German war veteran, Anne and her family fled from Germany in the middle 30s to escape persecution of the Jewish people. When the Nazis conquered Holland in 1940, Anne and her family had nowhere else to run. At first things went fairly well. Finally, however, in 1942 the Nazis started deporting Jewish people to death camps in the east. She and her family, along with four others, spent 25 months during World War II in rooms above her father's former office in Amsterdam. "So much has happened it's as if the whole world had suddenly turned upside down," Anne wrote in her diary on June 8, 1942. Betrayed by friends to the Nazis, Anne, her family, and the others living with them were arrested and deported to Nazi concentration camps. Seven months after she was arrested, Anne Frank died of typhus in March of 1945 at Bergen-Belsen concentration camp. She was 15 years old. Anne's father was the only family member who survived this terrible time in history.

Chapter Learning Objectives

In chapter 19 we will examine the use of characterization in *The Diary of Anne Frank.*

As a result of this chapter study you will be able to . . .

1. Using the perspective that Anne is a maturing young lady, discuss her views on boys, fate, loneliness, war, and parents. Show how she matures as a character.
2. Apply the biblical approach to Anne's words.
3. Pretend that Anne Frank did not die; pretend that she survived.

Look Ahead for Friday

- Turn in a final copy of essay
- Take Weekly Test

Background

Historically, for Jewish people, Germany was one of the most congenial countries in Europe. Enlightened and technologically advanced, Germany was one of the most civilized countries in the world. Germany was the home of Goethe, Beethoven, Einstein, and Schweitzer. All these factors made the rise of the anti-Semitic, anti-Jewish dictator Adolf Hitler seem even more incredible.

However, by the middle of the 1930s, Adolph Hitler's persecution of the Jews was well underway and it was obvious to the Franks that they had to move. The Netherlands seemed to be a safe place to move. The country was close to Germany and, if war came, would be neutral — as it had been in the last war. In 1940, the Franks were shocked when the Nazis conquered their new homeland.

The Holocaust, the systematic destruction of the Jewish people from 1933–1945, evolved slowly. The logistics of murdering eight million people were challenging. For one thing, Hitler and his henchman first had to define what "Jewish" meant. Was a person Jewish by birth? By religion? What if a Jew had converted to Christianity? What if a parent was Jewish and another parent was Christian? What would the German authorities do with a man like Mr. Frank who fought in the German army during World War II?

Once Jews had been identified, they needed to be concentrated in holding centers from which the Jews could then be shipped to death centers. These holding centers became the Jewish Ghettos of central Europe (e.g., Warsaw Ghetto).

Yes, the Nazis were committed to destroy systematically every Jewish person in Europe. To kill 8 million people and dispose of their bodies, however, was no small task. In fact, it was an extremely difficult one. Some moribund historians have argued that the technological challenges of killing so many people required greater technology than putting a man on the moon.

This daunting task was accomplished by the greatest scientists in Europe. Once, European scientists built massive cathedrals; now they built concentration camps. These killing centers included Auschwitz, Treblinka, and Bergen-Belsen, where Anne Frank died.

The victims would disembark at the concentration or death camps. Some were saved for labor; others immediately were put to death in gas chambers. Anne was chosen for labor. Later she was transferred to another camp, Bergen-Belsen, where she and her sister died of typhus.

Those who were selected for death were told they were going for "delousing" and a "shower." They were told to get undressed. Men and women were together. They were given receipts for their belongings. Many were given soap and a towel. The efficient Nazis kept the charade alive as long as possible.

Finally, once the door to the chamber was secure, poison gas escaped through the shower faucets. Within 30 minutes everyone was dead. It took another 30 minutes to remove the bodies and prepare the chamber for the next group of victims. The Nazis were efficient. On a particularly productive day, the Nazis could "process" 2,000 people at a time. At one point, Auschwitz was killing 20,000 people a day. Ultimately the Nazis were unable to kill all the Jews; they were able to kill 6 of the 8 million European Jews. There are virtually no European Jewish persons from ages 60 to 65 because over 90 percent of European Jewish children died in the Holocaust. Anne Frank was one of them.

Daily Assignment

- Warm-up: On Saturday, July 15, 1944 Anne Frank made a remarkable entry in her diary. Anne was 15 years old then and, with her family and others, had been hiding in an attic room for more than two years. Three weeks after this entry the hiding place was found and the Nazis sent all the inhabitants to concentration camps. Seven months later Anne died in the camp at Bergen-Belsen. That day she wrote: "It's really a wonder that I haven't dropped all my ideals, because they seem so absurd and impossible to carry out. Yet I keep them, because in spite of everything, I still believe that people are really good at heart. I simply can't build up my hopes on a foundation consisting of confusion, misery, and death. I see the world gradually being turned into wilderness. I hear the ever approaching thunder, which will destroy us too. I can feel the suffering of millions and yet, if I look up into the heavens, I think that it will all come right, that this cruelty too will end, and that peace and tranquility will return again." Respond to this quote. Is Anne right?
- Students will complete Concept Builder 19-A.
- Prayer journal: Students are encouraged to write in their prayer journal every day.
- Students need to review their material for the next assignment
- Students should systematically review their vocabulary words daily.

Anti-Semitism

The characters in *The Diary of Anne Frank* are dealing with one primary social conflict: the Holocaust. Discuss how each deals with this conflict in the chart below.

Character	Anne	Anne's Mom & Dad	Peter
Issue: Anti-Semitism	*Anne does not speak about this subject very much.*		

Sample Characterization Essay

The following is a characterization of a woman dying of pancreatic cancer:

Larry King was gently scolding Al Gore. CNN's *Larry King Live* was blaring from my mother's opaque Panasonic 25-inch screen. Electrons danced across this colander of 21st-century entertainment. Cable television munificence clashed with dancing electronic intruders. Bounteous contradictions were everywhere evident.

It did not matter, though, because my mother only accessed one-third of her available channels. The effort to ingress more exotic offerings in the upper channels was fatuous anyway. From Mom's perspective, she only needed CNN, the Weather Channel, and the History Channel. Even the local news no longer interested her. This was all the entertainment she needed, and to her, news was entertainment. Mom was dying of pancreatic cancer.

Lying under a crocheted brightly colored afghan knitted by her mother, affectionately called Big Mama by all other generations, Mom was obviously defeated by the cancer interlopers who had completely subdued her body and were now skirmishing with her spirit. With her blonde frosted wig slightly askew on her forehead, Mom very much appeared the defeated warrior.

She needed the bright color in the afghan to tease vigor from her emaciated frame and color from her pallid skin. Big Mama had shamelessly knit bright chartreuse, gold, and pinks into her afghan. Her cacophonic choices doomed the afghan to family coffers or to the most destitute recipient who had no ardor for natural, appealing, subtle hues or had no affordable choice anyway. My mother's body, naturally big boned and pudgy until recently, unnaturally jutted out from loose-knitted perimeters. Her angular right knee was lassoed by a frayed portion of Big Mama's much-used, little-appreciated afghan. It looked like a reptile peeking through the burnished flora of a viscous jungle thicket.

The afghan suited my mother just fine now, though. She felt frayed, tattered, and very old. She also felt used and useless. In the dim hue of *Larry King Live*, the afghan and my mother had a bizarre, surrealistic demeanor that accurately depicted the environs of her crumbling world.

It started with a stomachache. Ordinary in scope and sequence, this stomachache nonetheless was an aberration in my mother's medical portfolio. Mom simply wasn't sick. Ever. Her delusion of immortality was so endemic to her personality that sickness was beyond the realm of possibilities.

Unfortunately, the stomachache ended, and the anemia began. In most medical communities, anemia is a sure sign that something is amiss in the gastrointestinal cosmos. In the Southern Arkansas universe, where my mother lived, medicine was more empathic than empirical, and anemia was perceived as too much fried chicken or turnip greens. This diagnosis worked well enough, perhaps better than conventional interventions in colds, flu, and the occasional gall bladder attack. However, in the really big things — like pancreatic cancer — normal rural southern medical practice was hopelessly dilatory and inevitably, therefore, nugatory.

My mother, who walked three miles a day and regularly ate chicken gizzards fried in old lard, shrugged her shoulders and forgot about the whole thing. In fact, even after Geritol and BC Powders failed, she refused to visit her doctor. To question a doctor-friend's diagnosis was worse than cancer. With confident sanguineness, old Dr. E.P. Donahue, throat reflector protruding from his head, oversized Masonic ring protruding from his left middle finger, pronounced Mom to be in remarkably good health. Dr. Donahue, who had delivered all three of Mom's boys, was infallible. The medical "pope," as it were, whose edicts once promulgated were infallible, had spoken. ...

No, my mother was fortunate to have him. He was pretty busy, but since he was a good friend of my mother's old neighbor Josephine Mae Stuart, he agreed to take my mom's case.

Five minutes after Dr. Johnny Joe opened my mother up, he determined that the villainous corporeality had begun in the pancreas, but it had progressed too far too quickly and it was not worth anyone's while for him to do anything but remove a particularly nefarious and ripe-with-cancer gall bladder. Deep inside my mother's liver, with his rubber-clad left hand, Dr. Johnny Joe had rolled the marble-size tumors between his thumb and index finger. "Wipe my mouth, nurse," he said with a sigh.

Mom's tumor-infected gall bladder was sent to Houston for tests, but Dr. Johnny Joe had already announced my mother's death sentence. It was over just that quickly. With buck season in full swing, Dr. Johnny Joe was still able to kill a four point later that afternoon. Mom went home to die. Mom did not know that her gall bladder had been removed until she received her hospital bill. She thought it would be impolite to say anything. Dr. Johnny Joe could have taken out her heart, and she would have still been grateful.

Southern medicine was like that. Doctors politely did as they pleased. We northerners want to know what our physicians do. We make them give us forms to sign, and we ask for long lectures. We look at their diplomas on their walls, and we want to know if they are board certified. All Mom wanted was a smile, a nod, and a pat on her hand. "Johnny Joe is a good boy," Mom said. "Josephine says he visits his mother every Saturday, and he tithes."

For the first time, my mother was hedged in. She could not fight this thing. Her chances of survival, Dr. T.J. Jackson, the oncologist, who was a Texas Longhorn fan — a grievous shortcoming only overcome by his obvious doctoring skills — adjudged, were zero. But she never wanted to hear the truth. Neither Dr. Johnny Joe nor Dr. Jackson told Mom. She did not want to know, and they were too polite to tell her. My blood boiled. I smelled malpractice here. Mom only smelled okra gumbo stewing in the kitchen.

It turns out, however, she knew anyway, and the okra gumbo probably did her more good anyway. Virginia Maria, her childhood Catholic friend who gambled with her on the grounded riverboats at Greenville, Mississippi, told her, "Nelle, I am so sorry to hear you are going to die. And probably before the July Bonanza Night!"

"I'm sorry to hear that I'm going to miss the July Bonanza Night, too," she calmly responded.

As if she were sipping a new brand of orange pekoe tea, to make her family happy, she tried a little chemotherapy. No one dared die of cancer in 1999 without having a little chemotherapy. Hospice care was for colored folks who did not have insurance, my mom said. She meant to have all the medical care Blue Cross and Blue Shield owed her. Unfortunately, it only succeeded in destroying what hair she had left and caused her to discard her last pack of Winston Lights.

"Do you have, Mr. Vice President," Larry King leaned across his desk, "anything else to add?"

Although we did not know it, this was the last few weeks of her life. Mom knew it. She had literally moved into her living room. She did not want to die in the backwaters of a bedroom. She did not want to die on the bed she and my father had shared. She did not want to die among dreams that never happened. She did not want to die on the periphery of life. She wanted to be in the middle of the action. Her living room controlled all accesses to her house. She was the gatekeeper and planned to man her station until she literally dropped dead. A captain at her helm. With her CB radio scanning for police gossip, with practically every light burning, with her television running day and night, Mom wanted to feel the ebullience of life until the bitter end. She intended to watch *Larry King Live* until the lights went out.

It was Christmas, and this was both the last Christmas I would be with my mother on this earth and the first one I had spent with her for two decades. The juxtaposition of these two portentous events seemed strangely ironical to me. I had lost my mother only to reclaim her in death.

I was not proud of the fact that I had not been home for Christmas in 22 years. I had too many kids, too many bills, and too little income to justify a two-day trip from my Pennsylvania farm to Southern Arkansas. Besides, who wanted to leave the postcard, snowy Pennsylvania Laurel Highlands to spend Christmas along the dirty black railroad ties of the Delta? Who wanted to replace the pristine Mennonite farms of Western PA with the cotton-strewn roads of Southern Arkansas?

"I want to tell you a few things, Jimmy (my name), before I join your dad," she said. Mom never said that she was "dying" or even "passing away." She was always going to join Dad, who had died 18 years earlier.

Daily Assignment

- Warm-up: After the Nazi invasion of the Netherlands in May 1940, the Dutch people were immediately faced with the question of choice: how to respond to the Nazi occupation. Tens of thousands of Dutch people followed Hitler, and millions more looked the other way. The Nazis needed Dutch collaborators to carry out their orders. What would have influenced someone to become a collaborator?
- Students will complete Concept Builder 19-B.
- Prayer journal.
- Students should outline all assigned essays for the week.

Anne's Autobiographical Incident

Complete the chart below.

Hiding in the Annex
Anne's family was hiding from imminent death and they knew it. That colored the entire book. There is a foreboding presence of death in the novel — yet, in spite of this, Anne is able to live a fairly normal life.
Incidents
Concerning Whom?
Anne's Response?

Sample Characterization Essay

The following is a characterization paper on Jo in *Little Women* by Louisa May Alcott:

Two of the strongest characters in *Little Women* are Jo and Laurie. Within the friendship of Jo and Laurie, *Little Women* finds its strength and direction and offers to the reader one of the most important and enduring human lessons of all time.

Jo is a tomboy. She is a tower of strength to a family full of strong, competent women. She is a woman who will not step down in the face of any crisis. For example, Jo willingly sells her beautiful hair to fund her mother's trip to visit her sick father. Jo does not wait to be told what to do. She takes things into her own hands. Jo is outspoken and without guile. What you see is what you get! Grouchy Aunt March appreciates this fact and likes Jo more than anyone.

Laurie is one of Jo's best friends. In many ways, Laurie exhibits many of the female characteristics of this play. For example, he is sensitive almost to a fault. He is romantic and moody. He is like Jo in that he has a quick temper and is outspoken, but in other ways Jo and Laurie are opposites. Jo embraces dramatic reality at all costs — she is willing to sacrifice all to satisfy her artistic passions. Laurie is less willing to do so.

These two very good but different friends find themselves growing together and apart at the same time. The way this fissure plays itself out in the novel determines much of the story's strength. Laurie falls romantically in love with Jo. Jo does not respond in kind. When Laurie asks Jo to marry him, she bluntly declines. The reader expects that the wonderful relationship is over, but it is not. Laurie and Jo persevere, rediscover themselves, and re-emerge at the end of the book closer friends than ever. This is an efficacious turn of events indeed and helps make *Little Women* the wonderful classic that it is! (Jessica Stobaugh)

Daily Assignment

- Warm-up: Otto Frank, Anne's father, took out some of the negative comments Anne made about her mother and a number of the other residents of the Secret Annex. He believed that Anne would have wanted him to do so. Do you think he was correct?
- Students will complete a daily Concept Builder 19-C.
- Prayer journal.
- Students should write rough drafts of all assigned essays.

Forming Conclusions

Complete the chart below.

Conclusion	Yes/No	Because . . .
In spite of living in austere, harsh surroundings, Anne still manages to be happy.	*Yes*	*She had terrific courage and optimism.*
Anne falls in love with a young man.		
Anne loves her father more than she loves her mother.		

Lesson 4

Grammar Review: Misused Words

Never say *try and fix it.* Always say *try to fix it.*

Very is overworked. Try a synonym such as *extremely* and *quite.*

Daily Assignment

- Warm-up: Most Germans claim that they did not know about the Holocaust (as it was occurring). Do you believe them? Who is responsible for the murder of 6 million people?
- Students will complete Concept Builder 19-D.
- Prayer journal.
- Review the assigned text. Keep vocabulary cards.
- This is the day that students should write, and then rewrite, the final drafts of their assigned essays.

My Autobiographical Incident

Identify and describe an incident that changed your life.

Life Before the Incident

Incident

Concerning Whom?

My Response?

Setting — *Anne Frank: The Diary of a Young Girl* (Anne Frank)

Chapter 20

First Thoughts

Without a doubt, the setting is critical to *Anne Frank: The Diary of a Young Girl.* The setting set the perimeter and tone for the entire literary piece. Certainly the story would have been entirely different if it were not written in World War II and had not occurred in a small apartment above a business.

Chapter Learning Objectives

In chapter 20 we will examine the use of setting in *The Diary of Anne Frank.*

As a result of this chapter study you will be able to . . .

1. Discuss the importance of setting to *Anne Frank: The Diary of a Young Girl.*
2. Analyze how Esther saved the Jewish nation from a terrible holocaust.
3. Compare and contrast ways the setting of *The Call of the Wild* by Jack London develops Buck and the way Anne Frank's setting affects her. Why is the setting critical to both books?

Look Ahead for Friday

- Turn in a final copy of essay
- Take Weekly Test

Setting

Daily Assignment

- Warm-up: Why do bad things happen to good people?
- Students will complete Concept Builder 20-A.
- Prayer journal: Students are encouraged to write in their prayer journal every day.
- Students need to review their material for the next assignment
- Students should systematically review their vocabulary words daily.

Elements of a Story

Analyze the following elements of *The Diary of Anne Frank.*

Elements	Yes/No	Because . . .
Characters Do the characters seem real?	*Yes*	*The characters manifest universal human characteristics with which it is easy for the reader to identify.*
Narration Is Anne a credible narrator?		
Setting Is the setting important? Does it seem real?		
Plot Does the story flow logically? Does it flow well?		
Theme Is there a theme?		

Sample Essay: Setting

The following is a short story where the setting is critical to the story itself:

Mom lived all of her 68 years in the same unpretentious small southeast Arkansas town with the oxymoronic name Back Corner. Back Corner neither backed up to anything nor was it on anyone's corner. It lay halfway between Memphis, Tennessee, and Vicksburg, Mississippi.

Back Corner had 5,002 residents. It began at the railroad stockyard north of Bubba Dempsey's Pepsi Plant and ended at the railroad roundhouse south of Tip Pugh's Rice Dryer. These two icons were metaphors for what drove the economy of this little town: railroads and agriculture. When the railroads stopped depositing customers and picking up cotton bales, Back Corner weakened and never really recovered.

The illness was not fatal, however, and as I sat this early December enjoying my mother's last few weeks alive, Back Corner was still about 5,002. By now the tired town had deteriorated primarily to a critical mass of old people not old enough to die and young people not old enough to move.

However, Back Corner once boasted of two hotels, the downtown Back Corner Hotel and the suburban Greystone Hotel. These two domiciles were juxtaposed between the Sam Peck Hotel in Greenville, Mississippi, and the Admiral Binbo Inn in Pine Bluff, Arkansas. Both were 60 miles away. Most visitors gladly traded the ebullience of the Sam Peck and Admiral Binbo for the starched sheets of the Greystone.

Most Back Corner residents refused to stay in hotels — even when traveling. Hotels were unnatural things. Folks had no business being so far from home that they had to sleep in a strange bed. The Baptist preacher said that only harlots and indigent businessmen slept in hotels. This was confirmed when the Greystone put small Philco televisions in every room. One wanted one in his town, however, if for no other reason than to criticize its occupants. The Greystone and Back Corner Hotels, with business acumen and humility, contritely bowed their heads and opened small cafes on their premises.

Both Greystone and Back Corner cuisine were approximately of the same species. The Back Corner Hotel, however, had bragging rights. Every Friday night the Back Corner Owls, our high school football team, ordered tough old steaks, greasy curly-Q fries, and thick chocolate milkshakes before the big game at the Back Corner.

In addition to our two motels, there was one drugstore that gave credit and dispensed viscous butterscotch sundaes to waiting patrons. There were two department stores: Wolchanski's and Martin's. Both stores faithfully displayed Pine Bluff fashions in their store windows. They blessed us all with elegance and alacrity.

Mom was born in a rambling clapboard house eight blocks from the Greystone. Her home sat on buckshot clay that cracked and buckled every summer. The smell of feces and mildew intensified every hot summer afternoon. Behind her house was a wood lot too often the victim of unscrupulous foresters. Enchanted trails and moss-covered paths that would pique the imagination of most children were compromised in my mother's forest by young locust trees unimpeded by shade and larger competition. Sunlight was everywhere abundant. Since there was no reason to grow up and clasp sunlight, the young locust trees grew out and selfishly deprived all the pretty things in the forest of luminosity and therefore life.

The small woodland was the home of cane rattlers who loved rest in the shadows of the thickets. On the swampy eastern edge, moccasins hissed warnings at mockingbirds, snapping turtles, and inquisitive little girls. My mother learned early the advantages of limitation and constraint. She learned to measure each step carefully, always looking at what was in front of her, controlling, as much as possible, where her next step would land.

Not all snakes were my mother's enemies, although she never discriminated between friend or foe as far as reptiles were concerned. One huge, black and red king snake named Uncle Roy, lived under the old piano. Big Momma kept the piano around to house Uncle Roy. An aggressive king snake brought all sorts of advantages — for example mice were noticeably absent. Even other snakes avoided Big Momma's house. Occasionally, Uncle Roy slept behind the family toilet during the summer and enjoyed the only cool place in Big Momma's house. This was even too much for Uncle Roy's most fervent supporters and eventually he retreated to the back of the ice box, full of block ice from Mr. Badgett's icehouse. The downside of having Uncle Roy in the family was the growth of a pervasive herpephobia that thrived in all my mother's clan. In spite of our most fervent pleas, and even after a severe invasion of field mice, my mother would not allow us to have a king snake pet.

My mother's childhood home was an old army officer barrack house moved by huge six-wheeled trucks from a World War I Greenville Airfield. Placed incautiously on eight concrete cinder blocks, it was a nature refuge for a menagerie of unwelcome visitors.

There was hardly any room at all in Mom's house. Three boys and six girls lived together in a three-bedroom house. Big Momma and Big Daddy lived in one room, the boys in another, and the girls in a final room. Gender, not chronology, determined domicile. Mercifully, there were more girls than boys.

Big Daddy had run away from his Louisiana home when he was eight. Living on the outskirts of early 20th-century southern towns, he experienced the essence of poverty. Southern cuisine and lifestyle is the epitome of conservation and economy. Practically nothing is discarded from any animal: intestines, gizzards, stomachs — it all was eaten.

Daily Assignment

- Warm-up: You are Jewish, 14, and on a train with Anne to Auschwitz Concentration Camp. What are you thinking? What are your first impressions of this concentration camp?
- Students will complete Concept Builder 20-B.
- Prayer journal.
- Students should outline all assigned essays for the week.

Plot Development

Fill these boxes concerning the plot of Anne's account.

Exposition

Anne's family realizes that they must go into hiding or risk deportation to work camps or worse.

Rising Action

Climax

Falling Action

Resolution

Lesson 3

Grammar Review: Writer in the Background

The skillful author writes in a way that does not draw attention to self. The author should write with economy and grace, drawing attention away from the medium (i.e., the author) and toward the subject. As a rule of thumb, a cogent style (convincing and compelling) is an appropriate style.

Determine why this first passage is written better that the second one.

1. As we start this century, America continues to decide its court cases, punish its criminals, and define its social policy according to race. As fires smolder in American cities, it is becoming abundantly clear that in the hearts of millions of Americans there is a consuming anger. Racial anger. One hundred forty years after the Emancipation Proclamation, 40 years after the civil rights victories of the 1960s, there is as much anger, misunderstanding, and disagreement among the races as there ever was. Nothing has been as enduring and damaging to the American nation as racial anger. Racial anger is as strong today as it was when the first African American slave stepped into Jamestown in 1619.
2. As we start this century, America continues to decide its court cases, and punish its criminals, define its social policy according to race. Can you imagine it? What is wrong with our country? As fires smolder in American cities, it is becoming abundantly clear that in the hearts of millions of Americans there is a consuming anger. You have seen it, haven't you? That angry look in the grocery line, that unforgiving look at the gas station. Yes, it is racial anger — and I mean racial anger with a capitol R! Do you know what I mean? One hundred forty years after the Emancipation Proclamation, 40 years after the civil rights victories of the 1960s, there is as much anger, misunderstanding, and disagreement among the races as there ever was. That is for sure! Nothing has been as enduring and damaging to the American nation as racial anger. Racial anger is as strong today in the A & P as it was when the first African American slave stepped into Jamestown in 1619.

Daily Assignment

- Warm-up: The following are portions of Anne's diary that her father removed. "What has their marriage become? ... It isn't an ideal marriage. Father is not in love. He kisses her as he kisses us (children). ... He sometimes looks at her teasingly and mockingly but never lovingly. ... She loves him as she loves no other and it is difficult to see this kind of love always unanswered." Why would he remove these? Do parents who love each other sometimes fight? Why?
- Students will complete a daily Concept Builder 20-C.
- Prayer journal.
- Students should write rough drafts of all assigned essays.

Sequencing

Place these events in the order in which they occur in *The Diary of Anne Frank.*

______ On the morning of Monday, July 6, 1942, the family moved into the hiding place.

______ Some time later, after first dismissing the shy and awkward Peter van Pels, she recognized a kinship with him and the two became close friends.

______ After sharing her room with Pfeffer, she found him to be insufferable and resented his intrusion, and she clashed with Auguste van Pels, whom she regarded as foolish.

______ Anne's closest friendship was with Bep Voskuijl, "the young typist . . . the two of them often stood whispering in the corner."

______ She received her first kiss from Peter, but her infatuation with him began to wane as she questioned whether her feelings for him were genuine.

______ On the morning of August 4, 1944, the Annex was stormed by the German Security Police (Grüüne Polizei) following a tip-off from an informer who was never identified.

______ On July 13, the Franks were joined by the van Pels family: Hermann, Auguste, and 16-year-old Peter, and then in November by Fritz Pfeffer, a dentist and friend of the family.

______ She regarded Hermann van Pels and Fritz Pfeffer as selfish, particularly in regard to the amount of food they consumed.

Student Essay: The Setting in *The Diary Of Anne Frank*

Anne Frank, the Diary of a Young Girl, brings to life the story of a young teenage Jewish girl and her family in hiding from the Nazis during World War II. As narrator, Anne writes in her diary every couple of days, giving readers an ideal picture of her life. In 1942, when the first entry is written, Anne is about 13 years old, living in a peaceful Jewish home. When her father learns that they are to be taken away, the entire family goes into hiding. The diary, chronicling two years of her life, shows how Anne matures. She matures and changes in regard to her attitude to her parents and her fears.

Anne first begins to change in her attitude toward her parents. In her first entry, she feels like many other 12-year-old girls. Her mother is beautiful and her father is wonderful. However, as the story continues, teenage hormones come into play. She writes in January 1943, "I'd like to stamp my feet, scream, give Mummy a good shaking, cry, and I don't know what else, because of the horrible words, mocking looks, and accusations that are leveled at me repeatedly every day." In this, readers see that Anne is suffering from almost a typical situation in a teen's life. She feels alone, dejected, and unloved, all of which are most likely not true, but seem very real to her. Throughout the diary, her feelings don't seem to change much, since she is still growing and maturing. The change in Anne's perception of her mother happens early in the novel, as she moves from being a preteen to a young lady.

Another way Anne changes is through conquering her fears. Upon arrival, Anne seems in a constant fear of discovery, and then death. She knows, as does the entire family, that if they make too much noise during the day, they could be suspected and soon after discovered. Thieves are daring, and strike the shop below their hiding place several times. When police respond, there is a fresh terror at being discovered by them. After one particular scare, she writes that her "hand still shakes, although it's two hours since we had the shock." However, despite their numerous scares, Anne becomes hopeful. Upon learning of an attempt on Hitler's life, "The prospect that I may be sitting on school benches next October makes me feel far too cheerful to be logical! Oh, dearie me, hadn't I just told you that I didn't want to be too hopeful?" Anne believes, when writing this, that she will survive this war, and that she will soon be a normal girl again.

Anne Frank, her diary published several years after her death in 1944, chronicles in her diary her last years, spent in hiding. Written during her teenage years, her emotions often run high, her moods vary greatly, and she herself begins the maturation process of a young girl into a young lady. She ends her diary, the last entry before she and her family are discovered, with hope, ready to go out into the world, just like a normal girl. (Sheridan)

Daily Assignment

- Warm-up: Anne wrote this about her mom. "If she had just one aspect of an understanding mother, either tenderness or friendliness or patience or anything else, I would keep trying to approach her. But this unfeeling nature, these mocking ways. To love that becomes more impossible each day." Do you really think Anne meant this? Do you think she would have removed those words later? Do you think or write some things that you later regret? Why do we do things like that?
- Students will complete Concept Builder 20-D.
- Prayer journal.
- Review the assigned text. Keep vocabulary cards.
- This is the day that students should write, and then rewrite, the final drafts of their assigned essays.

Theme

Themes are formed from all the elements in the novel. Fill the circles with incidents from the book.

Plot:

The struggle to survive in close quarters with the same people

Setting:

Theme: Maturation

Characters Conflict:

Characters Development:

Plot — *Silas Marner* (George Eliot)

Chapter 21

First Thoughts

This short novel is the story of how a young, unloved child restores faith and hope to a brokenhearted recluse. This old man had been rejected by society and then rejected society himself. George Eliot, whose real name was Mary Ann Evans, wrote *Silas Marner*. In her day, Evans/Eliot was the most popular writer in England — more popular even than Charles Dickens. Her writings exhibit theism (but certainly not Christian theism).

Chapter Learning Objectives

In chapter 21 we will examine the use of coincidence in *Silas Marner* by George Eliot.

As a result of this chapter study you will be able to . . .

1. Analyze the use of coincidence.
2. Discuss the way George Eliot describes organized religion.
3. Research Eliot's (Evan's) life. Compare and contrast her own childhood to Eppie's childhood.

Look Ahead for Friday

- Turn in a final copy of essay
- Take Weekly Test

Lesson 1

Plot: Coincidence

Coincidence plays a large part in the plot. In fact, the plot would not progress at all without coincidence. Silas coincidentally is out of his cottage when Dunstan passes the cottage. Eppie coincidentally sees the light in the cottage. Molly coincidentally dies before Godfrey is exposed.

Does the story lose all credibility?

Are the coincidences necessary and appropriate to the plot's development?

Use evidence from the text to support your position.

The following is from *Silas Marner*, chapter 12, which exhibits some of the more blatant coincidences of the entire book:

While Godfrey was taking droughts of forgetfulness from the sweet presence of Nancy, willingly losing all sense of that hidden bond which at other moments galled and fretted him so as to mingle irritation with the very sunshine, Godfrey's wife was walking with slow uncertain steps through the snow-covered Raveloe lanes, carrying her child in her arms. This journey on New Year's Eve was a premeditated act of vengeance which she had kept in her heart ever since Godfrey, in a fit of passion, had told her he would sooner die than acknowledge her as his wife. There would be a great party at the Red House on New Year's Eve, she knew: her husband would be smiling and smiled upon, hiding her existence in the darkest corner of his heart. But she would mar his pleasure: she would go in her dingy rags, with her faded face, once as handsome as the best, with her little child that had its father's hair and eyes, and disclose her-self to the Squire as his eldest son's wife. It is seldom that the miserable can help regarding their misery as a wrong inflicted by those who are less miserable. Molly knew that the cause of her dingy rags was not her husband's neglect, but the demon Opium to whom she was enslaved, body and soul, except in the lingering mother's tenderness that refused to give him her hungry child. She knew this well; and yet, in the moments of wretched unbenumbed consciousness, the sense of her want and degradation transformed itself continually into bitterness toward Godfrey. He was well off; and if she had her rights she would be well off too. The belief that he repented his marriage, and suffered from it, only aggravated her vindictiveness. Just and self-reproving thoughts do not come to us too thickly, even in the purest air and with the best lessons of heaven and earth; how should those white-winged delicate messengers make their way to Molly's poisoned chamber, inhabited by no higher memories than those of a barmaid's paradise of pink ribbons and gentlemen's jokes?

She had set out at an early hour, but had lingered on the road, inclined by her indolence to believe that if she waited under a warm shed the snow would cease to fall. She had waited longer than she knew, and now that she found herself belated in the snow-hidden ruggedness of the long lanes, even the animation of a vindictive purpose could not keep her spirit from failing. It was seven o'clock, and by this time she was not very far from Raveloe, but she was not familiar enough with those monotonous lanes to know how near she was to her journey's end. She needed comfort, and she knew but one comforter — the familiar demon in her bosom; but she hesitated a moment, after drawing out the black remnant, before she raised it to her lips. In that moment the mother's love pleaded for painful consciousness rather than oblivion — pleaded to be left in aching weariness, rather than to have the encircling arms benumbed so that they could not feel the dear burden. In another moment Molly had flung something away, but it was not the black remnant — it was an empty phial. And she walked on again under the breaking cloud, from which there came now and then the light of a quickly veiled star, for a freezing wind had sprung up since the snowing had ceased. But she walked always more and more drowsily, and clutched more and more automatically the sleeping child at her bosom.

Slowly the demon was working his will, and cold and weariness were his helpers. Soon she felt nothing but a supreme immediate longing that curtained off all futurity — the longing to lie down and sleep. She had arrived at a spot where her footsteps were no longer checked by a hedgerow, and she had wandered vaguely, unable to distinguish any objects, notwithstanding the wide whiteness around her, and the growing starlight. She sank down against a straggling furze bush, an easy pillow enough; and the bed of snow, too, was soft. She did not feel that the bed was cold, and did not heed whether the child would wake and cry for her. But her arms had not yet relaxed their instinctive clutch; and the little one slumbered on as gently as if it had been rocked in a lace-trimmed cradle.

But the complete torpor came at last: the fingers lost their tension, the arms unbent: then the little head fell away from the bosom, and the blue eyes opened wide on the cold starlight. At first there was a little peevish cry of "mammy," and an effort to regain the pillowing arm and bosom; but mammy's ear was deaf, and the pillow seemed to be slipping away backward. Suddenly, as the child rolled downward on its mother's knees, all wet with snow, its eyes were caught by a bright glancing light on the white ground, and, with the ready transition of infancy, it was immediately absorbed in watching the bright living thing running toward it, yet never arriving. That bright living thing must be caught, and in an instant the child has slipped on all-fours, and held out one little hand to catch the gleam. But the gleam would not be caught in that way, and now the head was held up to see where the cunning gleam came from. It came from a very bright place; and the little one, rising on its legs, toddled through the snow, the old grimy shawl in which it was wrapped trailing behind it, and the queer little bonnet dangling at its back — toddled on to the open door of Silas Marner's cottage, and right up to the warm hearth, where there was a bright fire of logs and sticks, which had thoroughly warmed the old sack (Silas's greatcoat) spread out on the bricks to dry. The little one, accustomed to be left to itself for long hours without notice from its mother, squatted down on the sack, and spread its tiny hands to-ward the blaze, in perfect contentment, gurgling and making many inarticulate communications to the cheerful fire, like a new-hatched gosling beginning to find itself comfortable. But presently the warmth had a lulling effect, and the little golden head sank down on the old sack, and the blue eyes were veiled by their delicate half-transparent lids.

But where was Silas Marner while this strange visitor had come to his hearth? He was in the cottage, but he did not see the child. During the last few weeks, since he had lost his money, he had contracted the habit of opening his door and looking out from time to time, as if he thought that his money might be somehow coming back to him, or that some trace, some news of it, might be mysteriously on the road, and be caught by the listening ear or the straining eye. It was chiefly at night, when he was not occupied in his loom, that he fell into this repetition of an act for which he could have assigned no definite purpose, and which can hardly be understood except by those who have undergone a bewildering separation from a supremely loved object. In the evening twilight, and later, whenever the night was not dark, Silas looked out on that narrow prospect round the Stone-pits, listening and gazing, not with hope, but with mere yearning and unrest.

This morning he had been told by some of his neighbors that it was New Year's Eve, and that he must sit up and hear the old year rung out and the new rung in, because that was good luck, and might bring his money back again. This was only a friendly Raveloe way of jesting with the half-crazy oddities of a miser, but it had perhaps helped to throw Silas into a more than usually excited state. Since the oncoming of twilight he had opened his door again and again, though only to shut it immediately at seeing all distance veiled by the falling snow. But the last time he opened it the snow had ceased, and the clouds were parting here and there. He stood and listened, and gazed for a long while — there was really something on the road coming toward him then, but he caught no sign of it; and the stillness and the wide trackless snow seemed to narrow his solitude, and touched his yearning with the chill of despair. He went in again, and put his right hand on the latch of the door to close it — but he did not close it: he was arrested, as he had been already since his loss, by the invisible wand of catalepsy, and stood like a graven image, with wide but sightless eyes, holding open his door, powerless to resist either the good or the evil that might enter there.

When Marner's sensibility returned, he continued the action which had been arrested, and closed his door, unaware of the chasm in his consciousness, unaware of any intermediate change, except that the light had grown dim, and that he was chilled and faint. He thought he had been too long standing at the door and looking out. Turning toward the hearth, where the two logs had fallen apart, and sent forth only a red uncertain glimmer, he seated himself on his fire-side chair, and was stooping to push his logs together, when, to his blurred vision, it seemed as if there were gold on the floor in front of the hearth. Gold! — his own gold — brought back to him as mysteriously as it had been taken away! He felt his heart beat violently, and for a few moments he was unable to stretch out his hand and grasp the restored treasure. The heap of gold seemed to glow and get larger beneath his agitated gaze. He leaned forward at last, and stretched forth his hand; but instead of the hard coin with the familiar resisting outline, his fingers encountered soft warm curls. In utter amazement, Silas fell on his knees and bent his head low to examine the marvel: it was a sleeping child — a round, fair thing, with soft yellow rings all over its head. Could this be his little sister come back to him in a dream — his little sister whom he had carried about in his arms for a year before she died, when he was a small boy without shoes or stockings? That was the first thought that darted across Silas's blank wonderment. Was it a dream? He rose to his feet again, pushed his logs together, and, throwing on some dried leaves and sticks, raised a flame; but the flame did not disperse the vision — it only lit up more distinctly the little round form of the child, and its shabby clothing. It was very much like his little sister. Silas sank into his chair powerless, under the double presence of an inexplicable surprise and a hurrying influx of memories. How and when had the child come in without his knowledge? He had never been beyond the door. But along with that question, and almost thrusting it away, there was a vision of the old home and the old streets leading to Lantern Yard — and within that vision another, of the thoughts which had been present with him in those far-off scenes. The thoughts were strange to him now, like old friendships impossible to revive; and yet he had a dreamy feeling that this child was somehow a message come to him from that far-off life: it stirred fibers that had never been moved in Raveloe — old quiverings of tenderness — old impressions of awe at the presentiment of some Power presiding over his life; for his imagination had not yet extricated itself from the sense of mystery in the child's sudden presence, and had formed no conjectures of ordinary natural means by which the event could have been brought about.

But there was a cry on the hearth: the child had awaked, and Marner stooped to lift it on his knee. It clung round his neck, and burst louder and louder into that mingling of inarticulate cries with "mammy" by which little children express the bewilderment of waking. Silas pressed it to him, and almost unconsciously uttered sounds of hushing tenderness, while he bethought himself that some of his porridge, which had got cool by the dying fire, would do to feed the child with if it were only warmed up a little.

He had plenty to do through the next hour. The porridge, sweetened with some dry brown sugar from an old store which he had refrained from using for himself, stopped the cries of the little one, and made her lift her blue eyes with a wide quiet gaze at Silas, as he put the spoon into her mouth. Presently she slipped from his knee and began to toddle about, but with a pretty stagger that made Silas jump up and follow her lest she should fall against anything that would hurt her. But she only fell in a sitting posture on the ground, and began to pull at her boots, looking up at him with a crying face as if the boots hurt her. He took her on his knee again, but it was some time before it occurred to Silas's dull bachelor mind that the wet boots were the grievance, pressing on her warm ankles. He got them off with difficulty, and baby was at once happily occupied with the primary mystery of her own toes, inviting Silas with much chuckling, to consider the mystery too. But the wet boots had at last suggested to Silas that the child had been walking on the snow, and this roused him from his entire oblivion of any ordinary means by which it could have entered or been brought into his house. Under the prompting of this new idea, and without waiting to form conjectures, he raised the child in his arms, and went to the door. As soon as he had opened it, there was the cry of "mammy" again, which Silas had not heard since the child's first hungry waking. Bending forward, he could just discern the marks made by the little feet on the virgin snow, and he followed their track to the furze bushes. "Mammy!" the little one cried again and again, stretching itself forward so as almost to escape from Silas's arms, before he himself was aware that there was something more than the bush before him — that there was a human body, with the head sunk low in the furze, and half-covered with the shaken snow.[1]

---

1 George Eliot, *Silas Marner;* http://etext.lib.virginia.edu/toc/modeng/public/Eli2Sil.html.

Daily Assignment

- Warm-up: Eppie is raised by Silas. But Silas is an old, single, eccentric man. Is he the best father for Eppie? Or would Eppie's biological father be a better father? Offer evidence to support your answer.
- Students will complete Concept Builder 21-A.
- Prayer journal: Students are encouraged to write in their prayer journal every day.
- Students need to review their material for the next assignment
- Students should systematically review their vocabulary words daily.

Active Reading

Read this excerpt from *Silas Marner* (chapter 1) by George Eliot, and then answer the following questions.

And Raveloe was a village where many of the old echoes lingered, undrowned by new voices. Not that it was one of those barren parishes lying on the outskirts of civilization — inhabited by meagre sheep and thinly-scattered shepherds: on the contrary, it lay in the rich central plain of what we are pleased to call Merry England, and held farms which, speaking from a spiritual point of view, paid highly-desirable tithes. But it was nestled in a snug well-wooded hollow, quite an hour's journey on horseback from any turnpike, where it was never reached by the vibrations of the coach-horn, or of public opinion. It was an important-looking village, with a fine old church and large churchyard in the heart of it, and two or three large brick and stone homesteads, with well-walled orchards and ornamental weathercocks, standing close upon the road, and lifting more imposing fronts than the rectory, which peeped from among the trees on the other side of the churchyard — a village which showed at once the summits of its social life, and told the practiced eye that there was no great park and manor-house in the vicinity, but that there were several chiefs in Raveloe who could farm badly quite at their ease, drawing enough money from their bad farming, in those war times, to live in a rollicking fashion, and keep a jolly Christmas, Whitsun, and Easter tide.

It was fifteen years since Silas Marner had first come to Raveloe; he was then simply a pallid young man, with prominent short-sighted brown eyes, whose appearance would have had nothing strange for people of average culture and experience, but for the villagers near whom he had come to settle it had mysterious peculiarities which corresponded with the exceptional nature of his occupation, and his advent from an unknown region called "North'-ard." So had his way of life — he invited no comer to step across his door-sill, and he never strolled into the village to drink a pint at the Rainbow, or to gossip at the wheelwright's: he sought no man or woman, save for the purposes of his calling, or in order to supply himself with necessaries; and it was soon clear to the Raveloe lasses that he would never urge one of them to accept him against her will — quite as if he had heard them declare that they would never marry a dead man come to life again. This view of Marner's personality was not without another ground than his pale face and unexampled eyes; for Jem Rodney, the mole-catcher, averred that one evening as he was returning homeward he saw Silas Marner leaning against a stile with a heavy bag on his back, instead of resting the bag on the stile as a man in his senses would have done; and that, on coming up to him, he saw that Marner's eyes were set like a dead man's, and he spoke to him, and shook him, and his limbs were stiff, and his hands clutched the bag as if they'd been made of iron; but just as he had made up his mind that the weaver was dead, he came all right again, like, as you might say, in the winking of an eye, and said "Good night," and walked off. All this Jem swore he had seen, more by token that it was the very day he had been mole-catching on Squire Cass's land, down by the old saw-pit. Some said Marner must have been in a "fit," a word which seemed to explain things otherwise incredible; but the argumentative Mr. Macey, clerk of the parish, shook his head, and asked if anybody was ever known to go off in a fit and not fall down. A fit was a stroke, wasn't it? and it was in the nature of a stroke to partly take away the use of a man's limbs and throw him on the parish, if he'd got no children to look to. No, no; it was no stroke that would let a man stand on his legs, like a horse between the shafts, and then walk off as soon as you can say "Gee!" But there might be such a thing as a man's soul being loose from his body, and going out and in, like a bird out of its nest and back; and that was how folks got over-wise, for they went to school in this shell-less state to those who could teach them more than their neighbors could learn with their five senses and the parson. And where did Master Marner get his knowledge of herbs from — and charms too, if he liked to give them away?

What sort of town is Raveloe? Why is this setting important?

Lesson 2

Grammar Review: Overworked Words

Effective words: avoid such overworked words as *good*, *little*, and *rather*.

Splitting an infinitive is no longer considered incorrect. However, it should be avoided when it produces an awkward construction and the adverb functions more effectively in another location.[1] Compare the following:

It was impossible to slowly eat after the 12-hour fast.

It was impossible to eat slowly after the 12-hour fast.

Revise awkward constructions that split an infinitive. However, *splitting an infinitive* is sometimes not only natural but desirable.[2] Compare the following:

Susan forgot to totally shut the oven door.

Susan forgot totally to shut the oven door.

---

1 *Gregg Reference Manual*, Ninth Edition (New York: Glencoe McGraw-Hill, 2001), p. 254.

2 *Harbrace College Handbook*, Revised 13th Edition (New York: Harcourt Brace, 1998), p. 55.

Daily Assignment

- Warm-up: The story of Silas Marner's life has a mythic dimension to it. Silas undergoes a spiritual journey that is a variation on the great religious myth of Western culture. In the Christian myth, man is expelled from a garden, saved by the birth of the Christ-child, and promised a life in bliss in the heavenly city of Jerusalem described in the Book of Revelations. Silas travels a similar path from expulsion to redemption, but the symbolism is reversed. He is expelled from a city, saved by a child, and ends up in a garden (as seen in the final chapter when Eppie and Aaron grow a garden just outside his cottage). In the course of this journey, which occupies over thirty years of Silas's life, he travels from a stern, Bible-centered Calvinistic religion, in which the central concern is the "Assurance of salvation," to a more tolerant, nondogmatic version of Christianity in which the emphasis falls not on the idea of salvation but on tolerance and solidarity with others in a cooperative human community —Brian Aubrey. Agree or disagree with this comment.
- Students will complete Concept Builder 21-B.
- Prayer journal.
- Students should outline all assigned essays for the week.

Coincidence

Coincidence plays a large part in the plot. In fact, the plot would not progress at all without coincidence.

Complete the following chart.

Example of Coincidence	Purpose	Is it necessary? Why?
"He [Dunstan] knocked loudly, rather enjoying the idea that the old fellow would be frightened by sudden noise. He heard no movement in reply: all was silence in the cottage. . . . Dunstan knocked still more loudly, and, without pausing for a reply, pushed his fingers through the latch-hole, intending to shake the door and pull the latch-string up and down, not doubting that the door was fastened. But, to his surprise, at this double motion the door opened, and he found himself in front of a bright fire, which lit up every corner of the cottage — the bed, the loom, the three chairs, and the table — and showed him that Marner was not there." (32–33; ch. 4)	*Eliot wanted to have Dunstan commit an injustice against Silas so that, later, Dunstan would die and Eliot could make a moral statement.*	*Probably, because it was the only way Eliot could advance the plot. Besides, it is quite plausible that such an event might occur.*
"Suddenly, as the child rolled downward on its mother's knees, its eyes were caught by a bright glancing light on the white ground, and, with the ready transition of infancy, it was immediately absorbed in watching the bright living thing running towards it, yet never arriving. . . . It came from a bright place; and the little one, rising on its legs, toddled through the snow . . . toddled on to the open door of Silas Marner's cottage, and right up to the warm Hearth." (94; ch. 12)		
"Slowly the demon [opium] was working his will, and cold and weariness were his helpers. Soon she [Molly] felt nothing but a supreme immediate longing that curtained off all futurity — the longing to lie down and sleep. "Mammy!" the little one cried again and again, stretching itself forward so as to almost escape from Silas's arms, before he himself was aware that there was something more that the bush before — that there was a human body, with the head sunk low in the furze, and half-covered with snow." (94, 97; ch. 12)		

Lesson 3

Coincidence in *Uncle Tom's Cabin*

Many readers criticize Stowe's handling of subplots in *Uncle Tom's Cabin*. For example, George Harris's sister, Madame de Thoux, happens to meet George Shelby, who happens to be traveling with Cassy, who turns out to be Eliza's mother. Is this use of coincidence necessary? Or a distraction?

Chapter XLII
"An Authentic Ghost Story"

For some remarkable reason, ghostly legends were uncommonly rife, about this time, among the servants on Legree's place.

It was whisperingly asserted that footsteps, in the dead of night, had been heard descending the garret stairs, and patrolling the house. In vain the doors of the upper entry had been locked; the ghost either carried a duplicate key in its pocket, or availed itself of a ghost's immemorial privilege of coming through the keyhole, and promenaded as before, with a freedom that was alarming.

Authorities were somewhat divided, as to the outward form of the spirit, owing to a custom quite prevalent among negroes — and, for aught we know, among whites, too — of invariably shutting the eyes, and covering up heads under blankets, petticoats, or whatever else might come in use for a shelter, on these occasions. Of course, as everybody knows, when the bodily eyes are thus out of the lists, the spiritual eyes are uncommonly vivacious and perspicuous; and, therefore, there were abundance of full-length portraits of the ghost, abundantly sworn and testified to, which, as if often the case with portraits, agreed with each other in no particular, except the common family peculiarity of the ghost tribe — the wearing of a *white sheet.* The poor souls were not versed in ancient history, and did not know that Shakespeare had authenticated this costume, by telling how

"The sheeted dead

Did squeak and gibber in the streets of Rome."*

* Hamlet, Act I, scene 1, lines 115-116

And, therefore, their all hitting upon this is a striking fact in pneumatology, which we recommend to the attention of spiritual media generally.

Be it as it may, we have private reasons for knowing that a tall figure in a white sheet did walk, at the most approved ghostly hours, around the Legree premises — pass out the doors, glide about the house — disappear at intervals, and, reappearing, pass up the silent stairway, into that fatal garret; and that, in the morning, the entry doors were all found shut and locked as firm as ever.

Legree could not help overhearing this whispering; and it was all the more exciting to him, from the pains that were taken to conceal it from him. He drank more brandy than usual; held up his head briskly, and swore louder than ever in the daytime; but he had bad dreams, and the visions of his head on his bed were anything but agreeable. The night after Tom's body had been carried away, he rode to the next town for a carouse, and had a high one. Got home late and tired; locked his door, took out the key, and went to bed.

After all, let a man take what pains he may to hush it down, a human soul is an awful ghostly, unquiet possession, for a bad man to have. Who knows the metes and bounds of it? Who knows all its awful perhapses — those shudderings and tremblings, which it can no more live down than it can outlive its own eternity! What a fool is he who locks his door to keep out spirits, who has in his own bosom a spirit he dares not meet alone — whose voice, smothered far down, and piled over with mountains of earthliness, is yet like the forewarning trumpet of doom!

But Legree locked his door and set a chair against it; he set a night-lamp at the head of his bed; and put his pistols there. He examined the catches and fastenings of the windows, and then swore he "didn't care for the devil and all his angels," and went to sleep.

Well, he slept, for he was tired — slept soundly. But, finally, there came over his sleep a shadow, a horror, an apprehension of something dreadful hanging over him. It was his mother's shroud, he thought; but Cassy had it, holding it up, and showing it to him. He heard a confused noise of screams and groanings; and, with it all, he knew he was asleep, and he struggled to wake himself. He was half awake. He was sure something was coming into his room. He knew the door was opening, but he could not stir hand or foot. At last he turned, with a start; the door *was* open, and he saw a hand putting out his light.

It was a cloudy, misty moonlight, and there he saw it! — something white, gliding in! He heard the still rustle of its ghostly garments. It stood still by his bed; — a cold hand touched his; a voice said, three times, in a low, fearful whisper, "Come! come! come!" And, while he lay sweating with terror, he knew not when or how, the thing was gone. He sprang out of bed, and pulled at the door. It was shut and locked, and the man fell down in a swoon.

After this, Legree became a harder drinker than ever before. He no longer drank cautiously, prudently, but imprudently and recklessly.

There were reports around the country, soon after that he was sick and dying. Excess had brought on that frightful disease that seems to throw the lurid shadows of a coming retribution back into the present life. None could bear the horrors of that sick room, when he raved and screamed, and spoke of sights which almost stopped the blood of those who heard him; and, at his dying bed, stood a stern, white, inexorable figure, saying, "Come! come! come!"

By a singular coincidence, on the very night that this vision appeared to Legree, the house-door was found open in the morning, and some of the negroes had seen two white figures gliding down the avenue towards the high-road.

It was near sunrise when Cassy and Emmeline paused, for a moment, in a little knot of trees near the town.

Cassy was dressed after the manner of the Creole Spanish ladies — wholly in black. A small black bonnet on her head, covered by a veil thick with embroidery, concealed her face. It had been agreed that, in their escape, she was to personate the character of a Creole lady, and Emmeline that of her servant.

Brought up, from early life, in connection with the highest society, the language, movements and air of Cassy, were all in agreement with this idea; and she had still enough remaining with her, of a once splendid wardrobe, and sets of jewels, to enable her to personate the thing to advantage.

She stopped in the outskirts of the town, where she had noticed trunks for sale, and purchased a handsome one. This she requested the man to send along with her. And, accordingly, thus escorted by a boy wheeling her trunk, and Emmeline behind her, carrying her carpet-bag and sundry bundles, she made her appearance at the small tavern, like a lady of consideration.

The first person that struck her, after her arrival, was George Shelby, who was staying there, awaiting the next boat.

Cassy had remarked the young man from her loophole in the garret, and seen him bear away the body of Tom, and observed with secret exultation, his rencontre with Legree. Subsequently she had gathered, from the conversations she had overheard among the negroes, as she glided about in her ghostly disguise, after nightfall, who he was, and in what relation he stood to Tom. She, therefore, felt an immediate accession of confidence, when she found that he was, like herself, awaiting the next boat.

Cassy's air and manner, address, and evident command of money, prevented any rising disposition to suspicion in the hotel. People never inquire too closely into those who are fair on the main point, of paying well — a thing which Cassy had foreseen when she provided herself with money.

In the edge of the evening, a boat was heard coming along, and George Shelby handed Cassy aboard, with the politeness which comes naturally to every Kentuckian, and exerted himself to provide her with a good state-room.

Cassy kept her room and bed, on pretext of illness, during the whole time they were on Red River; and was waited on, with obsequious devotion, by her attendant.

When they arrived at the Mississippi river, George, having learned that the course of the strange lady was upward, like his own, proposed to take a state-room for her on the same boat with himself — good-naturedly compassionating her feeble health, and desirous to do what he could to assist her.

Behold, therefore, the whole party safely transferred to the good steamer Cincinnati, and sweeping up the river under a powerful head of steam.

Cassy's health was much better. She sat upon the guards, came to the table, and was remarked upon in the boat as a lady that must have been very handsome.

From the moment that George got the first glimpse of her face, he was troubled with one of those fleeting and indefinite likenesses, which almost every body can remember, and has been, at times, perplexed with. He could not keep himself from looking at her, and watching her perpetually. At table, or sitting at her state-room door, still she would encounter the young man's eyes fixed on her, and politely withdrawn, when she showed, by her countenance, that she was sensible to the observation.

Cassy became uneasy. She began to think that he suspected something; and finally resolved to throw herself entirely on his generosity, and intrusted him with her whole history.

George was heartily disposed to sympathize with any one who had escaped from Legree's plantation — a place that he could not remember or speak of with patience,— and, with the courageous disregard of consequences which is characteristic of his age and state, he assured her that he would do all in his power to protect and bring them through.

The next state-room to Cassy's was occupied by a French lady, named De Thoux, who was accompanied by a fine little daughter, a child of some twelve summers.

This lady, having gathered, from George's conversation, that he was from Kentucky, seemed evidently disposed to cultivate his acquaintance; in which design she was seconded by the graces of her little girl, who was about as pretty a plaything as ever diverted the weariness of a fortnight's trip on a steamboat.

George's chair was often placed at her state-room door; and Cassy, as she sat upon the guards, could hear their conversation.

Madame de Thoux was very minute in her inquiries as to Kentucky, where she said she had resided in a former period of her life. George discovered, to his surprise, that her former residence must have been in his own vicinity; and her inquiries showed a knowledge of people and things in his vicinity, that was perfectly surprising to him.

"Do you know," said Madame de Thoux to him, one day, "of any man, in your neighborhood, of the name of Harris?"

"There is an old fellow, of that name, lives not far from my father's place," said George. "We never have had much intercourse with him, though."

"He is a large slave-owner, I believe," said Madame de Thoux, with a manner which seemed to betray more interest than she was exactly willing to show.

"He is," said George, looking rather surprised at her manner.

"Did you ever know of his having — perhaps, you may have heard of his having a mulatto boy, named George?"

"O, certainly —George Harris — I know him well; he married a servant of my mother's, but has escaped, now, to Canada."

"He has?" said Madame de Thoux, quickly. "Thank God!"

George looked a surprised inquiry, but said nothing.

Madame de Thoux leaned her head on her hand, and burst into tears.

"He is my brother," she said.

"Madame!" said George, with a strong accent of surprise.

"Yes," said Madame de Thoux, lifting her head, proudly, and wiping her tears, "Mr. Shelby, George Harris is my brother!"

"I am perfectly astonished," said George, pushing back his chair a pace or two, and looking at Madame de Thoux.

"I was sold to the South when he was a boy," said she. "I was bought by a good and generous man. He took me with him to the West Indies, set me free, and married me. It is but lately that he died; and I was going up to Kentucky, to see if I could find and redeem my brother."

"I heard him speak of a sister Emily, that was sold South," said George.

"Yes, indeed! I am the one," said Madame de Thoux — "tell me what sort of a —"

"A very fine young man," said George, "notwithstanding the curse of slavery that lay on him. He sustained a first rate character, both for intelligence and principle. I know, you see," he said; "because he married in our family."

"What sort of a girl?" said Madame de Thoux, eagerly.

"A treasure," said George; "a beautiful, intelligent, amiable girl. Very pious. My mother had brought her up, and trained her as carefully, almost, as a daughter. She could read and write, embroider and sew, beautifully; and was a beautiful singer."

"Was she born in your house?" said Madame de Thoux.

"No. Father bought her once, in one of his trips to New Orleans, and brought her up as a present to mother. She was about eight or nine years old, then. Father would never tell mother what he gave for her; but, the other day, in looking over his old papers, we came across the bill of sale. He paid an extravagant sum for her, to be sure. I suppose, on account of her extraordinary beauty."

George sat with his back to Cassy, and did not see the absorbed expression of her countenance, as he was giving these details.

At this point in the story, she touched his arm, and, with a face perfectly white with interest, said, "Do you know the names of the people he bought her of?"

"A man of the name of Simmons, I think, was the principal in the transaction. At least, I think that was the name on the bill of sale."

"O, my God!" said Cassy, and fell insensible on the floor of the cabin.

George was wide awake now, and so was Madame de Thoux. Though neither of them could conjecture what was the cause of Cassy's fainting, still they made all the tumult which is proper in such cases — George upsetting a wash-pitcher, and breaking two tumblers, in the warmth of his humanity; and various ladies in the cabin, hearing that somebody had fainted, crowded the state-room door, and kept out all the air they possibly could, so that, on the whole, everything was done that could be expected.

Poor Cassy! when she recovered, turned her face to the wall, and wept and sobbed like a child — perhaps, mother, you can tell what she was thinking of! Perhaps you cannot — but she felt as sure, in that hour, that God had had mercy on her, and that she should see her daughter — as she did, months afterwards — when — but we anticipate.[1]

---

1 Harriet Beecher Stowe, *Uncle Tom's Cabin*, 1852; www.gutenberg.org/files/203/203-h/203-h.htm#2HCH0042.

Daily Assignment

- Warm-up: What does this quote mean? "...the past becomes dreamy because its symbols have all vanished, and the present too is dreamy because it is linked with no memories."-- *Silas Marner*, Chapter 1.
- Students will complete a daily Concept Builder 21-C.
- Prayer journal.
- Students should write rough drafts of all assigned essays.

Forming Conclusions

As he or she reads a text, every reader forms conclusion. What conclusions did you form about the novel *Silas Marner*?

Conclusion	Yes/No	Because . . .
Silas was unjustly accused of something he did not do, but he should not have reacted the way he did.		
Silas is an unhappy and lonely person until he meets Eppie.		
Eppie chooses her adopted father over her biological father.		
Silas lives happily ever after.		

Student Essay: Coincidence

Incidents of coincidence comprise much of *Silas Marner*. The author, Mary Anne Evans (also known as George Eliot), uses numerous unrelated, coincidental events to advance the plot. These events, far from lessening the novel's credibility, support its theme and overall effectiveness.

Even the beginning contains coincidence. In the exposition, we learn that Marner "had fallen . . . into a mysterious rigidity and suspension of consciousness . . ." which recurs twice in this chapter. Evans also introduces the character William Dane, "with whom [Silas] had long lived in such close friendship that it was the custom . . . to call them David and Jonathan." Surely that this friend should be in reality an enemy, bent on Silas's ruin, and that he alone should witness Silas's third *cataleptic* fit, thus enabling him to commit a crime while providing material evidence against Silas, would be a claim to arouse incredulity. Yet Eliot writes exactly this. The coincidence continues when Silas joins his church in praying before throwing lots, the accredited procedure for divining guilt. "The lots declared that Silas Marner was guilty."

The timing of certain events also appears quite unlikely. Marner's grief and bitterness transform him into a friendless miser, whose gold a neighbor steals. This theft is quite unheard of — "hoarding was common . . . in those days; but . . . neighbors . . . had not imaginations bold enough to lay a plan of burglary." Coincidentally, he steals it before the infant Eppie wanders into Marner's cottage. Perceiving Eppie as a sort of restitution for his treasure, Silas learns to love again. If his gold had not been stolen, or if circumstances had been different, such could not be the case. For instance, Eppie's mother dies. Had she survived, Marner would return her child. Quite probably, no other infant in the village has a father too self-centered to own her, as Eppie does.

These and other coincidences bear tints of either fantasy or supernatural power. As it happens, the story has a beautiful theistic theme of God's wisdom and love, as well as man's foolishness and need to trust his Maker. By describing a sequence of unlikely events that bring someone through a struggle with doubt and bitterness to a strengthened state of faith and love, Evans supports the idea of a loving deity wiser than man. At first, she uses coincidence to give Marner a reason to lose his trust in God. In doing so, Silas also distrusts mankind, as he learns what Dane had done. "You stole the money," he tells him, "and you have woven a plot to lay the sin at my door. But you may prosper, for all that: there is no just God that governs the earth righteously, but a God of lies, that bears witness against the innocent." In the mutual rejection of Marner and his community, the former becomes heterodox to a faulty religious sect. Yet through his unlikely foster fatherhood of Eppie, he cares for others once again and renews his faith in God. "Since the time the child was sent to me and I've come to love her as myself, I've had light enough to trusten by; and now, she says she'll never leave me, I think I shall trusten till I die."

Mary Ann Evan's tale is beautiful. Through a well-developed, wonderfully developed plot, she pushes the idea of man's finite mind, and his need to trust in Someone Else. In the stream of unlikely "coincidences," God, in a love-lit picture, is portrayed to us. (Bethany)

Daily Assignment

- Warm-up: What does this quote mean? "As the child's mind was growing into knowledge, his mind was growing into memory: as her life unfolded, his soul, long stupefied in a cold narrow prison, was unfolding too, and trembling gradually into full consciousness."— *Silas Marner*, Chapter 14.
- Students will complete Concept Builder 21-D.
- Prayer journal.
- Review the assigned text. Keep vocabulary cards.
- This is the day that students should write, and then rewrite, the final drafts of their assigned essays.

Plot Development

Complete the following chart focused on Silas Marner.

Every prose fiction work has a story, or plot. These include exposition, rising action, climax, falling action, and resolution. Complete this chart. For example, in Margaret Wise Brown's children's classic *The Runaway Bunny*, the exposition occurs when the reader learns that the principal characters are a baby bunny and his mom. We also learn that the young bunny is planning to run away. During the rising action we see that no matter where the bunny runs, the mommy bunny pursues and catches him. The climax occurs when the little bunny realizes that he cannot run away from his mom. The falling action occurs rather quickly, as the little bunny finally understands that he cannot escape the pursuing love of his mother. Finally, the resolution occurs when the little bunny happily accepts a carrot and decides to stay at home permanently.

Exposition: Introduction of Characters and Initial Action
Silas Marner is a member of a small Christian congregation in Lantern Yard, England, who is accused of stealing the congregation's funds while sitting with a very ill elder of the group. Two clues are given against him: a pocket-knife and the discovery of the bag formerly containing the money in his own house. Silas says that he last used the knife to cut some string for his friend William, who leads the campaign against him. Silas is unjustly convicted and the woman he was to marry breaks the engagement and later marries his former best friend, William. The reader wonders if William made up the charges to get Silas's girl. With his life shattered and his heart broken, he leaves Lantern Yard.
Rising Action: Initial and Subsequent Incidences That Advance the Plot
Climax: The Turning Point
Falling Action: Subsequent Incidences That Offer Some Resolution
Resolution: The Concluding Resolution of the Plot

Tone: Irony and Sentimentality — *Silas Marner* (George Eliot)

Chapter 22

First Thoughts

This short novel is the story of redemption, salvation, and restoration without a Christian framework for those laudable events. Silas Marner is restored to his joy and fortune in spite of his Christian faith — not because of his Christian faith. He is no Hester Prynne (in *The Scarlet Letter*) staying connected to the community no matter what the shortcomings of this community may be. He is no Huw (in *How Green Was My Valley*) who rejects any pretense of unforgiveness. Within the perimeters of his perceived injustice, Silas creates a naturalistic world within his secular but still morally theistic ethical system. In other words, Silas keeps the good works aspect of theism while rejecting the God who made these good works possible. This presages even more disturbing developments for the future works of literature.

Chapter Learning Objectives

In chapter 22 we will examine the use of irony and sentimentality (tone) in *Silas Marner* by George Eliot.

As a result of this chapter study you will be able to . . .

1. Decide if Eliot used too much sentimentality
2. Compare a biblical figure to Godfrey Cass. Then, discuss Godfrey's weaknesses.
3. Analyze the way Eliot uses irony.
4. Compare the use of sentimentality in this novel with *Pride and Prejudice* by Jane Austen.

Look Ahead for Friday

- Turn in a final copy of essay
- Take Weekly Test

Lesson 1

Irony and Sentimentality

Some critics argue that *Silas Marner* strays into sentimentality. While the reader may fervently desire for Silas to be a loving, attentive father, the chances of that really happening are slim.

Did Eliot use too much sentimentality?

The following is chapter 1 from *The Cash Boy* by Horatio Alger, and is an example of sentimentality. Determine whether or not sentimentality distracts the reader from more important issues. Is the scene and tone appropriate to the story?

Tom Pinkerton, son of Deacon Pinkerton, had just returned from Brooklyn, and while there had witnessed a match game between two professional clubs. On his return he proposed that the boys of Crawford should establish a club, to be known as the Excelsior Club of Crawford, to play among themselves, and on suitable occasions to challenge clubs belonging to other villages. This proposal was received with instant approval.

"I move that Tom Pinkerton address the meeting," said one boy.

"Second the motion," said another.

As there was no chairman, James Briggs was appointed to that position, and put the motion, which was unanimously carried.

Tom Pinkerton, in his own estimation a personage of considerable importance, came forward in a consequential manner, and commenced as follows:

"Mr. Chairman and boys. You all know what has brought us together. We want to start a club for playing baseball, like the big clubs they have in Brooklyn and New York."

"How shall we do it?" asked Henry Scott.

"We must first appoint a captain of the club, who will have power to assign the members to their different positions. Of course you will want one that understands about these matters."

"He means himself," whispered Henry Scott, to his next neighbor; and here he was right.

"Is that all?" asked Sam Pomeroy.

"No; as there will be some expenses, there must be a treasurer to receive and take care of the funds, and we shall need a secretary to keep the records of the club, and write and answer challenges."

"Boys," said the chairman, "you have heard Tom Pinkerton's remarks. Those who are in favor of organizing a club on this plan will please signify it in the usual way." All the boys raised their hands, and it was declared a vote.

"You will bring in your votes for captain," said the chairman.

Tom Pinkerton drew a little apart with a conscious look, as he supposed, of course, that no one but himself would be thought of as leader. Slips of paper were passed around, and the boys began to prepare their ballots. They were brought to the chairman in a hat, and he forthwith took them out and began to count them.

"Boys," he announced, amid a universal stillness, "there is one vote for Sam Pomeroy, one for Eugene Morton, and the rest are for Frank Fowler, who is elected." There was a clapping of hands, in which Tom Pinkerton did not join. Frank Fowler, who is to be our hero, came forward a little, and spoke modestly as follows:

"Boys, I thank you for electing me captain of the club. I am afraid I am not very well qualified for the place, but I will do as well as I can." The speaker was a boy of fourteen. He was of medium height for his age, strong and sturdy in build, and with a frank prepossessing countenance, and an open, cordial manner, which made him a general favorite. It was not, however, to his popularity that he owed his election, but to the fact that both at bat and in the field he excelled all the boys, and therefore was the best suited to take the lead.

The boys now proceeded to make choice of a treasurer and secretary. For the first position Tom Pinkton{sic} received a majority of the votes. Though not popular, it was felt that some office was due him.

For secretary, Ike Stanton, who excelled in penmanship, was elected, and thus all the offices were filled.

The boys now crowded around Frank Fowler, with petitions for such places as they desired.

"I hope you will give me a little time before I decide about positions, boys," Frank said; "I want to consider a little."

"All right! Take till next week," said one and another, "and let us have a scrub game this afternoon."

The boys were in the middle of the sixth inning, when some one called out to Frank Fowler: "Frank, your sister is running across the field. I think she wants you."

Frank dropped his bat and hastened to meet his sister.

"What's the matter, Gracie?" he asked in alarm.

"Oh, Frank!" she exclaimed, bursting into tears. "Mother's been bleeding at the lungs, and she looks so white. I'm afraid she's very sick."

"Boys," said Frank, turning to his companions, "I must go home at once. You can get some one to take my place, my mother is very sick."

When Frank reached the little brown cottage which he called home, he found his mother in an exhausted state reclining on the bed.

"How do you feel, mother?" asked our hero, anxiously.

"Quite weak, Frank," she answered in a low voice

"I have had a severe attack."

"Let me go for the doctor, mother."

"I don't think it will be necessary, Frank. The attack is over, and I need no medicines, only time to bring back my strength."

But three days passed, and Mrs. Fowler's nervous prostration continued. She had attacks previously from which she rallied sooner, and her present weakness induced serious misgivings as to whether she would ever recover. Frank thought that her eyes followed him with more than ordinary anxiety, and after convincing himself that this was the case, he drew near his mother's bedside, and inquired:

"Mother, isn't there something you want me to do?"

"Nothing, I believe, Frank."

"I thought you looked at me as if you wanted to say something."

"There is something I must say to you before I die."

"Before you die, mother!" echoed Frank, in a startled voice.

"Yes. Frank, I am beginning to think that this is my last sickness."

"But, mother, you have been so before, and got up again."

"There must always be a last time, Frank; and my strength is too far reduced to rally again, I fear."

"I can't bear the thought of losing you, mother," said Frank, deeply moved.

"You will miss me, then, Frank?" said Mrs. Fowler.

"Shall I not? Grace and I will be alone in the world."

"Alone in the world!" repeated the sick woman, sorrowfully, "with little help to hope for from man, for I shall leave you nothing. Poor children!"

"That isn't what I think of," said Frank, hastily.

"I can support myself."

"But Grace? She is a delicate girl," said the mother, anxiously. "She cannot make her way as you can."

"She won't need to," said Frank, promptly; "I shall take care of her."

"But you are very young even to support yourself. You are only fourteen."

"I know it, mother, but I am strong, and I am not afraid. There are a hundred ways of making a living."

"But do you realize that you will have to start with absolutely nothing? Deacon Pinkerton holds a mortgage on this house for all it will bring in the market, and I owe him arrears of interest besides."

"I didn't know that, mother, but it doesn't frighten me."

"And you will take care of Grace?"

"I promise it, mother."

"Suppose Grace were not your sister?" said the sick woman, anxiously scanning the face of the boy.

"What makes you suppose such a thing as that, mother? Of course she is my sister."

"But suppose she were not," persisted Mrs. Fowler, "you would not recall your promise?"

"No, surely not, for I love her. But why do you talk so, mother?" and a suspicion crossed Frank's mind that his mother's intellect might be wandering.

"It is time to tell you all, Frank. Sit down by the bedside, and I will gather my strength to tell you what must be told."

"Grace is not your sister, Frank!"

"Not my sister, mother?" he exclaimed. "You are not in earnest?"

"I am quite in earnest, Frank."

"Then whose child is she?"

"She is my child."

"Then she must be my sister — are you not my mother?"

"No, Frank, I am not your mother!"[1]

1 Horatio Alger, *The Cash Boy*, http://etext.lib.virginia.edu/toc/modeng/public/AlgCash.html.

Daily Assignment

- Warm-up: What actors and actresses would you choose to play the characters in *Silas Marner*?
- Students will complete Concept Builder 22-A.
- Prayer journal: Students are encouraged to write in their prayer journal every day.
- Students need to review their material for the next assignment
- Students should systematically review their vocabulary words daily.

Active Reading

In *Silas Marner* by George Eliot, compare and contrast how Silas's views on religion and children changed before and after he was accused of stealing.

Before he was accused of stealing

Religion	Children

After he was accused of stealing

Religion	Children

Lesson 2

Grammar Review: Periods for Commas

Do not use periods for commas. Compare the following:

The robin was singing. Because he was happy. (The second clause is a fragment — an incomplete sentence.)

Because the robin was happy, he was singing. (The two clauses are combined to make a complete sentence.)

Daily Assignment

- Warm-up: Rewrite the ending of *Silas Marner*. This time, have Eppie choose her biological father.
- Students will complete Concept Builder 22-B.
- Prayer journal.
- Students should outline all assigned essays for the week.

Elements of a Story

Analyze the following elements of the novel *Silas Marner* by George Eliot.

Elements	Yes/No	Because . . .
Characters Do the characters seem real?	*Mostly*	*Some of the characters appear to be archetypes (i.e., type or stock characters) more than real people (e.g., Dunstan and Molly).*
Narration Is Silas a credible narrator?		
Setting Is the setting important? Does it seem real?		
Plot Does the story flow logically? Does it flow well?		
Theme Is there a theme?		

Lesson 3

Sentimentality in the Prodigal Son

In spite of the fact that the story of the prodigal son is full of emotion, Luke carefully avoids sentimentality by:

- Creating credible characters
- Creating a credible plot

In short, Luke creates an emotional tone supported by circumstances, characters, and other literary elements.

Jesus continued: "There was a man who had two sons. The younger one said to his father, 'Father, give me my share of the estate.' So he divided his property between them.

"Not long after that, the younger son got together all he had, set off for a distant country and there squandered his wealth in wild living. After he had spent everything, there was a severe famine in that whole country, and he began to be in need. So he went and hired himself out to a citizen of that country, who sent him to his fields to feed pigs. He longed to fill his stomach with the pods that the pigs were eating, but no one gave him anything.

"When he came to his senses, he said, 'How many of my father's hired servants have food to spare, and here I am starving to death! I will set out and go back to my father and say to him: Father, I have sinned against heaven and against you. I am no longer worthy to be called your son; make me like one of your hired servants.' So he got up and went to his father.

"But while he was still a long way off, his father saw him and was filled with compassion for him; he ran to his son, threw his arms around him and kissed him.

"The son said to him, 'Father, I have sinned against heaven and against you. I am no longer worthy to be called your son.'

"But the father said to his servants, 'Quick! Bring the best robe and put it on him. Put a ring on his finger and sandals on his feet. Bring the fattened calf and kill it. Let's have a feast and celebrate. For this son of mine was dead and is alive again; he was lost and is found.' So they began to celebrate.

"Meanwhile, the older son was in the field. When he came near the house, he heard music and dancing. So he called one of the servants and asked him what was going on. 'Your brother has come,' he replied, 'and your father has killed the fattened calf because he has him back safe and sound.'

"The older brother became angry and refused to go in. So his father went out and pleaded with him. But he answered his father, 'Look! All these years I've been slaving for you and never disobeyed your orders. Yet you never gave me even a young goat so I could celebrate with my friends. But when this son of yours who has squandered your property with prostitutes comes home, you kill the fattened calf for him!'

" 'My son,' the father said, 'you are always with me, and everything I have is yours. But we had to celebrate and be glad, because this brother of yours was dead and is alive again; he was lost and is found.' " (Luke 15:11–31; NIV).

Daily Assignment

- Warm-up: How is the Church treated in this novel? Why is Eliot so critical? Is this an accurate portrayal of the Church?
- Students will complete a daily Concept Builder 22-C.
- Prayer journal.
- Students should write rough drafts of all assigned essays.

Irony

Irony is the contrast between what is expected and what actually happens. In situational irony, the character expects one thing to happen and another thing happens. In dramatic irony, the reader knows more about a situation or a character than the characters does. Here are some examples of irony from the novel *Silas Marner* by George Eliot. Decide whether the examples are situational or dramatic irony.

Situation	Situational Irony	Dramatic Irony
Silas's best friend betrays him.	*Yes*	*No*
Silas thinks he has lost everything when his gold disappears, but later he finds that he has gained the world with Eppie.		
The squire thinks he "dodges a bullet" when his mistress dies, only to find that he lost the best thing he had (i.e., Eppie).		
Silas expects Eppie to choose her birth father over her adopted father. But she does not do that.		
That which was meant for bad for Silas turns out to be the best thing that could happen to him.		

Student Essay: Sentimentality

Many accuse Silas Marner of excessive sentimentality. Through a series of coincidences, the author, George Eliot, creates a very happy ending. Due to the darkness developed earlier in the story, numerous readers doubtless anticipate a melancholy end. Certainly they never expect the joyous change depicted halfway through the book. This change, however, is not unwarranted. It develops the theme and works quite well with the book as a whole.

Silas Marner loses faith in God and man when his church condemns him for a crime he didn't commit. Greed and bitterness consume him, as he becomes a friendless miser. "For the first time in his life, he had five bright guineas put into his hand; no man expected a share of them, and he loved no man that he should offer him a share." Marner so alienates himself from God and society, and so forsakes all love for either, that many people consider his redemption impossible. How remarkable that Silas, of his own volition, becomes a caring foster father! "They lived together in perfect love . . ." we read. Credulous, indeed, does Eliot seem to believe her readers.

Yet even as she describes his moral decay, Eliot reminds us of Marner's benevolent potential and the life he lived before his sad disgrace befell him. "His life, before he came to Raveloe, had been filled with the movement, the mental activity, and the close fellowship which . . . marked the life of an artisan early incorporated in a narrow religious sect. . . . He had seemed to love [money] little in the years when every penny had its purpose for him; for he loved the purpose then. But now, when all purpose was gone, that habit of looking towards the money and grasping it with a sense of fulfilled effort made a loam that was deep enough for the seeds of desire." When Silas loses his gold, he needs another loam to satisfy those seeds, and the infant Eppie suffices for that loam. "[She's] a lone thing — and I'm a lone thing," Silas says. "My money's gone, I don't know where — and this is come from I don't know where."

As she quietly satisfies our incredulity, Eliot prepares us for the emergence of her theme. The book supports a belief in a loving God, and men's need to trust Him due to their finite minds. She promotes this theme through a series of coincidences, which lead to Marner's retrieval of trust and love for God and man. Through coincidence, Marner's gold is lost. Through coincidence, an abandoned child finds him. The story's very unlikelihood points to God's directing hand. He engenders circumstances for Silas's ultimate good. "Since he had found Eppie on the hearth, the sense of presiding goodness and the human trust which come with all pure peace and joy had given him a dim impression that there had been some error, some mistake, which had thrown that dark shadow over the days of his best years." And as he realizes the truth, Silas says, "Since the time the child was sent to me and I've come to love her as myself, I've had light enough to trusten by; and now, she says she'll never leave me, I think I shall trusten till I die."

Marner's relationship with Eppie is both appropriate and necessary. Eliot's skillful characterization of her main character makes his vicissitude believable. And when Marner returns to a life of faith and love, we see God's care and wisdom. (Bethany)

Daily Assignment

- Warm-up: Do you think Americans would want to see a movie made on this book? Why or why not?
- Students will complete Concept Builder 22-D.
- Prayer journal.
- Review the assigned text. Keep vocabulary cards.
- This is the day that students should write, and then rewrite, the final drafts of their assigned essays.

Sentimentality

Sentimentality is an author's technique used to evoke empathy and emotion from a reader. Many critics think that it is unnecessary. What do you think?

Example of Sentimentality	Purpose	Is it necessary? Why?
"Silas Marner was lulling the child. She was perfectly quiet now, but not asleep — only soothed by sweet porridge and warmth into that wide-gazing calm which makes us older human beings, with our inward turmoil, feel a certain awe in the presence of a little child, such as we feel before some quiet majesty or beauty in the earth or sky — before a steady glowing planet, or a full-flowered eglantine, or the bending trees over a silent pathway." (99; ch. 13)	*To show the reader how profound this event was to the protagonist.*	*Because this event, is used by Eliot to develop her theme, It was necessary to evoke deep emotion in the reader.*
"Thank you, ma'am — thank you, sir, for your offers — they're very great, and far above my wish. For I should have no delight i' life any more if I was forced to go away from my father, and knew he was sitting at home, a-thinking of me and feeling lonely We've been used to be happy together every day, and I can't think o' no happiness without him. And he says he'd nobody i' the world till I was sent to him, and he'd have nothing when I was gone. And he's took care of me and loved me from the first, and I'll cleave to him as long as he lives, and nobody shall ever come in between him and me." (143; ch. 19)		

Theme — *Silas Marner* (George Eliot)

Chapter 23

First Thoughts

A great story includes characters, plot, and other literary components. It also has profound and eternal meeting. Its meaning, or theme, should transcend time and location.

Chapter Learning Objectives

In chapter 23 we will examine several themes in *Silas Marner* by George Eliot.

As a result of this chapter study you will be able to . . .

1. Discuss several themes in *Silas Marner* and show how George Eliot (i.e., Evans) uses plot, setting, and characterization to develop them.
2. Explore redemption. This is an important theme in Silas Marner. Using copious textual examples, discuss the biblical understanding of redemption.
3. Compare a character in *Silas Marner* to a biblical character.

Look Ahead for Friday

- Turn in a final copy of essay
- Take Weekly Test

Student Essay: Theme

The following is a paper written on one theme in Erich Remarque's *All Quiet on the Western Front*:

We see men living with their skulls blown open; we see soldiers run with their two feet cut off; they stagger on their splintered stumps into the next shell-hole . . . we find one man who has held the artery of his arm in his teeth for two hours in order not to bleed to death.

This picture of the World War I Western Front is seen through the eyes of 19-year-old soldier Paul Baumer. Paul, the narrator of the book *All Quiet on the Western Front*, invited the reader into his hellish, naturalistic vision of life.

Naturalism was a late 19th-century, early 20th-century worldview arguing that life was controlled by unguided, uninterested fate. Life, if it had meaning at all, could not conceptualize itself as being under the control of a loving God. Written by the militant pacifist Erich Remarque in 1929, *All Quiet on the Western Front* has a naturalist bent, but this did not cause Remarque to spare his reader any gruesome details. Remarque clearly wished his reader to enter his naturalistic world where man is abused by other men and ignored by God. In fact, men became animals. Clearly, this is a naturalistic approach to life. In the book, a young recruit actually barks at Paul as he tries to force him to stand up and fight. "He draws up his legs, crouches back against the wall and shows his teeth like a cur. I seize him by the arm and try to pull him up. He barks."

Much like Joseph Conrad's *Heart of Darkness*, where the jungle turned Kurtz into a monster, so also did the war to every soul at the front. Kurtz realized that there was no ultimate meaning in life and he called "The horror! The horror!" Remarque's Paul Baumer realized that life was nothing more than "Bombardment, barrage, curtain-fire, mines, gas, tanks, machine-guns, hand-grenades, words, words, but they hold the horror." These two horrors were the same. Gone was the world of Homer's *Iliad*. In *The Iliad* a lot of horrible things happened, but these things happened with the full knowledge of the gods. These same gods, however, were not neglectful in their interaction with man. They were only mischievous. The "god" in *All Quiet* was utterly malevolent.

The war, also known as nature, created this horror inside the very souls of the men who fought each other. It created "the heavy, dead lump of lead that lies somewhere in me." That theme is communicated to the reader with horrible specificity. (Peter Stobaugh)

Daily Assignment

- Warm-up: Poor Silas learns that he cannot change the past. No one can. Yet, when we are born again, we experience a sort of rewriting of our history. Explain.
- Students will complete Concept Builder 23-A.
- Prayer journal: Students are encouraged to write in their prayer journal every day.
- Students need to review their material for the next assignment
- Students should systematically review their vocabulary words daily.

Author Bias

Eliot clearly had biased views toward certain subjects, and she communicated these views in her writing. Complete the following chart to show how she did this in her own text.

Subject	Eliot's View	Textual Examples
Religion		
Rich People		
The Industrial Revolution		

Lesson 2

Themes: Sacrificial Love and Wisdom

It is common for an author to develop two or more themes in one short narrative, or even more themes in a larger literary work. In this biblical passage, Jeremiah, the author of 1 Kings, presents a story to illustrate two themes:

- Sacrificial love
- Wisdom

Now two prostitutes came to the king and stood before him. One of them said, "Pardon me, my lord. This woman and I live in the same house, and I had a baby while she was there with me. The third day after my child was born, this woman also had a baby. We were alone; there was no one in the house but the two of us.

"During the night this woman's son died because she lay on him. So she got up in the middle of the night and took my son from my side while I your servant was asleep. She put him by her breast and put her dead son by my breast. The next morning, I got up to nurse my son — and he was dead! But when I looked at him closely in the morning light, I saw that it wasn't the son I had borne."

The other woman said, "No! The living one is my son; the dead one is yours."

But the first one insisted, "No! The dead one is yours; the living one is mine." And so they argued before the king.

The king said, "This one says, 'My son is alive and your son is dead,' while that one says, 'No! Your son is dead and mine is alive.' "

Then the king said, "Bring me a sword." So they brought a sword for the king. He then gave an order: "Cut the living child in two and give half to one and half to the other."

The woman whose son was alive was deeply moved out of love for her son and said to the king, "Please, my lord, give her the living baby! Don't kill him!"

But the other said, "Neither I nor you shall have him. Cut him in two!"

Then the king gave his ruling: "Give the living baby to the first woman. Do not kill him; she is his mother."

When all Israel heard the verdict the king had given, they held the king in awe, because they saw that he had wisdom from God to administer justice (1 Kings 3:16–28; NIV).

Daily Assignment

- Warm-up: Mary Ann Evans, the author of *Silas Marner*, rejected her faith. Give an example of how this affected the way she wrote her novel.
- Students will complete Concept Builder 22-B.
- Prayer journal.
- Students should outline all assigned essays for the week.

My Own Bias

Our own biases determine our views on a subject. Complete the following chart.

Subjects	Eliot's View	My Own Bias	My View
Religion	*Eliot is negative toward religion. This is partly based upon her own bad experience with religion.*	*My faith is a central part of my life. My church is a big part of my life.*	*Therefore I do not share the views of Eliot.*
Rich People			
The Industrial Revolution			

Lesson 3

Grammar Review: Consistency

Spell out all single-digit numerals (one, two, etc.) and use number symbols (11, 12, etc.) for numbers greater than ten.

Daily Assignment

- Warm-up: It seems like everyone gets what he deserves in this novel. Explain.
- Students will complete Concept Builder 23-C.
- Prayer journal.
- Students should write rough drafts of all assigned essays and speech.

CONCEPT BUILDER 23-C

Family History

Our own biases determine our views on a subject. Complete the following chart.

Activity	You	Parents/Guardians	Grandparents
Favorite Movies			
Dating Activity			
Favorite Music			
Vocational Plans			
Religion			
Favorite Books			

Lesson 4

Student Essay

Silas Marner portrays several themes and messages; one of the more prominent is redemption. Silas, for example, is redeemed from his obsession for gold and his bitterness of his past when he finds Eppie and begins to love once again. Another example is Godfrey, whose guilt lays heavily on him until he confesses his immorality and is redeemed by it.

Silas's redemption is manifested mostly through the discovery of Eppie. His deep attachment and obsession with his gold pulls him inward until he is a mere shell of his former self, already hurt and scarred by the past. When Eppie enters his life, he is redeemed from any former faults or accusations because his time can now be put into something productive and hopeful, something that yields more then gold.

"Silas's face showed that sort of transfiguration, as he sat in his arm-chair and looked at Eppie. She had drawn her own chair towards his knees, and leaned forward, holding both his hands, while she looked up at him. On the table near them, lit by a candle, lay the recovered gold — the old long-loved gold, ranged in orderly heaps, as Silas used to range it in the days when it was his only joy. He had been telling her how he used to count it every night, and how his soul was utterly desolate till she was sent to him."

Godfrey also experiences redemption through Eppie by confessing his wickedness. His guilt placed a heavy burden on him even after marrying Nancy and when confessed, he finally receives the forgiveness and redemption he was searching for all along.

"Everything comes to light, Nancy, sooner or later. When God Almighty wills it, our secrets are found out. I've lived with a secret on my mind, but I'll keep it from you no longer. I wouldn't have you know it by somebody else, and not by me — I wouldn't have you find it out after I'm dead. I'll tell you now. It's been 'I will' and 'I won't' with me all my life — I'll make sure of myself now."

Nancy's utmost dread had returned. The eyes of the husband and wife met with awe in them, as at a crisis which suspended affection.

"Nancy," said Godfrey, slowly, "when I married you, I hid something from you — something I ought to have told you. That woman Marner found dead in the snow — Eppie's mother — that wretched woman — was my wife: Eppie is my child."

As we follow Silas's life story, we see him being treated badly and rejected by those he once trusted. This sends him into bitterness. When he finds Eppie and begins to care for her, he experiences the love that was originally meant for him. The plot twists and turns but eventually opens into the broad and satisfying theme that justice prevails even in the most doubtful situations. (Stacia)

Daily Assignment

- Warm-up: The home is a central motif in this novel. Discuss your home and why it is important to you.
- Students will complete Concept Builder 23-D.
- Prayer journal.
- Review the assigned text. Keep vocabulary cards.
- This is the day that students should write, and then rewrite, the final drafts of their assigned essay.

Comparison/Contrast

Eliot clearly had biased views toward certain subjects, and she communicates these views in her writing. Likewise, Llewellyn, in his book *How Green Was My Valley*, also has certain bias/opinions. Compare these views and opinions. Complete the following chart.

Subject	Eliot	Llewellyn
Religion	*Eliot rejected traditional religion and the church while embracing a watered down, subjective, Judeo-Christian morality.*	*While Llewellyn saw the limits of the Church, he in no way rejected the church.*
Rich People		
The Industrial Revolution		

Précis — "The Religious Life of the Negro" (Booker T. Washington)

Chapter 24

First Thoughts

Booker T. Washington is one of the greatest Americans of the 19th century. Born a slave, Washington became a famous humanitarian, scholar, and teacher. Washington advanced the controversial position that African Americans should accept their social status while striving to advance themselves economically and morally.

Chapter Learning Objectives

In chapter 24 we will write a précis of "The Religious Life of the Negro" by Booker T. Washington.

As a result of this chapter study you will be able to . . .

1. Write a précis of "The Religious Life of the Negro" by Booker T. Washington.
2. Discuss Christian values Washington advanced in this essay even though he was not overtly writing a Christian essay.
3. Evaluate if Washington was too soft on prejudice in his essay.

Look Ahead for Friday

- Turn in a final copy of essay
- Take Weekly Test

Lesson 1

Précis Writing

One of the most important tasks before any reader is reading and understanding difficult books. Different kinds of books require different ways of reading. Difficult books that have layers of meaning require a much closer reading than books that do not. For instance, it would be foolish to look for deep meaning in Robert Louis Stevenson's *Treasure Island*, but it would be an entirely different matter if a person were reading C.S. Lewis' *The Screwtape Letters*.

Most readers are familiar with what is meant by a paraphrase, or a summary, which merely repeats the substance of the original passage in simpler language, but in approximately the same space. Paraphrasing and summarizing are processes of substituting easy phrases for those that present textual difficulties. In other words, a paraphrase and a summary are merely restatements of what is in the text.

A précis, on the other hand, often requires a rearrangement of ideas. The précis writer must assimilate the essence of the passage under discussion. It is easy, when one first begins to experiment with précis writing, to miss the theme of the text. A précis is a crystallization of the text in a precise, but profound way. A précis addresses intent as well as substance.

How does one write a précis?

First of all, it is necessary to read the passage attentively, and usually more than once, in an effort to grasp the central idea. This preliminary reading is concerned about details. Often it helps to read the passage aloud, for such a procedure necessitates slowness and may focus attention on some item that would otherwise be missed. At this stage, it is actually very helpful to write a paraphrase or summary of the text. Only on the second or subsequent readings do readers typically ferret out thematic concepts and syllogisms.

Daily Assignment

- Warm-up: By the last years of his life, Washington had moved away from many of his accommodationist policies. Speaking out with a new frankness, Washington attacked racism. In 1915 he joined ranks with former critics to protest the stereotypical portrayal of blacks in a new movie, "Birth of a Nation." Some months later he died at age 59. A man who overcame near-impossible odds himself, Booker T. Washington is best remembered for helping black Americans rise up from the economic slavery that held them down long after they were legally free citizens (National Park Service). Have you ever changed your mind about something? Why?
- Students will complete Concept Builder 24-A.
- Prayer journal: Students are encouraged to write in their prayer journal every day.
- Students need to review their material for the next assignment
- Students should systematically review their vocabulary words daily.

Active Reading

Read this excerpt from "The Religious Life of the Negro" by Booker T. Washington, and then answer the following questions:

In everything that I have been able to read about "The Religious Life of the Negro," it has seemed to me that writers have been too much disposed to treat it as something fixed and unchanging. They have not sufficiently emphasized the fact that the Negro people, in respect to their religious life, have been, almost since they landed in America, in a process of change and growth.

The Negro came to America with the pagan idea of his African ancestors; he acquired under slavery a number of Christian ideas, and at the present time he is slowly learning what those ideas mean in practical life. He is learning, not merely what Christians believe, but what they must do to be Christians.

The religious ideas which the Negroes brought with them to America from Africa were the fragments of a system of thought and custom, which, in its general features, is common to most barbarous people. What we call "fetishism" is, I suppose, merely the childish way of looking at and explaining the world, which did not, in the case of the people of West Africa, preclude a belief in the one true God, although He was regarded by them as far away and not interested in the little affairs of men.

But the peculiarity of their primitive religion, as I have learned from a very interesting book written by one who has been many years a missionary in Africa, consists in this, that it sought for its adherents a purely "physical salvation."

In the religion of the native African there was, generally speaking, no place of future reward or punishment, no heaven and no hell, as we are accustomed to conceive them. For this reason, the Negro had little sense of sin. He was not tortured by doubts and fears, which are so common and, we sometimes feel, so necessary a part of the religious experiences of Christians. The evils he knew were present and physical.

During the period of servitude in the New World, the Negro race did not wholly forget the traditions and habits of thought that it brought from Africa. But it added to its ancestral stock certain new ideas.

Slavery, with all its disadvantages, gave the Negro race, by way of recompense, one great consolation, namely, the Christian religion and the hope and belief in a future life. The slave, to whom on this side of the grave the door of hope seemed closed, learned from Christianity to lift his face from earth to heaven, and that made his burden lighter. In the end, the hope and aspiration of the race in slavery fixed themselves on the vision of the resurrection, with its "long white robes and golden slippers."

This hope and this aspiration, which are the theme of so many of the old Negro hymns, found expression in the one institution that slavery permitted to the Negro people the Negro Church. It was natural and inevitable that the Negro Church, coming into existence as it did under slavery, should permit the religious life of the Negro to express itself in ways almost wholly detached from morality. There was little in slavery to encourage the sense of personal responsibility.

1. What is Washington's view of the indigenous (native) African religions?

2. What is Washington's views of the Church?

Lesson 2

"The Raven"

Frequently the interpretation of an important part of a passage, or of the passage as a whole, will depend upon the clear understanding of a single word or a phrase. Consider, for example, Edgar Allan Poe's poem "The Raven." The refrain "Quoth the Raven, 'Nevermore' " is a critical phrase used in this poem. Its purpose and effect on the substance and theme of the poem is central to understanding the poem. Thus, a précis would address this element. Read the excerpt from the poem below:

Once upon a midnight dreary, while I pondered, weak and weary,
Over many a quaint and curious volume of forgotten lore,
While I nodded, nearly napping, suddenly there came a tapping,
As of some one gently rapping, rapping at my chamber door.
"'Tis some visitor," I muttered, "tapping at my chamber door —
Only this, and nothing more."

Ah, distinctly I remember it was in the bleak December,
And each separate dying ember wrought its ghost upon the floor.
Eagerly I wished the morrow — vainly I had sought to borrow
From my books surcease of sorrow — sorrow for the lost Lenore —
For the rare and radiant maiden whom the angels name Lenore —
Nameless here for evermore. …

And the Raven, never flitting, still is sitting, still is sitting
On the pallid bust of Pallas just above my chamber door;
And his eyes have all the seeming of a demon's that is dreaming,
And the lamplight o'er him streaming throws his shadow on the floor;
And my soul from out that shadow that lies floating on the floor
Shall be lifted — nevermore![1]

1 www.dailywriting.net/Poe.htm.

Daily Assignment

- Warm-up: Why do you think many Civil Rights leaders are pastors?
- Students will complete Concept Builder 24-B.
- Prayer journal.
- Students should outline all assigned essays for the week.

Comparing Views

Compare/contrast these two views with your own views.

Subjects	Washington's View	Malcolm X's View	My View
White-Black Relations	*African Americans should accept racial prejudice as inevitable and learn to live in this world..*	*Dubois took a more aggressive view and invited his community to reject the white world and to create an alternative community.*	
Violence	*There is no justification for violence of any kind.*	*Violence was justified and necessary.*	
Race Mixing	*Rejected this idea.*	*Rejected this idea.*	
Religion	*Christianity was at the heart of the African American life.*	*Christianity was a "white man's" faith. Therefore, African Americans should reject it.*	
Furture	*Very optimistic because he saw African Americans gaining new skills and knowledge that would help their cause.*	*Very pessimistic. Saw a future race war.*	

Lesson 3

Discerning Fundamental Metaphors of a Literary Piece

Often the entire meaning of a passage will depend upon some fundamental simile or metaphor. What is the central metaphor or simile in the following poem by Anne Bradstreet?

In Reference to Her Children, 2 June 1659

I had eight birds hatcht in one nest,
Four Cocks were there, and Hens the rest.
I nurst them up with pain and care,
No cost nor labour did I spare
Till at the last they felt their wing,
Mounted the Trees and learned to sing.
Chief of the Brood then took his flight
To Regions far and left me quite.
My mournful chirps I after send
Till he return, or I do end.
Leave not thy nest, thy Dame and Sire,
Fly back and sing amidst this Quire.
My second bird did take her flight
And with her mate flew out of sight.
Southward they both their course did bend,
And Seasons twain they there did spend,
Till after blown by Southern gales
They Norward steer'd with filled sails.
A prettier bird was no where seen,
Along the Beach, among the treen.
I have a third of colour white
On whom I plac'd no small delight,
Coupled with mate loving and true,
Hath also bid her Dame adieu.
And where Aurora first appears,
She now hath percht to spend her years.
One to the Academy flew
To chat among that learned crew.
Ambition moves still in his breast
That he might chant above the rest,
Striving for more than to do well,
That nightingales he might excell.
My fifth, whose down is yet scarce gone,
Is 'mongst the shrubs and bushes flown
And as his wings increase in strength
On higher boughs he'll perch at length.
My other three still with me nest
Until they're grown, then as the rest,
Or here or there, they'll take their flight,
As is ordain'd, so shall they light.
If birds could weep, then would my tears
Let others know what are my fears
Lest this my brood some harm should catch
And be surpris'd for want of watch
Whilst pecking corn and void of care
They fall un'wares in Fowler's snare;
Or whilst on trees they sit and sing
Some untoward boy at them do fling,
Or whilst allur'd with bell and glass
The net be spread and caught, alas;
Or lest by Lime-twigs they be foil'd;
Or by some greedy hawks be spoil'd.
O would, my young, ye saw my breast
And knew what thoughts there sadly rest.
Great was my pain when I you bred,
Great was my care when I you fed.
Long did I keep you soft and warm
And with my wings kept off all harm.
My cares are more, and fears, than ever,
My throbs such now as 'fore were never.
Alas, my birds, you wisdom want
Of perils you are ignorant.

Oft times in grass, on trees, in flight,
Sore accidents on you may light.
O to your safety have an eye,
So happy may you live and die.
Mean while, my days in tunes I'll spend
Till my weak lays with me shall end.
In shady woods I'll sit and sing
And things that past, to mind I'll bring.
Once young and pleasant, as are you,
But former toys (no joys) adieu!
My age I will not once lament
But sing, my time so near is spent,
And from the top bough take my flight
Into a country beyond sight
Where old ones instantly grow young
And there with seraphims set song.
No seasons cold, nor storms they see
But spring lasts to eternity.
When each of you shall in your nest
Among your young ones take your rest,
In chirping languages oft them tell
You had a Dame that lov'd you well,
That did what could be done for young
And nurst you up till you were strong
And 'fore she once would let you fly
She shew'd you joy and misery,
Taught what was good, and what was ill,
What would save life, and what would kill.
Thus gone, amongst you I may live,
And dead, yet speak and counsel give.
Farewell, my birds, farewell, adieu,
I happy am, if well with you.[1]

1 www.vcu.edu/engweb/webtexts/Bradstreet/reference.htm.

Daily Assignment

- Warm-up: Washington, born a slave, had every reason to be angry at his white captors, yet, there is no evidence that he had any rancor in his heart. Why?
- Students will complete Concept Builder 24-C.
- Prayer journal.
- Students should write rough drafts of all assigned essays and speech.

Persuasive Appeal

Complete the chart below based on Washington's views, historical insights, and your own views.

Argument:
Religion was very important to African Americans.

Thesis Statement:
To many slaves, and then freed African Americans, religion was vitally important because it was a very personal way to express feelings and hope in a way that others could not deny.

Reasons and Evidence

Counter-arguments

Response to Counter-arguments

Lesson 4

Grammar Review: Specific, Definite Language

Use specific, definite language. Compare the following:

The new car costs too much.

The 2003 Impala costs too much – $28,000.

Daily Assignment

- Warm-up: Some critics argue that Washington "sold out" to whites and did not advance the cause of his people enough. What do you think?
- Students will complete Concept Builder 24-D.
- Prayer journal.
- Review the assigned text. Keep vocabulary cards.
- This is the day that students should write, and then rewrite, the final drafts of their assigned essay.

Persuasive Essay

Booker T. Washington was a great American. However, within the African American community, some were critical of him. In particular, he wrote an essay, "The Religious Life of the African American Negro," where he argued that African Americans should accept their social position (segregation) for the greater good of educational and religious advancement. In other words, Washington seemed to suggest that African Americans should accept racial prejudice as inevitable (at least for now) and simply go on and live their lives the best way that they could. Agree or disagree with Booker T. Washington.

Thesis:

Argument 1:

Reason/Evidence:

Argument 2:

Reason/Evidence:

Argument 3:

Reason/Evidence:

Conclusion:

Characterization — *Anne of Green Gables* (L. Maude Montgomery)

Chapter 25

First Thoughts

Maude Montgomery was born at Clifton, Prince Edward Island, Canada, in November of 1874. When her mother died, Montgomery was in an orphanage for a while — but that was the extent of any similarity between her life and Anne Shirley's. Her father remarried and Mrs. Montgomery grew up with her father and her stepmother in Prince Edward Island. In 1911, she married Rev. Ewen Macdonald and moved to Ontario, where she raised three children. Marrying at age 37, Mrs. Montgomery had already established herself as a published author. She published her first book, *Anne of Green Gables,* in 1908 and continued to write prolifically. She died in 1942 and was buried at Prince Edward Island.

Chapter Learning Objectives

In chapter 25 we will discuss characterization in *Anne of Green Gables* by Maude Montgomery.

As a result of this chapter study you will be able to . . .

1. Use copious references from the text to discuss the way Maude Montgomery develops her protagonist Anne Shirley.
2. Discuss how the author of the Book of Job creates his main character (i.e., Job).
3. *Anne of Green Gables* is replete with rich characters. Discuss how Montgomery uses at least three characters (or foils) to develop Anne.

Look Ahead for Friday

- Turn in a final copy of essay
- Take Weekly Test

Lesson 1

Characterization

Characterization is the art of creating characters for a narrative. Characters may be presented by means of description, through their actions, speech, or thoughts. Maude Montgomery normally created young, adventurous female protagonists, the most-well known of whom was Anne Shirley. Observe the skillful way Montgomery introduces her colorful character, Anne Shirley:

Chapter 2
Matthew Cuthbert Is Surprised

Matthew Cuthbert and the sorrel mare jogged comfortably over the eight miles to Bright River. It was a pretty road, running along between snug farmsteads, with now and again a bit of balsamy fir wood to drive through or a hollow where wild plums hung out their filmy bloom. The air was sweet with the breath of many apple orchards and the meadows sloped away in the distance to horizon mists of pearl and purple; while

"The little birds sang as if it were
The one day of summer in all the year."

Matthew enjoyed the drive after his own fashion, except during the moments when he met women and had to nod to them — for in Prince Edward island you are supposed to nod to all and sundry you meet on the road whether you know them or not.

Matthew dreaded all women except Marilla and Mrs. Rachel; he had an uncomfortable feeling that the mysterious creatures were secretly laughing at him. He may have been quite right in thinking so, for he was an odd-looking personage, with an ungainly figure and long iron-gray hair that touched his stooping shoulders, and a full, soft brown beard which he had worn ever since he was twenty. In fact, he had looked at twenty very much as he looked at sixty, lacking a little of the grayness.

When he reached Bright River there was no sign of any train; he thought he was too early, so he tied his horse in the yard of the small Bright River hotel and went over to the station house. The long platform was almost deserted; the only living creature in sight being a girl who was sitting on a pile of shingles at the extreme end. Matthew, barely noting that it *was* a girl, sidled past her as quickly as possible without looking at her. Had he looked he could hardly have failed to notice the tense rigidity and expectation of her attitude and expression. She was sitting there waiting for something or somebody and, since sitting and waiting was the only thing to do just then, she sat and waited with all her might and main.

Matthew encountered the stationmaster locking up the ticket office preparatory to going home for supper, and asked him if the five-thirty train would soon be along.

"The five-thirty train has been in and gone half an hour ago," answered that brisk official. "But there was a passenger dropped off for you — a little girl. She's sitting out there on the shingles. I asked her to go into the ladies' waiting room, but she informed me gravely that she preferred to stay outside. 'There was more scope for imagination,' she said. She's a case, I should say."

"I'm not expecting a girl," said Matthew blankly. "It's a boy I've come for. He should be here. Mrs. Alexander Spencer was to bring him over from Nova Scotia for me."

The stationmaster whistled.

"Guess there's some mistake," he said. "Mrs. Spencer came off the train with that girl and gave her into my charge. Said you and your sister were adopting her from an orphan asylum and that you would be along for her presently. That's all I know about it — and I haven't got any more orphans concealed hereabouts."

"I don't understand," said Matthew helplessly, wishing that Marilla was at hand to cope with the situation.

"Well, you'd better question the girl," said the station-master carelessly. "I dare say she'll be able to explain — she's got a tongue of her own, that's certain. Maybe they were out of boys of the brand you wanted."

He walked jauntily away, being hungry, and the unfortunate Matthew was left to do that which was harder for him than bearding a lion in its den — walk up to a girl — a strange girl — an orphan girl — and demand of her why she wasn't a boy. Matthew groaned in spirit as he turned about and shuffled gently down the platform towards her.

She had been watching him ever since he had passed her and she had her eyes on him now. Matthew was not looking at her and would not have seen what she was really like if he had been, but an ordinary observer would have seen this: A child of about eleven, garbed in a very short, very tight, very ugly dress of yellowish-gray wincey. She wore a faded brown sailor hat and beneath the hat, extending down her back, were two braids of very thick, decidedly red hair. Her face was small, white and thin, also much freckled; her mouth was large and so were her eyes, which looked green in some lights and moods and gray in others.

So far, the ordinary observer; an extraordinary observer might have seen that the chin was very pointed and pronounced; that the big eyes were full of spirit and vivacity; that the mouth was sweet-lipped and expressive; that the forehead was broad and full; in short, our discerning extraordinary observer might have concluded that no commonplace soul inhabited the body of this stray woman-child of whom shy Matthew Cuthbert was so ludicrously afraid.

Matthew, however, was spared the ordeal of speaking first, for as soon as she concluded that he was coming to her she stood up, grasping with one thin brown hand the handle of a shabby, old-fashioned carpet-bag; the other she held out to him.

"I suppose you are Mr. Matthew Cuthbert of Green Gables?" she said in a peculiarly clear, sweet voice. "I'm very glad to see you. I was beginning to be afraid you weren't coming for me and I was imagining all the things that might have happened to prevent you. I had made up my mind that if you didn't come for me tonight I'd go down the track to that big wild cherry-tree at the bend, and climb up into it to stay all night. I wouldn't be a bit afraid, and it would be lovely to sleep in a wild cherry-tree all white with bloom in the moonshine, don't you think? You could imagine you were dwelling in marble halls, couldn't you? And I was quite sure you would come for me in the morning, if you didn't tonight."

Matthew had taken the scrawny little hand awkwardly in his; then and there he decided what to do. He could not tell this child with the glowing eyes that there had been a mistake; he would take her home and let Marilla do that. She couldn't be left at Bright River anyhow, no matter what mistake had been made, so all questions and explanations might as well be deferred until he was safely back at Green Gables.

"I'm sorry I was late," he said shyly. "Come along. The horse is over in the yard. Give me your bag."

"Oh, I can carry it," the child responded cheerfully. "It isn't heavy. I've got all my worldly goods in it, but it isn't heavy. And if it isn't carried in just a certain way the handle pulls out — so I'd better keep it because I know the exact knack of it. It's an extremely old carpet-bag. Oh, I'm very glad you've come, even if it would have been nice to sleep in a wild cherry-tree. We've got to drive a long piece, haven't we? Mrs. Spencer said it was eight miles. I'm glad because I love driving. Oh, it seems so wonderful that I'm going to live with you and belong to you. I've never belonged to anybody — not really. But the asylum was the worst. I've only been in it four months, but that was enough. I don't suppose you ever were an orphan in an asylum, so you can't possibly understand what it is like. It's worse than anything you could imagine. Mrs. Spencer said it was wicked of me to talk like that, but I didn't mean to be wicked. It's so easy to be wicked without knowing it, isn't it? They were good, you know — the asylum people. But there is so little scope for the imagination in an asylum — only just in the other orphans. It was pretty interesting to imagine things about them — to imagine that perhaps the girl who sat next to you was really the daughter of a belted earl, who had been stolen away from her parents in her infancy by a cruel nurse who died before she could confess. I used to lie awake at nights and imagine things like that, because I didn't have time in the day. I guess that's why I'm so thin — I am dreadful thin, ain't I? There isn't a pick on my bones. I do love to imagine I'm nice and plump, with dimples in my elbows."

With this Matthew's companion stopped talking, partly because she was out of breath and partly because they had reached the buggy. Not another word did she say until they had left the village and were driving down a steep little hill, the road part of which had been cut so deeply into the soft soil, that the banks, fringed with blooming wild cherry-trees and slim white birches, were several feet above their heads.

The child put out her hand and broke off a branch of wild plum that brushed against the side of the buggy.

"Isn't that beautiful? What did that tree, leaning out from the bank, all white and lacy, make you think of?" she asked.

"Well now, I dunno," said Matthew.

"Why, a bride, of course — a bride all in white with a lovely misty veil. I've never seen one, but I can imagine what she would look like. I don't ever expect to be a bride myself. I'm so homely nobody will ever want to marry me — unless it might be a foreign missionary. I suppose a foreign missionary mightn't be very particular. But I do hope that some day I shall have a white dress. That is my highest ideal of earthly bliss. I just love pretty clothes. And I've never had a pretty dress in my life that I can remember — but of course it's all the more to look forward to, isn't it? And then I can imagine that I'm dressed gorgeously. This morning when I left the asylum I felt so ashamed because I had to wear this horrid old wincey dress. All the orphans had to wear them, you know. A merchant in Hopeton last winter donated three hundred yards of wincey to the asylum. Some people said it was because he couldn't sell it, but I'd rather believe that it was out of the kindness of his heart, wouldn't you? When we got on the train I felt as if everybody must be looking at me and pitying me. But I just went to work and imagined that I had on the most beautiful pale blue silk dress — because when you are imagining you might as well imagine something worth while — and a big hat all flowers and nodding plumes, and a gold watch, and kid gloves and boots. I felt cheered up right away and I enjoyed my trip to the Island with all my might. I wasn't a bit sick coming over in the boat. Neither was Mrs. Spencer although she generally is. She said she hadn't time to get sick, watching to see that I didn't fall overboard. She said she never saw the beat of me for prowling about. But if it kept her from being seasick it's a mercy I did prowl, isn't it? And I wanted to see everything that was to be seen on that boat, because I didn't know whether I'd ever have another opportunity. Oh, there are a lot more cherry-trees all in bloom! This Island is the bloomiest place. I just love it already, and I'm so glad I'm going to live here. I've always heard that Prince Edward Island was the prettiest place in the world, and I used to imagine I was living here, but I never really expected I would. It's delightful when your imaginations come true, isn't it? But those red roads are so funny. When we got into the train at Charlottetown and the red roads began to flash past I asked Mrs. Spencer what made them red and she said she didn't know and for pity's sake not to ask her any more questions. She said I must have asked her a thousand already. I suppose I had, too, but how you going to find out about things if you don't ask questions? And what does make the roads red?"

Green Gables farmhouse in Cavendish, Prince Edward Island. Photo by Chensyuan, 2006 (CC BY-SA 3.0).

"Well now, I dunno," said Matthew.

"Well, that is one of the things to find out sometime. Isn't it splendid to think of all the things there are to find out about? It just makes me feel glad to be alive — it's such an interesting world. It wouldn't be half so interesting if we know all about everything, would it? There'd be no scope for imagination then, would there? But am I talking too much? People are always telling me I do. Would you rather I didn't talk? If you say so I'll stop. I can stop when I make up my mind to it, although it's difficult."

Matthew, much to his own surprise, was enjoying himself. Like most quiet folks he liked talkative people when they were willing to do the talking themselves and did not expect him to keep up his end of it. But he had never expected to enjoy the society of a little girl. Women were bad enough in all conscience, but little girls were worse. He detested the way they had of sidling past him timidly, with sidewise glances, as if they expected him to gobble them up at a mouthful if they ventured to say a word. That was the Avonlea type of well-bred little girl. But this freckled witch was very different, and although he found it rather difficult for his slower intelligence to keep up with her brisk mental processes he thought that he "kind of liked her chatter." So he said as shyly as usual:

"Oh, you can talk as much as you like. I don't mind."

"Oh, I'm so glad. I know you and I are going to get along together fine. It's such a relief to talk when one wants to and not be told that children should be seen and not heard. I've had that said to me a million times if I have once. And people laugh at me because I use big words. But if you have big ideas you have to use big words to express them, haven't you?"

"Well now, that seems reasonable," said Matthew.

"Mrs. Spencer said that my tongue must be hung in the middle. But it isn't — it's firmly fastened at one end. Mrs. Spencer said your place was named Green Gables. I asked her all about it. And she said there were trees all around it. I was gladder than ever. I just love trees. And there weren't any at all about the asylum, only a few poor weeny-teeny things out in front with little whitewashed cagey things about them. They just looked like orphans themselves, those trees did. It used to make me want to cry to look at them. I used to say to them, 'Oh, you poor little things! If you were out in a great big woods with other trees all around you and little mosses and Junebells growing over your roots and a brook not far away and birds singing in you branches, you could grow, couldn't you? But you can't where you are. I know just exactly how you feel, little trees.' I felt sorry to leave them behind this morning. You do get so attached to things like that, don't you? Is there a brook anywhere near Green Gables? I forgot to ask Mrs. Spencer that."

"Well now, yes, there's one right below the house."

"Fancy. It's always been one of my dreams to live near a brook. I never expected I would, though. Dreams don't often come true, do they? Wouldn't it be nice if they did? But just now I feel pretty nearly perfectly happy. I can't feel exactly perfectly happy because — well, what color would you call this?"

She twitched one of her long glossy braids over her thin shoulder and held it up before Matthew's eyes. Matthew was not used to deciding on the tints of ladies' tresses, but in this case there couldn't be much doubt.

"It's red, ain't it?" he said.

The girl let the braid drop back with a sigh that seemed to come from her very toes and to exhale forth all the sorrows of the ages.

"Yes, it's red," she said resignedly. "Now you see why I can't be perfectly happy. Nobody could who has red hair. I don't mind the other things so much — the freckles and the green eyes and my skinniness. I can imagine them away. I can imagine that I have a beautiful rose-leaf complexion and lovely starry violet eyes. But I cannot imagine that red hair away. I do my best. I think to myself, 'Now my hair is a glorious black, black as the raven's wing.' But all the time I know it is just plain red and it breaks my heart. It will be my lifelong sorrow. I read of a girl once in a novel who had a lifelong sorrow but it wasn't red hair. Her hair was pure gold rippling back from her alabaster brow. What is an alabaster brow? I never could find out. Can you tell me?"

"Well now, I'm afraid I can't," said Matthew, who was getting a little dizzy. He felt as he had once felt in his rash youth when another boy had enticed him on the merry-go-round at a picnic.

"Well, whatever it was it must have been something nice because she was divinely beautiful. Have you ever imagined what it must feel like to be divinely beautiful?"

"Well now, no, I haven't," confessed Matthew ingenuously.

"I have, often. Which would you rather be if you had the choice — divinely beautiful or dazzlingly clever or angelically good?"

"Well now, I — I don't know exactly."

"Neither do I. I can never decide. But it doesn't make much real difference for it isn't likely I'll ever be either. It's certain I'll never be angelically good. Mrs. Spencer says — oh, Mr. Cuthbert! Oh, Mr. Cuthbert!! Oh, Mr. Cuthbert!!!"

That was not what Mrs. Spencer had said; neither had the child tumbled out of the buggy nor had Matthew done anything astonishing. They had simply rounded a curve in the road and found themselves in the "Avenue."

The "Avenue," so called by the Newbridge people, was a stretch of road four or five hundred yards long, completely arched over with huge, wide-spreading apple-trees, planted years ago by an eccentric old farmer. Overhead was one long canopy of snowy fragrant bloom. Below the boughs the air was full of a purple twilight and far ahead a glimpse of painted sunset sky shone like a great rose window at the end of a cathedral aisle.

Its beauty seemed to strike the child dumb. She leaned back in the buggy, her thin hands clasped before her, her face lifted rapturously to the white splendor above. Even when they had passed out and were driving down the long slope to Newbridge she never moved or spoke. Still with rapt face she gazed afar into the sunset west, with eyes that saw visions trooping splendidly across that glowing background. Through Newbridge, a bustling little village where dogs barked at them and small boys hooted and curious faces peered from the windows, they drove, still in silence. When three more miles had dropped away behind them the child had not spoken. She could keep silence, it was evident, as energetically as she could talk.

"I guess you're feeling pretty tired and hungry," Matthew ventured to say at last, accounting for her long visitation of dumbness with the only reason he could think of. "But we haven't very far to go now — only another mile."

She came out of her reverie with a deep sigh and looked at him with the dreamy gaze of a soul that had been wondering afar, star-led.

"Oh, Mr. Cuthbert," she whispered, "that place we came through — that white place — what was it?"

"Well now, you must mean the Avenue," said Matthew after a few moments' profound reflection. "It is a kind of pretty place."

"Pretty? Oh, pretty doesn't seem the right word to use. Nor beautiful, either. They don't go far enough. Oh, it was wonderful — wonderful. It's the first thing I ever saw that couldn't be improved upon by imagination. It just satisfies me here" — she put one hand on her breast — "it made a queer funny ache and yet it was a pleasant ache. Did you ever have an ache like that, Mr. Cuthbert?"

"Well now, I just can't recollect that I ever had."

"I have it lots of time — whenever I see anything royally beautiful. But they shouldn't call that lovely place the Avenue. There is no meaning in a name like that. They should call it — let me see — the White Way of Delight. Isn't that a nice imaginative name? When I don't like the name of a place or a person I always imagine a new one and always think of them so. There was a girl at the asylum whose name was Hepzibah Jenkins, but I always imagined her as Rosalia DeVere. Other people may call that place the Avenue, but I shall always call it the White Way of Delight. Have we really only another mile to go before we get home? I'm glad and I'm sorry. I'm sorry because this drive has been so pleasant and I'm always sorry when pleasant things end. Something still pleasanter may come after, but you can never be sure. And it's so often the case that it isn't pleasanter. That has been my experience anyhow. But I'm glad to think of getting home. You see, I've never had a real home since I can remember. It gives me that pleasant ache again just to think of coming to a really truly home. Oh, isn't that pretty!"

They had driven over the crest of a hill. Below them was a pond, looking almost like a river so long and winding was it. A bridge spanned it midway and from there to its lower end, where an amber-hued belt of sand-hills shut it in from the dark blue gulf beyond, the water was a glory of many shifting hues — the most spiritual shadings of crocus and rose and ethereal green, with other elusive tintings for which no name has ever been found. Above the bridge the pond ran up into fringing groves of fir and maple and lay all darkly translucent in their wavering shadows. Here and there a wild plum leaned out from the bank like a white-clad girl tip-toeing to her own reflection. From the marsh at the head of the pond came the clear, mournfully-sweet chorus of the frogs. There was a little gray house peering around a white apple orchard on a slope beyond and, although it was not yet quite dark, a light was shining from one of its windows.

"That's Barry's pond," said Matthew.

"Oh, I don't like that name, either. I shall call it — let me see — the Lake of Shining Waters. Yes, that is the right name for it. I know because of the thrill. When I hit on a name that suits exactly it gives me a thrill. Do things ever give you a thrill?"

Matthew ruminated.

"Well now, yes. It always kind of gives me a thrill to see them ugly white grubs that spade up in the cucumber beds. I hate the look of them."

"Oh, I don't think that can be exactly the same kind of a thrill. Do you think it can? There doesn't seem to be much connection between grubs and lakes of shining waters, does there? But why do other people call it Barry's pond?"

"I reckon because Mr. Barry lives up there in that house. Orchard Slope's the name of his place. If it wasn't for that big bush behind it you could see Green Gables from here. But we have to go over the bridge and round by the road, so it's near half a mile further."

"Has Mr. Barry any little girls? Well, not so very little either — about my size."

"He's got one about eleven. Her name is Diana."

"Oh!" with a long indrawing of breath. "What a perfectly lovely name!"

"Well now, I dunno. There's something dreadful heathenish about it, seems to me. I'd ruther Jane or Mary or some sensible name like that. But when Diana was born there was a schoolmaster boarding there and they gave him the naming of her and he called her Diana."

"I wish there had been a schoolmaster like that around when I was born, then. Oh, here we are at the bridge. I'm going to shut my eyes tight. I'm always afraid going over bridges. I can't help imagining that perhaps just as we get to the middle, they'll crumple up like a jack-knife and nip us. So I shut my eyes. But I always have to open them for all when I think we're getting near the middle. Because, you see, if the bridge did crumple up I'd want to see it crumple. What a jolly rumble it makes! I always like the rumble part of it. Isn't it splendid there are so many things to like in this world? There we're over. Now I'll look back. Good night, dear Lake of Shining Waters. I always say good night to the things I love, just as I would to people I think they like it. That water looks as if it was smiling at me."

When they had driven up the further hill and around a corner Matthew said:

"We're pretty near home now. That's Green Gables over —"

"Oh, don't tell me," she interrupted breathlessly, catching at his partially raised arm and shutting her eyes that she might not see his gesture. "Let me guess. I'm sure I'll guess right."

She opened her eyes and looked about her. They were on the crest of a hill. The sun had set some time since, but the landscape was still clear in the mellow afterlight. To the west a dark church spire rose up against a marigold sky. Below was a little valley and beyond a long, gently-rising slope with snug farmsteads scattered along it. From one to another the child's eyes darted, eager and wistful. At last they lingered on one away to the left, far back from the road, dimly white with blossoming trees in the twilight of the surrounding woods. Over it, in the stainless southwest sky, a great crystal-white star was shining like a lamp of guidance and promise.

"That's it, isn't it?" she said, pointing.

Matthew slapped the reins on the sorrel's back delightedly.

"Well now, you've guessed it! But I reckon Mrs. Spencer described it so's you could tell."

"No, she didn't — really she didn't. All she said might just as well have been about most of those other places. I hadn't any real idea what it looked like. But just as soon as I saw it I felt it was home. Oh, it seems as if I must be in a dream. Do you know, my arm must be black and blue from the elbow up, for I've pinched myself so many times today. Every little while a horrible sickening feeling would come over me and I'd be so afraid it was all a dream. Then I'd pinch myself to see if it was real — until suddenly I remembered that even supposing it was only a dream I'd better go on dreaming as long as I could; so I stopped pinching. But it is real and we're nearly home."

With a sigh of rapture she relapsed into silence. Matthew stirred uneasily. He felt glad that it would be Marilla and not he who would have to tell this waif of the world that the home she longed for was not to be hers after all. They drove over Lynde's Hollow, where it was already quite dark, but not so dark that Mrs. Rachel could not see them from her window vantage, and up the hill and into the long lane of Green Gables. By the time they arrived at the house Matthew was shrinking from the approaching revelation with an energy he did not understand. It was not of Marilla or himself he was thinking of the trouble this mistake was probably going to make for them, but of the child's disappointment. When he thought of that rapt light being quenched in her eyes he had an uncomfortable feeling that he was going to assist at murdering something — much the same feeling that came over him when he had to kill a lamb or calf or any other innocent little creature.

The yard was quite dark as they turned into it and the poplar leaves were rustling silkily all round it.

"Listen to the trees talking in their sleep," she whispered, as he lifted her to the ground. "What nice dreams they must have!"

Then, holding tightly to the carpet-bag which contained "all her worldly goods," she followed him into the house.[1]

---

1 Maude Montgomery, *Anne of Green Gables*; www.cs.cmu.edu/~rgs/anne-table.html

Daily Assignment

- Warm-up: How does Montgomery make Anne so charming?
- Students will complete Concept Builder 25-A.
- Prayer journal: Students are encouraged to write in their prayer journal every day.
- Students need to review their material for the next assignment
- Students should systematically review their vocabulary words daily.

Active Reading

Read this excerpt from *Anne of Green Gables* (chapter 1) by Lucy Maud Montgomery, and then answer the following questions:

Mrs. Rachel Lynde lived just where the Avonlea main road dipped down into a little hollow, fringed with alders and ladies' eardrops and traversed by a brook that had its source away back in the woods of the old Cuthbert place; it was reputed to be an intricate, headlong brook in its earlier course through those woods, with dark secrets of pool and cascade; but by the time it reached Lynde's Hollow it was a quiet, well-conducted little stream, for not even a brook could run past Mrs. Rachel Lynde's door without due regard for decency and decorum; it probably was conscious that Mrs. Rachel was sitting at her window, keeping a sharp eye on everything that passed, from brooks and children up, and that if she noticed anything odd or out of place she would never rest until she had ferreted out the whys and wherefores thereof.

There are plenty of people in Avonlea and out of it, who can attend closely to their neighbor's business by dint of neglecting their own; but Mrs. Rachel Lynde was one of those capable creatures who can manage their own concerns and those of other folks into the bargain. She was a notable housewife; her work was always done and well done; she "ran" the Sewing Circle, helped run the Sunday-school, and was the strongest prop of the Church Aid Society and Foreign Missions Auxiliary. Yet with all this Mrs. Rachel found abundant time to sit for hours at her kitchen window, knitting "cotton warp" quilts — she had knitted sixteen of them, as Avonlea housekeepers were wont to tell in awed voices — and keeping a sharp eye on the main road that crossed the hollow and wound up the steep red hill beyond. Since Avonlea occupied a little triangular peninsula jutting out into the Gulf of St. Lawrence with water on two sides of it, anybody who went out of it or into it had to pass over that hill road and so run the unseen gauntlet of Mrs. Rachel's all-seeing eye.

She was sitting there one afternoon in early June. The sun was coming in at the window warm and bright; the orchard on the slope below the house was in a bridal flush of pinky-white bloom, hummed over by a myriad of bees. Thomas Lynde — a meek little man whom Avonlea people called "Rachel Lynde's husband" — was sowing his late turnip seed on the hill field beyond the barn; and Matthew Cuthbert ought to have been sowing his on the big red brook field away over by Green Gables. Mrs. Rachel knew that he ought because she had heard him tell Peter Morrison the evening before in William J. Blair's store over at Carmody that he meant to sow his turnip seed the next afternoon. Peter had asked him, of course, for Matthew Cuthbert had never been known to volunteer information about anything in his whole life. …

She was sitting there one afternoon in early June. The sun was coming in at the window warm and bright; the orchard on the slope below the house was in a bridal flush of pinky-white bloom, hummed over by a myriad of bees. Thomas Lynde — a meek little man whom Avonlea people called "Rachel Lynde's husband" — was sowing his late turnip seed on the hill field beyond the barn; and Matthew Cuthbert ought to have been sowing his on the big red brook field away over by Green Gables. Mrs. Rachel knew that he ought because she had heard him tell Peter Morrison the evening before in William J. Blair's store over at Carmody that he meant to sow his turnip seed the next afternoon. Peter had asked him, of course, for Matthew Cuthbert had never been known to volunteer information about anything in his whole life.

1. What is the narrative point of view?

2. Describe Rachel.

3. Describe Matthew.

Lesson 2

Characterization in the Bible: Ahab

The author of 1 Kings (Jeremiah) uses direct commentary, storytelling, and dialogue to develop his nefarious villain, King Ahab.

In the thirty-eighth year of Asa king of Judah, Ahab son of Omri became king of Israel, and he reigned in Samaria over Israel twenty-two years. Ahab son of Omri did more evil in the eyes of the LORD than any of those before him. He not only considered it trivial to commit the sins of Jeroboam son of Nebat, but he also married Jezebel daughter of Ethbaal king of the Sidonians, and began to serve Baal and worship him. He set up an altar for Baal in the temple of Baal that he built in Samaria. Ahab also made an Asherah pole and did more to arouse the anger of the LORD, the God of Israel, than did all the kings of Israel before him (1 Kings 16:29–33; NIV).

So Obadiah went to meet Ahab and told him, and Ahab went to meet Elijah. When he saw Elijah, he said to him, "Is that you, you troubler of Israel?"

"I have not made trouble for Israel," Elijah replied. "But you and your father's family have. You have abandoned the LORD's commands and have followed the Baals. Now summon the people from all over Israel to meet me on Mount Carmel. And bring the four hundred and fifty prophets of Baal and the four hundred prophets of Asherah, who eat at Jezebel's table."

So Ahab sent word throughout all Israel and assembled the prophets on Mount Carmel. Elijah went before the people and said, "How long will you waver between two opinions? If the LORD is God, follow him; but if Baal is God, follow him."

But the people said nothing. (1 Kings 18:16–21).

Daily Assignment

- Warm-up: Do you think this novel is a children's novel, or can it be enjoyed by readers of all ages? Explain.
- Students will complete Concept Builder 25-B.
- Prayer journal.
- Students should outline all assigned essays for the week.

Characterization

Complete the following chart about Anne's character.

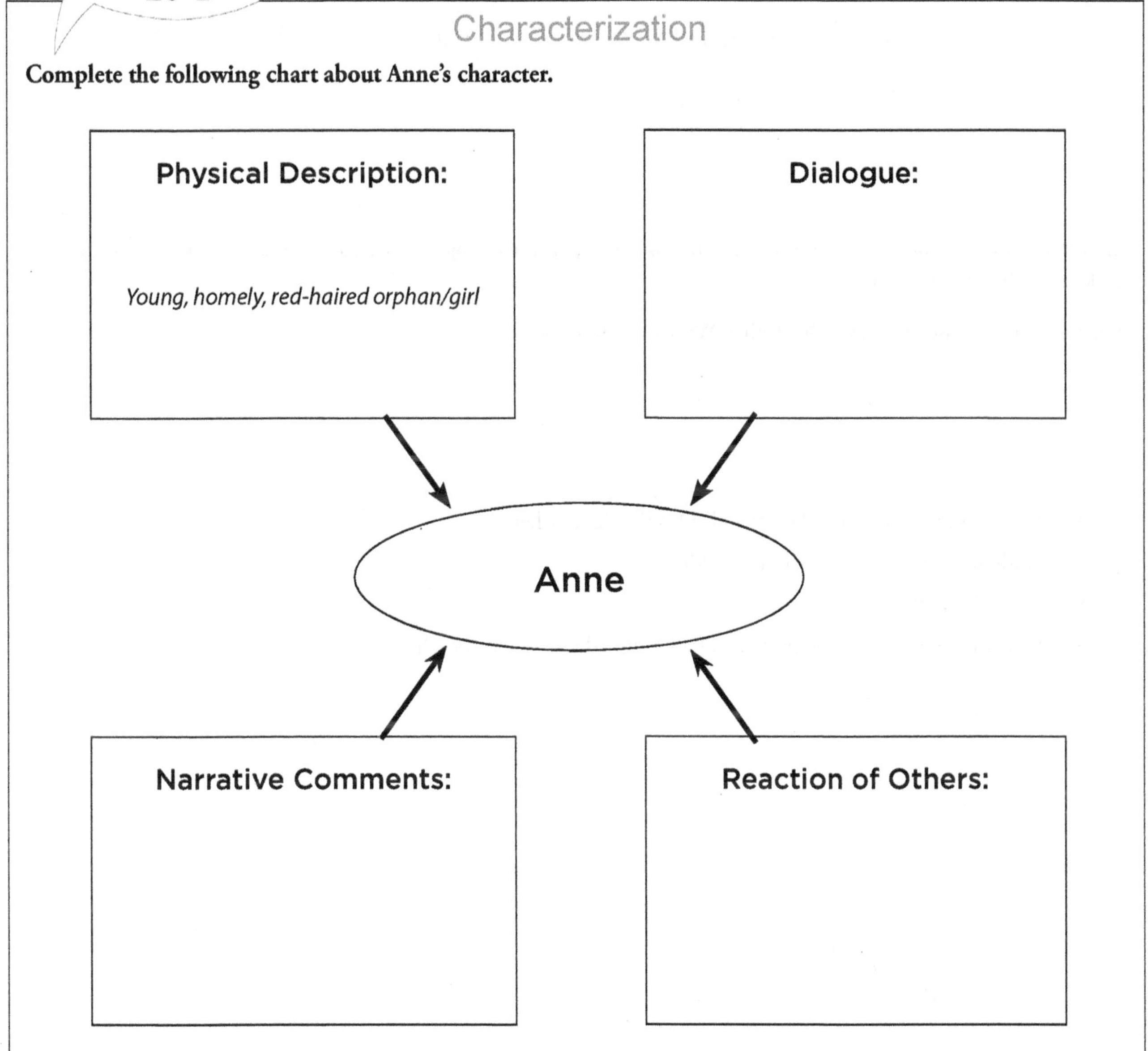

Lesson 3

Grammar Review: Quotations

In formal writing, a quotation that is in apposition or that is the direct object of a verb is preceded by a comma, and enclosed with quotation marks.

The missionary paused to pray, "Our Father, Who art in heaven."

Daily Assignment

- Warm-up: Do you have a best friend? Describe him or her.
- Students will complete Concept Builder 25-C.
- Prayer journal.
- Students should write rough drafts of all assigned essays and speech.

Elements of a Story

Analyze the following elements of the novel *Anne of Green Gables* by Lucy Maud Montgomery.

Elements	Yes/No	Because . . .
Characters Do the characters seem real?	*Yes*	*They all seem like the people we would meet in our neighborhood.*
Narration Is Anne a credible narrator?		
Setting Is the setting important? Does it seem real?		
Plot Does the story flow logically? Does it flow well?		
Theme Is there a theme?		

Student Essay

L.M. Montgomery's *Anne of Green Gables* is the story of a lively, romantic young girl, Anne Shirley. In the words of Matthew, Anne's caretaker, Anne is such a "real interesting little thing." To bring the character of Anne Shirley to life, Miss Montgomery used vivid descriptions, dialogue, and strong foils.

Anne's outward appearance makes up a huge part of her personality. Her most distinguishing trait is her carrot red hair, which is her "lifelong sorrow." Montgomery also describes her as skinny, homely, with large, thoughtful green eyes. "Her face was small, white and thin, also much freckled; her mouth was large and so were her eyes, which looked green in some lights and moods and gray in others" (chapter 2). Further descriptions include:

> "An extraordinary observer might have seen that the chin was very pointed and pronounced; that the big eyes were full of spirit and vivacity; that the mouth was sweet-lipped and expressive; that the forehead was broad and full; in short, our discerning extraordinary observer might have concluded that no commonplace soul inhabited the body of this stray woman-child." (chapter 2)

By giving strong descriptions of Anne, Montgomery brings her alive for the reader.

Another huge component of the characterization of Anne was dialogue. Through Anne's dialogue one learns more about the history of Anne as well as Anne's personality. One example of this is found in chapter 5, as Anne tells Marilla about herself.

> "I was eleven last March," said Anne, resigning herself to bald facts with a little sigh. "And I was born in Bolingbroke, Nova Scotia. My father's name was Walter Shirley, and he was a teacher in the Bolingbroke High School. My mother's name was Bertha Shirley. Aren't Walter and Bertha lovely names?" (chapter 5)

Anne's dialogue is also made up of an impressive vocabulary and flowery phrases, which reflect her romantic personality. This can be seen in the following conversation:

> "Well, that is another hope gone. 'My life is a perfect graveyard of buried hopes.' That's a sentence I read in a book once, and I say it over to comfort myself whenever I'm disappointed in anything."
>
> "I don't see where the comforting comes in myself," said Marilla.
>
> "Why, because it sounds so nice and romantic, just as if I were a heroine in a book, you know. I am so fond of romantic things, and a graveyard full of buried hopes is about as romantic a thing as one can imagine isn't it? I'm rather glad I have one." (chapter 5)

Through dialogue, Anne's priorities and perspective of life are seen. "It just makes me feel glad to be alive — it's such an interesting world. It wouldn't be half so interesting if we know all about everything, would it? There'd be no scope for imagination then, would there?" (chapter 2)

Lastly, Anne is developed through the use of foils. Two such strong foils were Diana Barry, her "bosom friend" and Gilbert Blythe, her worst enemy. These two foils showed the extreme side of Anne's nature. Diana she loves with a passion; Gilbert she hates with a passion. Diana is the completion of Anne's fervent wish to have a bosom friend, and their friendship is a solemn one.

> "We must join hands — so," said Anne gravely. "It ought to be over running water. We'll just imagine this path is running water. I'll repeat the oath first. I solemnly swear to be faithful to my bosom friend, Diana Barry, as long as the sun and moon shall endure" (chapter 12).

Diana is everything Anne is not: she has dark "raven" hair, dimples, and is a stark realist. Anne is everything Diana is not: Anne is academically smart, imaginative, and romantic. Diana complements Anne and helps in developing her character. While Diana brings out Anne's best side, Gilbert Blythe brings out the stubborn side of Anne. After Gilbert teases Anne about her hair, Anne flies into a rage and vows to never speak to him again (chapter 15). " 'I shall never forgive Gilbert Blythe,' said Anne firmly. . . . 'The iron has entered into my soul, Diana." For a good part of the rest of the book, Anne keeps her word and Gilbert Blythe became her hated rival and proof of her tenacious stubbornness.

Through the use of detailed descriptions, L.M. Montgomery develops Anne's outward appearance. Through rich dialogue, she develops Anne's person. Through the use of foils, she brings out Anne's strengths and weakness. All three things together make up the charming character of Anne of Green Gables. (Daphnide)

Daily Assignment

- Warm-up: Do you identify with Anne? Why or why not?
- Students will complete Concept Builder 25-D.
- Prayer journal.
- Review the assigned text. Keep vocabulary cards.
- This is the day that students should write, and then rewrite, the final drafts of their assigned essay.

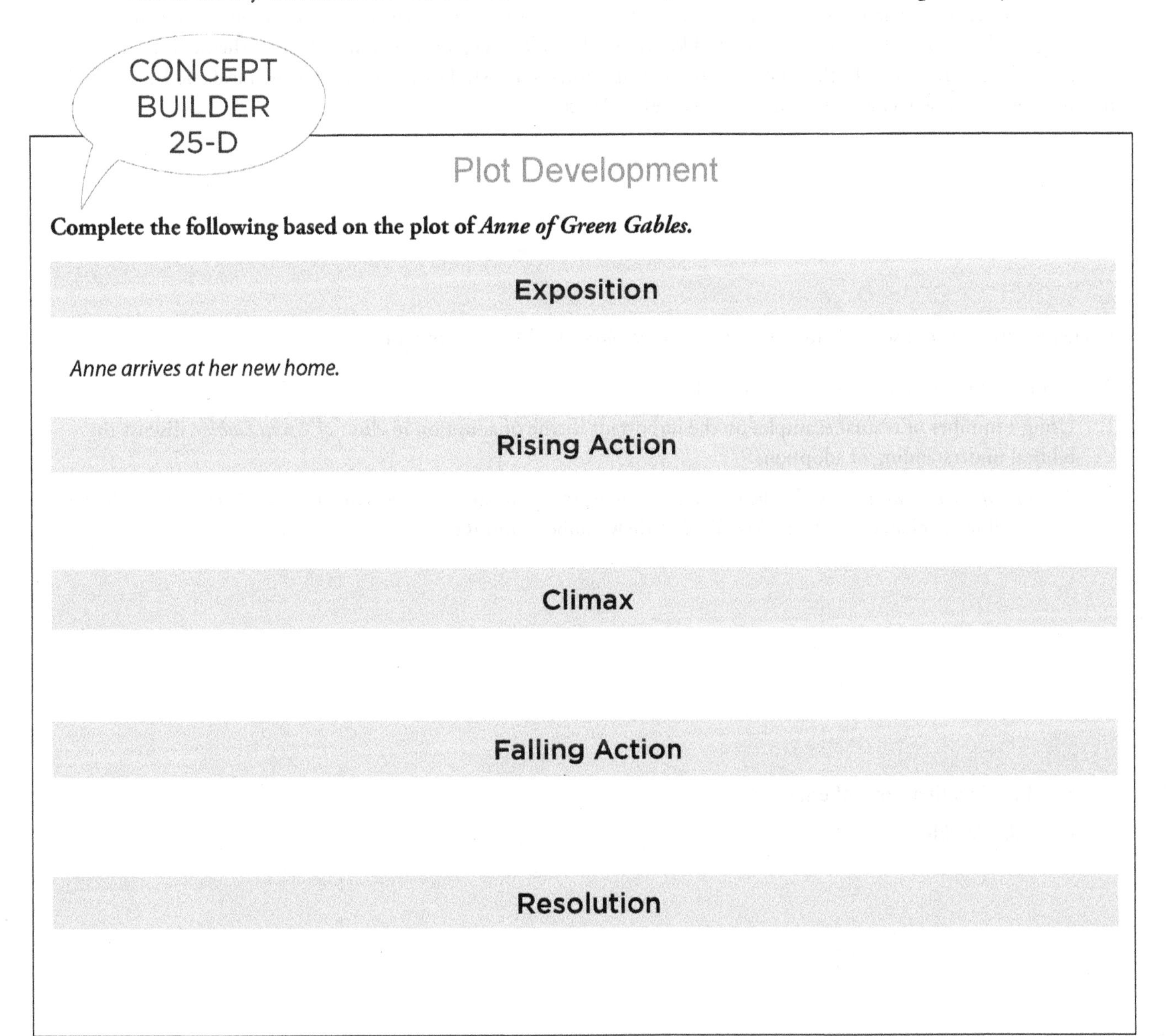

CONCEPT BUILDER 25-D

Plot Development

Complete the following based on the plot of *Anne of Green Gables*.

Exposition

Anne arrives at her new home.

Rising Action

Climax

Falling Action

Resolution

Theme — *Anne of Green Gables* (L. Maude Montgomery)

Chapter 26

First Thoughts

A great story includes characters, plot, and other literary components. It also has profound and eternal meaning. Its meaning, or theme, should transcend time and location. The following paper demonstrates one theme in Joseph Conrad's *Heart of Darkness.* In this book, the thoughtful protagonist Marlow is looking for the idealistic Kurtz who has disappeared while trying to enlighten the natives in Africa.

Chapter Learning Objectives

In chapter 26 we will discuss themes in *Anne of Green Gables* by Maude Montgomery.

As a result of this chapter study you will be able to . . .

1. Using a number of textual examples on the important theme of adoption in *Anne of Green Gables,* discuss the biblical understanding of adoption.
2. As *Anne of Green Gables* unfolds, the characters change in significant and permanent ways. Discuss these changes in the following characters: Anne, Marilla, Matthew, Gilbert, and Rachel.

Look Ahead for Friday

- Turn in a final copy of essay
- Take Weekly Test

Sample Essay: Theme

> One evening coming in with a candle I was startled to hear him say a little tremulously, "I am lying here in the dark wishing for death." The light was within a foot of his eyes. I forced myself to murmur, "Oh, nonsense!" and stood over him as if transfixed. Anything approaching the change that came over his features I have never seen before and hope never to see again. Oh, I wasn't just touched. I was fascinated. It was as though a veil had been rent. I saw on that ivory face the expression of somber pride, of ruthless power, of craven terror — of an intense and hopeless despair. Did he live his life again in every detail of desire, temptation, and surrender during that supreme moment of complete knowledge? He cried in a whisper at some image, at some vision — he cried out twice, a cry that was not more than a breath: "The horror! The horror!"[1]

The adventuresome protagonist Marlow found the lost Kurtz, only to lose him again on his deathbed. *Heart of Darkness*, by Joseph Conrad, has many different themes. One theme Conrad develops is a suspicion of modernity, a worldview that argues that science and human knowledge can solve almost anything.

Joseph Conrad wrote *Heart of Darkness* in the early 19th century when Western culture was full of optimism. The Industrial Revolution was well underway, advances had occurred in medicine, and the horseless carriage — the automobile — was even developed. Human ingenuity and progress seemed to have no end! In *Heart of Darkness*, we see Conrad, a Polish-born English novelist, exhibiting the vulnerability, limits, and flaws of human knowledge.

Heart of Darkness is a story that takes place in the mind of the protagonist, Charlie Marlow. With money from an aunt, Charlie Marlow, a young man who wants an adventure, sets off to the Congo River. He hears rumors of a man named Kurtz. Kurtz, a missionary, had disappeared into the jungle wilderness of interior Congo. Marlow is first fascinated, and then obsessed, with finding Kurtz. Like most modern men enthralled with knowledge, Marlow desperately wants, or needs, to find him and talk with him. He wants to know how he disappeared and why. He is on a modern, Hegelian search for truth — truth that arises from the struggle. This search, however, takes Marlow where he scarcely wished to go.

The reader comes to know Kurtz through Marlow's prying around and gleaning information from everyone he meets. Slowly, Marlow's detective work reveals a very disturbing picture of an evil man. Kurtz appears to be a man with vision. He is driven. He is a man of substance, morality, and, most of all, of predictability. Marlow knows what he wants and goes after it. This is a comforting thought to the modern Marlow, who is far more comfortable with the praxis, than the subjective, and whose worldview offers an answer to everything.

What Marlow found, however, was spontaneous and unpredictable. Kurtz's story was not scripted by a Rational God or a Theistic God. His story was scripted by a Naturalistic God. At the end of the book, Charlie finds Kurtz. Kurtz is very sick and depressed. Marlow talks to a man who had been with Kurtz for a long time, and he tells Marlow what he knows. He tells him that Kurtz is a monster — that he is the most ruthless and remorseless of all the cannibals in the jungle. Kurtz had started out with a clear mind but slowly became this ruthless monster. Kurtz had begun as a modern man, a scientific hero, a man who believed that knowledge could do everything. He went to an uncivilized land full of superstition and folklore. In other words, Kurtz was a "missionary" for "modernism" in a culture that was based on feelings and other abstractions. African society at this time was prehistoric. Ironically, the pre-civilized African culture had changed Kurtz's sophisticated culture, not vice versa. Kurtz, a child of science, a child of modernity, had his life pulled from him when he realized science was not the way to find happiness. To a large extent, it killed him.

". . . supreme moment of complete knowledge. . . ." The "knowledge" is the realization that science cannot fix the whole world, and that is what drove Kurtz to become this "monster." It was the "The horror! The horror!" (Peter Stobaugh)

1 Joseph Conrad, *Heart of Darkness*, http://etext.lib.virginia.edu/toc/modeng/public/ConDark.html.

Daily Assignment

- Warm-up: Anne is not perfect. For one thing, she struggles with anger. Do you have a problem with anger? How do you handle it?
- Students will complete Concept Builder 26-A.
- Prayer journal: Students are encouraged to write in their prayer journal every day.
- Students need to review their material for the next assignment
- Students should systematically review their vocabulary words daily.

Making Judgments

Readers really should make judgments about what they read. Read the following issues and make your judgments based on the text.

Issue	Yes/No	Because . . .
Anne is a very spirited young lady, but she is still kindhearted.		
Marilla has some rough edges, but she really is a good woman.		
Rachel is a mean-spirited, evil woman.		
Matthew is a gentle, loving man, always ready to give to others before he thinks of himself.		
Gilbert is a mean, spiteful boy.		

Lesson 2

Theme: Affirming Love

In this memorable scene from Anne of Green Gables, Anne is finishing her education. Marilla and Matthew are obviously tired and aged. Anne observes that life would have been better if they would have adopted a boy. Matthew quickly respond:

"If I had been the boy you sent for," said Anne wistfully, "I'd be able to help you so much now and spare you in a hundred ways. I could find it in my heart to wish I had been, just for that."

"Well now, I'd rather have you than a dozen boys, Anne," said Matthew patting her hand. "Just mind you that — rather than a dozen boys. Well now, I guess it wasn't a boy that took the Avery scholarship, was it? It was a girl — my girl — my girl that I'm proud of."

Matthew's affirming, unconditional love is obvious.

Chapter XXXVI
"The Glory and the Dream"

On the morning when the final results of all the examinations were to be posted on the bulletin board at Queen's, Anne and Jane walked down the street together. Jane was smiling and happy; examinations were over and she was comfortably sure she had made a pass at least; further considerations troubled Jane not at all; she had no soaring ambitions and consequently was not affected with the unrest attendant thereon. For we pay a price for everything we get or take in this world; and although ambitions are well worth having, they are not to be cheaply won, but exact their dues of work and self-denial, anxiety and discouragement. Anne was pale and quiet; in ten more minutes she would know who had won the medal and who the Avery. Beyond those ten minutes there did not seem, just then, to be anything worth being called Time.

"Of course you'll win one of them anyhow," said Jane, who couldn't understand how the faculty could be so unfair as to order it otherwise.

"I have not hope of the Avery," said Anne. "Everybody says Emily Clay will win it. And I'm not going to march up to that bulletin board and look at it before everybody. I haven't the moral courage. I'm going straight to the girls' dressing room. You must read the announcements and then come and tell me, Jane. And I implore you in the name of our old friendship to do it as quickly as possible. If I have failed just say so, without trying to break it gently; and whatever you do *don't* sympathize with me. Promise me this, Jane."

Jane promised solemnly; but, as it happened, there was no necessity for such a promise. When they went up the entrance steps of Queen's they found the hall full of boys who were carrying Gilbert Blythe around on their shoulders and yelling at the tops of their voices, "Hurrah for Blythe, Medalist!"

For a moment Anne felt one sickening pang of defeat and disappointment. So she had failed and Gilbert had won! Well, Matthew would be sorry — he had been so sure she would win.

And then!

Somebody called out:

"Three cheers for Miss Shirley, winner of the Avery!"

"Oh, Anne," gasped Jane, as they fled to the girls' dressing room amid hearty cheers. "Oh, Anne I'm so proud! Isn't it splendid?"

And then the girls were around them and Anne was the center of a laughing, congratulating group. Her shoulders were thumped and her hands shaken vigorously. She was pushed and pulled and hugged and among it all she managed to whisper to Jane:

"Oh, won't Matthew and Marilla be pleased! I must write the news home right away."

Commencement was the next important happening. The exercises were held in the big assembly hall of the Academy. Addresses were given, essays read, songs sung, the public award of diplomas, prizes and medals made.

Matthew and Marilla were there, with eyes and ears for only one student on the platform — a tall girl in pale green, with faintly flushed cheeks and starry eyes, who read the best essay and was pointed out and whispered about as the Avery winner.

"Reckon you're glad we kept her, Marilla?" whispered Matthew, speaking for the first time since he had entered the hall, when Anne had finished her essay.

"It's not the first time I've been glad," retorted Marilla. "You do like to rub things in, Matthew Cuthbert."

Miss Barry, who was sitting behind them, leaned forward and poked Marilla in the back with her parasol.

"Aren't you proud of that Anne-girl? I am," she said.

Anne went home to Avonlea with Matthew and Marilla that evening. She had not been home since April and she felt that she could not wait another day. The apple blossoms were out and the world was fresh and young. Diana was at Green Gables to meet her. In her own white room, where Marilla had set a flowering house rose on the window sill, Anne looked about her and drew a long breath of happiness.

"Oh, Diana, it's so good to be back again. It's so good to see those pointed firs coming out against the pink sky — and that white orchard and the old Snow Queen. Isn't the breath of the mint delicious? And that tea rose — why, it's a song and a hope and a prayer all in one. And it's good to see you again, Diana!"

"I thought you like that Stella Maynard better than me," said Diana reproachfully. "Josie Pye told me you did. Josie said you were infatuated with her."

Anne laughed and pelted Diana with the faded "June lilies" of her bouquet.

"Stella Maynard is the dearest girl in the world except one and you are that one, Diana," she said. "I love you more than ever — and I've so many things to tell you. But just now I feel as if it were joy enough to sit here and look at you. I'm tired, I think — tired of being studious and ambitious. I mean to spend at least two hours tomorrow lying out in the orchard grass, thinking of absolutely nothing."

"You've done splendidly, Anne. I suppose you won't be teaching now that you've won the Avery?"

"No. I'm going to Redmond in September. Doesn't it seem wonderful? I'll have a brand new stock of ambition laid in by that time after three glorious, golden months of vacation. Jane and Ruby are going to teach. Isn't it splendid to think we all got through even to Moody Spurgeon and Josie Pye?"

"The Newbridge trustees have offered Jane their school already," said Diana. "Gilbert Blythe is going to teach, too. He has to. His father can't afford to send him to college next year, after all, so he means to earn his own way through. I expect he'll get the school here if Miss Ames decides to leave."

Anne felt a queer little sensation of dismayed surprise. She had not known this; she had expected that Gilbert would be going to Redmond also. What would she do without their inspiring rivalry? Would not work, even at a coeducational college with a real degree in prospect, be rather flat without her friend the enemy?

The next morning at breakfast it suddenly struck Anne that Matthew was not looking well. Surely he was much grayer than he had been a year before.

"Marilla," she said hesitatingly when he had gone out, "is Matthew quite well?"

"No, he isn't," said Marilla in a troubled tone. "He's had some real bad spells with his heart this spring and he won't spare himself a mite. I've been real worried about him, but he's some better this while back and we've got a good hired man, so I'm hoping he'll kind of rest and pick up. Maybe he will now you're home. You always cheer him up."

Anne leaned across the table and took Marilla's face in her hands.

"You are not looking as well yourself as I'd like to see you, Marilla. You look tired. I'm afraid you've been working too hard. You must take a rest, now that I'm home. I'm just going to take this one day off to visit all the dear old spots and hunt up my old dreams, and then it will be your turn to be lazy while I do the work."

Marilla smiled affectionately at her girl.

"It's not the work — it's my head. I've got a pain so often now — behind my eyes. Doctor Spencer's been fussing with glasses, but they don't do me any good. There is a distinguished oculist coming to the Island the last of June and the doctor says I must see him. I guess I'll have to. I can't read or sew with any comfort now. Well, Anne, you've done real well at Queen's I must say. To take First Class License in one year and win the Avery scholarship — well, well, Mrs. Lynde says pride goes before a fall and she doesn't believe in the higher education of women at all; she says it unfits them for woman's true sphere. I don't believe a word of it.

Speaking of Rachel reminds me — did you hear anything about the Abbey Bank lately, Anne?"

"I heard it was shaky," answered Anne. "Why?"

"That is what Rachel said. She was up here one day last week and said there was some talk about it. Matthew felt real worried. All we have saved is in that bank — every penny. I wanted Matthew to put it in the Savings Bank in the first place, but old Mr. Abbey was a great friend of father's and he'd always banked with him. Matthew said any bank with him at the head of it was good enough for anybody."

"I think he has only been its nominal head for many years," said Anne. "He is a very old man; his nephews are really at the head of the institution."

"Well, when Rachel told us that, I wanted Matthew to draw our money right out and he said he'd think of it. But Mr. Russell told him yesterday that the bank was all right."

Anne had her good day in the companionship of the outdoor world. She never forgot that day; it was so bright and golden and fair, so free from shadow and so lavish of blossom. Anne spent some of its rich hours in the orchard; she went to the Dryad's Bubble and Willowmere and Violet Vale; she called at the manse and had a satisfying talk with Mrs. Allan; and finally in the evening she went with Matthew for the cows, through Lovers' Lane to the back pasture. The woods were all gloried through with sunset and the warm splendor of it streamed down through the hill gaps in the west. Matthew walked slowly with bent head; Anne, tall and erect, suited her springing step to his.

"You've been working too hard today, Matthew," she said reproachfully. "Why won't you take things easier?"

"Well now, I can't seem to," said Matthew, as he opened the yard gate to let the cows through. "It's only that I'm getting old, Anne, and keep forgetting it. Well, well, I've always worked pretty hard and I'd rather drop in harness."

"If I had been the boy you sent for," said Anne wistfully, "I'd be able to help you so much now and spare you in a hundred ways. I could find it in my heart to wish I had been, just for that."

"Well now, I'd rather have you than a dozen boys, Anne," said Matthew patting her hand. "Just mind you that — rather than a dozen boys. Well now, I guess it wasn't a boy that took the Avery scholarship, was it? It was a girl — my girl — my girl that I'm proud of."

He smiled his shy smile at her as he went into the yard. Anne took the memory of it with her when she went to her room that night and sat for a long while at her open window, thinking of the past and dreaming of the future. Outside the Snow Queen was mistily white in the moonshine; the frogs were singing in the marsh beyond Orchard Slope. Anne always remembered the silvery, peaceful beauty and fragrant calm of that night. It was the last night before sorrow touched her life; and no life is ever quite the same again when once that cold, sanctifying touch has been laid upon it.

Daily Assignment

- Warm-up: Anne remains eternally optimistic and thinks cheerfully about her future. Can you think of someone you know like that?
- Students will complete Concept Builder 26-B.
- Prayer journal.
- Students should outline all assigned essays for the week.

Characterization of Anne

Characters are developed by reactions of others to them. In the following chart, discuss how Anne develops as a character.

Creation of Anne as a Character

Reaction to Marilla and Matthew

In Anne's relationship with her adopted parents, for the first time in her life she finds sustaining unconditional love. This transforms her as a character. In fact, no other relationship(s) are as important.

Reaction of Rachel and other adults

Reaction of Diana and other children

Lesson 3

Grammar Review: Using Unnecessary Words

The word *personally* is usually used in a redundant fashion. Consider the following:

Personally, I prefer the Gospel of John to the Gospel of Luke.

Daily Assignment

- Warm-up: Striving to make Matthew and Marilla proud, Anne devotes herself to her studies wholeheartedly and earns the prestigious Avery Scholarship, which grants her enough money to attend a four-year college the following fall. When Anne learns that Marilla is likely to go blind, she decides to stay at Green Gables and teach nearby so she can care for Marilla, giving up her aspirations for a four-year degree. Did Anne do the right thing? Can you think of another solution?
- Students will complete Concept Builder 26-C.
- Prayer journal.
- Students should write rough drafts of all assigned essays and speech.

Sequencing the Plot

The sequence is the order of events in a plot. It is never coincidental; every author has a purpose in sequencing his events. What is the sequence of events as they emerge in *Anne of Green Gables?*

Event 1

Event 2

Event 3

Event 4

Event 5

Event 6

Resolution

Student Essay

Lucy M. Montgomery, author of Anne of Green Gables, writes in her classic novel of a young orphan girl with fiery red hair and a temper to match it. Throughout the story, Anne, as well as her friends, changes from a lonely, misbehaved girl to a beautiful young lady. This theme of growing up is aided by the plot, setting, and characters throughout the book.

One way Montgomery communicates her theme of growing up is through her plot. In actuality, there is no definite plot, but rather simply the course of Anne's years at Green Gables. As Anne grows, she slowly changes. At 11 years old, Anne loses her temper easily, flying into rages when insulted. First, Anne calls Rachel Lynde "a rude impolite, unfeeling woman," and later smashes a slate over Gilbert Blythe's head after he calls her carrots. However, as the story progresses, Anne matures and becomes able to overlook such insults, such as when Josie Pye tell her that "a red-haired fairy is just as ridiculous as a fat one." Thus, the theme of maturity is shown through the plot.

Also, the setting causes Anne to mature. Before her move to Green Gables, Anne is a "lonely, heart-hungry, [and] friendless child" who lives on her imagination. When living at Green Gables, Anne meets real friends, and leaves the ones in the mirror behind. The beautiful Canadian countryside stimulates her imagination and she and her bosom friend Diana Barry never grow tired of walking through it. As they grow, the two pretend less and simply talk more, as girls do. Despite stopping to pretend, Anne's imagination still persists, and the setting plays a part in it.

Finally, the characters of Montgomery's book change Anne. Marilla, as the mother figure in Anne's life, primarily brings Anne up, disciplining her as any child. Matthew, Marilla's brother, is shy, but occasionally "insists" upon spoiling Anne, without "interfering with [her] methods." These two characters in particular bring about most change in Anne, simply because they raise her, and she deeply desires to please them.

The story of Anne Shirley in *Anne of Green Gables* communicates a theme of growing up and maturing. The author, Lucy M. Montgomery, writes of an orphan who slowly matures throughout the story. Throughout it, there are three main factors that help Anne mature: the plot, setting, and characters. As Anne matures and develops, the theme of maturity is developed as well. (Sheridan)

Daily Assignment

- Warm-up: Later when Gilbert hears of Anne's decision to stay home with Marilla, he gives up his post as the teacher at Avonlea school so that Anne can teach there and be closer to Marilla. Did Gilbert do the right thing? Can you think of another solution?
- Students will complete Concept Builder 26-D.
- Prayer journal.
- Review the assigned text. Keep vocabulary cards.
- This is the day that students should write, and then rewrite, the final drafts of their assigned essay.

Making Inferences

An inference is a conclusion or summary drawn from information. What inferences can you draw from this book?

Title: *Anne of Green Gables*

Details from the story	What I know from reading or experience	Inference
After some mishaps, Anne takes much joy in life, and adapts quickly, thriving in the environment of Prince Edward Island. She is something of a chatterbox, and drives the prim, duty-driven Marilla to distraction, although shy Matthew falls for her immediately.	*My little sister is like Anne and I know that she means well. Montgomery obviously is fond of her protagonist, too.*	*Clearly, Anne will do just fine. She will develop into a winsome, wholesome character.*
The book ends with Matthew's death. Anne shows her devotion to Marilla and Green Gables by deciding to stay at home and help Marilla, whose eyesight is diminishing. To show his friendship, Gilbert Blythe gives up his teaching position in the Avonlea School to work at White Sands School instead, thus enabling Anne to teach at the Avonlea School and stay at Green Gables all through the week. After this kind act, Anne and Gilbert become friends.		

Plot — *Ivanhoe* (Sir Walter Scott)

Chapter 27

First Thoughts

Walter Scott was born in 1771 in Edinburgh, Scotland. He was one of Scotland's most popular adventure novelists. He began his writing career by writing long narrative poems (as Alfred Lord Tennyson had done). His "The Lay of the Last Minstrel" (1805) and "The Lady of the Lake" (1810) were extremely popular throughout Scotland and the English-speaking world. However, by around 1813, Lord Byron had overtaken him in popularity and with literary success as a narrative poet, and Scott turned to novels to rejuvenate his career (and to replenish his pocketbook). His *Waverly* (1814), a historical novel set during the Scottish Rebellion of 1745, became a huge success, and Scott began a long career as a historical novelist.

Chapter Learning Objectives

In chapter 27 we will discuss the plot in *Ivanhoe* by Sir Walter Scott.

As a result of this chapter study you will be able to . . .

1. Discuss the plot of *Ivanhoe*. In your discussion reference the structure of the plot: rising action, climax, falling action.
2. Examine Ivanhoe and other literary figures (e.g., *Beowulf*) who exhibit Christ-like tendencies. On the other hand, they are war-like. Discuss the ways that Ivanhoe is Christ-like and the ways that he is not.
3. Write a 3,000-word adventure story.

Look Ahead for Friday

- Turn in a final copy of essay
- Take Weekly Test

Lesson 1

Sample Essay: Plot

A great story has a well-conceived, well-designed plot. *Ivanhoe* is clearly such a novel.

The following is an essay about the plot in Stephen Crane's *Red Badge of Courage*:

The Red Badge of Courage has a plot that is tied very closely to one character: Henry Fleming. The setting is the Civil War. However, the plot is the story of Henry Fleming's transformation from a naive, romantic farm boy to a hardened, naturalistic soldier in the Civil War. Before exploring the plot, consideration should be given to the author.

Stephen Crane (1871–1900) was an American novelist and poet, one of the first American authors in the naturalistic style of writing. Crane is known for his pessimistic and often brutal portrayals of the human condition. In *The Red Badge of Courage*, Crane's protagonist changes. He begins the novel as a romantic but changes to a naturalist. The rising action of the plot is connected to the early stages of romantic disillusionment. The climax occurs when Henry Fleming abandons his romanticism for cynical naturalism. In the falling action or resolution section he begins his new role as a naturalist.

Romanticism, a movement in the literature of virtually every country of Europe, the United States, and Latin America, lasted from about 1750 to about 1870, is characterized by reliance on the imagination and subjectivity of approach, freedom of thought and expression, and an idealization of nature. Naturalism regarded human behavior as being controlled by instinct, emotion, or social and economic conditions. Naturalism rejected the concept of free will.

The Red Badge of Courage is a story of a romantic youth who leaves home, his mother, and everything familiar to him, to become a solder of the Union Army. This romantic youth has a fear that haunts him. He is afraid that he will be afraid when he is in the midst of battle. Cowardice to a romantic is an anathema; cowardice to a naturalist is ordinary.

At first, during the first battle, the young protagonist stood strong and fought proudly. However, as men around him died violent deaths, he faltered. His world collapsed! Giving into his survival instincts, a naturalistic urge, he ran away from the battle. At, first he felt no shame, but after seeing dead bodies, wounded men, and determined soldiers moving to the front, he felt shame, and the transformation from being a romantic to being a naturalist began. The shame first came as he felt like a coward. Later, the shame turned to embarrassment. He became a machine, doing only what he was told. The badge of courage he wore on his head was not a badge of heroism so much as it was a badge of cynical recognition that he had no control over his fate. Therefore, why not live and let live? Capturing a hill or lying in bed — a person could die or live in either place. There was no fear, but there was no anticipation or joy either. Fleming's transformation from romanticism to naturalism is at the heart of *The Red Badge of Courage.* (Timothy Stobaugh)

Daily Assignment

- Warm-up: Compare and contrast Rowena and Rebecca in *Ivanhoe*.
- Students will complete Concept Builder 27-A.
- Prayer journal: Students are encouraged to write in their prayer journal every day.
- Students need to review their material for the next assignment
- Students should systematically review their vocabulary words daily.

Active Reading

Read this excerpt from *Ivanhoe* (chapter 1) by Sir Walter Scott, and then answer the following questions:

In that pleasant district of merry England which is watered by the river Don, there extended in ancient times a large forest, covering the greater part of the beautiful hills and valleys which lie between Sheffield and the pleasant town of Doncaster. The remains of this extensive wood are still to be seen at the noble seats of Wentworth, of Warncliffe Park, and around Rotherham. Here haunted of yore the fabulous Dragon of Wantley; here were fought many of the most desperate battles during the Civil Wars of the Roses; and here also flourished in ancient times those bands of gallant outlaws, whose deeds have been rendered so popular in English song.

Such being our chief scene, the date of our story refers to a period towards the end of the reign of Richard I., when his return from his long captivity had become an event rather wished than hoped for by his despairing subjects, who were in the meantime subjected to every species of subordinate oppression. The nobles, whose power had become exorbitant during the reign of Stephen, and whom the prudence of Henry the Second had scarce reduced to some degree of subjection to the crown, had now resumed their ancient license in its utmost extent; despising the feeble interference of the English Council of State, fortifying their castles, increasing the number of their dependents, reducing all around them to a state of vassalage, and striving by every means in their power, to place themselves each at the head of such forces as might enable him to make a figure in the national convulsions which appeared to be impending.

The situation of the inferior gentry, or Franklins, as they were called, who, by the law and spirit of the English constitution, were entitled to hold themselves independent of feudal tyranny, became now unusually precarious. If, as was most generally the case, they placed themselves under the protection of any of the petty kings in their vicinity, accepted of feudal offices in his household, or bound themselves by mutual treaties of alliance and protection, to support him in his enterprises, they might indeed purchase temporary repose; but it must be with the sacrifice of that independence which was so dear to every English bosom, and at the certain hazard of being involved as a party in whatever rash expedition the ambition of their protector might lead him to undertake. On the other hand, such and so multiplied were the means of vexation and oppression possessed by the great Barons, that they never wanted the pretext, and seldom the will, to harass and pursue, even to the very edge of destruction, any of their less powerful neighbours, who attempted to separate themselves from their authority, and to trust for their protection, during the dangers of the times, to their own inoffensive conduct, and to the laws of the land.

1. What is the setting? Is it important?

2. What is the narrative point of view?

3. What is a central conflict in the plot?

Lesson 2

Plot

One criticism of *Ivanhoe* is that there is not much plot — that Scott spends too much time on the other elements and wanders aimlessly toward a conclusion.

CHAPTER III

Then (sad relief!) from the bleak coast that hears
The German Ocean roar, deep-blooming, strong,
And yellow hair'd, the blue-eyed Saxon came.
Thomson's Liberty

In a hall, the height of which was greatly disproportioned to its extreme length and width, a long oaken table, formed of planks rough-hewn from the forest, and which had scarcely received any polish, stood ready prepared for the evening meal of Cedric the Saxon. The roof, composed of beams and rafters, had nothing to divide the apartment from the sky excepting the planking and thatch; there was a huge fireplace at either end of the hall, but as the chimneys were constructed in a very clumsy manner, at least as much of the smoke found its way into the apartment as escaped by the proper vent. The constant vapour which this occasioned, had polished the rafters and beams of the low-browed hall, by encrusting them with a black varnish of soot. On the sides of the apartment hung implements of war and of the chase, and there were at each corner folding doors, which gave access to other parts of the extensive building.

The other appointments of the mansion partook of the rude simplicity of the Saxon period, which Cedric piqued himself upon maintaining. The floor was composed of earth mixed with lime, trodden into a hard substance, such as is often employed in flooring our modern barns. For about one quarter of the length of the apartment, the floor was raised by a step, and this space, which was called the dais, was occupied only by the principal members of the family, and visitors of distinction. For this purpose, a table richly covered with scarlet cloth was placed transversely across the platform, from the middle of which ran the longer and lower board, at which the domestics and inferior persons fed, down towards the bottom of the hall. The whole resembled the form of the letter T, or some of those ancient dinner-tables, which, arranged on the same principles, may be still seen in the antique Colleges of Oxford or Cambridge. Massive chairs and settles of carved oak were placed upon the dais, and over these seats and the more elevated table was fastened a canopy of cloth, which served in some degree to protect the dignitaries who occupied that distinguished station from the weather, and especially from the rain, which in some places found its way through the ill-constructed roof.

The walls of this upper end of the hall, as far as the dais extended, were covered with hangings or curtains, and upon the floor there was a carpet, both of which were adorned with some attempts at tapestry, or embroidery, executed with brilliant or rather gaudy colouring. Over the lower range of table, the roof, as we have noticed, had no covering; the rough plastered walls were left bare, and the rude earthen floor was uncarpeted; the board was uncovered by a cloth, and rude massive benches supplied the place of chairs.

In the centre of the upper table, were placed two chairs more elevated than the rest, for the master and mistress of the family, who presided over the scene of hospitality, and from doing so derived their Saxon title of honour, which signifies "the Dividers of Bread."

To each of these chairs was added a footstool, curiously carved and inlaid with ivory, which mark of distinction was peculiar to them. One of these seats was at present occupied by Cedric the Saxon, who, though but in rank a thane, or, as the Normans called him, a Franklin, felt, at the delay of his evening meal, an irritable impatience, which might have become an alderman, whether of ancient or of modern times.

It appeared, indeed, from the countenance of this proprietor, that he was of a frank, but hasty and choleric temper. He was not above the middle stature, but broad-shouldered, long-armed, and powerfully made, like one accustomed to endure the fatigue of war or of the chase; his face was broad, with large blue eyes, open and frank features, fine teeth, and a well formed head, altogether expressive of that sort of good-humour which often lodges with a sudden and hasty temper. Pride and jealousy there was in his eye, for his life had been spent in asserting rights which were constantly liable to invasion; and the prompt, fiery, and resolute disposition of the man, had been kept constantly upon the alert by the circumstances of his situation. His long yellow hair was equally divided on the top of his head and upon his brow, and combed down on each side to the length of his shoulders; it had but little tendency to grey, although Cedric was approaching to his sixtieth year.

Cover of Classics Comics No.2 (*Ivanhoe*) book, 1946 (PD-US).

His dress was a tunic of forest green, furred at the throat and cuffs with what was called minever; a kind of fur inferior in quality to ermine, and formed, it is believed, of the skin of the grey squirrel. This doublet hung unbuttoned over a close dress of scarlet which sat tight to his body; he had breeches of the same, but they did not reach below the lower part of the thigh, leaving the knee exposed. His feet had sandals of the same fashion with the peasants, but of finer materials, and secured in the front with golden clasps. He had bracelets of gold upon his arms, and a broad collar of the same precious metal around his neck. About his waist he wore a richly-studded belt, in which was stuck a short straight two-edged sword, with a sharp point, so disposed as to hang almost perpendicularly by his side. Behind his seat was hung a scarlet cloth cloak lined with fur, and a cap of the same materials richly embroidered, which completed the dress of the opulent landholder when he chose to go forth. A short boar-spear, with a broad and bright steel head, also reclined against the back of his chair, which served him, when he walked abroad, for the purposes of a staff or of a weapon, as chance might require.

Several domestics, whose dress held various proportions betwixt the richness of their master's, and the coarse and simple attire of Gurth the swine-herd, watched the looks and waited the commands of the Saxon dignitary. Two or three servants of a superior order stood behind their master upon the dais; the rest occupied the lower part of the hall. Other attendants there were of a different description; two or three large and shaggy greyhounds, such as were then employed in hunting the stag and wolf; as many slow-hounds of a large bony breed, with thick necks, large heads, and long ears; and one or two of the smaller dogs, now called terriers, which waited with impatience the arrival of the supper; but, with the sagacious knowledge of physiognomy peculiar to their race, forbore to intrude upon the moody silence of their master, apprehensive probably of a small white truncheon which lay by Cedric's trencher, for the purpose of repelling the advances of his four-legged dependants. One grisly old wolf-dog alone, with the liberty of an indulged favourite, had planted himself close by the chair of state, and occasionally ventured to solicit notice by putting his large hairy head upon his master's knee, or pushing his nose into his hand. Even he was repelled by the stern command, "Down, Balder, down! I am not in the humour for foolery."

In fact, Cedric, as we have observed, was in no very placid state of mind. The Lady Rowena, who had been absent to attend an evening mass at a distant church, had but just returned, and was changing her garments, which had been wetted by the storm. There were as yet no tidings of Gurth and his charge, which should long since have been driven home from the forest and such was the insecurity of the period, as to render it probable that the delay might be explained by some depreciation of the outlaws, with whom the adjacent forest abounded, or by the violence of some neighbouring baron, whose consciousness of strength made him equally negligent of the laws of property. The matter was of consequence, for great part of the domestic wealth of the Saxon proprietors consisted in numerous herds of swine, especially in forest-land, where those animals easily found their food.

Besides these subjects of anxiety, the Saxon thane was impatient for the presence of his favourite clown Wamba, whose jests, such as they were, served for a sort of seasoning to his evening meal, and to the deep draughts of ale and wine with which he was in the habit of accompanying it. Add to all this, Cedric had fasted since noon, and his usual supper hour was long past, a cause of irritation common to country squires, both in ancient and modern times. His displeasure was expressed in broken sentences, partly muttered to himself, partly addressed to the domestics who stood around; and particularly to his cupbearer, who offered him from time to time, as a sedative, a silver goblet filled with wine — "Why tarries the Lady Rowena?"

"She is but changing her head-gear," replied a female attendant, with as much confidence as the favourite lady's-maid usually answers the master of a modern family; "you would not wish her to sit down to the banquet in her hood and kirtle? and no lady within the shire can be quicker in arraying herself than my mistress."

This undeniable argument produced a sort of acquiescent umph! on the part of the Saxon, with the addition, "I wish her devotion may choose fair weather for the next visit to St John's Kirk;—but what, in the name of ten devils," continued he, turning to the cupbearer, and raising his voice as if happy to have found a channel into which he might divert his indignation without fear or control — "what, in the name of ten devils, keeps Gurth so long afield? I suppose we shall have an evil account of the herd; he was wont to be a faithful and cautious drudge, and I had destined him for something better; perchance I might even have made him one of my warders."

Oswald the cupbearer modestly suggested, "that it was scarce an hour since the tolling of the curfew;" an ill-chosen apology, since it turned upon a topic so harsh to Saxon ears.

"The foul fiend," exclaimed Cedric, "take the curfew-bell, and the tyrannical bastard by whom it was devised, and the heartless slave who names it with a Saxon tongue to a Saxon ear! The curfew!" he added, pausing, "ay, the curfew; which compels true men to extinguish their lights, that thieves and robbers may work their deeds in darkness! — Ay, the curfew; — Reginald Front-de-Boeuf and Philip de Malvoisin know the use of the curfew as well as William the Bastard himself, or e'er a Norman adventurer that fought at Hastings. I shall hear, I guess, that my property has been swept off to save from starving the hungry banditti, whom they cannot support but by theft and robbery. My faithful slave is murdered, and my goods are taken for a prey — and Wamba — where is Wamba? Said not some one he had gone forth with Gurth?"

Oswald replied in the affirmative.

"Ay? why this is better and better! he is carried off too, the Saxon fool, to serve the Norman lord. Fools are we all indeed that serve them, and fitter subjects for their scorn and laughter, than if we were born with but half our wits. But I will be avenged," he added, starting from his chair in impatience at the supposed injury, and catching hold of his boar-spear; "I will go with my complaint to the great council; I have friends, I have followers — man to man will I appeal the Norman to the lists; let him come in his plate and his mail, and all that can render cowardice bold; I have sent such a javelin as this through a stronger fence than three of their war shields! — Haply they think me old; but they shall find, alone and childless as I am, the blood of Hereward is in the veins of Cedric. — Ah, Wilfred, Wilfred!" he exclaimed in a lower tone, "couldst thou have ruled thine unreasonable passion, thy father had not been left in his age like the solitary oak that throws out its shattered and unprotected branches against the full sweep of the tempest!" The reflection seemed to conjure into sadness his irritated feelings. Replacing his javelin, he resumed his seat, bent his looks downward, and appeared to be absorbed in melancholy reflection.

From his musing, Cedric was suddenly awakened by the blast of a horn, which was replied to by the clamorous yells and barking of all the dogs in the hall, and some twenty or thirty which were quartered in other parts of the building. It cost some exercise of the white truncheon, well seconded by the exertions of the domestics, to silence this canine clamour.

"To the gate, knaves!" said the Saxon, hastily, as soon as the tumult was so much appeased that the dependants could hear his voice. "See what tidings that horn tells us of — to announce, I ween, some hership and robbery which has been done upon my lands."

Returning in less than three minutes, a warder announced "that the Prior Aymer of Jorvaulx, and the good knight Brian de Bois-Guilbert, commander of the valiant and venerable order of Knights Templars, with a small retinue, requested hospitality and lodging for the night, being on their way to a tournament which was to be held not far from Ashby-de-la-Zouche, on the second day from the present."

"Aymer, the Prior Aymer? Brian de Bois-Guilbert?" — muttered Cedric; "Normans both; — but Norman or Saxon, the hospitality of Rotherwood must not be impeached; they are welcome, since they have chosen to halt — more welcome would they have been to have ridden further on their way — But it were unworthy to murmur for a night's lodging and a night's food; in the quality of guests, at least, even Normans must suppress their insolence. — Go, Hundebert," he added, to a sort of major-domo who stood behind him with a white wand; "take six of the attendants, and introduce the strangers to the guests' lodging. Look after their horses and mules, and see their train lack nothing. Let them have change of vestments if they require it, and fire, and water to wash, and wine and ale; and bid the cooks add what they hastily can to our evening meal; and let it be put on the board when those strangers are ready to share it. Say to them, Hundebert, that Cedric would himself bid them welcome, but he is under a vow never to step more than three steps from the dais of his own hall to meet any who shares not the blood of Saxon royalty. Begone! see them carefully tended; let them not say in their pride, the Saxon churl has shown at once his poverty and his avarice."

The major-domo departed with several attendants, to execute his master's commands.

"The Prior Aymer!" repeated Cedric, looking to Oswald, "the brother, if I mistake not, of Giles de Mauleverer, now lord of Middleham?"

Oswald made a respectful sign of assent. "His brother sits in the seat, and usurps the patrimony, of a better race, the race of Ulfgar of Middleham; but what Norman lord doth not the same? This Prior is, they say, a free and jovial priest, who loves the wine-cup and the bugle-horn better than bell and book: Good; let him come, he shall be welcome. How named ye the Templar?"

"Brian de Bois-Guilbert."

"Bois-Guilbert," said Cedric, still in the musing, half-arguing tone, which the habit of living among dependants had accustomed him to employ, and which resembled a man who talks to himself rather than to those around him — "Bois-Guilbert? that name has been spread wide both for good and evil. They say he is valiant as the bravest of his order; but stained with their usual vices, pride, arrogance, cruelty, and voluptuousness; a hard-hearted man, who knows neither fear of earth, nor awe of heaven. So say the few warriors who have returned from Palestine.—Well; it is but for one night; he shall be welcome too.—Oswald, broach the oldest wine-cask; place the best mead, the mightiest ale, the richest morat, the most sparkling cider, the most odoriferous pigments, upon the board; fill the largest horns — Templars and Abbots love good wines and good measure. — Elgitha, let thy Lady Rowena, know we shall not this night expect her in the hall, unless such be her especial pleasure."

"But it will be her especial pleasure," answered Elgitha, with great readiness, "for she is ever desirous to hear the latest news from Palestine."

Cedric darted at the forward damsel a glance of hasty resentment; but Rowena, and whatever belonged to her, were privileged and secure from his anger. He only replied, "Silence, maiden; thy tongue outruns thy discretion. Say my message to thy mistress, and let her do her pleasure. Here, at least, the descendant of Alfred still reigns a princess." Elgitha left the apartment.

"Palestine!" repeated the Saxon; "Palestine! how many ears are turned to the tales which dissolute crusaders, or hypocritical pilgrims, bring from that fatal land! I too might ask — I too might enquire — I too might listen with a beating heart to fables which the wily strollers devise to cheat us into hospitality — but no — The son who has disobeyed me is no longer mine; nor will I concern myself more for his fate than for that of the most worthless among the millions that ever shaped the cross on their shoulder, rushed into excess and blood-guiltiness, and called it an accomplishment of the will of God."

He knit his brows, and fixed his eyes for an instant on the ground; as he raised them, the folding doors at the bottom of the hall were cast wide, and, preceded by the major-domo with his wand, and four domestics bearing blazing torches, the guests of the evening entered the apartment.[1]

1 www.gutenberg.org/files/82/82-h/82-h.htm#2HCH0002.

Daily Assignment

- Warm-up: Many of the characters in *Ivanhoe* enter the plot disguised. Why does Scott do that?
- Students will complete Concept Builder 27-B.
- Prayer journal.
- Students should outline all assigned essays for the week.

Symbolism

Ivanhoe **is full of adventure and is a historical romance; however, Ivanhoe does represent virtue and goodness. Draw symbols that represent the words below.**

America	Islam	Christianity
Terrorist	Goodness	Evil
Homeschooling	Love	Family

Lesson 3

Grammar Review: Document Design

Most academic papers should be printed using a font that looks like typewriter type (size 10 or 12 Courier or Times Roman or even Arial). Using a variety of fonts detracts from the content of your paper unless you have specific reasons for changing the font: use of italics for designating titles of book, magazines, or other long literary works; occasional use of enlarged font to set off sections of long papers, etc.

Daily Assignment

- Warm-up: When you think about "knights and damsels in distress," what do you think? What is your earliest impression of these events?
- Students will complete a daily Concept Builder 27-C.
- Prayer journal.
- Students should write rough drafts of all assigned essays.

Elements of a Story

Analyze the following elements of the novel *Ivanhoe* by Sir Walter Scott.

Elements	Yes/No	Because . . .
Characters Do the characters seem real?	*No*	*Most of the characters are "type" characters or archetypes. They represent a personality or worldview rather than a human being.*
Setting Is the setting important? Does it seem real?		
Plot Does the story flow logically? Does it flow well?		
Theme Is there a theme?		

Student Essay: Plot in *Ivanhoe*

The intriguing plot of *Ivanhoe* is composed of the rising action, climax, and falling action. The first part of the story focuses on the return of King Richard to England. He makes his appearance at a jousting tournament, disguised as the Black Knight. In the course of this tournament, Ivanhoe, who had accompanied the king on the crusades, also disguises himself as the Disinherited Knight. When Ivanhoe reveals himself, the stage is set for the climax. In the climax, the Black Knight defeats an ambush led by Waldemar Fitzurse. After his victory, the Black Knight exposes himself as King Richard. From this point, all the events in the story lead to the ending. The rising action, climax, and falling action combine to form the adventurous plot of *Ivanhoe.*

The rising action encompasses the return of King Richard to England, while he is disguised as the Black Knight. The author, Sir Walter Scott, uses a jousting tournament for the Black Knight to make his appearance. The beginning of chapter 7 emphasizes the significance of King Richard's return to England. "The condition of the English nation was at this time sufficiently miserable. . . . Prince John, in league with Philip of France, Coeur-de-Lion's mortal enemy, was using every species of influence with the Duke of Austria to prolong the captivity of his brother Richard, to whom he stood indebted for so many favours. In the meantime, he was strengthening his own faction in the kingdom of which he proposed to dispute the succession, in case of the King's death, with the legitimate heir, Arthur, Duke of Brittany, son of Geoffrey Plantagenet, the elder brother of John." The tournament also sets the stage for when Ivanhoe, camouflaged as the Disinherited Knight, will reveal his true identity. Ivanhoe, who had accompanied King Richard in the crusades, was against Prince John taking over the throne. At the end of the tournament, when Ivanhoe's identity is revealed, a threat to Prince John's plans appears. Through the return of King Richard and the revealing of Ivanhoe, the rising action is accomplished.

The climax of *Ivanhoe* occurs when the Black Knight defeats an ambush led by Waldemar Fitzurse and identifies himself as King Richard. Previously, upon learning of the ambush, King Richard had sent a letter to the captors in chapter 20. In it, he asks them to free their prisoners. After he lists the prisoners, the Black Knight explains what he will do if they do not liberate the captives. "Failing of which, we do pronounce to you, that we hold ye has robbers and traitors, and will wager our bodies against ye in battle, siege, or otherwise, and do our utmost to your annoyance and destruction." As the captors do not free the prisoners, King Richard carries out his promise. As his promise to liberate the prisoners is fulfilled, the Black Knight reveals himself as King Richard. After King Richard defeats Fitzurse and exposes his true identity, the climax of *Ivanhoe* is fulfilled.

After the climax, the rest of the events in Ivanhoe are the falling action. The end of chapter 29 gives a precise summary of what happens to Ivanhoe. "Ivanhoe distinguished himself in the service of Richard, and was graced with further marks of the royal favour." King Richard is on the throne of England and Ivanhoe is in his service.

The adventurous plot of *Ivanhoe* is created with the rising action, climax, and falling action. With these, the author explains King Richard's secretive return to England and triumphant return to the royal throne. The plot also includes the revealing of the Black Knight, who is King Richard. Suspense, intrigue, and betrayal are the cornerstones in the plot of *Ivanhoe.* (Claire)

Daily Assignment

- Warm-up: Many readers enjoy Scott's story but are distracted by his wordy style. What do you think?
- Students will complete Concept Builder 27-D.
- Prayer journal.
- Review the assigned text. Keep vocabulary cards.
- This is the day that students should write, and then rewrite, the final drafts of their assigned essays.

Journey Motif

A motif is a theme or tone that permeates a literary work. The central motif of this novel is the journey motif. Ivanhoe is on a journey home, and then a journey from place to place.

Create an imaginary journey from your home to another location. On that journey, identify landmarks that you will pass along this journey, and imagine what dangers will seek to keep you from your destination. If necessary, pretend!

Home

Landmarks	Dangers
My neighbor's mailbox	*My neighbor's mean dog!*

Destination

Worldviews of Protagonist — *Ivanhoe* (Sir Walter Scott)

Chapter 28

First Thoughts

Many of Walter Scott's works were historical romances about his homeland, but his best and most famous novel, 1819's *Ivanhoe*, had nothing to do with Scotland at all. Set in England in the last years of the 12th century, *Ivanhoe* tells the story of a noble knight involved with King Richard I — known to history as "Richard the Lion-Hearted" — and his return to England from the Crusades. This Ivanhoe, not to be confused with the Ivanhoe in the King Arthur legends, is a quintessential hero.

Chapter Learning Objectives

In chapter 28 we will discuss the worldview in *Ivanhoe* by Sir Walter Scott.

As a result of this chapter study you will be able to . . .

1. Discuss how Scott uses the plot and characters to communicate his worldview in *Ivanhoe*.
2. Compare the way Scott presents women (one-dimensional and somewhat shallow) with the way the virtuous woman is presented in Proverbs 31.
3. Evaluate if Christians should read literature that has aberrant worldviews.

Look Ahead for Friday

- Turn in a final copy of essay
- Take Weekly Test

Sample Essay: Worldview

Sir Walter Scott, like most of his contemporaries, was a theist. Even though his novel had romantic tendencies, it clearly was a theistic novel. Ivanhoe exemplifies, defends, and promotes Judeo-Christian values. He is the personification of the values of Sir Walter Scott.

The following is an essay describing a similar situation in Ernest Hemingway's novels:

"What have we done to have that happen to us?" This was a question that all of Hemingway's protagonists asked. What had they done to deserve what life allotted to them? This question demonstrates a self-centeredness that exemplifies naturalism.

Naturalists readily accepted the role of victim. It was convenient and consistent with a worldview that invited its participants to be weak. In *Farewell to Arms*, protagonist Frederick Henry, for instance, always found something to whine about. He readily accepted the victim role and blamed the world for his misfortunes. No consideration was given to Henry's making horrendous personal choices.

This worldview penchant effectively communicates Hemingway's personal life, a life full of self-centered self-reflection. His terse Grammar Review exemplifies this worldview. Hemingway was a master at writing. He used an economical Grammar Review that often seems simple and almost childlike to the reader. However, his method was calculated and used to great effect. In his writing, using simple language to capture scenes precisely, Hemingway provided neutral descriptions of plot events. He avoided describing his characters' emotions and thoughts directly; he let the reader see the character's response. Avoiding editorial comment, Hemingway made the reading of a text approximate as closely as possible the actual experience.

Hemingway strongly condemned economic and political injustices, and his characters reflect this viewpoint. He did this, however, from a realistic/naturalistic worldview. His stories and characters were his vehicles to make his political points. For instance, *For Whom the Bells Toll* is a political statement about the Spanish Civil War.

Even though Hemingway wrote many stories and novels, there are three characters that stand out as quintessential characters of Hemingway. They seem to be the men who Hemingway himself wished that he could be. They were Harry in *Snows of Kilimanjaro*, Robert Wilson in "The Short and Happy Life of Francis Macomber," and finally, Henry in *A Farewell to Arms*. All the characters in these literary pieces share the same feelings of hopelessness. All three characters reflect the worldview of Hemingway's world.

The character Harry in *Snows of Kilimanjaro* was wronged by his surroundings. Harry had gangrene in his leg. Ironically, he got this disease from a scratch from a thorn. The scratch became infected, and then his life was in danger. He was wronged because it was a little scratch and he forgot to put iodine on it and then his leg was rotting off. All he could do was sit there and listen to a woman, whom he truly hated, chatter away at him. To a brave naturalist (defined as someone who quietly accepted his hellish existence), this was a fate worse than death. On reflection, the reader realizes that while Hemingway pretended to say little and to carry a big metaphysical stick, he says plenty through his characters' foibles. For instance, while the unfortunate Harry quietly listened to his wife, in his own mind he was speaking volumes, mainly excursions into self-pity. In fact, his wife told him lies — for instance, that a truck was on the way to save him. However, always the skeptic, he did not believe her. He also told himself lies. For instance, it would be out of character for "God" to deliver him. No, he realized how foolish life really was and how cruel nature could be.

As Harry realized that life was cruel, so did Henry in *A Farewell to Arms*. Henry was an American ambulance driver in the Italian front. Henry lost his desire to fight in the war. Like the protagonist in *Red Badge of Courage*, by Stephen Crane, he abandoned his romanticism for naturalism.

Hemingway cleverly communicates his worldview in his stories and characters. (Peter Stobaugh)

Daily Assignment

- Warm-up: If you had to play a character in a movie based on *Ivanhoe*, which one would you choose? Why?
- Students will complete Concept Builder 28-A.
- Prayer journal: Students are encouraged to write in their prayer journal every day.
- Students need to review their material for the next assignment
- Students should systematically review their vocabulary words daily.

Active Reading - Imagery

Read "The Walrus and The Carpenter" from *Alice in Wonderland* by Lewis Carroll, and then answer the questions below:

The sun was shining on the sea,
Shining with all his might:
He did his very best to make
The billows smooth and bright—
And this was odd, because it was
The middle of the night.

The moon was shining sulkily,
Because she thought the sun
Had got no business to be there
After the day was done—
"It's very rude of him," she said,
"To come and spoil the fun!"

The sea was wet as wet could be,
The sands were dry as dry.
You could not see a cloud, because
No cloud was in the sky:
No birds were flying overhead—
There were no birds to fly.

The Walrus and the Carpenter
Were walking close at hand;
They wept like anything to see
Such quantities of sand:
"If this were only cleared away,"
They said, "it would be grand!"

"If seven maids with seven mops
Swept it for half a year.
Do you suppose," the Walrus said,
"That they could get it clear?"
"I doubt it," said the Carpenter,
And shed a bitter tear.

"O Oysters, come and walk with us!"
The Walrus did beseech.
"A pleasant walk, a pleasant talk,
Along the briny beach:
We cannot do with more than four,
To give a hand to each."

1. This poem is full of word pictures and imagery. Are the images real?

2. Do you consider it too long or too short?

3. How are the metaphors developed?

4. Do they resonate with your experience?

Lesson 2

Worldview Model

Daily Assignment

- Warm-up: Did you like the ending of Ivanhoe? If not, write a more satisfying ending. If you liked the ending, why did you like it?
- Students will complete Concept Builder 28-B.
- Prayer journal.
- Students should outline all assigned essays for the week.

The Antagonist

There are several antagonists (foils opposed to the protagonist) in *Ivanhoe*. Check the categories that apply to these and other antagonists in movies and books.

Name of Villain	All bad	Mostly bad	Equally bad and good	Character changes in the story
Reginald Front-de-Boeuf				
Waldemar Fitzurse				
Prince John				
Sleeping Beauty witch				
Stepmother in *Cinderella*				
Grinch Who Stole Christmas				

Lesson 3

Grammar Review: Misused Words

Like and *as* have different usages. Although *like* is widely used in spoken English, *as*, *as if*, and *as though* are preferred for written English.

Use *like* to express similarity (Susan is *like* a sister to me).

As a conjunction, use *as* to express sameness of degree, quantity, or manner (Do *as* I say, not *as* I do.);

As a preposition, use *as* to express equivalence (Think of me *as* your best teacher.)

Daily Assignment

- Warm-up: Would *Ivanhoe* make a good movie? Why or why not?
- Students will complete a daily Concept Builder 28-C.
- Prayer journal.
- Students should write rough drafts of all assigned essays.

Author's Worldview

Sir Walter Scott, through his plot and characters, communicates a particular world view. Compare that world view with your world view by answering yes or no to the following statements.

Statement	Sir Walter Scott	Myself
A person should be brave all the time.	*Yes*	*Yes*
A person can lie if it advances his purposes.		
A person should never lie under any circumstances.		
If one works hard enough, one will succeed.		
A person should not make hasty decisions.		
Be careful what you wish — it just might come true!		
The good guys always win.		
Bad things happen to good people.		
Women and men are equal in all ways.		
Do what feels good.		
Do what is right, whether if feels good or not.		
Do unto others as you would have them do unto you.		
Obey your parents.		
Be faithful to your spouse.		
Keep your word.		
Change your mind if it suits your purposes.		
Children are to be seen, not heard.		
Traditions are important.		
Animals are as important as humans.		
Friendship is important.		
Kill or be killed.		

Student Essay: Worldview in *Ivanhoe*

Sir Walter Scott expresses his theistic worldview through the main character in *Ivanhoe*. Dictionary.com defines *theism* as "the belief in one God as the creator and ruler of the universe without rejection of revelation." The character of Ivanhoe acts valiantly and with chivalry because he believes he is morally obligated to do so. This is similar to David, Joshua, and Gideon in the Bible. These godly men acted with courage against the enemy because they believed in and stood under a righteous God. By having his central character act because of his belief in a moral absolute, Scott creates a likeness to important figures in the Bible.

Ivanhoe exhibits courage in his quest for the just to prevail. This main character fights against evil with the belief that there is always a right and a wrong. In chapter 22, Scott uses Ivanhoe's father Cedric to present the belief of right and wrong. " 'God's will be done,' said Cedric in a voice tremulous with passion." God, as presented in this statement, is the right. Ivanhoe, in chapter 28, demonstrates his valiance and belief in right and wrong when he appears to fight for the life of a Jewess. "I am a good knight and noble, come hither to sustain with lance and sword the just and lawful quarrel of this damsel, Rebecca, daughter of Issac of York; to uphold the doom pronounced against her to be false and truthless, and to defy Sir Brian de Bois-Guilbert as a traitor, murderer, and liar; as I will prove in this field with my body against his, by the aid of God, of Our Lady, and of Monsignuer Saint George, the good knight." Ivanhoe not only has courage, but he also believes that God will aid him in fighting evil.

Gideon, David, and Joshua compare to Ivanhoe in their belief to act courageously because of a righteous God. David exemplifies this belief in 1 Samuel 17:37, when he defeats a giant as a boy because of his faith in God. "And David said, 'The Lord who delivered me from the paw of the lion and from the paw of the bear will deliver me from the hand of this Philistine' " (NIV). Joshua also fought valiantly for the glory of God. In Joshua 23:3, Joshua explains to Israel's leaders how he was able to fight bravely. "You have seen all that the LORD your God has done to all these nations because of you, for the LORD your God is He who has fought for you" (NKJV). In Judges 6, in a conversation with Gideon, the Lord shows how Gideon will save Israel. "So he said to Him, 'O my Lord, how can I save Israel? Indeed my clan is the weakest in Manasseh, and I am the least in my father's house.' And the LORD said to him, 'Surely I will be with you, and you shall defeat the Midianites as one man' " (NKJV). These three men of God demonstrate their belief in a righteous and incorruptible God through their actions and bravery.

Ivanhoe relates to the biblical figures of Gideon, David, and Joshua through his valiance, chivalry, and belief in fighting for truth, justice, and a cause greater than himself. By this connection, Scott's theistic worldview is obvious. The men believe in one God who rules supremely over the universe. (Claire)

Daily Assignment

- Warm-up: Some critics argue that there are too many characters in *Ivanhoe*. Agree or disagree and explain your answer.
- Students will complete Concept Builder 28-D.
- Prayer journal.
- Review the assigned text. Keep vocabulary cards.
- This is the day that students should write, and then rewrite, the final drafts of their assigned essays.

Making Moral Decisions

Characters in *Ivanhoe* are constantly asked to make moral decisions. Likewise, we as believers have to make moral decisions, too. Complete the chart below.

Moral Dilemma	What will I do?	Why?
A student in Sunday school tells a racial joke that is inappropriate. What will you do?	*I will ask him to stop. If he does not, I will tell someone in authority.*	*I will follow Matthew 18, but the behavior must stop.*
In World War II, some Christians hid Jewish people from their German captors, even though it was against the law. What would you do?		
You buy a notebook in a store. The cashier gives you back too much change. What will you do?		

Tone: Suspense — *Shane* (Jack Warner Schaefer)

Chapter 29

First Thoughts

Shane is one of the most popular movies and books of the 20th century. On one level, Shane is a superb cowboy-and-Indians story. On another level, this tale of the mysterious stranger who rides in from the distant hills and rides off again, is a stock archetype story (prototype or representative), replicated in several different genres and narratives. The protagonist is desperate to escape his past. The gunfighter Shane changes into the farmer Shane at a little farmstead, where he is befriended by the farmer's young son. However, the scheming cattle barons make his escape impossible. Mystery man Shane helps the farmers stand up to the cowboy bullies sent by the ranchers. Matters get out of hand when the head rancher, frustrated by Shane's presence and mettle, calls in a ruthless gunman from nearby Cheyenne to bring matters to a head. Shane is more than a match. This archetypal story is a powerful well-written piece of fiction for several reasons. While the storyline is common and predictable — the brave gunfighter saves the sedentary farmer and his family — the characters are well-developed and complicated. Shane wants to retire and cannot. Joe is a hard-working farmer who is really brave — even though his son does not know it until the end of the novel. Shane's relationship with the wife is subtle and skillfully developed by the author. All these conspire to make this novel a well-written piece of fiction.

Chapter Learning Objectives

In chapter 29 we will examine the way Jack Schaefer creates suspense in *Shane.*

As a result of this chapter study you will be able to . . .

1. Discuss how Schaefer develops suspense in *Shane's* plot.
2. Discuss how Samuel builds suspense in the story of David and Goliath (1 Samuel 18).
3. Compare the way suspense is created in *Shane* and in *Call of the Wild.*

Look Ahead for Friday

- Turn in a final copy of essay
- Take Weekly Test

Lesson 1

Suspense: "The Tell-Tale Heart"

In one of the most memorable scenes in the book, Shane leaves the peace-loving Starratts to confront the Fletchers. The ensuing fight is one of the most unforgettable and suspenseful in literature.

Read the following short story, and determine how writer Edgar Allan Poe builds suspense.

TRUE! nervous, very, very dreadfully nervous I had been and am; but why WILL you say that I am mad? The disease had sharpened my senses, not destroyed, not dulled them. Above all was the sense of hearing acute. I heard all things in the heaven and in the earth. I heard many things in hell. How then am I mad? Hearken! and observe how healthily, how calmly, I can tell you the whole story.

It is impossible to say how first the idea entered my brain, but, once conceived, it haunted me day and night. Object there was none. Passion there was none. I loved the old man. He had never wronged me. He had never given me insult. For his gold I had no desire. I think it was his eye! Yes, it was this! One of his eyes resembled that of a vulture — a pale blue eye with a film over it. Whenever it fell upon me my blood ran cold, and so by degrees, very gradually, I made up my mind to take the life of the old man, and thus rid myself of the eye for ever.

Now this is the point. You fancy me mad. Madmen know nothing. But you should have seen me. You should have seen how wisely I proceeded — with what caution — with what foresight, with what dissimulation, I went to work! I was never kinder to the old man than during the whole week before I killed him. And every night about midnight I turned the latch of his door and opened it oh, so gently! And then, when I had made an opening sufficient for my head, I put in a dark lantern all closed, closed so that no light shone out, and then I thrust in my head. Oh, you would have laughed to see how cunningly I thrust it in! I moved it slowly, very, very slowly, so that I might not disturb the old man's sleep. It took me an hour to place my whole head within the opening so far that I could see him as he lay upon his bed. Ha! would a madman have been so wise as this? And then when my head was well in the room I undid the lantern cautiously — oh, so cautiously — cautiously (for the hinges creaked), I undid it just so much that a single thin ray fell upon the vulture eye. And this I did for seven long nights, every night just at midnight, but I found the eye always closed, and so it was impossible to do the work, for it was not the old man who vexed me but his Evil Eye. And every morning, when the day broke, I went boldly into the chamber and spoke courageously to him, calling him by name in a hearty tone, and inquiring how he had passed the night. So you see he would have been a very profound old man, indeed, to suspect that every night, just at twelve, I looked in upon him while he slept.

Upon the eighth night I was more than usually cautious in opening the door. A watch's minute hand moves more quickly than did mine. Never before that night had I felt the extent of my own powers, of my sagacity. I could scarcely contain my feelings of triumph. To think that there I was opening the door little by little, and he not even to dream of my secret deeds or thoughts. I fairly chuckled at the idea, and perhaps he heard me, for he moved on the bed suddenly as if startled. Now you may think that I drew back — but no. His room was as black as pitch with the thick darkness (for the shutters were close fastened through fear of robbers), and so I knew that he could not see the opening of the door, and I kept pushing it on steadily, steadily.

I had my head in, and was about to open the lantern, when my thumb slipped upon the tin fastening, and the old man sprang up in the bed, crying out, "Who's there?"

I kept quite still and said nothing. For a whole hour I did not move a muscle, and in the meantime I did not hear him lie down. He was still sitting up in the bed, listening; just as I have done night after night hearkening to the death watches in the wall.

Presently, I heard a slight groan, and I knew it was the groan of mortal terror. It was not a groan of pain or of grief — oh, no! It was the low stifled sound that arises from the bottom of the soul when overcharged with awe.

I knew the sound well. Many a night, just at midnight, when all the world slept, it has welled up from my own bosom, deepening, with its dreadful echo, the terrors that distracted me. I say I knew it well. I knew what the old man felt, and pitied him although I chuckled at heart. I knew that he had been lying awake ever since the first slight noise when he had turned in the bed. His fears had been ever since growing upon him. He had been trying to fancy them causeless, but could not. He had been saying to himself, "It is nothing but the wind in the chimney, it is only a mouse crossing the floor," or, "It is merely a cricket which has made a single chirp." Yes he has been trying to comfort himself with these suppositions; but he had found all in vain. ALL IN VAIN, because Death in approaching him had stalked with his black shadow before him and enveloped the victim. And it was the mournful influence of the unperceived shadow that caused him to feel, although he neither saw nor heard, to feel the presence of my head within the room.

When I had waited a long time very patiently without hearing him lie down, I resolved to open a little — a very, very little crevice in the lantern. So I opened it — you cannot imagine how stealthily, stealthily — until at length a single dim ray like the thread of the spider shot out from the crevice and fell upon the vulture eye.

It was open, wide, wide open, and I grew furious as I gazed upon it. I saw it with perfect distinctness — all a dull blue with a hideous veil over it that chilled the very marrow in my bones, but I could see nothing else of the old man's face or person, for I had directed the ray as if by instinct precisely upon the spot.

And now have I not told you that what you mistake for madness is but over-acuteness of the senses? Now, I say, there came to my ears a low, dull, quick sound, such as a watch makes when enveloped in cotton. I knew that sound well too. It was the beating of the old man's heart. It increased my fury as the beating of a drum stimulates the soldier into courage.

But even yet I refrained and kept still. I scarcely breathed. I held the lantern motionless. I tried how steadily I could maintain the ray upon the eye. Meantime the hellish tattoo of the heart increased. It grew quicker and quicker, and louder and louder, every instant. The old man's terror must have been extreme! It grew louder, I say, louder every moment! — do you mark me well? I have told you that I am nervous: so I am. And now at the dead hour of the night, amid the dreadful silence of that old house, so strange a noise as this excited me to uncontrollable terror. Yet, for some minutes longer I refrained and stood still. But the beating grew louder, louder! I thought the heart must burst. And now a new anxiety seized me — the sound would be heard by a neighbour! The old man's hour had come! With a loud yell, I threw open the lantern and leaped into the room. He shrieked once — once only. In an instant I dragged him to the floor, and pulled the heavy bed over him. I then smiled gaily, to find the deed so far done. But for many minutes the heart beat on with a muffled sound. This, however, did not vex me; it would not be heard through the wall. At length it ceased. The old man was dead. I removed the bed and examined the corpse. Yes, he was stone, stone dead. I placed my hand upon the heart and held it there many minutes. There was no pulsation. He was stone dead. His eye would trouble me no more.

If still you think me mad, you will think so no longer when I describe the wise precautions I took for the concealment of the body. The night waned, and I worked hastily, but in silence.

I took up three planks from the flooring of the chamber, and deposited all between the scantlings. I then replaced the boards so cleverly so cunningly, that no human eye — not even his — could have detected anything wrong. There was nothing to wash out — no stain of any kind — no blood spot whatever. I had been too wary for that.

When I had made an end of these labors, it was four o'clock — still dark as midnight. As the bell sounded the hour, there came a knocking at the street door. I went down to open it with a light heart, — for what had I now to fear? There entered three men, who introduced themselves, with perfect suavity, as officers of the police. A shriek had been heard by a neighbour during the night; suspicion of foul play had been aroused; information had been lodged at the police office, and they (the officers) had been deputed to search the premises.

I smiled,—for what had I to fear? I bade the gentlemen welcome. The shriek, I said, was my own in a dream. The old man, I mentioned, was absent in the country. I took my visitors all over the house. I bade them search — search well. I led them, at length, to his chamber. I showed them his treasures, secure, undisturbed. In the enthusiasm of my confidence, I brought chairs into the room, and desired them here to rest from their fatigues, while I myself, in the wild audacity of my perfect triumph, placed my own seat upon the very spot beneath which reposed the corpse of the victim.

The officers were satisfied. My MANNER had convinced them. I was singularly at ease. They sat and while I answered cheerily, they chatted of familiar things. But, ere long, I felt myself getting pale and wished them gone. My head ached, and I fancied a ringing in my ears; but still they sat, and still chatted. The ringing became more distinct: I talked more freely to get rid of the feeling; but it continued and gained definitiveness — until, at length, I found that the noise was NOT within my ears.

No doubt I now grew VERY pale; but I talked more fluently, and with a heightened voice. Yet the sound increased — and what could I do? It was A LOW, DULL, QUICK SOUND — MUCH SUCH A SOUND AS A WATCH MAKES WHEN ENVELOPED IN COTTON. I gasped for breath, and yet the officers heard it not. I talked more quickly, more vehemently but the noise steadily increased. I arose and argued about trifles, in a high key and with violent gesticulations; but the noise steadily increased. Why WOULD they not be gone? I paced the floor to and fro with heavy strides, as if excited to fury by the observations of the men, but the noise steadily increased. O God! What COULD I do? I foamed — I raved — I swore! I swung the chair upon which I had been sitting, and grated it upon the boards, but the noise arose over all and continually increased. It grew louder — louder — louder! And still the men chatted pleasantly, and smiled. Was it possible they heard not? Almighty God! — no, no? They heard! — they suspected! — they KNEW! — they were making a mockery of my horror! — this I thought, and this I think. But anything was better than this agony! Anything was more tolerable than this derision! I could bear those hypocritical smiles no longer! I felt that I must scream or die! — and now — again — hark! louder! louder! louder! LOUDER! —

"Villains!" I shrieked, "dissemble no more! I admit the deed! — tear up the planks! — here, here! — it is the beating of his hideous heart!" [1]

1 Edgar Allan Poe, "The Tell-Tale Heart"; www.classicreader.com/read.php/sid.6/bookid.10/.

Daily Assignment

- Warm-up: Did you like *Shane*? Why or why not?
- Students will complete Concept Builder 29-A.
- Prayer journal: Students are encouraged to write in their prayer journal every day.
- Students need to review their material for the next assignment
- Students should systematically review their vocabulary words daily.

Predicting or Foreshadowing

Most authors are quite intentional about the way they structure their literary piece. A clever reader, however, will discern the outcome/resolution long before the literary piece ends. Find as many hints as possible in *Shane* (if possible before you finish reading it) and offer an informed prediction.

Shane Arrives

Foreshadowing Incident 1

A stranger named Shane drifts into an isolated western valley. It soon becomes apparent that he is a former gunslinger, and he finds himself drawn into a conflict between the humble farmer Joe Starrett and powerful cattle baron Rufus Ryker, who wants to force Starrett and every other homesteader in the valley off the land.

Foreshadowing Incident 2

Foreshadowing Incident 3

Shane Rides into the Sunset

Lesson 2

Sample Essay: Suspense

The following is a discussion of the way that Edith Wharton creates suspense in her novel *Ethan Frome.*

In *Ethan Frome,* stream of consciousness is Edith Wharton's primary means of creating suspense. *Stream of consciousness,* a narrative technique — by definition, omniscient narration — where the author tells the story by providing thoughts of the character, not by dialogue or plot actions, occurs when the author reveals the plot, character relationships, and thematic principles through what is going on inside a character's mind.

> As he drew near the farm he saw, through the thin screen of larches at the gate, a light twinkling in the house above him. "She's up in her room," he said to himself, "fixing herself up for supper." He remembered Zeena's sarcastic stare when Mattie, on the evening of her arrival, had come down to supper with smoothed hair and a ribbon at her neck.

Stream of consciousness makes *Ethan Frome* into the great novel that it is. Edith Wharton wrote numerous novels, as well as short stories, poems, essays, and travel books. Author David Marc states, "In her novels she explored the suffering caused by changing economic forces and Victorian-era social codes." The novel is somewhat autobiographical. Edith struggled in a bad marriage, but unlike Ethan, she chose divorce over suicide. Stream of consciousness is the way Wharton explores the hellish theme of unrequited love.

Ethan Frome is set in the hard winter environment of the small fictional town of Starkfield, Massachusetts. It is a horrible, tragic, love story. Ethan, a poor New England farmer, lived in a small country home with his mother. His mother became very sick and she sent for her distant cousin, Zeena, to come and care for her. Zeena cared for Ethan's mother, and when Ethan's mother finally died, he felt an obligation to Zeena, so he married her. This marriage of convenience caused both to suffer. Soon Zeena became ill and grew very bitter toward Ethan. Since she could not do chores around the house, she sent for cousin Mattie. It was a cool but fateful spring morning when Ethan picked up Mattie at the train station. They experienced unspoken love at first sight. Tension grew between Mattie and Ethan when they both recognized their love for each other, but it was nothing compared to the tension that resulted when Zeena discovered their infatuation. Zeena decided that Mattie must leave. On the way to the train station, Ethan and Mattie tried to die together by sledding down a hill into a tree.

This incredibly passionate love story is not created by outward physical emotions: rather, it is through passion that takes place in the soul and mind. It is the deep feeling inside the two, carefully developed by the author, that later compelled them to the tree:

> Frome's heart was beating fast. He had been straining for a glimpse of the dark head under the cherry-colored scarf and it vexed him that another eye should have been quicker than his. The leader of the reel, who looked as if he had Irish blood in his veins, danced well, and his partner caught his fire. As she passed down the line, her light figure swinging from hand to hand in circles of increasing swiftness, the scarf flew off her head and stood out behind her shoulders, and Frome, at each turn, caught sight of her laughing panting lips, the cloud of dark hair about her forehead, and the dark eyes which seemed the only fixed points in a maze of flying lines.

It was their thoughts, not their behavior, that communicated their love for each other. They guarded their actions to keep their love hidden from Zeena. Wharton used stream of consciousness to show Ethan's love to Mattie and also to build suspense. Since readers see only one perspective, they are unaware of what will happen next.

Almost the whole love story takes place inside Ethan's mind. Wharton shows this by allowing readers to read his thought and feelings. "The motions of her mind were as incalculable as the flit of a bird in the branches. The fact that he had no right to show his feelings, and thus provoke the expression of hers, made him attach a fantastic importance to every change in her look and tone. Now he thought she understood him, and feared; now he was sure she did not, and despaired." This is the perfect example of Ethan showing his love mentally but not physically

All this mental insight builds suspense. Readers begin to feel that something will happen. At the same time, Wharton uses dialogue to build suspense:

> Through the stillness they heard the church clock striking five.
>
> "Oh, Ethan, it's time!" she cried.
>
> He drew her back to him. "Time for what? You don't suppose I'm going to leave you now?"
>
> "If I missed my train where'd I go?"
>
> "Where are you going if you catch it?"
>
> She stood silent, her hands lying cold and relaxed in his.
>
> "What's the good of either of us going anywheres without the other one now?" he said.
>
> She remained motionless, as if she had not heard him. Then she snatched her hands from his, threw her arms about his neck, and pressed a sudden drenched cheek against his face. "Ethan! Ethan! I want you to take me down again!"
>
> "Down where?"
>
> "The coast. Right off," she panted. "So 't we'll never come up any more."

Ethan and Mattie did not die that day when they crashed into the tree. Instead they were badly injured. Ethan's left side was crushed, and he could never again stand straight up. He hobbled to the side on a crooked leg. For the remainder of her life, the invalid Mattie's once-beautiful face was full of horrific scars. All three, living in a naturalistic hell, finished their lives together. As Mrs. Halls says, ". . . there's not much difference between the Fromes up at the farm and the Fromes down in the graveyard; 'cept that down there they're all quiet. . . ." (Peter Stobaugh)

Daily Assignment

- Warm-up: Did Shane do the right thing (supporting the family with violence)?
- Students will complete Concept Builder 29-B.
- Prayer journal.
- Students should outline all assigned essays for the week.

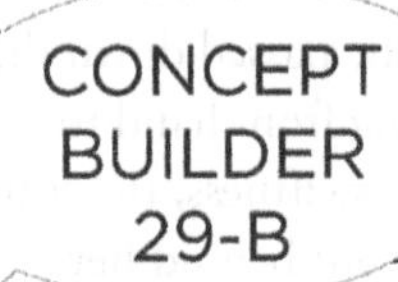

Foils

Foils are used by an author to develop his main character, in this case, Shane. Discuss how the author uses foils to develop Shane.

Foil	Joe	Marian	Joey	Ryker
How the author develops Shane	*Joe invites Shane to a cause. He is a moral, stubborn farmer who needs help. This brings out the best in Shane.*			

Lesson 3

Grammar Review: Problems in Style

"A clear straightforward style is preferable to an ornate one. An ornate or flowery style makes reading slow and calls attention to your words rather than your ideas. . . . In some cultures shaped by different traditions, being direct and straightforward might be considered rude, but that is not true in the United States . . . consider your word choice."[1]

When *literary analysis* deliberately emphasizes use of new vocabulary, students should be careful to use the new words correctly, considering the tone of the writing, and should keep their writing as clear and straightforward as possible. The writer's work should not resemble the reading of a thesaurus.

1 John C. Hodges, *Harbrace College Handbook* Harcourt Brace & Company, 1198, p. 92.

Daily Assignment

- Warm-up: Did you like the ending? If not, write a more satisfying ending. If you liked the ending, why did you like it?
- Students will complete Concept Builder 29-C.
- Prayer journal.
- Students should write rough drafts of all assigned essays and speech.

CONCEPT BUILDER 29-C

Generalizations

Slowly, as the story unfolds, the reader makes observations, forms conclusions, and ultimately makes generalizations about Shane. Note some of those here.

Fact/Observation 1	Shane is not afraid to be connected to poor, unimportant people.
Fact/Observation 2	
Fact/Observation 3	
Fact/Observation 4	

Generalization: Shane is a very brave man, a fair man, and a just man.

Student Essay

"The stranger nodded again. 'Call me Shane,' he said." *Shane*, written by Jack Schaeffer, is a story set in the Wild West. It is a tense story full of suspense that keeps the reader riveted to the story. This suspense revolves around the mysterious character of Shane and his actions. Schaeffer uses first-person account, detailed descriptions, and a slow progression of events to create this suspense.

The story is told as a memory flashback through the eyes of a young boy, Bob. "He rode into our valley in the summer of '89. I was a kid then, barely topping the backboard of father's old chuck-wagon." This first-person accounts builds suspense because the events enfold as if the reader is there witnessing it. With first person, the reader cannot easily figure out where the story is progressing. This method of suspense is clearly seen in the entrance of Shane.

"In that clear Wyoming air I could see him plainly, though he was still several miles away. . . . He came steadily, on straight through the town without slackening pace, until he reached the fork a half-mile below our place. . . . He hesitated briefly, studying the choice and moved again steadily on our side."

"He drew rein not twenty feet from me. His glance hit me, dismissed me, flicked over our place."

As for Shane himself, he exudes a suspenseful air through detailed descriptions of his dress and manners. In both of these things, he is unlike any other cowboy in the area. "As he came near, what impressed me first was his clothes. "He wore dark trousers of some serge material. . . . His shirt was finespun linen, rich brown in color . . . his hat was not the familiar Stetson, not the familiar gray or muddy tan. It was a plain black, sort in texture, unlike any hat I had ever seen." Along with his unusually nice clothes, his manner is equally unusual. This from Bob's mother expresses the general impression Shane makes on people: "He's so nice and polite and sort of gentle. Not like most men I've met out here. But there's something about him. Something underneath the gentleness." Shane is also always described as being tense and alert while maintaining a clam façade. "Yet even in this easiness was a suggestion of tension. It was the easiness of a coiled spring, of a trap set."

Along with Shane's mysterious character, slow progression of events is crucial to the suspense. Schaeffer gives a minute-by-minute description of the events, keeping the reader on edge. This method is especially effective in describing the many bar fights in the story.

"Shane was just taking hold of the bottle Will had fetched him. His hand closed on it and the knuckles showed white. He moved slowly, almost unwillingly, to face Chris. In that moment there was nothing . . . for him but that mocking man only a few feet away . . . The big room was so quiet the stillness fairly hurt. Chris stepped back involuntarily, one pace, two, then pulled up erect. And still nothing happened."

The slow progression of events keeps a tension between the story and the reader. The reader is eager to find out more as the story inches along, captivating the reader's attention. This energy between the story and the reader keeps the suspense level high.

The story of *Shane* is built on suspense. To achieve this suspense, Jack Schaeffer used first-person account, detailed descriptions, and the slow progression of events. "He was the man who rode into our little valley out of the heart of the great glowing West and when his work was done rode back whence he had come and he was Shane." (Daphnide)

Daily Assignment

- Warm-up: What Hollywood actor would you like to see as Shane? Why?
- Students will complete Concept Builder 29-D.
- Prayer journal.
- Review the assigned text. Keep vocabulary cards.
- This is the day that students should write, and then rewrite, the final drafts of their assigned essay.

Theme

The theme is the central purpose of a literary piece. It is the central idea that an author wants to share with a reader. The author mostly uses the plot and characters to advance a theme.

The author develops several plots, but, notably, is the plot of "redemption." Shane is literally healed and redeemed by helping a family overcome adversity. How does the author develop this theme?

Plot Details	Character Details
A conflict — farmers vs. the ranchers — exists before the story begins.	*Shane is a man struggling with his violent past.*
Shane is obviously shy and quiet. He seems to be hiding something.	
Shane has an awkward relationship with Marian.	
The ranchers are openly antagonistic to the farmers.	
One of the farmers is killed.	
Shane will have to fight the ranchers himself or Joe will.	
Theme - Redemption	

Character: Internal Conflict — *Shane* (Jack Warner Schaefer)

Chapter 30

First Thoughts

Shane is full of characters who change. Most of them change because of internal conflict.

Chapter Learning Objectives

In chapter 30 we will examine the way Jack Schaefer uses internal conflict to change characters in *Shane.*

As a result of this chapter study you will be able to . . .

1. Discuss how several characters in the novel *Shane* change because of internal conflict.
2. Discuss the internal conflict that Moses must have felt when he returned to Egypt.
3. Compare the way Bob changes in *Shane* and the way Huw changes in *How Green Was My Valley.*

Look Ahead for Friday

- Turn in a final copy of essay
- Take Weekly Test

Lesson 1

Literary Analysis: Internal Conflict in a Character

Internal conflict is a form of conflict that a character experiences in his mind.

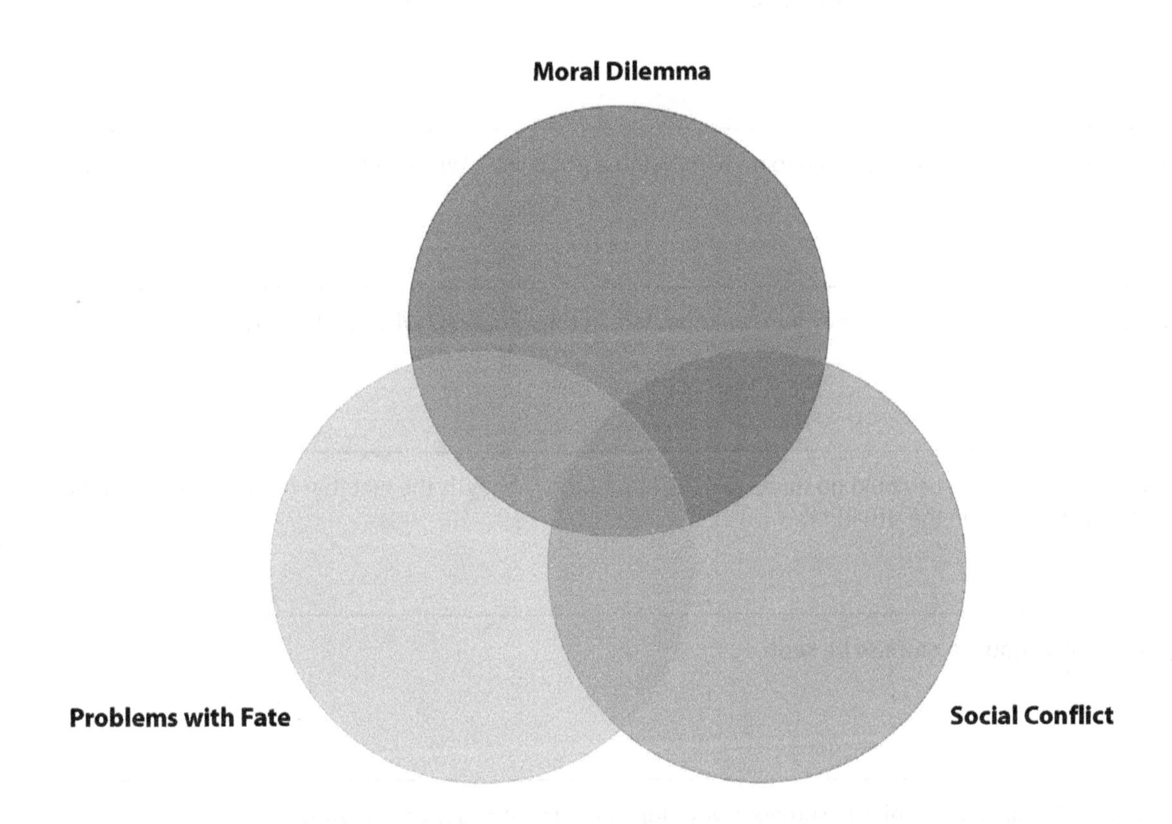

Daily Assignment

- Warm-up: Is Shane too good to be true? Does he seem like a real person? Why or why not?
- Students will complete Concept Builder 30-A.
- Prayer journal: Students are encouraged to write in their prayer journal every day.
- Students need to review their material for the next assignment
- Students should systematically review their vocabulary words daily.

Moral Dilemma

Shane has a moral dilemma, yet it is not unlike many dilemmas we face. Solve the following dilemma.

Joe is a 14-year-old boy who wanted to go to camp very much. His father promised Joe he could go if he saved up the money for it himself. So Joe worked hard at his paper route and saved up the 40 dollars it cost to go to camp, and a little more besides. But just before camp was going to start, his father changed his mind. There was a family emergency and Joe's father asked Joe to give him the money he had saved from the paper route.

Should Joe refuse to give his father the money? Why or why not?

Does the father have the right to tell Joe to give him the money? Why or why not?

Does giving the money have anything to do with being a good son?. Why or why not?

Is the fact that Joe earned the money himself important in this situation? Why or why not?

The father promised Joe he could go to camp if he earned the money. Is the fact that the father promised the most important thing in the situation?

In general, why should a promise be kept?

Is it important to keep a promise to someone you don't know well and probably won't see again?

In thinking back over the dilemma, what would you say is the most responsible thing for Joe to do in this situation? Why?

Lesson 2

Biblical Example of Internal Conflict

Judas Iscariot

Notice the way Judas struggles with his previous bad choice. The conflict is entirely internal.

Early in the morning, all the chief priests and the elders of the people made their plans how to have Jesus executed. So they bound him, led him away and handed him over to Pilate the governor.

When Judas, who had betrayed him, saw that Jesus was condemned, he was seized with remorse and returned the thirty pieces of silver to the chief priests and the elders. "I have sinned," he said, "for I have betrayed innocent blood."

"What is that to us?" they replied. "That's your responsibility."

So Judas threw the money into the temple and left. Then he went away and hanged himself.

The chief priests picked up the coins and said, "It is against the law to put this into the treasury, since it is blood money." So they decided to use the money to buy the potter's field as a burial place for foreigners. That is why it has been called the Field of Blood to this day. Then what was spoken by Jeremiah the prophet was fulfilled: "They took the thirty pieces of silver, the price set on him by the people of Israel, and they used them to buy the potter's field, as the Lord commanded me" (Matt. 27:1–10; NIV).

Daily Assignment

- Warm-up: Tell the *Shane* story from the perspective of the ranchers.
- Students will complete Concept Builder 30-B.
- Prayer journal.
- Students should outline all assigned essays for the week.

Moral Dilemma

Your 15-year-old pet, a black lab, is still healthy but struggling. He requires a costly operation to survive. Your family has the money, but they wonder what would be the best solution. Choose one of the solutions below and explain why you chose it.

Solution	What is the best choice and why?
The family simply finds the money to pay for the operation.	
The family decides to put the dog to sleep.	

Lesson 3

Grammar Review: Wordy

Avoid unnecessary words; do not be wordy. Compare the following:

There is no doubt but that the soldier regretted his action.

The soldier no doubt regretted his action.

Daily Assignment

- Warm-up: Compare Shane to a hero you have.
- Students will complete Concept Builder 30-C.
- Prayer journal.
- Students should write rough drafts of all assigned essays and speech.

Character Conflicts

Shane struggles through several internal/external struggles. List these below.

Conflict	Internal/External Conflict	Outcome
To stay and help the farmers or not.	*Shane will lose his anonymity (internal conflict).*	*He puts the welfare of the farmer and his family before his own desires.*
To give in and be friendly with the farmer's wife or not.		
To be close to the boy but not too close; Shane knows he will leave someday.		
To honor the farmer's courage but to save the farmer's life.		
To fight the evil ranchers or not.		

Lesson 4

Student Essay: Internal Conflict in *Shane*

Multiple characters in the novel *Shane* experience internal conflict as the storyline progresses. Shane, the mysterious former gunfighter who comes to work on the Starretts' farm, doesn't wish to fight, yet he feels the need to do so when men threaten the Starrett family. Marian Starrett faces internal conflict as she grows to love both Shane and her husband but must choose between them. Her husband Joe seeks to measure up to his friend Shane. As the plot develops, so do the main characters of Shane, Marian, and Joe.

Shane came to the Starretts' farm in the beginning of the book seeking to leave his gunfighting past. In chapter 6, Shane keeps himself from fighting a man although the man has ridiculed him. "Quietly he walked, the bottle forgotten in his hand, so close by Chris as almost to brush him yet apparently not even seeing him, through the doors and was gone." He is unable to avoid fights, however, when he begins to realize the harm the Starrett family is facing. A powerful man named Fletcher wishes to own their farm and will do anything to get it. When Fletcher hires Wilson, a professional gunfighter, Shane feels the need to protect the Starretts. In chapter 14, he goes to the town saloon and engages in a gunfight with Wilson. "Time stopped and there was nothing in all the world but two men looking into eternity in each other's eyes. And the room rocked in the sudden blur of action indistinct in its incredible swiftness and the roar of their guns was a single sustained blast." Shane wins. Through the internal conflict Shane faces, his love for the Starretts causes him to use the gunfighting skills he wished to forget.

As Shane stays and works on the Starretts' farm, Marian Starrett begins to fall in love with Shane. She faces internal conflict as she must decide between her husband and Shane. In chapter 8, Marian's love for Shane becomes apparent when he asks her if she needs him. " 'And you?' Shane's lips barely moved and I was not sure of the words. Mother hesitated. Then her head went up. 'Yes. It's only fair to say it. I need you too.' " Another time Marian's love for Shane is shown is in chapter 13. "She was watching Shane, her throat curving in a lovely proud line, her eyes wide with a sweet warmth shining in them." Although Marian loves Shane, she decides to stay with her husband. In chapter 15, Marian reminds Joe Starrett of the roots they have made together. "See, Joe. See what I mean. We have roots here now that we can never tear loose." Marian chooses to stay with her husband as the story ends, ending the internal conflict that began with her love for Shane.

Joe Starrett struggles throughout the story to measure up to Shane. In chapter 13, Shane and Joe argue over Shane going to fight Wilson. Shane punches Joe, causing him to become unconscious. Afterward, as Shane and Marian are talking, Shane explains why Joe should not try to measure up to him. " 'Tell him no man need be ashamed of being beat by Shane.' The name sounded queer like that, the man speaking of himself. It was the closest he ever came to boasting. And then you understood that there was not the least hint of a boast. He was stating a fact, simple and elemental as the power that dwelled in him." Shane understands that Joe feels the need to compete with him. Yet he also explains why Joe should not go through the internal conflict he is experiencing.

The characters of Shane, Marian, and Joe develop as they go through internal conflict. Shane desires to quit gunfighting but feels the need to fight for those he loves. Marian must decide between Shane and Joe. Joe tries to measure up to Shane. These three internal conflicts end when Shane leaves the Starretts' farm. (Claire)

Daily Assignment

- Warm-up: Did you guess the ending of *Shane*? Is it predictable? Why or why not?
- Students will complete Concept Builder 30-D.
- Prayer journal.
- Review the assigned text. Keep vocabulary cards.
- This is the day that students should write, and then rewrite, the final drafts of their assigned essay.

Social Conflict

***Shane* has several central conflicts that propel the plot forward. Complete the following chart.**

Conflict	Participants	Resolution
Farmers versus the ranchers	*The ranchers do not want the farmers to fence the open range. The open range is critical to the ranchers' financial survival.*	*The farmers this time at least win.*
Poor, ordinary people versus the privileged, wealthy people.		
Shane, the gunfighter, versus ordinary farmers who are not by trade gunmen.		
The farmer's wife who urges the strong, righteous Shane to protect her husband.		

Literary Review: Drama — *A Midsummer Night's Dream* (William Shakespeare)

Chapter 31

First Thoughts

For the remainder of this curriculum, you will be introduced to several other literary genres, and you will be invited to write literary critiques of these works. These genres include: drama, letters, a poem, and a short story.

Our first selection is a play. *A Midsummer Night's Dream* is one of William Shakespeare's most popular and well-written plays. During Shakespeare's time, theater was entertainment (before it was art), much like television functions today. Theater was not merely the pastime of the elite and the educated. It belonged to the people. Shakespeare wrote and performed during the reigns of Queen Elizabeth and King James. The Elizabethan theater highlighted the spoken word. The Elizabethan audience was attentive to the spoken word. They had to be. Theater used few stage properties and almost no scenery. Its outdoor circular theaters surrounded a bare horseshoe-shaped stage. Characters were developed at a fast pace, and what they said indicated who they were. There was neither narrator nor fancy bulletin to help the unwary listener. The audience worked for their treat. Thus, the playwright constantly had to keep his audience interested through the use of bright costumes, numerous action scenes, and frequent scene changes. *A Midsummer Night's Dream* had it all: fairies, creatures, and unicorns. They all invite the reader/viewer to a world of intrigue and entertainment.

Chapter Learning Objectives

In chapter 31 we will analyze an entire literary piece: William Shakespeare's *A Midsummer Night's Dream*.

As a result of this chapter study you will be able to . . .

1. Write a literary analysis of the entire play *A Midsummer Night's Dream*.
2. Analyze what vulgarity is.
3. Discuss the purpose of Puck in this comedy.

Look Ahead for Friday

- Turn in a final copy of essay
- Take Weekly Test

Lesson 1

Sample Play Review (Not a Full Literary Analysis)

Plays have been around since biblical times. They are best understood as they are read orally. Try it!

The following is a play review of *A Midsummer Night's Dream.*

William Shakespeare wrote the comedy *A Midsummer Night's Dream* in 1595. This play is best known for its famous line, "Lord what fools these mortals be!" (Act III, Scene ii). It is a story of fairies, kings, queens, actors, and lovers. Shakespeare combined a child's fairyland with adult troubles, creating a hilarious plot that both children and adults enjoyed.

Last year a local middle school put on this extraordinary comedy. Though middle schoolers are not known to be sensational actors/actresses, these few performed adequately. One of the most amazing players was Kurt Focht, who played the part of Nick Bottom. In the play, Nick is a traveling actor who happens to get the part of a donkey. The fairy queen (who has been put under a spell by the fairy king) sees Nick (who is disguised as a donkey) and unintentionally falls in love with him. Even though Kurt did not have a very large part, he performed it so splendidly that he stole the entire play. His performance and character were memorable.

One of the weaknesses of the performance as a whole was the way the lines were delivered. Most of the novice actors were unfamiliar with Old English dialect. When the lines were spoken, they were delivered in a haltingly, clumsy way. Many times the listener was forced to strain to hear the performers.

However, the performance was a hit. In the end it reached its goal of putting the audience in a fit of laughter, which seemed to delight the performers exceedingly. (Jessica Stobaugh)

Daily Assignment

- Warm-up: Compare *A Midsummer Night's Dream* to another Shakespeare play you have read or seen.
- Students will complete Concept Builder 31-A.
- Prayer journal: Students are encouraged to write in their prayer journal every day.
- Students need to review their material for the next assignment
- Students should systematically review their vocabulary words daily.

Grammar Review: Cogency and Focus

Rewrite the following passages with more cogency and focus.

A. In a morbid condition of the brain, dreams often have a singular actuality, vividness, and extraordinary semblance of reality. At times monstrous images are created, but the setting and the whole picture are so truth-like and filled with details so delicate, so unexpectedly, but so artistically consistent, that the dreamer, were he an artist like Pushkin or Turgenev even, could never have invented them in the waking state. Such sick dreams always remain long in the memory and make a powerful impression on the overwrought and deranged nervous system. (from *Crime and Punishment*)

A. Rewrite

B. Later on, when he recalled that time and all that happened to him during those days, minute by minute, point by point, he was superstitiously impressed by one circumstance, which, though in itself not very exceptional, always seemed to him afterwards the predestined turning-point of his fate. He could never understand and explain to himself why, when he was tired and worn out, when it would have been more convenient for him to go home by the shortest and most direct way, he had returned by the Hay Market where he had no need to go. It was obviously and quite unnecessarily out of his way, though not much so. It is true that it happened to him dozens of times to return home without noticing what streets he passed through. But why, he was always asking himself, why had such an important, such a decisive and at the same time such an absolutely chance meeting happened in the Hay Market (where he had moreover no reason to go) at the very hour, the very minute of his life when he was just in the very mood and in the very circumstances in which that meeting was able to exert the gravest and most decisive influence on his whole destiny? As though it had been lying in wait for him on purpose! (from *Crime and Punishment*)

B. Rewrite

Lesson 2

Worldview Model

"A Midsummer Night's Dream" shines like "Romeo and Juliet" in darkness, but shines merrily. Lysander, one of the two nonentities who are its heroes, complains at the beginning about the brevity of love's course. . . .

So quick bright things come to confusion.

This, however, is at the beginning. Bright things will come to clarity in a playful, sparkling night while fountains gush and spangled starlight betrays the presence in a wood near Athens of magic persons who can girdle the earth in forty minutes and bring any cure for human woe. Nor will the woe to be cured have any power to elicit our anxiety. . . . There will be no pretense that reason and love keep company, or that because they do not death lurks at the horizon.

— Mark Van Doren, *Shakespeare*, 1939

If ever the son of man in his wanderings was at home and drinking by the fireside, he is at home in the house of Theseus. All the dreams have been forgotten, as a melancholy dream remembered throughout the morning might be forgotten in the human certainty of any other triumphant evening party; and so the play seems naturally ended. It began on the earth and it ends on the earth. Thus to round off the whole midsummer night's dream in an eclipse of daylight is an effect of genius. But of this comedy, as I have said, the mark is that genius goes beyond itself; and one touch is added which makes the play colossal. Theseus and his train retire with a crashing finale, full of humour and wisdom and things set right, and silence falls on the house. Then there comes a faint sound of little feet, and for a moment, as it were, the elves look into the house, asking which is the reality. "Suppose we are the realities and they the shadows." If that ending were acted properly any modern man would feel shaken to his marrow if he had to walk home from the theatre through a country lane.

— G.K. Chesterton, *Chesterton on Shakespeare*, 1971

Daily Assignment

- Warm-up: Summarize the plot of *A Midsummer Nights Dream.*
- Students will complete Concept Builder 31-B.
- Prayer journal.
- Students should outline all assigned essays for the week.

The Plot

Draw and label the three plots that are occurring in *A Midsummer Night's Dream*.

Lesson 3

Grammar Review: Exclamation Points

Exclamation points are used after emphatic interjections and after other expressions to show strong emotion, such as surprise or disbelief. Use an exclamation point when it is truly needed and not to make a superfluous point. Consider the following:

The play was good! (writer trying to make a superfluous point with a simple sentence)

"Get off the stage!" the audience yelled.

"Hallelujah!" What a glorious blessing!

Daily Assignment

- Warm-up: Did you like this play? Why? Why not? Explain.
- Students will complete a daily Concept Builder 31-C.
- Prayer journal.
- Students should write rough drafts of all assigned essays.

CONCEPT BUILDER 31-C

Plot Climax

Draw the climax of *A Midsummer Night's Dream* on this stage.

Student Essay: Analysis of *A Midsummer Night's Dream*

William Shakespeare's play *A Midsummer Night's Dream* is an entertaining comedy full of lovers, fairies, and actors. The play is very enjoyable for a number of reasons. It contains an engaging story line and interesting characters. Shakespeare also brings the action alive through the dialogue.

Shakespeare makes the plot interesting through the confusing yet humorous plot. The confusion the reader feels at times forces them to look deeper into the story and therefore causes them to become further interested in it. The story is mainly about four lovers. One couple loves each other. They are Hermia, the woman, and Lysander, the man. The other man is named Demetrius. He also is in love with Hermia, though she doesn't love him. The other woman is Helena, and she is madly in love with Demetrius, who has no feelings for Helena at all. The fairies, while trying to help the lovers in this complicated situation, accidentally make it worse. They possess magic cream that, when applied to a person's eyelids, cause the person to fall in love with the first living thing they see when they awaken. The fairies mean to help Helena by applying this cream to Demetrius' eyelids so that he will see her first thing when he awakens. Accidentally, the fairies apply it to Lysander instead and when he awakens, the first thing he sees is Helena. He then loses his faithful love to Hermia. Then the fairies, realizing their mistake, apply the cream to Demetrius, and he also falls deeply in love with Helena. This angers Hermia to lose her lover, and it also angers Helena, thinking that the men are making fun of her, and don't really love her. All the lovers are then in a huge argument, all because of the fairies' cream. This confusing and humorous plot is enjoyable to read.

Shakespeare makes the characters colorful and interesting through developing them all with different personalities. Their differences give the play variety, and are revealed in the character's dialogue. A perfect example of the differences in characters is the contrast between Helena, the woman who is madly in love with Demetrius, and Demetrius, who is completely uninterested in Helena. Helena shows that she is a woman controlled by her emotions, and Demetrius, on the other hand, is curt, sensible, and not at all sensitive to the feelings of others. Here their different personalities show as Helena is chasing Demetrius through the woods against his will.

HELENA: Stay though thou kill me, sweet Demetrius.

DEMETRIUS: I charge thee, hence, and do not haunt me thus.

HELENA: O, wilt thou darkling leave me? Do not so.

DEMETRIUS: Stay, on thy peril. I alone will go.

Shakespeare brings the action alive through the dialogue, so the play is enjoyable to read. Through the descriptive dialogue, the reader can visualize what is happening.

Here the reader can tell through the dialogue that tension is rising between the characters as they argue.

DEMETRIUS: Relent, sweet Hermia, Lysander, yield thy crazed title to my certain right.

LYSANDER: You have her father's love, Demetrius. Let me have Hermia's. Do you marry him.

EGEUS: Scornful Lysander, true, he hath my love; And what is mine my love shall render him. And she is mine, and all my right of her I do estate unto Demetrius.

Here the reader can visualize through the dialogue that the characters are running around trying to find each other. They are very confused because the fairies are finding each other difficult through calling to the men in their enemy's voice, and leading them in the wrong direction.

LYSANDER: Where art thou, proud Demetrius, speak thou now.

ROBIN (in Demetrius' voice): Here, villain, drawn and ready. Where art thou?

LYSANDER: I will be with thee straight.

ROBIN (in Demetrius' voice): Follow me, then, to plainer ground.

Enter Demetrius

DEMETRIUS: Lysander, speak again. Thou runaway, thou coward, art thou fled? Speak! In some bush? Where dost thou hide thy head?

ROBIN (in Lysander's voice): Thou coward, art thou bragging to the stars, Telling the bushes that thou look'st for wars, And wilt not come? Come, recreant! Come, thou child! I'll whip thee with a rod. He is defiled That draws a sword on thee.

DEMETRIUS: Yea, art thou there?

ROBIN (in Lysander's voice): Follow my voice. We'll try no manhood here.

A Midsummer Night's Dream is a very entertaining play by William Shakespeare. Shakespeare makes his play interesting by creating colorful characters and an interesting, humorous plot. He writes descriptive dialogue that gives the reader a good visual picture of what is happening. (Jaime)

Daily Assignment

- Warm-up: Share a dream you had that seemed real until you woke.
- Students will complete Concept Builder 31-D.
- Prayer journal.
- Review the assigned text. Keep vocabulary cards.
- This is the day that students should write, and then rewrite, the final drafts of their assigned essays.

Theme Development

The theme of a story is a lesson the author wishes to share with his readers. Complete the following chart considering a theme centered around love.

A Theme of Love is developed by . . .

Characterization

The characters are colorful, round, and strong. They feel their world deeply. They connect with other characters.

Plot

Setting

Literary Review: Letters — "Letters" (C.S. Lewis)

Chapter 32

First Thoughts

Letter writing is quickly becoming a lost art. With the advent of e-mail and telecommunications, most Americans do not write letters anymore. However, throughout history letter writing has been a powerfully effective way to communicate. For example, Paul's letters to the churches in the New Testament were a powerful and effective means to communicate the gospel.

Chapter Learning Objectives

In chapter 32 we will examine C.S. Lewis's "Letters to Mr. Vanauken."

As a result of this chapter study you will be able to . . .

1. Examine the letters and discuss their style and structure. In other words, how does Lewis persuade his friend to give his life to Christ?
2. Write a letter to a friend or acquaintance who does not know the Lord.
3. Discuss the influence of C.S. Lewis on the conversion of Chuck Colson.

Look Ahead for Friday

- Turn in a final copy of essay
- Take Weekly Test

Lesson 1

Literary Analysis: Internal Conflict in a Character

The following personal letters are from C.S. Lewis to a friend. Lewis is trying to persuade his friend, Mr. Vanauken, to commit his life to Christ.

Dear Mr. Vanauken,

The contradiction "we must have faith to believe and must believe to have faith" belongs to the same class as those by which the Eleatic philosophers proved that all motion is impossible. And there are many others. You can't swim unless you can support yourself in water and you can't support yourself in water unless you can swim. Or again, in an act of volition (e.g. getting up in the morning) is the very beginning of the act itself voluntary or involuntary? If voluntary then you must have willed it, you were willing it already, it was not really the beginning. If involuntary, then the continuation of the act (being determined by the first movement) is involuntary too. But in spite of this we do swim, and we do get out of bed.

I do not think there is a demonstrative proof (like Euclid) of Christianity, nor of the existence of matter, nor of the good will and honesty of my best and oldest friends. I think all three (except perhaps the second) far more probable than the alternatives. The case for Christianity in general is well given by Chesterton; and I tried to do something in my Broadcast Talks. As to why God doesn't make it demonstrably clear; are we sure that He is even interested in the kind of Theism which would be a compelled logical assent to a conclusive argument? Are we interested in it in personal matters? I demand from my friend a trust in my good faith which is certain without demonstrative proof. It wouldn't be confidence at all if he waited for rigorous proof. Hang it all, the very fairy tales embody the truth. Othello believed in Desdemona's innocence when it was proved: but that was too late. `His praise is lost who stays till all commend.' The magnanimity, the generosity which will trust on a reasonable probability, is required of us. But supposing one believed and was wrong after all? Why, then you would have paid the universe a compliment it doesn't deserve. Your error would even so be more interesting and important than the reality. And yet how could that be? How could an idiotic universe have produced creatures whose mere dreams are so much stronger, better, subtler than itself?

Note that life after death which still seems to you the essential thing, was itself a late revelation. God trained the Hebrews for centuries to believe in Him without promising them an afterlife, and, blessings on Him, he trained me in the same way for about a year. It is like the disguised prince in a fairy tale who wins the heroine's love before she knows he is anything more than a woodcutter. What would be a bribe if it came first had better come last.

It is quite clear from what you say that you have conscious wishes on both sides. And now, another point about wishes. A wish may lead to false beliefs, granted. But what does the existence of the wish suggest? At one time I was much impressed by Arnold's line "Nor does the being hungry prove that we have bread." But surely tho' it doesn't prove that one particular man will get food, it does prove that there is such a thing as food! i.e. if we were a species that didn't normally eat, weren't designed to eat, would we feel hungry? You say the materialist universe is "ugly." I wonder how you discovered that! If you are really a product of a materialistic universe, how is it you don't feel at home there? Do fish complain of the sea for being wet? Or if they did, would that fact itself not strongly suggest that they had not always, or would not always be, purely aquatic creatures? Notice how we are perpetually surprised at Time. ("How time flies! Fancy John being grown-up and married! I can hardly believe it!") In heaven's name, why? Unless, indeed, there is something about us that is not temporal.

Total humility is not in the Tao because the Tao (as such) says nothing about the Object to which it would be the right response: just as there is no law about railways in the acts of Q. Elizabeth. But from the degree of respect which the Tao demands for ancestors, parents, elders, and teachers, it is quite clear what the Tao would prescribe towards an object such as God. But I think you are already in the meshes of the net! The Holy Spirit is after you. I doubt if you'll get away!

Dear Vanauken,

My prayers are answered. No: a glimpse is not a vision. But to a man on a mountain road by night, a glimpse of the next three feet of road may matter more than a vision of the horizon. And there must perhaps be always just enough lack of demonstrative certainty to make free choice possible: for what could we do but accept if the faith were like the multiplication table? There will be a counter attack on you, you know, so don't be too alarmed when it comes. The enemy will not see you vanish into God's company without an effort to reclaim you.

Be busy learning to pray and (if you have made up your mind on the denominational question) get confirmed.

Blessings on you and a hundred thousand welcomes. Make use of me in any way you please: and let us pray for each other always.[1]

The following letter from Paul is to Philemon (from the Holman Christian Standard Bible):

Paul, a prisoner of Christ Jesus, and Timothy, our brother: To Philemon, our dear friend and co-worker, to Apphia our sister, to Archippus our fellow soldier, and to the church that meets in your house.

Grace to you and peace from God our Father and the Lord Jesus Christ.

I always thank my God when I mention you in my prayers, because I hear of your love and faith toward faith that you have toward the Lord Jesus and for all the saints. [I pray] that your participation in the faith may become effective through knowing every good thing that is in us for [the glory of] Christ. For I have great joy and encouragement from your love, because the hearts of the saints have been refreshed through you, brother.

For this reason, although I have great boldness in Christ to command you to do what is right, I appeal, instead, on the basis of love. I, Paul, as an elderly man and now also as a prisoner of Christ Jesus, appeal to you for my child, whom I fathered while in chains — Onesimus. Once he was useless to you, but now he is useful to both you and me. I am sending him — a part of myself — back to you. I wanted to keep him with me, so that in my imprisonment for the gospel he might serve me in your place. But I didn't want to do anything without your consent, so that your good deed might not be out of obligation, but of your own free will. For perhaps this is why he was separated [from you] for a brief time, so that you might get him back permanently, no longer as a slave, but more than a slave — as a dearly loved brother. This is especially so to me, but even more to you, both in the flesh and in the Lord.

So if you consider me a partner, accept him as you would me. And if he has wronged you in any way, or owes you anything, charge that to my account. I, Paul, write this with my own hand: I will repay it — not to mention to you that you owe me even your own self. Yes, brother, may I have joy from you in the Lord; refresh my heart in Christ. Since I am confident of your obedience, I am writing to you, knowing that you will do even more than I say. But meanwhile, also prepare a guest room for me, for I hope that through your prayers I will be restored to you.

Epaphras, my fellow prisoner in Christ Jesus, greets you, and so do Mark, Aristarchus, Demas, and Luke, my co-workers.

The grace of the Lord Jesus Christ be with your spirit (Philemon 1–25; HCSB).

1 www.discovery.org/cslewis/articles/writingspblcdmn/letters.php.

Daily Assignment

- Warm-up: Describe a significant religious experience that you have had.
- Students will complete Concept Builder 32-A.
- Prayer journal: Students are encouraged to write in their prayer journal every day.
- Students need to review their material for the next assignment
- Students should systematically review their vocabulary words daily.

Active Reading

Read the following personal letter from C.S. Lewis to a friend, and then answer the following questions:

Dear Mr. Vanauken,

My own position at the threshold of Christianity was exactly the opposite of yours. You wish it were true; I strongly hoped it was not. At least, that was my conscious wish: you may suspect that I had unconscious wishes of quite a different sort and that it was these which finally shoved me in. True: but then I may equally suspect that under your conscious wish that it were true, there lurks a strong unconscious wish that it were not. What this works out to is that all the modern thinking, however useful it may be for explaining the origin of an error which you already know to be an error, is perfectly useless in deciding which of two beliefs is the error and which is the truth. For (a.) One never knows all one's wishes, and (b.) In very big questions, such as this, even one's conscious wishes are nearly always engaged on both sides. What I think one can say with certainty is this: the notion that everyone would like Christianity to be true, and that therefore all atheists are brave men who have accepted the defeat of all their deepest desires, is simply impudent nonsense. Do you think people like Stalin, Hitler, Haldane, Stapledon (a corking good writer, by the way) would be pleased on waking up one morning to find that they were not their own masters, that they had a Master and a Judge, that there was nothing even in the deepest recesses of their thoughts about which they could say to Him "Keep out! Private. This is my business?" Do you? Rats! Their first reaction would be (as mine was) rage and terror. And I very much doubt whether even you would find it simply pleasant. Isn't the truth this: that it would gratify some of our desires (ones we feel in fact pretty seldom) and outrage a good many others? So let's wash out all the wish business. It never helped anyone to solve any problem yet. I don't agree with your picture of the history of religion. Christ, Buddha, Mohammed and others elaborating on an original simplicity. I believe Buddhism to be a simplification of Hinduism and Islam to be a simplification of Christianity. Clear, lucid, transparent, simple religion (Tao plus a shadowy, ethical god in the background) is a late development, usually arising among highly educated people in great cities. What you really start with is ritual, myth, and mystery, the death and return of Balder or Osiris, the dances, the initiations, the sacrifices, the divine kings. Over against that are the Philosophers, Aristotle or Confucius, hardly religion at all. The only two systems in which the mysteries and the philosophies come together are Hinduism and Christianity: there you get both the Metaphysics and Cult (continuous with primeval cults). That is why my first step was to be sure that one or the other of these had the answer. For the reality can't be one that appeals either only to savages or only to high brows. Real things aren't like that (e.g. matter is the first most obvious thing you meet milk, chocolates, apples, and also the object of quantum physics). There is no question of just a crowd of disconnected religions. The choice is between (a.) The materialist world picture: which I can't believe. (b.) The real archaic primitive religions; which are not moral enough. (c.) The (claimed) fulfillment of these in Hinduism. (d.) The claimed fulfillment of these in Christianity. But the weakness of Hinduism is that it doesn't really merge the two strands. Unredeemable savage religion goes on in the village; the Hermit philosophizes in the forest: and neither really interfaces with the other. It is only Christianity which compels a high brow like me to partake of a ritual blood feast, and also compels a central African convert to attempt an enlightened code of ethics. Have you ever tried Chesterton's The Everlasting Man? The best popular apologetic I know. Meanwhile, the attempt to practice Tao is certainly the right line. Have you read the Analects of Confucius? He ends up by saying, "This is the Tao. I do not know if anyone has ever kept it." That's significant: one can really go direct from there to the Epistle of the Romans. I don't know if any of this is the least use. Be sure to write again, or call, if you think I can be of any help.

1. Notice the way that Lewis uses rhetorical questions and dialogue. Why?

2. Circle examples of each.

Lesson 2

Biblical Letter

Philemon 1

Paul, a prisoner of Christ Jesus, and Timothy our brother,

To Philemon our dear friend and fellow worker — also to Apphia our sister and Archippus our fellow soldier —and to the church that meets in your home:

Grace and peace to you from God our Father and the Lord Jesus Christ.

I always thank my God as I remember you in my prayers, because I hear about your love for all his holy people and your faith in the Lord Jesus. I pray that your partnership with us in the faith may be effective in deepening your understanding of every good thing we share for the sake of Christ. Your love has given me great joy and encouragement, because you, brother, have refreshed the hearts of the Lord's people.

Paul's Plea for Onesimus

Therefore, although in Christ I could be bold and order you to do what you ought to do, yet I prefer to appeal to you on the basis of love. It is as none other than Paul — an old man and now also a prisoner of Christ Jesus — that I appeal to you for my son Onesimus, who became my son while I was in chains. Formerly he was useless to you, but now he has become useful both to you and to me.

I am sending him — who is my very heart — back to you. I would have liked to keep him with me so that he could take your place in helping me while I am in chains for the gospel. But I did not want to do anything without your consent, so that any favor you do would not seem forced but would be voluntary. Perhaps the reason he was separated from you for a little while was that you might have him back forever — no longer as a slave, but better than a slave, as a dear brother. He is very dear to me but even dearer to you, both as a fellow man and as a brother in the Lord.

So if you consider me a partner, welcome him as you would welcome me. If he has done you any wrong or owes you anything, charge it to me. I, Paul, am writing this with my own hand. I will pay it back — not to mention that you owe me your very self. I do wish, brother, that I may have some benefit from you in the Lord; refresh my heart in Christ. Confident of your obedience, I write to you, knowing that you will do even more than I ask.

And one thing more: Prepare a guest room for me, because I hope to be restored to you in answer to your prayers.

Epaphras, my fellow prisoner in Christ Jesus, sends you greetings. And so do Mark, Aristarchus, Demas and Luke, my fellow workers.

The grace of the Lord Jesus Christ be with your spirit (Philemon 1–25; NIV).

Daily Assignment

- Warm-up: Persuade your parents to let you go to Disneyland.
- Students will complete Concept Builder 32-B.
- Prayer journal.
- Students should outline all assigned essays for the week.

Writing a Letter

Write an informal letter to an unsaved friend, convincing him to give his life to Christ. Begin with a greeting. Offer some arguments, and evidence to support your arguments. Then, discuss one counter-argument (opposing view) and finish with a summary and prayer.

Greeting/Introduction

Argument 1

Evidence 1

Argument 2

Evidence 2

Counter-argument

Refutation

Conclusion

Prayer

Lesson 3

Grammar Review: Wordy

Avoid using *and/or* in formal writing. Consider the following:

We will go to school tomorrow and/or the football game.

We will go to school tomorrow and to the football game.

Daily Assignment

- Warm-up: Persuade your best friend to eat pizza from the wide (not sharp) end.
- Students will complete Concept Builder 32-C.
- Prayer journal.
- Students should write rough drafts of all assigned essays and speech.

Analyze Lewis' Letter

Take excerpts from the text of C.S. Lewis' letter to complete the boxes below.

Greeting/Introduction

My own position at the threshold of Christianity was exactly the opposite of yours. You wish it were true; I strongly hoped it was not. At least, that was my conscious wish: you may suspect that I had unconscious wishes of quite a different sort and that it was these which finally shoved me in. True: but then I may equally suspect that under your conscious wish that it were true, there lurks a strong unconscious wish that it were not. What this works out to is that all the modern thinking, however useful it may be for explaining the origin of an error which you already know to be an error, is perfectly useless in deciding which of two beliefs is the error and which is the truth.

Argument

Evidence

Conclusion

Prayer

Student Essay: Style of Persuasion in C.S. Lewis's "Letters"

C.S. Lewis, in his "Letters," urges Mr. Vanauken, a personal friend of his, to commit his life to Christianity. Lewis writes his "Letters" in a personal and persuasive style, identifying with his friend while using logic to help convince Mr. Vanauken of the validity of Christianity"

> My own position at the threshold of Christianity was exactly the opposite of yours. You wish it were true, I strongly hoped it was not. At least, that was my conscious wish: you may suspect that I had unconscious wishes of quite a different sort and that it was these which finally shoved me in. . . . Do you think people like Stalin, Hitler, Haldane, Stapleton (a corking good writer, by the way) would have been pleased on waking up one morning to find that they were not their own masters. . . ? (page 1)

Throughout his letter, Lewis constantly refers to Mr. Vanauken by name and talks about what he is likely thinking. He empathizes with Mr. Vakauken's opinions and feelings while gently pushing him toward Christianity, talking to his friend as if he is a real person with a soul. From the opening sentences to the concluding paragraphs of his letters, Lewis strives to identify on a personal level with his friend.

Yet Lewis does not restrict his letters to only personal pleadings. Lewis also uses logic to help explain the validity of Christianity. In fact, a great deal of his letters are devoted to laying out the reasons why Mr. Vakauken should rest assured that Christianity is authentic:

> And I very much doubt whether even you would find it [the fact that God exists] simply pleasant. Isn't the truth this: that it would gratify some of our desires (ones that we feel in fact pretty seldom) and outrage a good many others? So let's wash all the wish business. It never helped anyone to solve any problem yet. I don't agree with your picture of the history of religion. Christ, Buddha, Mohammed and others elaborating on an original simplicity. . . . That is why my first step was to be sure that one or the other of these [religions] had the answer. For reality can't be one that appeals either only to savages or only to high brows. Real things aren't like that. . . . You say the materialist universe is 'ugly'. I wonder how you discovered that! If you're really a product of a materialistic universe, how is it that you don't feel at home there? Do fish complain of the sea for being wet? Or if they did, would the fact itself not strongly suggest that they have not always, or would not always be, purely aquatic creatures? . . . Notice how we are perpetually surprised at Time. . . . In heaven's name why? Unless, indeed, there is something about is that is not temporal. (pages 1–3)

Here, Lewis argues gently but persuasively for reasons why Christianity might be true. He lightly chides Mr. Vakauken for not being totally honest with himself, then launches into his argument. Using compelling logic and raising valid points, Lewis draws his conclusion: that man isn't a temporal product of the universe. He uses logic to help convince Mr. Vakauken of the validity of Christianity.

Thus, in his Letters, C.S. Lewis communicates and connects with his friend on a personal level while using logic to help convince him of the authenticity of Christianity. (JB)

Daily Assignment

- Warm-up: Write a letter to someone you love. Tell him/her why.
- Students will complete Concept Builder 32-D.
- Prayer journal.
- Review the assigned text. Keep vocabulary cards.
- This is the day that students should write, and then rewrite, the final drafts of their assigned essay.

Background History

First, tell who these people are. Then, look in a reference book and check your answer.

Person in History	Who I think he is . . .	Who he really is. . .
Confucius		
Aristotle		
Hitler		

Poetry — "The Midnight Ride of Paul Revere" (Henry Wadsworth Longfellow)

Chapter 33

First Thoughts

During his lifetime, Longfellow was loved and admired both at home and abroad. In 1884, he was honored by the placing of a memorial bust in Poets' Corner of Westminster Abbey in London. He was the first American to be so recognized. Sweetness, gentleness, simplicity, and a romantic vision shaded by melancholy are the characteristic features of Longfellow's poetry. His poetry was not merely good; it was read by almost every literate American. Perhaps no American poet has captured the American heart like Longfellow did.

Chapter Learning Objectives

In chapter 33 we will learn how to write a literary analysis of a poem and will examine Henry David Longfellow's "Midnight Ride of Paul Revere."

As a result of this chapter study you will be able to . . .

1. Write a literary analysis of "The Midnight Ride of Paul Revere."
2. Discuss biblical examples of storytelling.
3. Write a narrative poem about a famous, intriguing, or even difficult event in your family's life, using Longfellow's narrative poem celebrating a famous historical event as an example

Look Ahead for Friday

- Turn in a final copy of essay
- Take Weekly Test

"The Midnight Ride of Paul Revere"

Listen my children and you shall hear
Of the midnight ride of Paul Revere,
On the eighteenth of April, in Seventy-five;
Hardly a man is now alive
Who remembers that famous day and year.

He said to his friend, "If the British march
By land or sea from the town tonight,
Hang a lantern aloft in the belfry arch
Of the North Church tower as a signal light, —
One if by land, and two if by sea;
And I on the opposite shore will be,
Ready to ride and spread the alarm
Through every Middlesex village and farm,
For the country folk to be up and to arm."
Then he said "Good-night!" and with muffled oar
Silently rowed to the Charlestown shore,
Just as the moon rose over the bay,
Where swinging wide at her moorings lay
The Somerset, British man-of-war;
A phantom ship, with each mast and spar
Across the moon like a prison bar,
And a huge black hulk, that was magnified
By its own reflection in the tide.

Meanwhile, his friend through alley and street
Wanders and watches, with eager ears,
Till in the silence around him he hears
The muster of men at the barrack door,
The sound of arms, and the tramp of feet,
And the measured tread of the grenadiers,
Marching down to their boats on the shore.

Then he climbed the tower of the Old North Church,
By the wooden stairs, with stealthy tread,
To the belfry chamber overhead,
And startled the pigeons from their perch
On the sombre rafters, that round him made
Masses and moving shapes of shade, —
By the trembling ladder, steep and tall,
To the highest window in the wall,
Where he paused to listen and look down
A moment on the roofs of the town
And the moonlight flowing over all.
Beneath, in the churchyard, lay the dead,
In their night encampment on the hill,
Wrapped in silence so deep and still
That he could hear, like a sentinel's tread,
The watchful night-wind, as it went
Creeping along from tent to tent,
And seeming to whisper, "All is well!"
A moment only he feels the spell
Of the place and the hour, and the secret dread
Of the lonely belfry and the dead;
For suddenly all his thoughts are bent
On a shadowy something far away,
Where the river widens to meet the bay, —
A line of black that bends and floats
On the rising tide like a bridge of boats.

Meanwhile, impatient to mount and ride,
Booted and spurred, with a heavy stride
On the opposite shore walked Paul Revere.
Now he patted his horse's side,
Now he gazed at the landscape far and near,

Then, impetuous, stamped the earth,
And turned and tightened his saddle girth;
But mostly he watched with eager search
The belfry tower of the Old North Church,
As it rose above the graves on the hill,
Lonely and spectral and sombre and still.
And lo! as he looks, on the belfry's height
A glimmer, and then a gleam of light!
He springs to the saddle, the bridle he turns,
But lingers and gazes, till full on his sight
A second lamp in the belfry burns.
A hurry of hoofs in a village street,
A shape in the moonlight, a bulk in the dark,
And beneath, from the pebbles, in passing, a spark
Struck out by a steed flying fearless and fleet;
That was all! And yet, through the gloom and the light,
The fate of a nation was riding that night;
And the spark struck out by that steed, in his flight,
Kindled the land into flame with its heat.
He has left the village and mounted the steep,
And beneath him, tranquil and broad and deep,
Is the Mystic, meeting the ocean tides;
And under the alders that skirt its edge,
Now soft on the sand, now loud on the ledge,
Is heard the tramp of his steed as he rides.
It was twelve by the village clock
When he crossed the bridge into Medford town.
He heard the crowing of the cock,
And the barking of the farmer's dog,
And felt the damp of the river fog,
That rises after the sun goes down.
It was one by the village clock,
When he galloped into Lexington.
He saw the gilded weathercock
Swim in the moonlight as he passed,
And the meeting-house windows, black and bare,
Gaze at him with a spectral glare,
As if they already stood aghast
At the bloody work they would look upon.
It was two by the village clock,
When he came to the bridge in Concord town.
He heard the bleating of the flock,
And the twitter of birds among the trees,
And felt the breath of the morning breeze
Blowing over the meadow brown.
And one was safe and asleep in his bed
Who at the bridge would be first to fall,
Who that day would be lying dead,
Pierced by a British musket ball.
You know the rest. In the books you have read
How the British Regulars fired and fled, —
How the farmers gave them ball for ball,
From behind each fence and farmyard wall,
Chasing the redcoats down the lane,
Then crossing the fields to emerge again
Under the trees at the turn of the road,
And only pausing to fire and load.
So through the night rode Paul Revere;
And so through the night went his cry of alarm
To every Middlesex village and farm, —
A cry of defiance, and not of fear,
A voice in the darkness, a knock at the door,
And a word that shall echo for evermore!
For, borne on the night-wind of the Past,
Through all our history, to the last,
In the hour of darkness and peril and need,
The people will waken and listen to hear
The hurrying hoof-beats of that steed,
And the midnight message of Paul Revere.[1]

1 www.online-literature.com/henry_longfellow/946/.

Daily Assignment

- Warm-up: What is your favorite poem? Why?
- Students will complete Concept Builder 33-A.
- Prayer journal: Students are encouraged to write in their prayer journal every day.
- Students need to review their material for the next assignment
- Students should systematically review their vocabulary words daily.

Writing Poetry

Read the poem and then answer the following questions.

Fork

This strange thing must have crept
Right out of hell.
It resembles a bird's foot

Work around the cannibal's neck.
As you hold it in your hand,
As you stab with it into a piece of meat,
It is possible to imagine the rest of the bird:
Its head which like your fist
Is large, bald, beakless and blind.
— by Charles Simic

1. What is the central image Simic presents?

2. What metaphors does he use to compare the fork?

3. Is this poem humorous? Why?

4. Create a similar poem entitled: "The Spoon."

Lesson 2

Literary Analysis: Poetry

The following list offers helpful guidelines to use to write an analysis of poetry:

1. Get involved with the poem. Mark it up! What words should be accented? Unaccented?
2. Consider the title of the poem carefully. Is it a correct title?
3. Read through the poem several times, both silently and aloud. What does it sound like? What does it mean? Rewrite the poem in prose.
4. Are there difficult or confusing words? Define them.
5. What mood is evoked in the poem? How is this mood accomplished? Is there a refrain?
6. Are there divisions within the poem? Why? Do they seem appropriate?
7. Finally, can you compare this poem to another written by the same author or another author?

Daily Assignment

- Warm-up: What makes a great poem?
- Students will complete Concept Builder 33-B.
- Prayer journal.
- Students should outline all assigned essays for the week.

Writing Poetry

Read the poem and then answer the following questions.

Star

Star,
If you are
A love compassionate,
You will walk with us this year.
We face a glacial distance, who are here
Huddld
At your feet.
— by William Burford

1. Why is the word "Star" on the top?

2. Why is huddld misspelled?

3. Using the above poem as a model, write a poem entitled "A Church."

Lesson 3

Grammar Review: Review

Using a solid, thorough, advanced grammar text, review Diction Grammar Guidelines, including good usage, exactness, conciseness, clarity, and completeness.

Daily Assignment

- Warm-up: Imagine you are in your yard. Describe your surroundings.
- Students will complete Concept Builder 33-C.
- Prayer journal.
- Students should write rough drafts of all assigned essays and speech.

CONCEPT BUILDER 33-C

Concrete Poems

The following is a concrete poem:

Tornadoes come and crash
They speak with wind
Hushed lives gather
Hiding from howls
Waiting for quiet
The all is well
Until then
We pray
Amen
Yes

Create a concrete poem with one of the following titles:

Clouds
Forest
River

The Plot of the Midnight Ride

"The Midnight Ride of Paul Revere" is a poem about the Revolutionary War battles of Lexington and Concord in Boston. Henry Longfellow, the author, accents his poem with many strong literary aspects that make the poem captivating. He uses descriptive words to show the emotions and actions of the characters. All of these characteristics make Longfellow's poetry an engrossing poem.

The plot of "The Midnight Ride of Paul Revere" is laid out nicely. Longfellow opens the poem with Paul Revere talking to the watchmen at the North Church. They have made a plan to signal each other if the British should come and attack. In the rising action, Paul is anxiously waiting for the watchman's signal so that he may warn the people of Boston. The watchman is scanning the city and the ocean. When the climax approaches, the signal, two lanterns hung on the church tower, warns Paul that the British are coming by sea. The anxious feelings of Paul are given to the reader as he rides into Boston, warning the town. In the falling action and conclusion, Longfellow briefly talks about the battle and ends with saying that Paul Revere's story will last throughout history.

> Meanwhile, impatient to mount and ride,
> Booted and spurred, with a heavy stride
> On the opposite shore walked Paul revere.
> Now he patted his horse's side,
> Now he gazed at the landscape far and near,
> Then, impetuous, stamped the earth,
> And turned and tightened his saddle girth;
> But mostly he watched with eager search
> The belfry tower of the Old North Church,
> As it rose above the graves on the hill,
> Lonely and spectral and somber and still.
> And lo! As he looks, on the belfry's height
> A glimmer, and then a gleam of light!
> He springs to the saddle, the bridle he turns,
> But lingers and gazes, till full on his sight
> A second lamp in the belfry burns.

Throughout the poem, the reader can identify a tone of anxious suspense.

Both the watchman and Paul Revere are described with words that relay anxiety. As the poem progresses, suspense builds. The reader wonders when the watchman will give Paul the signal to gallop into Boston and warn the townspeople to take up arms. When the signal is given, suspense is still held. Paul rushes into the town, yelling the warning. A small description of the battle is given, showing the bravery of the townspeople. The tone of Longfellow's poem keeps the reader captivated, even though everyone knows the outcome of the story already.

> So through the night rode Paul Revere;
> And so through the night went his cry of alarm
> To every Middlesex village and farm, —
> A cry of defiance, and not of fear,
> A voice in the darkness, a knock at the door,
> And a work that shall echo evermore!

In "The Midnight Ride of Paul Revere," there is also an evident theme of bravery. Without the bravery of the men who warned the people of Boston, the British would have captured the city. The portrayal of this fretful account also shows the bravery of the men of Boston. Since America did not have an actual army at this time, their defense consisted of volunteers briefly trained. The bravery of these Boston men showed other Americans that they could, indeed, defeat the British.

> Who at the bridge would be first to fall,
> Who that day would be lying dead,
> Pierced by a British musket ball.
> You know the rest. In the books you have read
> How the British Regulars fired and fled, —
> How the farmers gave them ball for ball,
> From behind each fence and farmyard wall,
> Chasing the redcoats sown the lane,
> Then crossing the fields to emerge again.

All of the characteristics of "The Midnight Ride of Paul Revere" set Longfellow's poetry apart from others. This piece is easy to comprehend and captivates the reader. It is also an account of an important time in American history. This depiction of Paul Revere's ride also helps the reader to get an insight of the frightful night on April 18, 1775. (Megan)

Daily Assignment

- Warm-up: Describe "loneliness."
- Students will complete Concept Builder 33-D.
- Prayer journal.
- Review the assigned text. Keep vocabulary cards.
- This is the day that students should write, and then rewrite, the final drafts of their assigned essay.

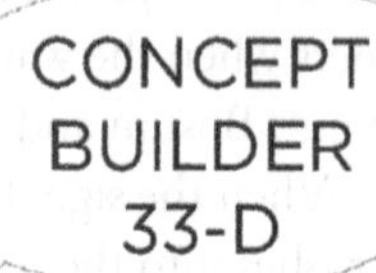

Poetry Descriptions

Read the poem and then answer the following questions.

SEASON of mists and mellow fruitfulness,
Close bosom-friend of the maturing sun;
Conspiring with him how to load and bless
With fruit the vines that round the thatch-eaves run;
To bend with apples the moss'd cottage-trees,
And fill all fruit with ripeness to the core;
To swell the gourd, and plump the hazel shells
With a sweet kernel; to set budding more,
And still more, later flowers for the bees,
Until they think warm days will never cease;
For Summer has o'erbrimm'd their clammy cells.

— by John Keats

1. What season is Keats describing?

2. Draw a picture of this poem.

3. Give two examples of effective descriptions in this poem.

Short Story — "The Lady or the Tiger?" (Frank Stockton)

Chapter 34

First Thoughts

The short story is more than a short story; it is a story that makes a succinct point, or promotes a focused point within a 500–15,00 word limitation.

Chapter Learning Objectives

In chapter 34 we will write a literary analysis of the short story "The Lady or the Tiger?" by Frank Stockton.

As a result of this chapter study you will be able to . . .

1. Write a literary analysis of "The Lady or the Tiger?" by Frank Stockton. Discuss the plot, theme, tone, setting, narration, and characters.
2. Explain how "The Lady or the Tiger?" is disturbingly anti-Christian.
3. Analyze the ending of this short story.

Look Ahead for Friday

- Turn in a final copy of essay
- Take Weekly Test

Lesson 1

The Lady or the Tiger?

In the very olden time, there lived a semi-barbaric king, whose ideas, though somewhat polished and sharpened by the progressiveness of distant Latin neighbors, were still large, florid, and untrammeled, as became the half of him which was barbaric. He was a man of exuberant fancy, and, withal, of an authority so irresistible that, at his will, he turned his varied fancies into facts. He was greatly given to self-communing; and, when he and himself agreed upon any thing, the thing was done. When every member of his domestic and political systems moved smoothly in its appointed course, his nature was bland and genial; but whenever there was a little hitch, and some of his orbs got out of their orbits, he was blander and more genial still, for nothing pleased him so much as to make the crooked straight, and crush down uneven places.

Among the borrowed notions by which his barbarism had become semified was that of the public arena, in which, by exhibitions of manly and beastly valor, the minds of his subjects were refined and cultured.

But even here the exuberant and barbaric fancy asserted itself. The arena of the king was built, not to give the people an opportunity of hearing the rhapsodies of dying gladiators, nor to enable them to view the inevitable conclusion of a conflict between religious opinions and hungry jaws, but for purposes far better adapted to widen and develop the mental energies of the people. This vast amphitheatre, with its encircling galleries, its mysterious vaults, and its unseen passages, was an agent of poetic justice, in which crime was punished. Or virtue rewarded, by the decrees of an impartial and incorruptible chance.

When a subject was accused of a crime of sufficient importance to interest the king, public notice was given that on an appointed day the fate of the accused person would be decided in the king's arena — a structure which well de-served its name; for, although its form and plan were borrowed from afar, its purpose emanated solely from the brain of this man, who, every barleycorn a king, knew no tradition to which he owed more allegiance than pleased his fancy, and who ingrafted on every adopted form of human thought and action the rich growth of his barbaric idealism.

When all the people had assembled in the galleries, and the king, surrounded by his court, sat high up on his throne of royal state on one side of the arena, he gave a signal, a door beneath him opened, and the accused subject stepped out into the amphitheatre. Directly opposite him, on the other side of the enclosed space, were two doors, exactly alike and side by side. It was the duty and the privilege of the person on trial, to walk directly to these doors and open one of them. He could open either door he pleased: he was subject to no guidance or influence but that of the aforementioned impartial and incorruptible chance. If he opened the one, there came out of it a hungry tiger, the fiercest and most cruel that could be procured, which immediately sprang upon him, and tore him to pieces, as a punishment for his guilt. The moment that the case of the criminal was thus decided, doleful iron bells were clanged, great wails went up from the hired mourners posted on the outer rim of the arena, and the vast audience, with bowed heads and downcast hearts, wended slowly their homeward way, mourning greatly that one so young and fair, or so old and respected, should have merited so dire a fate.

But, if the accused person opened the other door, there came forth from it a lady, the most suitable to his years and station that his majesty could select among his fair subjects; and to this lady he was immediately married, as a reward of his innocence. It mattered not that he might already possess a wife and family, or that his affections might be engaged upon an object of his own selection: the king allowed no such subordinate arrangements to interfere with his great scheme of retribution and reward. The exercises, as in the other instance, took place immediately, and in the arena. Another door opened beneath the king, and a priest, followed by a band of choristers' and dancing maidens blowing joyous airs on golden horns and treading on measure, advanced to where the pair stood side by side; and the wedding was promptly and cheerily solemnized. Then the gay brass bells rang forth their merry peals, the people shouted glad hurrahs, and the innocent man, preceded by children strewing flowers on his path, led his bride to his home.

This was the king's semi-barbaric method of administering justice. Its perfect fairness is obvious. The criminal could not know out of which door would come the lady: he opened either he pleased, without having the slightest idea whether, in the next instant, he was to be devoured or married. On some occasions the tiger came out of one door, and on some out of the other. The decisions of this tribunal were not only fair, they were positively determinate: the accused person was instantly punished if he found himself guilty; and, if innocent, he was rewarded on the spot, whether he liked it or not. There was no escape from the judgments of the king's arena.

The institution was a very popular one. When the people gathered together on one of the great trial days, they never knew whether they were to witness a bloody slaughter or a hilarious wedding. This element of uncertainty lent an interest to the occasion which it could not otherwise have attained. Thus, the masses were entertained and pleased, and the thinking part of the community could bring no charge of unfairness against this plan; for did not the accused person have the whole matter in his own hands?

This semi-barbaric king had a daughter as blooming as his most florid fancies, and with a soul as fervent and imperious as his own. As is usual in such cases, she was the apple of his eye, and was loved by him above all humanity. Among his courtiers was a young man of that fineness of blood and lowness of station common to the conventional heroes of romance who love royal maidens. This royal maiden was well satisfied... for he was handsome and brave to a degree unsurpassed in all this kingdom .... This love affair moved on happily for many months, until one day the king happened to discover its existence. He did not hesitate nor waver in regard to his duty in the premises. The youth was immediately cast into prison, and a day was appointed for his trial in the king's arena. This, of course, was an especially important occasion; and his majesty, as well as all the people, was greatly interested in the workings and development of this trial. Never before had such a case occurred; never before had a subject dared to love the daughter of a king. In after-years such things became commonplace enough; but then they were, in no slight degree, novel and startling.

The tiger-cages of the kingdom were searched for the most savage and relentless beasts, from which the fiercest monster might be selected for the arena; and the ranks of maiden youth and beauty throughout the land were carefully surveyed by competent judges, in order that the young man might have a fitting bride in case fate did not determine for him a different destiny. Of course, everybody knew that the deed with which the accused was charged had been done. He had loved the princess, and neither he, she, nor any one else thought of denying the fact; but the king would not think of allowing any fact of this kind to interfere with the workings of the tribunal, in which he took such great delight and satisfaction. No matter how the affair turned out, the youth would be disposed of; and the king would take an aesthetic pleasure in watching the course of events, which would determine whether or not the young man had done wrong in allowing himself to love the princess.

The appointed day arrived. From far and near the people gathered, and thronged the great galleries of the arena; and crowds, unable to gain admittance, massed themselves against its outside walls. The king and his court were in their places, opposite the twin doors — those fateful portals, so terrible in their similarity.

All was ready. The signal was given. A door beneath the royal party opened, and the lover of the princess walked into the arena. Tall, beautiful, fair, his appearance was greeted with a low hum of admiration and anxiety. Half the audience had not known so grand a youth had lived among them. No wonder the princess loved him! What a terrible thing for him to be there!

As the youth advanced into the arena, he turned, as the custom was, to bow to the king: but he did not think at all of that royal personage; his eyes were fixed upon the princess, who sat to the right of her father. Had it not been for the moiety of barbarism in her nature, it is probable that lady would not have been there; but her intense and fervid soul would not allow her to be absent on an occasion in which she was so terribly interested. From the moment that the decree had gone forth, that her lover should decide his fate in the king's arena, she had thought of nothing, night or day, but this great event and the various subjects connected with it. Possessed of more power, influence, and force of character than any one who had ever before been interested in such a case, she had done what no other person had done — she had possessed herself of the secret of the doors. She knew in which of the two rooms, that lay behind those doors, stood the cage of the tiger, with its open front, and in which waited the lady. Through these thick doors, heavily curtained with skins on the inside, it was impossible that any noise or suggestion should come from within to the person who should approach to raise the latch of one of them; but gold, and the power of a woman's will, had brought the secret to the princess.

And not only did she know in which room stood the

lady ready to emerge, all blushing and radiant, should her door be opened, but she knew who the lady was. It was one of the fairest and loveliest of the damsels of the court who had been selected as the reward of the accused youth, should he be proved innocent of the crime of aspiring to one so far above him; and the princess hated her. Often had she seen, or imagined that she had seen, this fair creature throwing glances of admiration upon the person of her lover, and sometimes she thought these glances were perceived and even returned. Now and then she had seen them talking together; it was but for a moment or two, but much can be said in a brief space; it may have been on most unimportant topics, but how could she know that? The girl was lovely, but she had dared to raise her eyes to the loved one of the princess; and, with all the intensity of the savage blood transmitted to her through long lines of wholly barbaric ancestors, she hated the woman who blushed and trembled behind that silent door.

When her lover turned and looked at her, and his eye met hers as she sat there paler and whiter than any one in the vast ocean of anxious faces about her, he saw, by that power of quick perception which is given to those whose souls are one, that she knew behind which door crouched the tiger, and behind which stood the lady. He had expected her to know it. He understood her nature, and his soul was assured that she would never rest until she had made plain to herself this thing, hidden to all other lookers-on, even to the king. The only hope for the youth in which there was any element of certainty was based upon the success of the princess in discovering this mystery; and the moment he looked upon her, he saw she had succeeded, as in his soul he knew she would succeed.

Then it was that his quick and anxious glance asked the question: "Which?" It was as plain to her as if he shouted it from where he stood. There was not an instant to be lost. The question was asked in a rush; it must be answered in another.

Her right arm lay on the cushioned parapet before her. She raised her hand, and made a slight, quick movement toward the right. No one but her lover saw her. Every eye but his was fixed on the man in the arena.

He turned, and with a firm and rapid step he walked across the empty space. Every heart stopped beating, every breath was held, every eye was fixed immovably upon that man. Without the slightest hesitation, he went to the door on the right, and opened it.

Now, the point of the story is this: Did the tiger come out of that door, or did the lady?

The more we reflect upon this question, the harder it is to answer. It involves a study of the human heart, which leads us through devious mazes of passion, out of which it is difficult to find our way. Think of it, fair reader, not as if the decision of the question depended upon yourself, but upon that hot-blooded, semi-barbaric princess, her soul at a white heat beneath the combined fires of despair and jealousy. She had lost him, but who should have him?

How often, in her waking hours and in her dreams, had she started in wild horror, and covered her face with her hands, as she thought of her lover opening the door on the other side of which waited the cruel fangs of the tiger!

But how much oftener had she seen him at the other door! How in her grievous reveries had she gnashed her teeth, and torn her hair, when she saw his start of rapturous delight as he opened the door of the lady! How her soul had burned in agony when she had seen him rush to meet that woman, with her flushing cheek and sparkling eye of triumph; when she had seen him lead her forth, his whole frame kindled with the joy of recovered life; when she had heard the glad shouts from the multitude, and the wild ringing of the happy bells; when she had seen the priest, with his joyous followers, advance to the couple, and make them man and wife before her very eyes; and when she had seen them walk away together upon their path of flowers, followed by the tremendous shouts of the hilarious multitude, in which her one despairing shriek was lost and drowned!

Would it not be better for him to die at once, and go to wait for her in the blessed regions of semi-barbaric futurity?

And yet, that awful tiger, those shrieks, that blood!

Her decision had been indicated in an instant, but it had been made after days and nights of anguished deliberation. She had known she would be asked, she had decided what she would answer, and, without the slightest hesitation, she had moved her hand to the right.

The question of her decision is one not to be lightly considered, and it is not for me to presume to set myself up as the one person able to answer it. And so I leave it with all of you: Which came out of the opened door — the lady, or the tiger?[2]

2 www.eastoftheweb.com/short-stories/UBooks/LadyTige.shtml.

Daily Assignment

- Warm-up: What makes a great short story?
- Students will complete Concept Builder 34-A.
- Prayer journal: Students are encouraged to write in their prayer journal every day.
- Students need to review their material for the next assignment
- Students should systematically review their vocabulary words daily.

CONCEPT BUILDER 34-A

Conflict and Consequences Equal Suspense

Identify conflicts in "The Lady or the Tiger?" by Frank R. Stockton.

Character	Plot Event	Conflict	Suspense
Protagonist	Meets the young lady, wants to marry the young lady	Internal conflict: External conflict:	
King (Antagonist)	Meets the young man, offers a challenge to the young man	Internal conflict: External conflict:	

Lesson 2

Composition of the Short Story

Any student who wishes to express himself correctly and pleasingly, and desires a keener sense for the appreciation of literary work, must write. The way others have done the thing never appears in a forceful light until one sets himself at a task of like nature. Just so in the study of this text. To find and appreciate the better points of the short story, students must write stories of their own, patterned in a small way on the technique of the masterpieces.

The process of short story writing follows in a general way the following program. In the first place the class must have something interesting and suggestive to write about. Sometimes the class can suggest a subject; newspapers almost every day give incidents worthy of story treatment; happenings in the community often give the very best material for stories; and phases of the literature work may well be used in the development of students' themes. Change the type of character and place, reconstruct the plot, or require a different ending for the story, leaving the plot virtually as it is, and then assign to the class. Boys and girls should invariably be taught to see stories in the life about them, in the newspapers and magazines on their library tables, and in the masterpieces they study in their class work.

After the idea that the class wishes to develop has been definitely determined and the material for this development has been gathered and grouped about the idea, the class should select a viewpoint and proceed to write. Sometimes the author should tell the story, sometimes a third person who may be of secondary importance in the story should be given the role of the storyteller, sometimes the whole may be in dialogue. The class should choose a fitting method.

Young writers should be very careful about the beginning of a story. An action story should start with a striking incident that catches the reader's attention at once and forecasts subsequent happenings. In every case, this first incident must have in it the essence of the end of the story and should be perfectly logical to the reader after he has finished the reading. A story in which the setting is emphasized can well begin with a description and contain a number of descriptions and expositions, distributed with a sense of propriety throughout the theme. A good method to use in the opening of a character story is that of conversation. An excellent example of a sharp use of this device is Mrs. Freeman's *Revolt of Mother*, where the first paragraph is a single spoken word.

Every incident included in the story should be tested for its value in the development of the theme. An incident that does not amplify certain phases of the story has no right to be included, and great care should be used in an effort to incorporate just the material necessary for the proper evolution of the thought. The problem is not so much what can be secured to be included in the story, but rather, after making a thorough collection of the material, what of all these points should be cast out.

The ending must be a natural outgrowth of the development found in the body of the composition. Even in a story with a surprise ending, of which we are tempted to say that we have had no preparation for such a turn in the story, there must be hints — the subtler the better — that point unerringly and always toward the end. The end is presupposed in the beginning and the changing of one means the altering of the other.

Young writers have trouble in stopping at the right place. They should learn, as soon as possible, that to drag on after the logical ending has been reached spoils the best of stories. It is just as bad to stop before arriving at the true end. In other words, there is only one place for the ending of a story, and in no case can it be shifted without ruining the idea that has obtained throughout the theme.

There are certain steps in the development of story writing that should be followed if the best results are to be obtained. The first assignment should require only the writing of straight narrative. *The Arabian Nights Tales* and children's stories represent this type of writing and will give the teacher valuable aid in the presentation of this work. After the students have produced simple stories resembling the Sinbad Voyages, they should next add descriptions of persons and places and explanations of situations to develop clearness and interest in their original productions. Taking these themes in turn, students should be required to introduce plot incidents that complicate the simple happenings and divert the straightforward trend of the narrative. Now that the stories are well developed in their descriptions, expositions, and plot interests they should be tested for their emotional effects. Students should go through their themes, and by making the proper changes give in some cases a humorous and in others a pathetic or tragic effect. These few suggestions are given to emphasize the facts that no one conceives a story in all its details in a moment of inspiration, and that there is a way of proceeding that passes in logical gradations from the simplest to the most complex phases of story writing.[1]

1 L.A. Pittenger, *Short Stories* (New York: The Macmillan Company, 1914) p. 7.

Daily Assignment

- Warm-up: Will the protagonist get the girl? Or will he be eaten by the tiger? Offer textual evidence to support your conclusion.
- Students will complete Concept Builder 34-B.
- Prayer journal.
- Students should outline all assigned essays for the week.

Plot Development

Identify the exposition, rising action, climax, denouement, and resolution in "The Lady or the Tiger."

Exposition	*The three principal characters are introduced.*
Rising Action	
Climax	
Denouement	
Resolution	

Lesson 3

Grammar Review: Review

Continue using a thorough, advanced grammar text for reviewing Diction Guidelines, including good usage, exactness, conciseness, clarity, and completeness.

Daily Assignment

- Warm-up: Compare "The Lady or the Tiger?" with another short story you have read.
- Students will complete a daily Concept Builder 34-C.
- Prayer journal.
- Students should write rough drafts of all assigned essays.

Plot Development

Identify the plot development in "The Lady or the Tiger?"

Hint 1	*Among the borrowed notions by which his barbarism had become semified was that of the public arena, in which, by exhibitions of manly and beastly valor, the minds of his subjects were refined and cultured.*
Hint 2	
Hint 3	

Student Essay: A Review of "The Lady or the Tiger?"

Frank Stockton's "The Lady or the Tiger?" is a chilling story that causes the reader to consider the human heart. In this short story, Stockton describes a king who has a unique way of punishing the kingdom's criminals. The king is the story's antagonist, yet the protagonist is a much broader character. Although written in third person, the author does not give a definite ending, thus giving the story a tone of suspense all the way up to the end. Overall, Stockton builds on the themes of human nature and fate. He does this in a way that makes the reader pause and examine these two themes.

The story line describes an ancient, semi-barbaric king's method of punishing criminals. When an interesting criminal is found, he is taken to the king's arena. Once there, in front of many people, he opens one of two doors. Behind one door is a tiger that will kill him, and behind the other is a beautiful lady who he will wed. However, the man has no way of knowing which is behind each door. Stockton focuses on one particular "criminal." The king had recently discovered that his daughter and this man had been secretly in love. For this, he had the lover arrested. The man is taken to the arena. Knowing the princess found what was behind each door, he looked up to her. She signaled to the right door. Before though, the author describes the lady behind one door, a lady whom the princess was jealous of. At the end of the story, Stockton asks the reader if it was the lady or the tiger that was behind the door to the right. With this ending, the reader spends more time examining the story, characters, and tendencies of the human heart.

Although there are not many characters in "The Lady or the Tiger?" the character of the king is built upon the most. He is considered evil because he causes men to receive immoral and unjust punishment. The princess and her lover are both foils. These two characters are used to show the evil nature of the king. This short story is unusual as Stockton presents a clear antagonist instead of a clear protagonist.

Stockton creates the story to take place in an ancient kingdom. The storyline fits well into this setting, as the political system must be a monarchy, which has become less common in modern times. The king in the story has the right to decide the punishment of criminals. An ancient setting also works well as the place of punishment for the kingdom is the king's arena. In the present, barely any countries punish their criminals in such a public place. "The Lady or the Tiger?" storyline is historically correctly placed in a monarchy from long ago.

"The Lady or the Tiger?" is written in third-person narration, without a particular character telling the story. Although many books written in third person share more than any of the characters individually can tell, this is not entirely the case with Stockton's short story. Although he certainly could have told the reader what was behind the right door, Stockton chose not to. However, because the story was written in third person, the reader is able to learn of the princess's motion to the right door while also learning about the king's own feelings. The author wrote "The Lady or the Tiger?" using certain advantages of third-person narration yet retaining other assets.

"The Lady or the Tiger?" is written with a tone of suspense. The simple plot of this story is filled with tension, because of the unknown fate of the princess's lover. This suspenseful tone is carried out even past the ending of the story. Because Stockton never tells the reader what is behind the right door, one is left to decide for himself. This decision is made by the reader based on the suspense created at the very end of the story.

Stockton builds on the themes of human nature and fate in "The Lady or the Tiger?" The king's method of punishment is primarily based on fate. The criminals have no way of knowing what is behind each door; the consequence of either the lady or the tiger, Stockton implies, is fate. As the author gives the reader a chance to contemplate what is behind the right door, one contemplates human nature and the tendencies of the heart. In this short story, human nature has a hand in determining the fate of an individual.

"The Lady or the Tiger?" is a suspenseful story that shows the consequences of a ruthless king. Although written in third person, the reader is left to decide the ending, based on his or her understanding of the human heart. With this decision, the reader is introduced to Stockton's presentation of fate and human nature. (Claire)

Daily Assignment

- Warm-up: Why does the father create a contest to test his potential son-in-law?
- Students will complete Concept Builder 34-D.
- Prayer journal.
- Review the assigned text. Keep vocabulary cards.
- This is the day that students should write, and then rewrite, the final drafts of their assigned essays.

Descriptions

Explain what each word picture means, and then draw a physical picture of the word picture.

Word Picture	In Your Own Words	Picture
He was a man of exuberant fancy	*He was a man prone to excesses. When he created an event, it was usually full of surprises and excitement.*	
This semi-barbaric king had a daughter as blooming as his most florid fancies.		
Among his courtiers was a young man of that fineness of blood and lowness of station common to the conventional heroes of romance who love royal maidens.		

Appendices

Writing Tips

How do students produce concise, well-written essays?

GENERAL STATEMENTS

- Essays should be written in the context of the other social sciences. This means that essays should be written on all topics: science topics, history topics, social science topics, etc.
- Some essays should be rewritten, depending on the literary analysis and the purpose of the writing; definitely those essays that are to be presented to various readers or a public audience should be rewritten for their best presentation. Parents and other educators should discuss with their students which and how many essays will be rewritten. Generally speaking, I suggest that students rewrite at least one essay per week.
- Students should write something every day and read something every day. Students will be prompted to read assigned whole books before they are due. It is imperative that students read ahead as they write present essays or they will not be able to read all the material. Remember this, too: students tend to write what they read. Poor material — material that is too juvenile — will be echoed in the vocabulary and syntax of student essays.
- Students should begin writing literary analyses immediately after they are assigned. A suggested implementation schedule is provided. Generally speaking, students will write about one hour per day to accomplish the writing component of this course.
- Students should revise their papers as soon as they are evaluated. Follow the implementation schedule at the end of each course.

Every essay includes a *prewriting phase, an outlining phase, a writing phase, a revision phase,* and for the purposes of this course, *a publishing phase.*

PRE-WRITING THINKING CHALLENGE

Issue

State problem/issue in five sentences.

1.

2.

3.

4.

5.

State problem/issue in two sentences.

1.

2.

State problem/issue in one sentence.

1.

Name three or more subtopics of problem.

1.

2.

3.

Name three or more subtopics of the subtopics.

1.

2.

3.

What information must be known to solve the problem or to answer the question?

State the answer to the question/problem.

— In five sentences

1.

2.

3.

4.

5.

— In two sentences

1.

2.

— In one sentence

1.

Stated in terms of outcomes, what evidences do I see that confirm that I have made the right decision?

Once the problem/question is answered/solved, what one or two new problems/answers may arise?

ABBREVIATED PRE-WRITING THINKING CHALLENGE

What is the issue?

State problem/issue in five sentences.

1.

2.

3.

4.

5.

State problem/issue in two sentences.

1.

2.

State problem/issue in one sentence.

1.

Name three or more subtopics of problem.

1.

2.

3.

Name three or more subtopics of the subtopics.

1.

2.

3.

What information must be known to solve the problem or to answer the question?

State the answer to the question/problem — in five sentences — in two sentences — in one sentence.

Stated in terms of outcomes, what evidences do I see that confirms that I have made the right decision?

Once the problem or question is answered or solved, what are one or two new problems or answers that could arise?

PRE-WRITING PHASE

Often called the brainstorming phase, the pre-writing phase is the time you decide on exactly what your topic is. What questions must you answer? You should articulate a thesis (a one-sentence statement of purpose for why you are writing about this topic. The thesis typically has two to four specific points contained within it). You should decide what sort of essay this is — for instance, a definition, an exposition, a persuasive argument — and then design a strategy. For example, a clearly persuasive essay will demand that you state the issue and give your opinion in the opening paragraph.

Next, after a thesis statement, you will write an outline. No matter what length the essay may be, 20 pages or one paragraph, you should create an outline.

Outline

Thesis: In his poem "The Raven," Edgar Allan Poe uses literary devices to describe such weighty topics as death and unrequited love, which draw the reader to an insightful and many times emotional moment. (Note that this thesis informs the reader that the author will be exploring death and unrequited love.)

I. Introduction (Opens to the reader the exploration of the writing and tells the reader what to expect.)

II. Body (This particular essay will include two main points developed in two main paragraphs, one paragraph about death and one paragraph about emotions. The second paragraph will be introduced by means of a transition word or phrase or sentence.)

  A. Imagining Death

  B. Feeling Emotions

III. Conclusions (A paragraph that draws conclusions or solves the problem mentioned in the thesis statement.)

One of the best ways to organize your thoughts is to spend time in concentrated thinking, what some call brain-storming. Thinking through what you want to write is a way to narrow your topic.

Sample Outline:

Persuasive Paper with Three Major Points (Arguments)

I. Introduction: Thesis statement includes a listing or a summary of the three supportive arguments and introduces the paper.

II. Body

A. Argument 1

Evidence (transition words or phrases or sentences to the next topic)

B. Argument 2

Evidence (transition words or phrases or sentences to the next topic)

C. Argument 3

Evidence (transition words or phrases or sentences to the conclusion)

III. Conclusion: Restatement of arguments and evidence used throughout the paper (do not use the words in conclusion — just conclude).

NOTE: For greater detail and explanation of outlining, refer to a composition handbook. Careful attention should be paid to parallel structure with words or phrases, to correct form with headings and subheadings, to punctuation, and to pairing of information. Correct outline structure will greatly enhance the writing of any paper.

Sample Outline:

Expository Essay with Four Major Points

I. Introduction: Thesis statement includes a listing or mention of four examples or supports and introduces the paper; use transitional words or phrases at the end of the paragraph.

II. Body

A. Example 1

Application (transition words or phrases or sentences to the next topic)

B. Example 2

Application (transition words or phrases or sentences to the next topic)

C. Example 3

Application (transition words or phrases or sentences to the next topic)

D. Example 4

Application (transition words or phrases or sentences to the conclusion)

III. Conclusion: Restatement of thesis, drawing from the evidence or applications used in the paper (do not use the words in conclusion — just conclude).

NOTE: For greater detail and explanation of outlining, refer to a composition handbook. Careful attention should be paid to parallel structure with words or phrases, to correct form with headings and subheadings, to punctuation, and to pairing of information. Correct outline structure will greatly enhance the writing of any paper.

The Thinking Challenge

The following is an example of a Thinking Challenge approach to Mark Twain's *The Adventures of Huckleberry Finn:*

The Problem or The Issue or The Question:

Should Huck turn in his escaped slave-friend Jim to the authorities?

State problem/issue in five sentences, then in two sentences, and, finally, in one sentence.

Five Sentences:

Huck runs away with Jim. He does so knowing that he is breaking the law. However, the lure of friendship overrides the perfidy he knows he is committing. As he floats down the Mississippi River, he finds it increasingly difficult to hide his friend from the authorities and to hide his feelings of ambivalence. Finally he manages to satisfy both ambiguities.

Two Sentences:

Huck intentionally helps his slave friend Jim escape from servitude. As Huck floats down the Mississippi River, he finds it increasingly difficult to hide his friend from the authorities and at the same time to hide his own feelings of ambivalence.

One Sentence:

After escaping with his slave-friend Jim and floating down the Mississippi River, Huck finds it increasingly difficult to hide his friend from the authorities and at the same time to hide his own feelings of ambivalence.

Name three or more subtopics of problem.

Are there times when we should disobey the law?

What responsibilities does Huck have to his family?

What should Huck do?

Name three or more subtopics of the subtopics.

Are there times when we should disobey the law?

Who determines what laws are unjust?

Should the law be disobeyed publicly?

Who is injured when we disobey the law?

What responsibilities does Huck have to his family?

Who is his family? Jim? His dad?

Is allegiance to them secondary to Jim's needs?

Should his family support his civil disobedience?

What should Huck do?

Turn in Jim?

Escape with Jim?

Both?

What information must be known?

Laws? Jim's character? If he is bad, then should Huck save him?

State the answer to the question/problem in five, two, and one sentence(s).

Five Sentences:

Huck can escape with Jim with profound feelings of guilt. After all, he is helping a slave escape. This is important because it shows that Huck is still a moral, if flawed, character. Jim's freedom does outweigh any other consideration — including the laws of the land and his family's wishes. As the story unfolds, the reader sees that Huck is indeed a reluctant criminal, and the reader takes comfort in that fact.

Two Sentences:

Showing reluctance and ambivalence, Huck embarks on an arduous but moral adventure. Jim's freedom outweighs any other need or consideration.

One Sentence:

Putting Jim's freedom above all other considerations, Huck, the reluctant criminal, embarks on an arduous but moral adventure.

Once the problem or issue or question is solved, what are one or two new problems that may arise? What if Huck is wrong? What consequences could Huck face?

Every essay has a beginning (introduction), a middle part (body), and an ending (conclusion). The introduction must draw the reader into the topic and usually presents the thesis to the reader. The body organizes the material and expounds on the thesis (a one-sentence statement of purpose) in a cogent and inspiring way. The conclusion generally is a solution to the problem or issue or question or is sometimes a summary. Paragraphs in the body are connected with transitional words or phrases: furthermore, therefore, in spite of. Another effective transition technique is to mention in the first sentence of a new paragraph a thought or word that occurs in the last sentence of the previous paragraph. In any event, the body should be intentionally organized to advance the purposes of the paper. A disciplined writer always writes a rough draft. Using the well-thought-out outline composed during the pre-writing phase is an excellent way to begin the actual writing. The paper has already been processed mentally and only lacks the writing.

WRITING PHASE

The writer must make the first paragraph grab the reader's attention enough that the reader will want to continue reading.

The writer should write naturally, but not colloquially. In other words, the writer should not use clichés and everyday coded language. *The football players blew it* is too colloquial.

The writer should use as much visual imagery and precise detail as possible, should assume nothing, and should explain everything.

REWRITING PHASE

Despite however many rewrites are necessary, when the writer has effectively communicated the subject and corrected grammar and usage problems, he or she is ready to write the final copy.

Top Ten Most Frequent Essay Problems

Agreement between the Subject and Verb: Use singular forms of verbs with singular subjects and use plural forms of verbs with plural subjects.

WRONG: Everyone finished their homework.

RIGHT: Everyone finished his homework (Everyone is an indefinite singular pronoun.)

Using the Second Person Pronoun — "you," "your" should rarely, if ever, be used in a formal essay.

WRONG: You know what I mean (too informal).

Redundancy: Never use "I think" or "It seems to me"

WRONG: I think that is true.

RIGHT: That is true (We know you think it, or you would not write it!)

Tense consistency: Use the same tense (usually present) throughout the paper.

WRONG: I was ready to go, but my friend is tired.

RIGHT: I am ready to go but my friend is tired.

Misplaced Modifiers: Place the phrase or clause close to its modifier.

WRONG: The man drove the car with a bright smile into the garage.

RIGHT: The man with a bright smile drove the car into the garage.

Antecedent Pronoun Problems: Make sure pronouns match (agree) in number and gender with their antecedents.

WRONG: Mary and Susan both enjoyed her dinner.

RIGHT: Mary and Susan both enjoyed their dinners.

Parallelism: Make certain that your list/sentence includes similar phrase types.

WRONG: I like to take a walk and swimming.

RIGHT: I like walking and swimming

Affect vs. Effect: Affect is a verb; effect is a noun unless it means to achieve.

WRONG: His mood effects me negatively.

RIGHT: His mood affects me negatively.

RIGHT: The effects of his mood are devastating.

Dangling Prepositions: Rarely end a sentence with an unmodified preposition.

WRONG: Who were you speaking to?

RIGHT: To whom were you speaking?

Transitions: Make certain that paragraphs are connected with transitions (e.g., furthermore, therefore, in spite of).

RIGHT: Furthermore, Jack London loves to describe animal behavior.

LITERARY DEVICES

Read the following essay. Note the reader comments in the margins given to stimulate corrections in the essay.

LITERARY DEVICES IN EDGAR ALLEN POE'S POEMS

Edgar Allan Poe is a clever writer. To enhance his poetry, he **used** literary devices such as end rhyme, alliteration, assonance, and repetition. These devices are paths that one may follow while reading Poe's poetry. The reader is invited to walk with Poe as he describes such weighty topics as death and unrequited love. The above-mentioned literary devices **draws** the reader down Poe's trail to an insightful and many times emotional moment.

For example, in his poem *The Sleeper,* Poe uses end rhyme, alliteration, assonance, and repetition: A*t midnight, in the month of June,/I stand beneath the mystic moon* (lines 1&2). Later in lines 25 and 26 he uses alliteration with laudable results: *And wave the curtain canopy/so fitfully-so carefully.* Lines 5 and 6 include assonance, alliteration, and end rhyme. *And, softly dripping, drop by drop/Upon the quiet mountain top.* These literary devices naturally help Poe describe a very emotional and existential experience; namely, death. These devices draw the reader along the path to visualizing and imagining what death is like — which is really all we can do. In that sense, these literary devices are particularly important.

In the next two Poe poems, *Annabel Lee* and *To Helen*, Poe becomes romantic. He struggles with one of the most heart wrenching topics: unfulfilled or unrequited love.

Literary devices are critical to Poe's overall effect. In fact, in *Annabel Lee,* Poe uses alliteration in almost every verse: *It was many and many a year ago,/In a kingdom by the sea,/That a maiden there lived whom you may know/By the name of Annabel Lee;/And this maiden she lived with no other thought/Than to love and be loved by me.* Alliteration is important in *To Helen. Helen, thy beauty is to me/Like those Nicean barks of yore,/That gently, o'er a perfumed sea,/The weary, wayworn wanderer bore/To his own native shore.* A powerful visual and olfactory metaphor like *perfumed sea* to describe death requires equally powerful literary devices. Use of these devices draws the reader along the path to feeling the tremendous loss that Poe feels in each poem. His young wife, his beloved, is dead. There is a chasm across which no man can cross. **But** Poe tries to cross and to take us with him. Literary devices pull us into that path by evoking feelings and emotions too deep to utter.

I **don't** like Poe for the very reason he is so brilliant. I do not enjoy thinking about death. It is not a subject I enjoy exploring. It is not a road I am ready to walk. **But,** I must admit, by use of literary devices, Poe draws the reader into the dark maelstrom of death. His naked emotion and powerful images draw me into this vortex. However, I am glad that Jesus Christ is my savior and my death is **mitigated** by the fact that I shall live forever with our Lord.

NOVEL REVIEW

Book ______________________________ Student ______________________________

Author ______________________________ Date Of Reading ____________

I. Briefly describe:

Protagonist —

Antagonist —

Other characters used to develop protagonist —

If applicable, state why any of the book's characters remind you of specific Bible characters.

II. Setting:

III. Point of view: (circle one) first person, third person, third person omniscient

IV. Brief summary of the plot:

V. Theme (the quintessential meaning/purpose of the book in one or two sentences):

VI. Author's worldview: how do you know? What behaviors do(es) the character(s) manifest that lead you to this conclusion?

VII. Why did you like/dislike this book?

VIII. The next literary work I read will be . . .

SHORT STORY REVIEW

Short story ______________________ Student ______________________

Author ______________________ Date of Reading ____________

I. Briefly describe

Protagonist —

Antagonist —

Other characters used to develop protagonist —

If applicable, state why any of the story's characters remind you of specific Bible characters.

II. Setting

III. Point of view: (circle one) first person, third person, third person omniscient

IV. Brief summary of the plot

Identify the climax of the short story.

V. Theme (the quintessential meaning/purpose of the story in one or two sentences):

VI. Author's worldview:

How do you know this? What behaviors do(es) the character(s) manifest that lead you to this conclusion?

VII. Why did you like/dislike this short story?

VIII. The next literary work I read will be . . .

DRAMA REVIEW

Play______________________________ Student______________________________

Author______________________________ Date of Reading __________

I. Briefly describe

Protagonist —

Antagonist —

If applicable, state why any of the play's characters remind you of specific Bible characters.

II. Setting

III. Point of view: (circle one) first person, third person, third person omniscient

IV. Brief summary of the plot

Identify the climax of the play.

V. Theme (the quintessential meaning/purpose of the play in one or two sentences)

VI. Author's worldview

How do you know this? What behaviors do(es) the character(s) manifest that lead you to this conclusion?

VII. Why did you like/dislike this play?

VIII. The next literary work i will read will be . . .

NONFICTION REVIEW

Literary Work____________________________Student____

Author_________________________________ Date of Reading ____________

I. Write a précis of this book. In your précis, clearly state the author's thesis and supporting arguments.

II. Are you persuaded? Why or why not?

III. Why did you like/dislike this book?

IV. The next literary work I read will be . . .

PRAYER JOURNAL GUIDE

Journal Guide Questions

Bible Passage(s): ______________________________

____

____

1. Centering Time (a list of those things that I must do later):

2. Discipline of Silence (remain absolutely still and quiet).

3. Reading Scripture Passage (with notes on text):

4. Living in Scripture:

   A. How does the passage affect the person mentioned in the passage? How does he/she feel?

   B. How does the passage affect my life? What is the Lord saying to me through this passage?

5. Prayers of adoration and thanksgiving, intercession, and future prayer targets:

6. Discipline of Silence

PEER EVALUATION CHECKLIST

I. Organization

___ Is the writer's purpose clearly introduced? What is it?

___ Does the organization of the paper coincide with the outline?

___ Does the writer answer the Literary Analysis?

___ Does the introduction grab the reader's attention?

___ Is the purpose advanced by each sentence and paragraph? (Are there sentences that don't seem to belong in the paragraphs?)

___ Does the body (middle) of the paper advance the purpose?

___ Does the conclusion solve the purpose of the paper?

Comments regarding organization:

II. Mechanics

___ Does the writer use active voice?

___ Does the writer use the appropriate verb tense throughout the paper?

___ Is there agreement between all pronouns and antecedents?

___ Are there effective and appropriately used transitions?

Comments regarding other mechanical problems:

III. Argument

___ Are you persuaded by the arguments?

___ Does the author need stronger arguments? More arguments?

Other helpful comments:

COMPOSITION EVALUATION

EVALUATION TECHNIQUE 1

Based on 100 points

I. Grammar and Syntax: Is the composition grammatically correct?

(25 points) 20/25

Comments: See corrections. Watch agreement. Your verb usage could be a lot more precise. Look up "Subject/ Verb Agreement" in your grammar test, read about it, write the grammar rule, and then correct this part of your essay.

II. Organization: Does this composition exhibit well-considered organization? Does it flow? Transitions? Introduction and a conclusion?

(25 points) 25/25

Comments: Good job with transitional phrases and with having a strong introduction. Your thesis statement gives me a clear idea about the content of your paper. Your conclusion explains your thesis very thoroughly.

III. Content: Does this composition answer the question, argue the point well, and/or persuade the reader?

(50 points) 50/50

Comments: Excellent insights. I was fully persuaded to your point of view. You supported your thesis well with strong arguments. I especially was impressed with ______________

If the parent/educator does not wish to evaluate a student with a number grade, another option is to use a checklist:

*To be duplicated and placed on each essay.

COMPOSITION EVALUATION

EVALUATION CHECKLIST TECHNIQUE 2

I. Organization

___ Is the writer's purpose stated clearly in the introduction? Is there a thesis sentence? What is it?

___ Does the writer answer the literary analysis?

___ Does the introduction grab the reader's attention?

___ Is the purpose advanced by each sentence and paragraph?

___ Does the body (middle) of the paper advance the purpose?

___ Does the conclusion accomplish its purpose?

Other helpful comments for the writer:

II. Mechanics

___ Does the writer use active voice?

___ Does the writer use the appropriate verb tense throughout the paper?

___ Is there agreement between all pronouns and antecedents?

___ Is there appropriate subject/verb agreement?

___ Are the transitions effective and appropriate?

Other mechanical trouble spots:

III. Argument

___ Are you persuaded by the arguments?

Other helpful comments for the writer:

BOOK LIST FOR SUPPLEMENTAL READING (SOME ARE IN OTHER LIT BOOKS)

Note: Not all literature is suitable for all students; educators and students should choose literature appropriate to students' age, maturity, interests, and abilities.

Jane Austen, *Emma*

Charlotte Bronte, *Jame Eyre*

Thomas Bulfinch, *The Age of Fable*

Pearl S. Buck, *The Good Earth*

John Bunyan, *The Pilgrim's Progress*

Agatha Christie, *And Then There Were None*

Samuel T. Coleridge, *Rime of the Ancient Mariner*

Joseph Conrad, *Heart of Darkness, Lord Jim*

James F. Cooper, *The Last of the Mohicans, Deerslayer*

Stephen Crane, *The Red Badge of Courage*

Clarence Day, *Life with Father*

Daniel Defoe, *Robinson Crusoe*

Charles Dickens, *Great Expectations; A Christmas Carol; A Tale of Two Cities; Oliver Twist; Nicholas Nickleby*

Arthur C. Doyle, *The Adventures of Sherlock Holmes*

Alexander Dumas, *The Three Musketeers*

George Eliot, *Silas Marner*

T.S. Eliot, *Murder in the Cathedral*

Anne Frank, *The Diary of Anne Frank*

Oliver Goldsmith, *The Vicar of Wakefield*

Edith Hamilton, *Mythology*

Nathaniel Hawthorne, *The Scarlet Letter; The House of the Seven Gables*

Thor Heyerdahl, *Kon-Tiki*

J. Hilton *Lost Horizon; Goodbye, Mr. Chips*

Homer, *The Odyssey; The Iliad*

W.H. Hudson, *Green Mansions*

Victor Hugo, *Les Miserables; The Hunchback of Notre Dame*

Zora Neale Hurston, *Their Eyes Were Watching God*

Washington Irving, *The Sketch Book*

Rudyard Kipling, *Captains Courageous*

Harper Lee, *To Kill a Mockingbird*

Madeline L'Engle, *A Circle of Quiet; The Summer of the Great-Grandmother; A Wrinkle in Time*

C.S. Lewis, *The Screwtape Letters; Mere Christianity; The Chronicles of Narnia*

Jack London, *The Call of the Wild; White Fang*

George MacDonald, *The Curate's Awakening*

Sir Thomas Malory, *Le Morte d'Arthur*

Guy de Maupassant, Short stories

Herman Melville, Billy Budd; Moby Dick

Monsarrat, *The Cruel Sea*

Charles Nordhoff & James Norman Hall, *Mutiny on the Bounty*

Edgar Allen Poe, Poems and short stories

E. M.Remarque, *All Quiet on the Western Front*

Anne Rinaldi, *A Break with Charity: A Story about the Salem Witch Trials*

Carl Sanburg, *Abraham Lincoln*

William Saroyan, *The Human Comedy*

Sir Walter Scott, *Ivanhoe*

William Shakespeare, *Hamlet; Macbeth; Julius Caesar; As You Like It; Romeo and Juliet; A Midsummer Night's Dream*

George Bernard Shaw, *Pygmalion*

Sophocles, *Antigone*

Harriet Beecher Stowe, *Uncle Tom's Cabin*

John Steinbeck, *Of Mice and Men; The Grapes of Wrath*

Robert Louis Stevenson, *Dr. Jekyll and Mr. Hyde;* Treasure Island; *Kidnapped*

Irving Stone, *Lust for Life*

Jonathan Swift, *Gulliver's Travels*

Booth Tarkington, *Penrod*

J.R.R. Tolkien, *The Lord of the Rings Trilogy*

Mark Twain, *The Adventures of Huckleberry Finn; The Adventures of Tom Sawyer*

Jules Verne, *Master of the World*

Booker T. Washington, *Up from Slavery*

H.G. Wells, *The Complete Works of H.G. Wells*

Tennessee Williams, *The Glass Menagerie*

FOR OLDER STUDENTS

Chinua Achebe, *Things Fall Apart*

Aristotle, *Poeticus*

Edward Bellamy, *Looking Backward*

Jorge Luis Borges, (Colombia, Argentina) Various short stories

Stephen V. Benet, *John Brown's Body*

Charlotte Bronte, *Wuthering Heights*

Camus, *The Stranger*

Chaucer, *The Canterbury Tales; Beowulf*

Willa Cather, *My Antonia*

Miguel de Cervantes, *Don Quixote*

Fyodor Dostovesky, *Crime and Punishment; The Idiot; The Brothers Karamazov*

William Faulkner, *The Hamlet Trilogy*

F. Scott Fitzgerald, *The Great Gatsby*

John Galsworthy, *The Forsythe Saga*

Lorraine Hansberry, *A Raisin in the Sun*

Thomas Hardy, *The Return of the Native; The Mayor of Casterbridge*

A.E. Housman, *A Shropshire Lad*

Henrik Ibsen, *A Doll's House*

Charles Lamb, *The Essays of Elia*

Sinclair Lewis, *Babbitt: Arrowsmith*

Kamala Markandaya, *Nectar in a Sieve*

Gabriel Barcia Marquez, *100 Years of Solitude*

John P. Marquand, *The Late George Apley*

E. Lee Masters, *A Spoon River Anthology*

Somerset Maugham, *Of Human Bondage*

Arthur Miller, *The Crucible; Death of a Salesman*

Eugene O'Neill, *The Emperor Jones*

George Orwell, *Animal Farm; 1984*

Thomas Paine, *The Rights of Man*

Alan Paton, *Cry, the Beloved Country*

Plato, *The Republic*

Plutarch, *Lives*

O.E. Rolvaag, *Giants in the Earth*

Edmund Rostand, *Cyrano de Bergerac*

Mary Shelley, *Frankenstein*

Sophocles, *Oedipus Rex*

John Steinbeck, *The Pearl*

Ivan Turgenev, *Fathers and Sons*

William Thackeray, *Vanity Fair*

Leo Tolstoy, *War and Peace*

Edith Wharton, *Ethan Frome*

Walt Whitman, *Leaves of Grass*

Thornton Wilder, *Our Town*

Thomas Wolfe, *Look Homeward, Angel*

GLOSSARY OF LITERARY TERMS

Allegory: A story or tale with two or more levels of meaning — a literal level and one or more symbolic levels. The events, setting, and characters in an allegory are symbols for ideas or qualities.

Alliteration: The repetition of initial consonant sounds. The repetition can be juxtaposed (side by side; e.g., simply sad). An example: I conceive therefore, as to the business of being profound, that it is with writers, as with wells; a person with good eyes may see to the bottom of the deepest, provided any water be there; and that often, when there is nothing in the world at the bottom, besides dryness and dirt, though it be but a yard and a half under ground, it shall pass, however, for wondrous deep, upon no wiser a reason than because it is wondrous dark. (Jonathan Swift)

Allusion: A casual and brief reference to a famous historical or literary figure or event: You must borrow me Gargantua's mouth first. 'Tis a word too great for any mouth of this age's size. (Shakespeare)

Analogy: The process by which new or less familiar words, constructions, or pronunciations conform to the pattern of older or more familiar (and often unrelated) ones; a comparison between two unlike things. The purpose of an analogy is to describe something unfamiliar by pointing out its similarities to something that is familiar.

Antagonist: In a narrative, the character with whom the main character has the most conflict. In Jack London's "To Build a Fire" the antagonist is the extreme cold of the Yukon rather than a person or animal.

Archetype: The original pattern or model from which all other things of the same kind are made; a perfect example of a type or group. For example, the biblical character Joseph is often considered an archetype of Jesus Christ.

Argumentation: The discourse in which the writer presents and logically supports a particular view or opinion; sometimes used interchangeably with persuasion.

Aside: In a play, an aside is a speech delivered by an actor in such a way that other characters on the stage are presumed not to hear it; an aside generally reveals a character's inner thoughts.

Autobiography: A form of non-fiction in which a person tells his/her own life story. Notable examples of autobiography include those by Benjamin Franklin and Frederick Douglass.

Ballad: A song or poem that tells a story in short stanzas and simple words with repetition, refrain, etc.

Biography: A form of non-fiction in which a writer tells the life story of another person.

Character: A person or an animal who takes part in the action of a literary work. The main character is the one on whom the work focuses. The person with whom the main character has the most conflict is the antagonist. He is the enemy of the main character (protagonist). For instance, in *The Scarlet Letter*, by Nathaniel Hawthorne, Chillingsworth is the antagonist. Hester is the protagonist. Characters who appear in the story may perform actions, speak to other characters, be described by the narrator, or be remembered. Characters introduced whose sole purpose is to develop the main character are called foils.

Classicism: An approach to literature and the other arts that stresses reason, balance, clarity, ideal beauty, and orderly form in imitation of the arts of Greece and Rome.

Conflict: A struggle between opposing forces; can be internal or external; when occurring within a character is called internal conflict. An example of this occurs in *Mark Twain's Adventures of Huckleberry Finn*. In this novel Huck is struggling in his mind about whether to return an escaped slave, his good friend Jim, to the authorities. An external conflict is normally an obvious conflict between the protagonist and antagonist(s). London's "To Build a Fire" illustrates conflict between a character and an outside force. Most plots develop from conflict, making conflict one of the primary elements of narrative literature.

Crisis or **Climax:** The moment or event in the *plot* in which the conflict is most directly addressed: the main character "wins" or "loses"; the secret is revealed. After the climax, the denouement or falling action occurs.

Dialectic: Examining opinions or ideas logically, often by the method of question and answer

Discourse, forms of: Various modes into which writing can be classified; traditionally, writing has been divided into the following modes:

Exposition: Writing that presents information

Narration: Writing that tells a story

Description: Writing that portrays people, places, or things

Persuasion (sometimes also called Argumentation): Writing that attempts to convince people to think or act in a certain way

Drama: A story written to be performed by actors; the playwright supplies dialogue for the characters to speak and stage directions that give information about costumes, lighting, scenery, properties, the setting, and the character's movements and ways of speaking.

Dramatic monologue: A poem or speech in which an imaginary character speaks to a silent listener. Eliot's "The Love Song of J. Alfred Prufrock" is a dramatic monologue.

Elegy: A solemn and formal lyric poem about death, often one that mourns the passing of some particular person; Whitman's "When Lilacs Last in the Dooryard Bloom'd" is an elegy lamenting the death of President Lincoln.

Essay: A short, nonfiction work about a particular subject; essay comes from the Old French word *essai*, meaning "a trial or attempt"; meant to be explanatory, an essay is not meant to be an exhaustive treatment of a subject; can be classified as formal or informal, personal or impersonal; can also be classified according to purpose as either expository, argumentative, descriptive, persuasive, or narrative.

Figurative language: See metaphor, simile, analogy

Foil: A character who provides a contrast to another character and whose purpose is to develop the main character.

Genre: A division or type of literature; commonly divided into three major divisions, literature is either poetry, prose, or drama; each major genre can then be divided into smaller genres: poetry can be divided into lyric, concrete, dramatic, narrative, and epic poetry; prose can be divided into fiction (novels and short stories) and non-fiction (biography, autobiography, letters, essays, and reports); drama can be divided into serious drama, tragedy, comic drama, melodrama, and farce.

Gothic: The use of primitive, medieval, wild, or mysterious elements in literature; Gothic elements offended 18th-century classical writers but appealed to the romantic writers who followed them. Gothic novels feature writers who use places like mysterious castles where horrifying supernatural events take place; Poe's "The Fall of the House of Usher" illustrates the influence of Gothic elements.

Harlem Renaissance: Occurring during the 1920s, a time of African American artistic creativity centered in Harlem in New York City; Langston Hughes was a Harlem Renaissance writer.

Hyperbole: A deliberate exaggeration or overstatement; in Mark Twain's "The Notorious Jumping Frog of Calaveras County," the claim that Jim Smiley would follow a bug as far as Mexico to win a bet is hyperbolic.

Idyll: A poem or part of a poem that describes and idealizes country life; Whittier's "Snowbound" is an idyll.

Irony: A method of humorous or subtly sarcastic expression in which the intended meanings of the words used is the direct opposite of their usual sense.

Journal: A daily autobiographical account of events and personal reactions.

Kenning: Indirect way of naming people or things; knowledge or recognition; in Old English poetry, a metaphorical name for something.

Literature: All writings in prose or verse, especially those of an imaginative or critical character, without regard to their excellence and/or writings considered as having permanent value, excellence of form, great emotional effect, etc.

Metaphor (figure of speech): A comparison that creatively identifies one thing with another dissimilar thing and transfers or ascribes to the first thing some of the qualities of the second. Unlike a simile or analogy, metaphor asserts that one thing is another thing — not just that one is like another. Very frequently a metaphor is invoked by the verb to be:

Affliction then is ours;

We are the trees whom shaking fastens more. (George Herbert)

Then Jesus declared, "I am the bread of life" (John 6:35).

Jesus answered, "I am the Way and the truth and the life" (John 14:6).

Meter: A poem's rhythmical pattern, determined by the number and types of stresses, or beats, in each line; a certain number of metrical feet make up a line of verse; (pentameter denotes a line containing five metrical feet); the act of describing the meter of a poem is called scanning which involves marking the stressed and unstressed syllables, as follows:

Iamb: A foot with one unstressed syllable followed by one stressed syllable, as in the word abound.

Trochee: A foot with one stressed syllable followed by one unstressed syllable, as in the word spoken.

Anapest: A foot with two unstressed syllables followed by one stressed syllable, as in the word interrupt.

Dactyl: A foot with a stressed syllable followed by two unstressed syllables, as in the word accident.

Spondee: Two stressed feet: quicksand, heartbeat; occurs only occasionally in English.

Motif: A main idea element, feature; a main theme or subject to be elaborated on.

Narration: The way the author chooses to tell the story.

First person narration: A character refers to himself or herself using "I." Example: Huck Finn in *The Adventures of Huckleberry Finn* tells the story from his perspective. This is a creative way to bring humor into the plot.

Second person narration: Addresses the reader and/or the main character as "you" (and may also use first person narration, but not necessarily). One example is the opening of each of Rudyard Kipling's Just So Stories, in which the narrator refers to the child listener as "O Best Beloved."

Third person narration: Not a character in the story; refers to the story's characters as "he" and "she." This is probably the most common form of narration.

Limited narration: Only able to tell what one person is thinking or feeling. Example: in *A Separate Peace*, by John Knowles, we only see the story from Gene's perspective.

Omniscient narration: Charles Dickens employs this narration in most of his novels.

Reliable narration: Everything this narration says is true, and the narrator knows everything that is necessary to the story.

Unreliable narrator: May not know all the relevant information; may be intoxicated or mentally ill; may lie to the audience. Example: Edgar Allan Poe's narrators are frequently unreliable. Think of the delusions that the narrator of "The Tell-Tale Heart" has about the old man.

Narrative: In story form.

Onomatopoeia: Use of words that, in their pronunciation, suggest their meaning. "Hiss," for example, when spoken is intended to resemble the sound of steam or of a snake. Other examples include these: slam, buzz, screech, whirr, crush, sizzle, crunch, wring, wrench, gouge, grind, mangle, bang, blam, pow, zap, fizz, urp, roar, growl, blip, click, whimper, and, of course, snap, crackle, and pop.

Parallelism: Two or more balancing statements with phrases, clauses, or paragraphs of similar length and grammatical structure.

Plot: Arrangement of the action in fiction or drama — events of the story in the order the story gives them. A typical plot has five parts: exposition, rising action, crisis or climax, falling action, and resolution (sometimes called denouement).

Précis: Summary of the plot of a literary piece.

Protagonist: The enemy of the main character (antagonist).

Rhetoric: Using words effectively in writing and speaking.

Setting: The place(s) and time(s) of a story, including the historical period, social milieu of the characters, geographical location, descriptions of indoor and outdoor locales.

Scop: An Old English poet or bard.

Simile: A figure of speech in which one thing is likened to another dissimilar thing by the use of like, as, etc.

Sonnet: A poem normally of 14 lines in any of several fixed verse and rhyme schemes, typically in rhymed iambic pentameter; sonnets characteristically express a single theme or idea.

Structure: The arrangement of details and scenes that make up a literary work.

Style: An author's characteristic arrangement of words. A style may be colloquial, formal, terse, wordy, theoretical, subdued, colorful, poetic, or highly individual. Style is the arrangement of words in groups and sentences; diction, on the other hand, refers to the choice of individual words; the arrangement of details and scenes make up the structure of a literary work; all combine to influence the tone of the work; thus, diction, style, and structure make up the form of the literary work.

Theme: The one-sentence, major meaning of a literary piece, rarely stated but implied. The theme is not a moral, which is a statement of the author's didactic purpose of his literary piece. A *thesis statement* is very similar to the theme.

Tone: The attitude the author takes toward his subject; author's attitude is revealed through choice of details, through diction and style, and through the emphasis and comments that are made. Like theme and style, tone is sometimes difficult to describe with a single word or phrase; often it varies in the same literary piece to suit the moods of the characters and the situations. For instance, the tone or mood of Poe's "Annabel Lee."